Studies in Economic History

Aim and Scopes

This series from Springer provides a platform for works in economic history that truly integrate economics and history. Books on a wide range of related topics are welcomed and encouraged, including those in macro-economic history, financial history, labor history, industrial history, agricultural history, the history of institutions and organizations, spatial economic history, law and economic history, political economic history, historical demography, and environmental history.

Economic history studies have greatly developed over the past several decades through application of economics and econometrics. Particularly in recent years, a variety of new economic theories and sophisticated econometric techniques—including game theory, spatial economics, and generalized method of moment (GMM)—have been introduced for the great benefit of economic historians and the research community.

At the same time, a good economic history study should contribute more than just an application of economics and econometrics to past data. It raises novel research questions, proposes a new view of history, and/or provides rich documentation. This series is intended to integrate data analysis, close examination of archival works, and application of theoretical frameworks to offer new insights and even provide opportunities to rethink theories.

The purview of this new Springer series is truly global, encompassing all nations and areas of the world as well as all eras from ancient times to the present. The editorial board, who are internationally renowned leaders among economic historians, carefully evaluate and judge each manuscript, referring to reports from expert reviewers. The series publishes contributions by university professors and others well established in the academic community, as well as work deemed to be of equivalent merit.

More information about this series at http://www.springer.com/series/13279

Kazuhiko Yago • Yoshio Asai • Masanao Itoh
Editors

History of the IMF

Organization, Policy, and Market

Springer

Editors
Kazuhiko Yago
School of Commerce
Waseda University
Shinjuku-ku, Tokyo, Japan

Yoshio Asai
Faculty of Economics
Seijo University
Setagaya-ku, Tokyo, Japan

Masanao Itoh
School of Social Information Studies
Otsuma Women's University
Tama, Tokyo, Japan

ISSN 2364-1797 ISSN 2364-1800 (electronic)
Studies in Economic History
ISBN 978-4-431-55350-2 ISBN 978-4-431-55351-9 (eBook)
DOI 10.1007/978-4-431-55351-9

Library of Congress Control Number: 2015940572

Springer Tokyo Heidelberg New York Dordrecht London

Printed on acid-free paper

Springer Japan KK is part of Springer Science+Business Media (www.springer.com)

Preface: The IMF and the Postwar International Financial Order

This book aims to examine the foundation and evolution of the post-WWII international financial order, focusing on the International Monetary Fund (hereafter IMF). The volume deals mainly with the period from the start of the IMF in 1947 until the beginning of the 1960s, when the institution fully exercised its functions. In order to demonstrate our basic standpoint, let us examine previous studies on selected topics regarding this subject.

The Gold Standard and After: Was the Bretton Woods System an "Innovation"?

An understanding of the classical international gold standard as well as the interwar gold exchange standard is indispensable in putting the postwar international financial system in a larger historical context. Representative studies on the pre-WWI international gold standard describe it as a sort of global public good for peripheral countries, without any artificial structure (Bordo 1984; Kindleberger 1986). It was also a "Good Housekeeping Seal of Approval" for peripheral countries to access capital flows from the industrialized core regions (Bordo and Rockoff 1996). Following this view, official international cooperation on money and exchange had been promoted only in a limited scope during the gold standard era: a debate between Barry Eichengreen and Marc Flandreau sharply revealed this point (Eichengreen 1995; Flandreau 1997). Why could this gold standard operate without a legal structure and formal collaboration? Historians often refer to a "silent rule" or "rules of the game" that unofficially regulated the gold standard regime, although a great variety of views are still left among historians as for function of this "rules of game" (Bordo 1984). During the interwar period, the move toward international collaboration on money and exchange emerged but stayed in a burgeoning stage: the Tripartite Monetary Agreement in 1936 took steps toward exchange stability through international collaboration, but it could not bring about results through collaboration in the true sense of the word (Eichengreen 1992; Mouré 2002).

In contrast, the international monetary system founded by the Bretton Woods Conference during the late WWII period was, after Harold James, an "innovation" that emerged in the middle of the twentieth century, for the system involved a rule that could limit national sovereignty in exchange-rate and macroeconomic policies (James 1996, p. 9). The Bretton Woods Conference (officially the International Monetary and Financial Conference of the United and Associated Nations) was held in Bretton Woods, New Hampshire, the United States, 1–22 July 1944, with 44 participating countries. The Conference approved the final statement as well as the Agreements of the IMF and the International Bank for Reconstruction and Development, known as the World Bank (hereafter WB). Both Agreements of these institutions went into effect on 27 December 1945. After the founding assemblies of both institutions in March 1946, the WB opened its doors on 25 June 1946 and the IMF on 1 March 1947. The Bretton Woods system thus was created both artificially and officially.

However, the above-mentioned antagonism between the "silent rule" under the gold standard era and the "innovation" in the Bretton Woods System invokes, from our perspective, some questions: was the "silent rule" so automatically effective, and was the "innovation" such a new attempt? In fact, the "silent rule" for the participating countries in the gold standard system was not "silent" in the sense that central banks actively coordinated their bank rates in order to neutralize the negative effect of business cycle contagion (Toniolo 1988; Borio et al. 2008). The Bretton Woods System was also a product of diplomatic negotiation, often with obscure concessions (Steil 2013; Helleiner 2014). It is therefore hard to distinguish these systems, gold standard as an automatic market-based one and the Bretton Woods system as a legal-based one.

Our research in this volume attempts to cast doubt on the view of the Bretton Woods System as an "innovation" and to positively present an alternative historical view referring to a certain continuity in terms of the political character of the systems, in between the prewar and the postwar international financial orders. In the following chapters, we approach the rule-making process of the IMF from the viewpoint of international politics. In the IMF during the fixed-rate era, the countries with surplus international balances were privileged, while deficit countries were sanctioned, and socialist countries were kept aside. This system, however, was not set up this way from the beginning: the rules on lending and the Article 14 consultation had been elaborated upon through a struggle among member countries. This is why we focus on politics in the rule-setting phase during the 1950s, in which period the institutional framework of the IMF was set up.

Bretton Woods, System or Order?

An article by Michael Bordo, which represents a commonly accepted view on the Bretton Woods monetary system, asks "why Bretton Woods was statistically so stable and why it was short lived?" (Bordo 1993, p. 4). In fact, the IMF had 12 years of preparation before beginning to function fully and less than 10 years of heyday from 1959 to 1967. The answer according to Bordo was that the weakness of the Bretton Woods System was due to the system's having been built by combining the gold exchange standard on the one hand and the adjustable peg system on the other. The system depended solely on the United States and thus when the United States gave up its price stability policy in late 1960s, the system was led to collapse. The above interpretation of the Bretton Woods System by Bordo stands on the presupposition that the core of the System had been a fixed-rate system.

Contrary to above conventional views, international political economist David Andrews recently proposed the notion of the "Bretton Woods Order". Andrews made a distinction between the Bretton Woods *System* as an officially established international monetary system and the Bretton Woods *Order* as an unofficial international economic order: according to his thesis the Bretton Woods System collapsed but the Bretton Woods Order is still evolving until the present (Andrews 2008). The system built by the Bretton Woods Conference was, according to Andrews, an economic order seeking two goals at once: domestic economic policy and international trade development. Thus the objectives of the Bretton Woods Order stayed unchanged after the end of the Bretton Woods System as a monetary system (i.e., a fixed-rate system). In fact, he says, trade liberalization is still ongoing, without a thorough return to protectionism.

Andrew's view is inspired by the "embedded liberalism" thesis of John Ruggie (1982). This Ruggie theory, influential among international political scientists, describes post-WWII liberalism as a product of compromise between economic nationalism and multilateral economic liberalism, the latter totally different from the nineteenth-century liberalism. The interwar period gold standard collapsed, according to Ruggie, not because of the absence of a hegemon country but due to the leading states' lack of power to coordinate market forces to respond to social requirements. However, with agreement on the Atlantic Charter in 1941, two goals, namely, multilateralism for free trade on the one hand and domestic economic development with social insurance on the other, have been combined, to be incarnated in the Bretton Woods Agreement as well as the General Agreement on Tariffs and Trade (hereafter GATT). Even after the suspension of gold–dollar exchange in 1971, free trade is still developing. Moreover, Ruggie says, the flexible rate system has been introduced in order to avoid the contradiction between international macroeconomic policy and the international monetary system per se, which indicates the continuity of the double political goals of the Bretton Woods System. Ruggie's views has been echoed recently by Abdelal, who stresses European leadership in capital movement liberalization, as an example of the Ruggie thesis (Abdelal 2007).

This book shares the view of Ruggie and Andrews regarding historical continuity before and after introduction of the floating system in the early 1970s; however, the approach differs: our book pays special attention to the evolution of the international monetary system as an international public good, and above all the role played by the IMF. In our hypothesis, the IMF and the international market have not been "embedded" in a social order in Ruggie's sense; they had their own logic of evolution, influenced by economic and monetary conditions, at home as well as overseas.

The Bretton Woods System and National Economies

During the late half of the nineteenth century, the European and American nation states were establishing their proper domestic currency systems, and this domestic process went along with the formation of an international system of settlements based on the gold standard (Helleiner 2003). This means that, as recent historical studies have made clear, the international gold standard had been supported by the development of domestic currency systems, not by the gold bullion itself. As Robert Triffin stated, "the nineteenth century could be far more accurately described as the century of an emerging and growing credit-money standard, and of the euthanasia of gold and silver moneys, rather than as the century of the gold standard" (Triffin 1968, p. 21). In Japan as well, concessional trade during the late Tokugawa Shogunate and the early Meiji period had been settled by silver, but this was replaced soon after by the settlement by exchange bills following the establishment of the Yokohama Specie Bank. Finally the Japanese currency system was integrated into the international gold standard in 1897, along with the elaboration of the domestic currency system with the foundation of the Bank of Japan (1882) and the Convertible Bank Note Act (1884) (Ishii 1994).

Compared to the above achievements in financial history during the gold standard era, the relations between the international system and national economies in the Bretton Woods period still remain unclear. Was the international system stipulated in the Bretton Woods Agreement so powerful in shaping the postwar national economies, at least in the industrialized West? Did the postwar international financial system support the unprecedented growth of the capitalist world, or did the growth itself make the international system sustainable? Our study tries to answer these questions, focusing mainly on the tension in the rounds on exchange restrictions and lending between the IMF and member countries. It is also worth noting that before 1950 the only surplus country was essentially the United States, but in 1960 the situation totally changed with the US recording overall deficits of international accounts: the book also deals with the redefining of the system under the above changes that took place in the national economies.

Together with the above approach to the national economies, we pay special attention to the relation of the IMF with the markets. The counterparts for the IMF's operations being the member countries' exchange agencies, the Fund did not have official contact with the markets. Nevertheless, the IMF had to watch the movements of the markets carefully: The IMF's commitment to the pound sterling during the 1940s and the 1950s as well as the approval of the European Payments Union as opposed to the original ideal of the IMF were products of the Fund's recognition of the realities of the markets selecting their proper currencies of settlement. Moreover, as Chap. 6 explains, the IMF examined the use of international short-term capital markets to cope with the international liquidity problem. The above "market-oriented" aspect of the IMF is one of the major findings of this volume, as a critique of the Ruggie–Andrews thesis that treats the IMF mainly from the "embedded" social context, ignoring market conditions and constraints.

The IMF as One of the Actors, but an Independent One

Finally, we try to provide an answer to the following question: Whose role was the most decisive in the working of the Bretton Woods System: the IMF, the United States, or someone else? Our hypothesis is that the postwar international financial system was an amalgam produced by several actors, in which no participants could maintain their hegemony over the system. In order to approach this issue, our book places the role of the IMF in relation to the international monetary and the financial system as a whole, i.e. with other institutions and treaties. Although the IMF has been the central focus of the post-WWII international monetary system, the position of the IMF has changed from its foundation to the present: although the IMF was a main actor of the fixed-rate system, it was not even a supporting actor during the Marshall Plan period, and after the mid-1960s its initiative has been taken over by the G10. From our point of view, the work on the IMF by Harold James, a quasi-official history of the institution, could be criticized for describing the IMF as the main actor in the system at all times (James 1996). Contrary to this "IMF-centrism," recent historical studies on the Bank for International Settlements are trying to introduce an alternative view (Toniolo 2005; Yago 2013). Of course, all the "official" IMF histories, from Horsefield (1969) to De Vries (1986), and above all James (1996) and Boughton (2001) were very useful for our research, leading us to insightful topics. Our approach, however, differs from those official historians in putting the IMF in the midst of plural powers and interests, often from the points of view of member countries. In light of the above current of studies, this book approaches the IMF from multiple hypotheses to critique such an "IMF-centric" history. Although very important, the IMF was just *one of the actors* in the postwar international financial order.

On the other hand, we pay attention to the autonomous character of the IMF as an institution. The fact that the United States maintains its veto over important decision making in the IMF often leads to an image that the US could drive this institution freely, a view that of course is backed by some solid evidence. However, once established, the IMF as an institution generated its own interests and logic in policymaking, and the staff headed by the Managing Director represented those interests and logic. The US Government, on the other hand, did not represent one single interest: inside the government were plural antagonisms, between the Department of State and the Department of the Treasury, and even within the Treasury. We must also keep in mind the relation between the US Government and the Congress (Lavelle 2011). The American veto over IMF decisions, therefore, did not mean the dependence of the IMF on the US Government. Moreover, for the United States, the IMF was not the only gateway to the international financial arena. In this context, the work of Jeffrey Chwieroth, which pointed out an organizational change "from within" the IMF, has inspired our approach (Chwieroth 2010). After all, the IMF must be regarded as an *independent actor*.

Conclusion

In sum, our standpoint is simple and clear: the financial history approach, represented by Bordo, Eichengreen, or Flandreau, leans too much towards economics based explanation; the international political science approach, guided by Ruggie and Andrews, depends too much on historical or anecdotal description. The former approach describes history by logic, the latter develops logic by history; the former places less emphasis upon human networks, the latter pays less attention to markets and structural constraints. Our volume tries to synthesize the above two approaches, combining the strengths of both, relying upon archival sources.

Every chapter in this book explores archival sources, mainly from the IMF Archives but also from the national archives of the governments involved (the United States National Records and Archives, the Public Record Office of the United Kingdom, Archives Nationales de France, the Japanese Government Archives, etc.) as well as those of the central banks (the Bank of England, Banque de France, Bundesbank, Banca d'Italia, the Bank of Canada, the Bank of Japan, etc.).

Tokyo, Japan

Yoshio Asai
Kazuhiko Yago

References

Abdelal, Rawi. (2007). *Capital Rules, the construction of global finance*. Cambridge: Harvard University Press.

Andrews, David M. (2008). *Orderly change: international monetary relations since Bretton Woods*. Ithaca: Cornell University Press.

Bordo, Michael D. (1984). The gold standard: the traditional approach. In *A Retrospective on the classical gold standard*, ed. M.Bordo and A.Schwartz. Chicago: The University Chicago Press.

Bordo, Michael D. (1993). The Bretton Woods international monetary system: A historical overview. In *A Retrospective on the Bretton Woods system*, ed. M. Bordo and B. Eichengreen. Chicago: The University Chicago Press.

Bordo, Michael D., and Hugh Rockoff. (1996). The gold standard as a "Good housekeeping seal of approval". *The Journal of Economic History* 56(2): 389–428.

Borio, Claudio, Toniolo Gianni., and Clement Piet. (2008). *Past and future of Central Bank Cooperation*. New York: Cambridge University Press.

Boughton, James. (2001). *Silent Revolution, the International Monetary Fund, 1979–1989*. Washington: International Monetary Fund.

Chwieroth, Jeffrey. (2010). *Capital Ideas, the IMF and the rise of financial liberalization*. Princeton: Princeton University Press.

De Vries, Margaret. (1986). *The IMF in a changing world, 1945–85*. Washington, DC: International Monetary Fund.

Eichengreen, Barry. (1992). *Golden Fetters: The gold standard and the great depression, 1919–1939,* NBER series on long-term factors in economic development.

Eichengreen, Barry. (1995). Central banks cooperation and exchange rate commitments: The classical and interwar gold standards compared. *Financial History Review* 2(2): 99–117.

Flandreau, Marc. (1997). Central bank cooperation in historical perspective: A sceptical view. *Economic History Review* (50): 735–763.

Helleiner, Eric. (1994). *States and the reemergence of global finance*. Ithaca: Cornell University Press.
Helleiner, Eric. (2003). *The Making of national money*. Ithaca: Cornell University Press.
Helleiner, Eric. (2014). *Forgotten foundations of Bretton Woods, international development and the making of the postwar order*. Ithaca: Cornell University Press.
Horsefield, J. Keith. (1969). *The International Monetary Fund, 1945–1965*, vols. 1–3. Washington, D.C.: IMF.
Ishii, Kanji. (1994). Japanese foreign trade and the Yokohama Specie Bank, 1880–1913. In *Pacific banking, 1859–1959: East meets West*, ed. Olive Checkland, Shizuya Nishimura., and Norio Tamaki. London: St. Martin's Press.
James, Harold. (1996). *International monetary cooperation since Bretton Woods*. Oxford: IMF & Oxford University Press.
Kindleberger, Charles P. (1986). International public goods without international government. *American Economic Review* 76(1): 1–13.
Lavelle, Katheryn C. (2011). *Legislating international organization, the US Congress, the IMF, and the World Bank*. New York: Oxford University Press.
Mouré, Kenneth. (2002). *The Gold standard illusion, France, the Bank of France, and the international gold standard, 1914–1939*. Oxford: Oxford University Press.
Ruggie, John Gerard. (1982). International regimes, transactions, and change: Embedded liberalism in the postwar economic order. *International Organization* 36(2): 379–415.
Steil, Benn. (2013). *The battle of Bretton Woods: John Maynard Keynes, Harry Dexter White, and the making of a new world order*. Princeton: Princeton University Press.
Toniolo, Gianni, ed. (1988). *Central banks' independence in historical perspective*. Berlin/New York: W. de Gruyter.
Toniolo, Gianni. (2005). *Central bank cooperation at the Bank for International Settlements, 1930–1973, with the assistance of Piet Clement*. New York: Cambridge University Press.
Triffin, Robert. (1968). *Our International Monetary System: Yesterday, today and tomorrow*. New York: Random House.
Yago, Kazuhiko. (2013). *The Financial history of the Bank for International Settlements*. London: Routledge.

Contents

Biographies

Editors

Yoshio Asai is a Professor of Economic History at Seijo University. He is the author of *Sengo Kaikaku to Minshushugi* (Post-war Economic Reforms and Democracy) (2001) and a co-author of *Showa Zaiseishi, 1952–73* (History of Fiscal and Monetary Policies in Japan, 1952–73), Vol. 11 (1999), Vol. 12 (1992) and *Kinyu Kiki to Kakushin* (Financial Crises and Innovations) (2000).

Masanao Itoh Professor at Otsuma Women's University and Professor Emeritus at the University of Tokyo. His main writings are *Japanese Overseas Finance and Financial Policy 1914–1936* (Nagoya University Press, 1989, in Japanese), which was awarded the 31st Japan Economist Prize in 1990; *History of Fiscal and Monetary Policies in Japan 1974–1989*, Vol. 7, 11: International Finance and External Economic Affairs (Ministry of Finance, Toyo Keizai Inc., editor, 2003, 2004, in Japanese); *Japanese Overseas Finance and Financial Policy 1945–1974* and *The Formation and the End of the 360 Yen–Dollar Rate* (Nagoya University Press, 2009, in Japanese); and *Why Have the Financial Crises Been Repeated?* (Junpo-sha, 2010, in Japanese).

Kazuhiko Yago, Professor at Waseda University, Faculty of Commerce, defended his doctoral dissertation "L'épargne populaire comme fonds de placement public: Caisse des Dépôts et Consignations" at Université Paris X in 1996. Publications include: *Asian Imperial Banking History* (with Hubert Bonin and Nuno Valério), (Pickering and Chatto, 2014); *The Financial History of the Bank for International Settlements* (Routledge, 2012); and "La Banque du Japon dans le système monétaire international, 1945–1985", in Olivier Feiertag et Michel Margairaz, dirs., *Les banques centrales à l'échelle du monde* (Presses de la Fondation nationale des sciences politiques, 2012).

Authors

Piet Clement currently works as historian and head of the Library and Archives unit at the Bank for International Settlements in Basel, Switzerland. He obtained a Ph. D. in Modern History at the Katholieke Universiteit Leuven, Belgium in 1995, with a dissertation on Belgian public finance (1830–1940). His papers include: "Nazi Germany and the service of the Dawes and Young Loans" (*Financial History Review* 11(1): 33–50); "The term 'macroprudential': origins and evolution" (*BIS Quarterly Review*, March: 59–67); "A balancing act: 75 years of international monetary and financial cooperation, 1936–2011" (*Revue bancaire et financière*, 2010:7–8; 2011: 386–393).

Ayako Ishizaka, Professor at Aichi Shukutoku University, Faculty of Business. She studied economic history and received her doctorate in economics in 2000 from Nagoya University. Her publications include: "Disequilibrium between National and International Economic Accounts in the 1950s West Germany: Dilemma of the 'Social Market Economy'", in Gonjo, Yasuo, ed., *Neo-Liberalism and the Post-War Capitalism: The European and American Experiences from Historical Perspectives* (Nihon Keizai Hyouronsha, 2006, pp. 255–299); and "From Regional Surplus Nation to Global Capital Exporter: German as an Article XIV Member of the IMF (1952–1961), in *Rekishi to Keizai* (Journal of Political Economy and Economic History), 217 (Vol. LV, No. 1), Autumn 2012, pp. 1627.

Kanna Ito is an Associate Professor of St. Andrew's University, Faculty of Economics. She received her doctorate in economics in 2001 from Nagoya University. Her publications include: "Economic Revitalization and Birth of the State Ownership in Interwar Italy," in *Economic Science, Nagoya University*, 2008, vol. 56; "Foundation of the Post-war Italian Economy: Formation of the 1936 Banking Law and the State Holdings Company", in Isao Hirota et al. eds., *Social and Economic Policy of Contemporary Europe: Formation and Evolution* (Nihon Keizai Hyouronsha, 2006); "Industrial Relief in Italy under the Great Depression: SIP Group Dissolution by the IRI," in *Journal of Political Economy and Economic History*, 2001, no. 172.

Makoto Kishida is an Assistant Professor of Japanese Economic History in the College of Economics at Nihon University. He has written articles on the history of Anglo-Japanese/US-Japanese financial relations in the twentieth century. He is co-author of *Nihon Keizaishi, 1600–2000* (Economic History of Japan, 1600–2000) (Keio University Press, 2009). His recent publications include papers on Japan's foreign loan issues and its credit in the international capital market before the World War II.

Teru Nishikawa is an Associate Professor of Economics at Yokohama National University. He holds a PhD in Economics from the University of Tokyo, Japan. He is the author of Creation and Evolution of the IMF Economic Policy in the Bretton Woods Era (The University of Nagoya Press, 2014).

Yasutoshi Noshita is a Professor in the faculty of Political Science and Economics, Kokushikan University. He is the author of the book *Contemporary Development of Monetary Economic Analysis: In Search of the Managed Currency System of non-Keynesian Type* (in Japanese) (Nihon Keizaihyouronsha, 2001).

Catherine Schenk, FRHS, is Professor of International Economic History at the University of Glasgow. She gained her Ph.D. at the London School of Economics and has held academic posts at Royal Holloway, University of London, Victoria University of Wellington, and visiting positions at the International Monetary Fund and the Hong Kong Monetary Authority as well as the University of Hong Kong and Nottingham Business School campus in Seminyeh, Malaysia. She is an associate fellow in the international economics department at Chatham House in London. Her research focuses on international monetary and financial relations after 1945 with a particular emphasis on East Asia and the United Kingdom. She is the author of several books including *International Economic Relations since 1945* (2011) and *The Decline of Sterling: Managing the Retreat of an International Currency* (2010). Her current research interests include the development of international banking regulation since the 1960s and the causes of the sovereign debt crisis of the 1980s.

Ayumu Sugawara is an Associate Professor of Global Business History at Tohoku University. He obtained his Ph.D. in Economics from Kyoto University. His papers include "British Overseas Investments in Canada in the 1950s" (Shakai-Keizai Shigaku, Vol. 66, No. 2, 2001, in Japanese); "N.M. Rothschild & Sons' Mining Investments, 1952–1960" (Keieishigaku, Vol. 36, No. 1, 2001; in Japanese; and "American International Banking in Asia: The Case of IBC in China during the Inter-War Period" (Keizaigaku, Vol. 74, No. 4, 2014).

Isao Suto is a Professor of Economic History at Meiji University, Tokyo. He gained his Ph.D. in Economics from Nagoya University. His books include *Shaping of the Post-War Federal* Reserve *Policy: From New Deal to the Accord* (2008).

Masayoshi Tsurumi is a Professor in the Department of Economics, Hosei University. He obtained a Ph.D. from the Department of Economics at the University of Tokyo.

Abbreviations

BA	Banker's acceptance
BIS	Bank for International Settlements
BOE	Bank of England
ECA	Economic Cooperation Administration
ECAFE	Economic Commission for Asia and the Far East
ECOSOC	Economic and Social Council of the United Nations
EMA	European Monetary Agreement
EPU	European Payments Union
ERP	European Recovery Program
EXIM	Export-import Bank of Washington
FOMC	Federal Open Market Committee
FRB	Board of Governors of Federal Reserve System
FRBNY	Federal Reserve Bank of New York
G10	Group of Ten
GAB	General Agreement to Borrow
GATT	General Agreement on Tariffs and Trade
IBRD	International Bank for Reconstruction and Development (see WB)
IDA	International Development Association
IMF	International Monetary Fund
ITO	International Trade Organization
KMT	Guomintang (Chinese Nationalist Party)
MSA	Mutual Security Act
MSA	Mutual Security Agency
NAC	National Advisory Council on International Monetary and Financial Problems
NSC	National Security Council
OECD	Organization for Economic Cooperation and Development
OEEC	Organization for European Economic Cooperation
PRC	People's Republic of China
ROC	Republic of China
SDR	Special Drawing Rights

UN	United Nations
UNCTAD	United Nations Conference on Trade and Development
WB	World Bank (see IBRD)
WP3	OECD Economic Policy Committee Working Party Three

Part I
Foundation and Development of the IMF

Chapter 1
Pre-history of the IMF: Debates in the UK and Anglo-American Negotiation

Masanao Itoh

1 Introduction

According to a study by the IMF released in September 2008, around the time of the economic shock that followed the collapse of Lehman Brothers, over the 38-year period from 1970 through 2007 currency crises had occurred in 208 countries, bank crises in 124 countries, and national debt crises in 63 countries.[1] Since the 1970s financial crises had occurred in a wide variety of countries and regions—in developed countries, emerging newly industrialized states, and developing countries, and in Asia, Europe, North and South America, and Africa. Under such conditions, the Washington consensus and the role of IMF conditionality became a subject of consideration anew, as well as reconsideration of the role of the IMF in recent great moderation era.

In the 2009 G20 meeting in London, then-British Prime Minister Gordon Brown stated, "The old Washington consensus is over." Many argue that the Washington consensus arose in the 1970s with the exit of Keynesianism, spread during the 1980s, peaked in the 1990s, and either came to an end in the 2000s or survived until the global financial crisis of 2008 and 2009. One also could say that questions are being asked again about how to restore confidence in international institutions themselves or in the policies they propose.

In doing so, the age of the IMF system as an adjustable peg system, or the age of the so-called Bretton Woods system, often is mentioned as a standard of comparison. Since the subjects discussed at G20 meetings after the Lehman Brothers shock, such as whether a new reserve currency or intermediate currency should be created,

[1] IMF, WP08/224, Systemic Banking Crises: A New Database.

M. Itoh (✉)
School of Social Information Studies, Otsuma Women's University,
Tama, Tokyo 206-8540, Japan
e-mail: masaitoh@e.u-tokyo.ac.jp

K. Yago et al. (eds.), *History of the IMF*, Studies in Economic History,
DOI 10.1007/978-4-431-55351-9_1

how to regulate movement of capital, means of providing funds to countries faced with funds shortages, and supervision and regulation of private financial institutions, are the same topics discussed when forming the Bretton Woods system, it is not unexpected that the period of formation of the Bretton Woods system would emerge as a standard of comparison.

Already an extremely large number of topics related to the formation of the Bretton Woods system have been discussed. Among these, the view of Harrod (1951) and Gardner (1969) have served as standards for a very long period of time. This is the view that, despite the Keynes' proposal was superior to the White's, the Keynes proposal of a credit-creation function and a multilateral settlement system based on banking principles was defeated by the White's proposal based on the principle of contribution, which did not involve any particular credit-creation function or settlement system, due to the overwhelming economic power of the United States and wartime financial relations between the U.S. and Great Britain (in which debtor nation status, fiscal insolvency, and a current account deficit led to accumulation of pounds sterling).

However, the 1970s saw the beginning of opposition to this Keynesian myth. The fuse was lit by T. Balogh (1976), whose criticisms advanced through both focusing on the historical limitations of the Keynes' plan and reconsidering the U.S. proposal. Behind this development was progress in materials, such as the publication of Keynes' complete works and disclosure of primary materials in both Britain and the U.S., as well as criticism of Keynesian economics from the points of view of monetarism and rational expectations theory, which saw stagflation which commonly occurred in many developed nations as a result of Keynesian policies.

Regarding the first point, a focus on the historical limitations of the Keynes plan, A. van Dormael (1978) argued that there was continuity between the Keynes plan and Nazi bilateral settlement agreements, while R.F. Mikesell (1994) argued for the transitional nature of the multilateral settlement concept premised on an exchange concentration system. Also, D.E. Moggridge (1986), who conducted a detailed comparison with the age of the international gold standard, identified two abstract views of Keynes—one as a regulationist who argued for control through rules (in response to nonconformity between international finance and international economic policies)—and one as an elasticity pessimist. R. Skidelsky (2002) abstracted an image of Keynes as a defender of British interests. On the contrary, G.C. Peden (2004), through primary materials of the HM Treasury, revealed that Keynes' idealism brought conflicts repeatedly with the HM Treasury and the Bank of England in various scenes. Recently, as seen in Shigeru Yonekura (2006), the view also has arisen that Keynes had little understanding of the IMF Articles of Agreement.

The latter point, the review of the American proposal, saw a transition from R.F. Harrod's (1951) mythicized view of White as a believer in Keynesianism to R.W. Oliver's (1975) view of White's proposal as no more than an offshoot of the Inter-American Bank proposal and the image of White identified by S.W. Black (1991) as a person deeply opposed to Treasury Secretary Morgenthau and Treasury Principal Economist Bernstein (the first Director of the IMF Research Department).

Furthermore, in recent years the view even has appeared that White was a Soviet spy, as argued in J.E. Haynes and H. Klehr (1999).[2] In contrast, J.M. Boughton (2006) has expressed the opposite view that not only had Morgenthau continued to trust White but that his innovative, flexible, and future-oriented economic thought played a decisive role in the design of the IMF. Furthermore, from an extensive review of a large number of White's unpublished documents B. Steil (2013) has depicted him as a designer of the postwar order from his perspective as a patriot and defender of American interests.

Even today the fundamental issues of these arguments over the process of creation of the IMF system remain unresolved. The main reason for this can be thought of as the fact that even today there is insufficient understanding of the points of how the Allies' postwar plans resulted in the structure of the IMF, where among these plans the Allies were fundamentally in opposition to each other, and how this opposition was reflected in the agreement. This work will reconsider these points by looking mainly at the process of formation of the Keynes and White plans during the period prior to the Bretton Woods Agreements and identifying various confrontations that emerged during that process.

2 What Were the Disputes?

2.1 The Allies' Postwar Plans

It is well known that the Allies' postwar plans appeared in the August 1941 Atlantic Charter and the February 1942 Anglo-American Mutual Aid Agreement. Put simply, these postwar plans intended to realize the two goals of "freedom, nondiscrimination, and multilateralism" and "expanding equilibrium (economic recovery and full employment through expansionism)" among the Allies through international partnership and cooperation. However, it is not necessarily the case that there was a consensus, either among the Allies or domestically in the U.S. or Britain, of how such freedom, nondiscrimination, and multilateralism should be understood or how these three ideals should be linked to expanding equilibrium.

For example, even within the U.S., which had taken leadership on the Atlantic Charter, the State Department had adopted a free-trade position focusing more on free trade than on multilateral settlement under the Hull principles, while the

[2]While it is clear today from the archives of the former Soviet Union that White had provided documents and information to the Soviets, this does not necessarily mean that White was a spy. J.M. Boughton (2006) argues that Morgenthau continued to trust White and that it had been determined that he needed to appear to be friendly to the Soviet Union for the purposes of stability of the international currency system, and B. Steil (2013, p. 36) also rejects the theory that White was a spy, arguing that he provided the materials of his own accord without being ordered by anybody to do so and was not involved in any underground activities.

Treasury Department focused most of all on international currency issues, seeing these as important to creating some kind of system by which the dollar could function as an international currency. Its plan was to build a systemic framework for providing short-term exchange-rate stabilization funds needed to maintain fixed exchange rates and link it with the international investment bank plan for providing long-term exchange-rate stabilization loans (Honma 1991, Ch. 1). However, private U.S. banks were critical of these postwar plans of the Treasury Department, arguing that dollar loans by private banks were essential to postwar stability. Probably one issue that we should look at would be the relationship between these domestic disputes and the White plan that would be formed later.

In addition, from an observation at British postwar reconstruction plans from the postwar reconstruction plans defined in Article 7 of the February 1942 Anglo-American Mutual Aid Agreement one could conclude that in addition to recovery assistance by creditor nations, tariff reductions, and adoption of expansionist economic policies, international cooperation was envisioned in the form of permitting debtor nations to take protective measures to regulate imbalances in their international balances of payments. The British side managed to combine multilateralism with bilateralism. This once again brings up the subject of the relationship between such British interests and the Keynes plan, which was being prepared and elaborated upon.

2.2 *Release of the Keynes and White Plans*

Over the period of roughly one-half year from the Atlantic Charter to the Anglo-American Mutual Aid Agreement, the first through fourth drafts of the Keynes plan on a postwar international currency system and the first draft of the White plan were prepared. Then, following conclusion of the Anglo-American Mutual Aid Agreement, the second and third drafts of the White plan were prepared in March and April 1942, and then in August the fifth and sixth drafts of Keynes plan were prepared together with comments on White plan. White visited Britain in October, where he met privately with Keynes in London. The seventh draft of Keynes' plan was prepared in November, and following consideration by the U.S. based on this draft in April 1943 the U.S. State Department announced the Preliminary Draft Outline of Proposal for a United and Associated Nations Stabilization Fund and then the British government announced the Proposals by British Experts for an International Clearing Union. It is these documents that are referred to commonly as the White plan and the Keynes plan, respectively.

As outlined below, until the White and Keynes plans were finalized in this way each country's own proposal was subjected to a number of internal criticisms within the U.S. and British governments. Federal Reserve Bank of New York

(FRBNY) Vice President Williams criticized the White plan from a key currency approach, with the strong support of the U.S. financial sector. Following the preparation of the first draft of Keynes' plan, Thompson of the BOE foreign bureau repeatedly argued that the only practical approach to addressing the issue of sterling balances while maintaining the international status of the pound sterling was that of "planned bilateralism." Both plans incorporated such internal criticisms to a limited extent. Table 1.1 summarizes the Keynes and White plans as of April 1943.

The differences between the two proposals as of that time are summarized briefly below. The first concerns the fundamental nature of the organization to be set up. While the Keynes plan envisioned a multilateral clearing mechanism that would

Table 1.1 The Keynes and White plans

Keynes plan	White plan
1. The International Clearing Union (ICU) would be set up, with each country opening an account with this union and settling its external accounts through multilateral clearing.	1. A currency stabilization fund would be set up with funding from member countries, in gold or their own currencies, based on certain criteria.
2. No fund would be necessary for the ICU because for each credit account a country had with the union, the counterpart country would have a debit account.	2. Each country would be assigned a quota based on criteria such as its gold holdings and national income, and it would enjoy benefits such as voting rights and payment advantages in accordance with this quota.
3. Each member country would be assigned a quota based on its average exports and imports over the past 3 years, and a surcharge would apply to debit balances when they reached a certain threshold (25 % of the quota).	3. Each member country could, under certain conditions, purchase the currency of other member countries for gold or its own currency.
4. A monetary unit called a Bancor, which would indicate a fixed amount of gold, would be set up, and each country would link its own currency to this unit. The central bank of each country would open up a Bancor account with the union, through which mutual settlement of accounts and credit provision would be conducted.	4. A monetary unit called a Unitas, equivalent to USD10, would be set up and used to indicate the value of members' currencies.
5. Although in principle the value of the Bancor would be fixed, under certain conditions it would be permitted to be revalued or devalued.	5. Member countries would assume obligations including prompt elimination of the restrictions on current transactions, guarantee for the free exchange of their own currencies held by the fund, cooperation with the management of movements of capital of other countries, and elimination of bilateral clearing arrangements and multiple currency practices.
6. While Bancor could be purchased using gold, gold could not be purchased using Bancor.	

permit overdrafts, the White plan envisioned limited provision of credit based on the principle of contributions. Second, Keynes envisioned that the monetary unit used would be the bancor, with gold not having any currency status, while the White plan would use the unitas, a monetary unit with a value in dollars and with gold or each country's currency linked to the dollar. The third difference concerns funding quotas. While under the Keynes plan Britain would have had the largest quota, under the White plan the U.S. quota would be the largest.

The fourth concerns exchange rates. While the Keynes plan was flexible, permitting increases and decreases when certain conditions were met, the White plan envisioned fixed exchange rates like those under the gold standard. The fifth concerns currency markets. The Keynes plan assumed official convertibility centered on the central banks, while the White plan assumed exchange in the marketplace, based on market principles. Also, while the bancor would be an international currency, the unitas would be simply an accounting unit.

The sixth difference concerns the length of the transitional period. The Keynes plan envisioned a transition over 5 years, while the White plan envisioned a 3-year period. Even though Keynes' proposal called for a longer period, both plans intended to complete transitional measures over a short time. The seventh concerns restrictions on movement of capital. While the Keynes plan would have required strong restrictions on movement of capital, the White plan was ambiguous on this point. The eighth concerns the issue of adjustment for current account imbalances. Keynes' plan argued for symmetry, with both creditor and debtor nations bearing similar responsibility for such adjustments, while White's argued that countries with deficits should bear all responsibility for adjustment for current account imbalances.

When both plans were published, Keynes was highly optimistic about the superiority of his own plan: "It is fair to say that all of them (the European Allies) without exception, not only prefer the Clearing Union, but prefer it very strongly, and for what I, at any rate, would regard as sound, fundamental reasons. After all, there are several reasons why S.F. in its present form cannot look too attractive to a smallish country (April 1943, *The Collected Writings of John Maynard Keynes*, v. 25 ["v. 25" hereinafter], p. 240)." "It is clear that practically the whole world, with only one or two insignificant exceptions, if there are any at all, prefers the general schema of the Clearing Union to the Stabilisation Fund (June 9, 1943, v. 25, p. 283)."

However, Keynes' optimism was shattered by the defection of key members of the Sterling bloc, including Canada, India, and South Africa, from the British side and by the approaches of White and others to Allies and quasi-Allies through vigorous bilateral discussions. At the end of June 1943, Keynes prepared a document titled "Integration of the C.U. and the S.F.," whose main content is excerpted below (June 29, 1943, v. 25, pp. 308–309).

I

We accept the substance of White's essential conditions,
Namely:

(1) We agree to the subscription principle;
(2) We agree to the limitation of liability;
(3) We agree that no country shall be required to change the gold value of its currency against its will.

We also accept the U.S. formula for quotas and voting power, and the general shape of S.F. We are prepared to agree as a condition of the scheme, that the initial exchange rate between pound and dollar shall be £1 = $4.

II

Our own essential conditions are:

(i) The fund shall not deal in a mixed bag of currencies but only in unitas, holding of which will be acquired by members in exchange for their subscriptions and which will not be redeemable in gold.
(ii) As regarding the gold subscription, the original S.F. proposal, namely 12 1/2 per cent of the quota, would be acceptable. If this is to be modified, it must be in such a way as not to give the scheme too pronounced a gold-standard appearance and, more particularly, must not unduly qualify its expansionist possibilities by draining gold from countries whose reserves are relatively deficient already.
(iii) The balance of the subscription must be in the shape of a non-negotiable government security.
(iv) The provisions for elasticity in changing the value of a member's currency and for preserving sovereignty in this respect shall be reconsidered.
(v) The greatest objections to S.F. in its revised version is that a creditor country can go on absorbing great quantities of gold as heretofore, before any real pressure is put upon it.

(omission)

Even while arguing against "capitulating completely to dollar diplomacy" (July 19, 1943, v. 25, p. 318), as of June 1943 Keynes had been forced into a negotiation of conditions with the U.S. side. Ultimately, the April 1944 "Joint Statement by Experts" largely converged on the White plan, as seen in Table 1.2.

2.3 *Identifying the Basic Battle Lines*

Each of the two proposals for a postwar international currency mechanism included intricate overlapping battle lines on the subjects of philosophies, structures, and policies for the postwar international currency system.

Table 1.2 Excerpted from Joint Statement by Experts on the Establishment of an International Monetary Fund (April 22, 1944)

I. Purpose and policies of the International Monetary Fund
(omission)
II. Subscription to the Fund
1. Member countries shall subscribe in gold and in their local funds amounts (quotas) to be agreed, which will amount altogether to about $8 billion if all the United and Associated Nations subscribe to the Fund (corresponding to about $10 billion for the world as a whole).
(omission)
III. Transactions with the Fund
1. Member countries shall deal with the Fund only through their Treasury, central bank, stabilization fund or other fiscal agencies. The Fund's account in a member's currency shall be kept at the central bank of the member country.
2. A member shall be entitled to buy another member's currency from the Fund in exchange for its own currency on the following conditions:-
(omission)
3. The operations on the Fund's account will be limited to transactions for the purpose of supplying a member country on the member's initiative with another member's currency in exchange for its own currency or for gold.
(omission)
IV. Par values of member currencies
1. The par value of a member's currency shall be agreed with the Fund when it is admitted to membership and shall be expressed in terms of gold. All transactions between the Fund and members shall be at par subject to a fixed charge payable by the member making application to the Fund; and all transactions in member currencies shall be at rates within an agreed percentage of parity.
(omission)
V. Capital transactions
1. A member country may not use the Fund's resources to meet a large or sustained outflow of capital and the Fund may require a member country to exercise control to prevent such use of the resources of the Fund. (omission)
VI. Apportionment of scarce currencies
1. When it becomes evident to the Fund that the demand for a member country's currency may soon exhaust the Fund's holdings of the currency, the Fund shall so inform member countries and propose an equitable method of apportioning the scarce currency. When a currency is thus declared scarce, the Fund shall issue a report embodying the causes of the scarcity and containing recommendations designed to bring it to an end.
2. A decision by the Fund to apportion a scarce currency shall operate as an authorization to a member country, after consultation with the Fund, temporarily to restrict the freedom of exchange operations in the affected currency and, in determining the manner of restricting the demand and rationing the limited supply amongst its nationals, the member country shall have complete jurisdiction.
(omission)

Source: *The Collected Writings of John Maynard Keynes*, v. 25, pp. 469–477

The first battle line concerned issues related to the philosophies behind building postwar international trade and financial relations. This can be seen in the conflict between the multilateral and bilateral or unilateral approaches, or between the universal approach and the key currency approach. While at first glance it would seem that the multilateral approach corresponded to the universal approach while the bilateral or unilateral approach corresponded to the key currency approach, things were not so simple.

The Anglo-American Financial Agreement signed 1 year after the signing of the IMF Articles of Agreement and the Marshall Plan begun in 1948 clearly were bilateral in nature. Gardner's commonly accepted view of the Anglo-American Financial Agreement as a departure from multilateralism based on anticommunist ideology assumes this correspondence. However, the Anglo-American Financial Agreement also can be seen to supplement the IMF. From another point of view, the issue can be said to be that of whether these two battle lines should be seen as Keynes vs. White or as Keynes and White vs. Williams. Keynes, both a universalist and a defender of British interests, faced opposition in Britain from the Bank of England, which argued for even stricter bilateralism. White too, who was even more of a universalist than Keynes but also a defender of U.S. interests, faced opposition in the U.S. from private banks, which sought free movement of capital and freedom in their own overseas lending, and the Federal Reserve Bank of New York.

The second battle line involved issues related to the systems and nature of the mechanism to be created. Here the focal points were the well-known arguments between banking principles and fund principles and between official exchange and market exchange. Since after the end of World War II it was an objective fact that Britain faced the difficulties of its debtor nation status, fiscal collapse, and a current account deficit that resulted in accumulation of Sterling balances, the international currency system to be created needed to address this issue of accumulated Sterling balances. While Bretton Woods avoided addressing the issue of accumulated Sterling balances itself directly as a topic, since the issue was inseparable from the scarce currency clause through the conversion to dollars of pounds held by Sterling bloc nations, this conflict inevitably placed substantial restrictions on postwar British economic developments.

In fact, after signing of the IMF Articles of Agreement in July 1944 the Keynes-Robertson dispute and a subsequent dispute between Britain and the U.S. would develop concerning interpretation of Article 8. These disputes, focused on whether the market exchange of Paragraph 2 of Article 8 of the IMF Articles of Agreement or the public exchange of Paragraph 4 of that article should have priority, is said to have ended in a defeat for Keynes. Originally there had been differences between the British and U.S. sides on the order of paragraphs 2 and 4 (with the British proposal putting Paragraph 4 first). Keynes saw convertibility of currency as a duty of central banks, while Robertson saw it as a duty of the private sector. Put another way, Keynes considered convertibility to be based on multilateral settlement among central banks, and he believed that this would make it possible to restrict private-sector capital movements.

In concluding the Anglo-American Financial Agreement, the British side pledged to restore convertibility of the pound in 1 year, and convertibility resumed on July 18, 1947. However, this restoration lasted for only 1 month, and on August 20 Britain was forced to suspend convertibility as its restoration of trading on open currency markets was a spectacular failure. This is where the issue of the positioning of the Anglo-American Financial Agreement as seen above comes in. This also can be looked at together with the issue of whether the established IMF was considered a transitional mechanism for the postwar period or a permanent mechanism that would continue to function even after the postwar recovery period.

The third battle line concerned the policy choices for maintaining and operating the mechanism. One conflict was between giving priority to free trade and giving priority to free foreign exchange, or to put it another way the conflict between planning a currency system based on the real economy or one assuming autonomy in the monetary economy. To the British side, it definitely would not be desirable to prioritize free trade if the objective was to realize expanding equilibrium (economic recovery and full employment through expansionism).

At the same time, this brought about a conflict between the theory of responsibility of deficit countries and the theory of responsibility of surplus countries. This conflict would arise again in the 1971 Nixon Shock and in the 1985 Plaza Accord. While in both those cases the U.S. argued for the responsibility of surplus countries, at this postwar time it argued strongly for the complete opposite point of view, the responsibility of deficit countries.

The above battle lines were in existence prior to the formation of the IMF. There were intricate battle lines regarding philosophies, mechanisms, and policy choices for the IMF. There is a need to look anew at which of these were fundamental battle lines and at the relations between these battle lines.[3]

3 The Keynes Plan and the White Plan: Evolution and Elaboration

3.1 The Process of Formation of the Keynes Plan

It has been commonly understood that a rift developed between Keynes on one side and HM Treasury and the Bank of England (BOE) on the other in the process of British-American financial negotiations in October 1945 and later. Already it is clear to some extent that in the process from the first draft of Keynes plan for a postwar international currency system in September 1941 to his seventh draft in December 1942 various government departments including HM Treasury, the BOE and Oxford economists had made various criticisms of Keynes plan. Then, in April 1943 a Keynes plan significantly revised through the process of such debate was

[3] This identification of the issues draws further on the lines of argument concerning whether the Truman Doctrine of containment impacted the forms of the functions of the IMF and IBRD (Topic 2, The IBRD, the Anglo-American Financial Agreement, the Marshall Plan, and the IMF) and that concerning whether the IMF and the IBRD were the starting point of Anglo-American neoliberalism (Topic 3, Anglo-American Neoliberalism: the Result of Seeing Full Market Competition as the Core Issue of Liberalism and Free Movement of Capital as the Core Issue of Freedom).

conveyed to the U.S. government in the form of a British government white paper, "Proposals for an International Clearing Union." Since Keynes continued to play an active role as a central figure in nearly all aspects of negotiations with the U.S., at the time of this official government proposal the view came to be accepted that the conflict concerning Keynes plan within the British government had, to some degree, been resolved.

However, by tracing the debate on Keynes plan within the British government in further detail one can see that consistent criticism of the gap between the basic framework envisioned by Keynes and its actual functions continued to be expressed by the British government and the BOE. While of course in the background was a conflict of opinions concerning recognitions of Britain's actual situation, it would appear that another background factor concerned Keynes' own treatment of idealism and pragmatism. Keynes referred to his own postwar international currency plans as "my Utopia," and it is not clear whether he saw the process of revisions to his plan as voluntary improvements made through the process of debate or as compromises with criticism.

Let's look first of all at the responses of HM Treasury and the BOE to the Keynes plan from the time of the first draft in September 1941 to that of the fourth draft in January 1942. The first draft in September consisted of two memorandums entitled "Post-war Currency Policy" and "Proposals for an International Currency Union.[4] The former argued that the international gold standard was inappropriate as a means of rectifying imbalances in international balances of payments, and that creditor nations needed to play the main role in such rectification through restrictions on movements of capital. The latter argued for the establishment of a new international clearing bank and the development of a system of settlement of all international transactions between central banks through their own accounts with the international clearing bank.

HM Treasury and the BOE immediately criticized this plan. In response to these criticisms, in November 1941 Keynes released his second draft, titled "Proposal for an International Currency Union".[5] This second proposal was "to generalize the essential principle of banking … through the establishment of an International Clearing Bank" (v. 25, p. 44), and "the automatic register of the size and the whereabouts of the debtor and creditor positions allows definite criteria of which countries are entitled to special protection until they have re-adjusted their positions, and which are not" (ibid., p. 50). The readjustment of positions would be conducted through "unfettered multilateral clearing" (v. 25, p. 51). This second draft made it clear that the differences between the BOE and Keynes were fundamental. Originally, the BOE believed that it was essential to base any efforts to address the issue of sterling balances on existing bilateral payment agreements, and furthermore that current account imbalances should be rectified through various restrictions on international trade (i.e., the planned system). Keynes plan abandoned use

[4] The Collected Writings of John Maynard Keynes, v. 25 (Activities 1940–1944: Shaping the post-war world: The Clearing Union [Trans. Takashi Murano, 1992]), pp. 21–44.

[5] Ibid., pp. 42–71.

of these methods from the start. This was because Keynes considered their use were against his principles of multilateralism or universality.

In response to these criticisms, in December Keynes prepared his third draft, which deployed the main arguments of his second draft in greater detail. He sent it first to BOE Governor Norman.[6] The Keynes plan was an attempt to address the BOE's concerns that his plan might result in a crisis in the territories where sterling was the common currency. While the third draft continued to be the topic of discussion in various government ministries and agencies, Hopkins of HM Treasury came out with detailed critical observations of the proposal.[7] Keynes accepted part of Hopkins' critical observations, and in January 1942 he produced his fourth draft, which proposed the establishment of an international clearing union.

The BOE was the fiercest critic of Keynes' first through fourth drafts.[8] The BOE would keep up its criticism of Keynes' series of proposals, and this criticism continued until after the end of the Bretton Woods Conference.

For example, Thompson saw the Keynes plan as only a second best to reciprocal trade negotiations. "The danger which I see in Keynes' scheme, attractive as it is in many ways, is that the Board of Trade and the Americans will be prone to believe that monetary devices alone will solve our post-war exchange problem, while trade can be left free and indiscriminate."[9] Bolton was strongly critical, arguing that (i) Keynes' first draft was not a "Utopia" at all but contained notable flaws and limitations, (ii) if these were made public and Keynes made a director of the BOE, his "Utopia" would come to be considered a BOE project, (iii) the proposal was likely to be accepted uncritically in the U.S., and (iv) if the scheme should be printed, they may be compelled at a later stage to oppose it because of its unsoundness.[10] Furthermore, Cobbold argued that the difference between Keynes' approach and that of the BOE was in the way Keynes attempted to describe the initial steps that

[6] Ibid., pp. 75–100. The complete text of the December 19 letter to Norman is on pp. 99–108.

[7] The complete text of Sir Richard Hopkins, 'Critical observations on the Clearing Bank Plan' is in Peden (2004), pp. 247–260.

[8] The series of BOE documents criticizing the Keynes plan is collected in BOE Archives, ADM14. L.P. Thompson-McCausland's papers (1941–1965). Thompson (later Thompson-McCausland) joined the bank in October 1939. He was appointed assistant advisor to the governor in 1941 and advisor to the governor in 1949, retiring in September 1965. During this time with the bank, he mainly worked in the area of overseas finance. In 1941 he went to Washington with Keynes, where he worked mainly on wartime lending, and in 1943 he was sent to the U.S. again for the Bretton Woods Conference. He was a member of the British representative committee at the Geneva Conference in the summer of 1947 Geneva Conference and the Havana Conference (on setting up the GATT) in December of that year. He played a leading role in the debate on IMF reforms in the early 1960. In the above document, L.P.T refers to L.P. Thompson, G.L.F.B. to G.L.F. Bolton (BOE representative in the Washington Conference), and C.F.C. to C.F. Cobbold (a director of the Bank of England).

[9] BOE, ADM14. Keynes' Memoranda (1 & 2), L. P. T., 22nd Sep 41

[10] BOE, ADM14. On Mr. Keynes' Utopia (to C. F. C.), G. L. F. B., 30th Oct 41

they should take right away toward an ultimate goal while they emphasized the responsibility they were expected to fulfill for moving in the proper direction, avoiding initial errors.[11]

The most important topic to the BOE was how realistically to solve the issue of handling blocked pounds and accumulated pound balances likely to surface after World War II. Since the postwar British economy was fundamentally restricted by its debtor-nation status, fiscal collapse, and current-account deficit, it was not possible to solve the problem by avoiding this issue. The issue was reignited when acceptance of aid from the U.S. became a pressing topic in 1944 and later years, when after the signing of the Bretton Woods Accord negotiations on a British-American financial agreement were unavoidable. After Keynes' first January 1944 memorandum on U.S. aid to Britain, the BOE constantly opposed Keynes' proposal, and HM Treasury also began to criticize Keynes strongly. If facing head-on the current state of the British economy—its debtor-nation status, fiscal collapse, and current-account deficit—the Keynes plan from the start was the second-best proposal from the point of view of HM Treasury and the BOE, particularly the BOE.

In response, at this stage Keynes was in the position of a universalist or idealist attempting to break through the limitations of the classical gold standard and the gold standard restructured in the 1920s, through creation of a new international credit-creating agency. Keynes' answer to Hopkins' critical observations also included the arguments that Hopkins overemphasized the unique position of the U.S., that since over the short term countries with current-account surpluses would either lend those surpluses, buy gold with them, or deposit them in the clearing bank (i.e., increase their creditor positions) it was the responsibility required of such countries with current-account surpluses, and that stability in currency exchange was an important element behind achievement of postwar security and the clearing bank proposal was the most flexible proposal for foreign exchange markets based on this assumption (January 22, 1942, v. 25, pp. 103–108). In these arguments one can identify Keynes the universalist again.

The phase beginning with Keynes' fourth draft, which proposed the establishment of an international clearing union, would be a phase of internal adjustments through reconciliation between Britain and the U.S. of the two countries' own rough drafts, through a process that included the White plan sent to Keynes in July 1942, the preparation of Keynes' fifth draft and his response to the White plan that August, Morgenthau's meeting with White in October, and the meeting with Dominion representatives in November. Accordingly, we will look next at the process of formation of the White plan.

[11] BOE, ADM14, Post-War Policy (Bank's Memo and JMK) and memo., C. F. C., 24th Nov 41

3.2 The Process of Formation of the White Plan

The first rough draft of the White plan was written in December 1941. At that time, White held the post of chief of the finance division at the Treasury Department. Treasury Secretary Morgenthau instructed him to write a memo roughly five pages in length (Black 1991, pp. 35–38) that would become the December 30 document "Inter-Allied Monetary and Banking Action" (the first draft of the White plan) (van Dormael 1978, pp. 42–44; Mikesell 1994, p. 6). Based on this plan, beginning in January 1942 the Treasury Department played a central role in fairly in-depth discussions on a fund and bank, and in March 1942 the plan for an international stabilization fund (the second draft of the White plan) was prepared.

In this second draft, White described three international issues that the U.S. would face immediately after the end of World War II. The first was the need to avoid a breakdown of foreign exchange and a collapse of the currency and credit systems, the second was the need for a sound recovery of international trade, and the third was the need to supply considerable funds needed for world reconstruction, aid, and economic recovery. He also noted the need to establish agencies with the funding, power, and structure capable of addressing these three issues. This led later to the IMF, the World Bank (International Bank for Reconstruction and Development), and the International Trade Organization.[12]

Following minor revisions, this second draft was put together in April as the "Preliminary Draft Proposal for a United Nations Stabilization Fund and a Bank for Reconstruction and Development of the United and Associated Nations" (the third draft of the White plan). White's third draft is outlined below from the three perspectives of contributions, exchange rates, and provision of funds (Iwamoto 1999, pp. 251–253). First, member states would contribute amounts equivalent to at least USD5 billion in total. The share to be subscribed by each country would be decided in accordance with its gold holdings, gold production, national income, foreign trade, foreign investment, and external debt, and contributions would be made in gold, the countries' own currencies, and government securities. Of the total subscription of USD5.2 billion calculated in this way, the U.S. contributed slightly under USD3.2 billion and Britain slightly over USD600 million. Next, exchange rates between member countries' currencies would be fixed, and they could be changed only in the event of fundamental imbalances, and with the consent of four-fifths of the member countries. In the area of provision of funds, member countries could purchase currencies of other member countries held by the fund, paying for these using their own currencies. These were the key points of White plan as of this point in time.

White's third draft proposed that (i) the dollar should be in effect the sole core currency of the system; (ii) exchange rates should be fixed but could be adjusted (in the event of fundamental imbalances); and (iii) the fund should provide funding to cover shortages in member countries' payment of current account deficits in accor-

[12] White Archives, Box 6, Folder 6, "United Nations Stabilization Fund".

dance with their quotas. These were based on the assumptions that (iv) international trade should operate under a gold currency-change standard and (v) the fund should serve as a central storage institution for member countries' gold and foreign currency. It should be noted that this third draft already made point (iii) above clear when it called for restricting use of fund assets by debtor countries, restricting the possibility that unlimited U.S. funds would flow to debtor countries through the fund.

But where should one look for the background of this White plan? Boughton (2006, pp. 7–14) argues below that the first background factor is the role of gold in the system. In an unpublished 1942 paper,[13] White analyzed the gold-standard currency-exchange system and argued that such a system was best suited to an adjustable fixed exchange rate system as an innovative middle road between a strict gold standard and a completely managed currency system. Compared to Keynes, White clearly had more trust in the classical gold standard and in the automatic adjustment functions of the 1920s gold-standard currency-exchange system, and this was reflected in the White plan.

Second is the necessity of multilateral agreement and the role of silver bullion. Through steps including analysis of the 1933 London Monetary and Economic Conference, the Tripartite Agreement of 1936, and the 1937 default on Latin American debts to the U.S. White came to consider bilateral negotiation on financial policy to be largely meaningless.

In fact, when in 1935 White was first dispatched to London mainly to consult with HM Treasury on the issue of devaluation of the pound he got a true feel for the meaninglessness of bilateral discussions with HM Treasury, and a few months later he began studying methods of minimizing the shock to the U.S. economy of a rapid collapse of the pound. He concluded that the U.S. should build close trade relations with as many countries as possible and have those countries peg their own currencies to the dollar. In addition, when at the end of the 1930s Cuba and Mexico faced difficulties in paying their debts to the U.S., White proposed financial assistance in the form of the U.S. government providing silver to these countries, and furthermore he proposed a plan for a bank to hold silver in the Americas. This focus on the role of silver bullion in international settlement was reflected in the White plan.

Third is the role of the U.S. Exchange Stabilization Fund (ESF) established in January 1934.[14] In the mid-1930s, White proposed conversion of the ESF from a fund intended to stabilize the value of the dollar in gold to one that would stabilize the dollar's values in other currencies. In other words, he proposed using the ESF more broadly for the benefit of U.S. international finance, and when the Treasury Department accepted this proposal the ESF came to be used in regulation of financial markets with Mexico, Brazil, and other Latin American countries. Boughton notes, "White's experience with EFS lending also convinced him that the IMF should not extend credits automatically. His initial plan of April 1942 suggested that

[13] White Archives, Box 1, Folder 9, The Future of Gold, 1942.

[14] Bordo and Schwartz (2001) argue that expansionary use of the ESF was suggested in White's 1942 plan.

the Fund should respond to requests from borrowing countries by first making a careful independent assessment of the policy changes that the country should make to correct the underlying causes of its balance of payments problem." Boughton argues that that this was the prototype for the IMF conditionality that continued from the 1950s to the 1990s. While this proposal of White's was withdrawn in the face of Keynes' opposition, the policy of restrictions on use of fund assets by debtor countries was a result of his experience with the ESF.

The fourth concerns restrictions on movements of capital. It is well known that both Keynes and White recognized the need for restrictions on capital movement. Boughton notes, "Keynes drew a clear line between good capital flows—those that financed trade or real investment—and those that were speculative or volatile or that promoted capital flight. In contrast, the more nuanced practice regarding capital flows has been more in line with White's thinking, as revealed both his original plan for the Fund and his earlier work at the U.S. Treasury." There is no doubt that the 1935 inflow of gold to the U.S. and the franc crisis 3 years later convinced White of the necessity of restrictions on capital movements, but still White saw these restrictions as a necessary evil, calling them "the best of the bad choices".[15] In this way, Boughton infers that unlike Keynes White saw the line between real movements of capital and speculative ones as unclear.

White plan drew numerous criticisms from within the United States. The number of criticisms increased following the publication in April 1943 of both governments' proposals. Here we will examine the criticism from Deputy Governor Williams of the FRBNY (Honma 1991, pp. 92–95). The main points of Williams' critique of White were: (i) that the establishment of an international agency such as a supranational bank would give debtor nations decisive authority in international finance, (ii) that it would violate the principle of a balanced budget because the U.S. would bear the heaviest burden, (iii) that the U.S. would be unable to decide on terms of credit, (iv) that stabilization of foreign exchange would not be a fundamental solution to various difficulties in international finance, and (v) that universal currency stabilization by an international agency was an unrealistic approach and measures should be taken bilaterally through reciprocal agreements.

Here we can identify the relationship between White and Williams as analogous to that in Britain between Keynes and the BOE. While White squared off against Williams as a universalist, Williams' main goals were securing the interests of the U.S. banking sector and American leadership in the postwar recovery.[16]

[15] White Archives, Box 3, Folder 7, Memorandum from White to Morgenthau, April 30, 1938.

[16] The dispute reignited after the signing of the Bretton Woods Accord in July 1944 and as the dispute over "correcting" the accord through its ratification one year later. In this dispute, Williams told White frankly that the Bretton Woods Accord had lost the balance between idealism and pragmatism, but this subject is beyond the scope of this work.

3.3 *Reconciliation of the Two Plans and Convergence on White Plan*

After preparation of White's third draft in April 1942, the Treasury Department's offensive against the State Department advanced vigorously. In meetings between the two departments on May 25 and July 2, 1942, Morgenthau argued for having the Allies' finance ministers send financial experts to Washington to discuss American plans for the postwar international currency system. While the State Department was wary of this proposal, it approved informal meetings with Britain, China, Russia, and other leading Allies (Steil 2013, pp. 156–157). In this way, the White plan was sent to Britain in July 1942.

After receiving the White plan in July, Keynes began studying the plan. In an August 1942 memorandum, Keynes argued that while his and White plans might seem similar in appearance, the principles on which they were based differed fundamentally. He added the criticism that since White plan largely confined itself to adaptation of the gold standard, it would not be able to regulate the volumes of international currency as needed, and it would depend on the policies of countries that already held large gold reserves. At the same time, he described White's plan as containing a number of useful and suggestive proposals, and he said he was studying subjects including the issues of resolution of blocked pounds, restrictions on movements of capital, price stability of primary commodities, and gradual elimination of trade barriers. Based on these studies, Phillips sent Keynes' sixth draft to White on August 28, 1942.

During this period, Morgenthau and White visited London unofficially in October 1942, advancing reconciliation of White's and Keynes plans through steps including discussions with Keynes. However, Keynes was severely shocked when he received the White plans produced on February 18 (eight draft) and March 1 (ninth draft), 1943.[17] This was because they proposed the scarce currency clause, which had until then been nonexistent. This clause was to permit a country determined to have a shortage of a specific currency (specifically, the dollar) to restrict trading with the country whose currency it was short, through means such as import restrictions. A skeptical Keynes replied to Harrod, who saw this clause as a conciliatory or favorable approach to Britain on the U.S. side, "I cannot imagine that the State Department really would put forward as their own solution the rationing of purchases from a scarce currency country. You must remember that the evidence as to the extent to which the State Department have actually accepted this document of Harry White's is somewhat flimsy. I should expect that the moment emphatic attention was drawn to this alternative, it would be withdrawn (March 4, 1943, v. 25, p. 230)."

As mentioned at the start of this chapter, this plan of White's was published in April 1943 as the U.S. draft proposal for a United and Associated Nations Stabilization Fund. At the same time, Keynes plan too was published as the British

[17] Op. cit, p. 171.

government's proposal for an International Clearing Union. As we have seen above, for a while after its publication Keynes was confident in the comparative superiority of his own plan, and he believed that not only the Sterling bloc but also the nations of continental Europe would choose the clearing bank proposal. However, this confidence would collapse only a short time later. This was because it became clear that as a result of aggressive persuasive efforts on the part of the U.S. not just its neighbors but also key countries in the Dominion and the Sterling bloc had defected from the British side.

The July 24, 1943 letter from White to Keynes describes these circumstances clearly as follows: "We have almost completed our scheduled bilateral discussions on post-war monetary problems. Altogether we conferred with delegates of some 25 countries and also had several sessions of group discussions attended by delegates from about a score of countries. In the bilateral conference the most of the provisions in the Fund draft were discussed, and in almost every case the more important provisions in the Clearing Union draft were also considered…both proposals were rather fully discussed though the American proposal was the point of departure in the agenda. In our bilateral conference with the British group I think the salient points in both proposals were fully discussed and compared (July 24, 1943, v. 25, p. 335)."

In the lengthy official bilateral U.S.-British discussions held from September 21 to October 9, 1943—the so-called Washington Conference—the topics included the reliability of Fund use, minting of unitas, loan quotas, American lending limits, amounts of gold contributions, exchange-rate changes, and allocation of short currencies. However, Keynes' efforts to convert the Fund effectively into a bank, or put another way to incorporate into the Fund draft as much as possible the essentials of the Clearing Union draft, were unsuccessful. In addition, the rift between Keynes and the Bank of England widened over the course of this Washington Conference. On the subject of this rift, Sir Wilfrid Eady, Joint Second Secretary at HM Treasury, said that the Bank of England "derided" Keynes' view that it would be possible to block pre-zero-hour balances using exchange-rate controls based on stability fund capital, instead criticizing Keynes' view head-on, arguing, "we must make our own domestic arrangements with each of the holders of balances on the merits of the economic position and that so far from acquiring additional authority from the text of S.F. we (i.e., Britain) shall be embarrassed by the obligation to move towards multilateral clearing in 3 years (December 16, 1943, v. 25, p. 396)." Since the British wartime cabinet had ordered that this issue be deferred in the Washington Conference, this conflict did not surface during the conference. However, the issue of treatment of accumulated sterling balances that had been subjects of consideration in the White and Keynes plans through then would be left out from discussion of the agreement beginning with this conference.

In 1944, the conflict between Keynes and the BOE grew more acute. Lord Cherwell, an advisor to the Prime Minister, describes the circumstances as follows: "The Chancellor, though I believe, in favour of the proposals, is embarrassed by the existence of two rival factions in the Treasury. The one is headed by Lord Keynes, and supported by most of the Treasury, the Economic Section of the War Cabinet and officials of the Board of Trade. The other acts under the aegis of the Bank of England, and consists of Sir Hubert Henderson, an economist with Schachtian aspirations, and Sir Wilfred Eady, who after a variegated Civil Service experience has only recently joined the Treasury (February 9, 1944, v. 25, p. 408)."

In a letter dated February 23, 1944 to the Chancellor of the Exchequer, Keynes stated, "On the currency side-and much the same thing applies mutatis mutandis to the other topics-there are three alternatives. (I am here thinking of the normal, rather than of the transitional, period):-

(1) A Sterling currency bloc.
(2) An Anglo-American bloc offered as an international scheme.
(3) Dollar diplomacy

We regard the choice as between (1) and (2). The Americans regard it as between (2) and (3). They will not allow (1) (and it is only too easy for them to prevent it) except as a temporary expedient. We are not in fact strong enough to support (1) unaided. It follows that (2) is the only way of avoiding (3). The U.S. Treasury and State Department offer us (2) in a spirit of real disinterestedness; they do not like (3); but they will readily fall back on it-for, both politically and with the bankers, it is the line of least resistance-if they believe that we are throwing (2) over in favour of (1). The Bank is not facing any of the realities. They do not allow for the fact that our post-war domestic policies are impossible without further American assistance. They do not allow for the fact that the Americans are strong enough to offer inducements to many or most of our friends to walk out on us, if we ostentatiously set out to start up an independent shop. They do not allow for the fact that vast debt and exiguous reserves are not, by themselves, the best qualification for renewing old-time international banking (February 23, 1944, v. 25, pp. 411–412)."

At this stage in 1944, Keynes clearly had shifted to a position of trying to maintain the interests and authority of Britain and the London financial markets, based on the realities of the power relationship between Britain and the United States. White was doing the exact same thing.

4 Conclusion

In this chapter we have looked at the process of rethinking of the Keynes and White plans over the period from the conclusion of the Atlantic Charter in August 1941 to roughly April 1944. First, the prototypes of the Keynes and White plans were proposed beginning in autumn 1941, and over the period of roughly one and one-half years until both plans were published in April 1943 revisions to both of them proceeded basically through the process of adaptation to domestic reactions. To their domestic critics, both Keynes and White appeared as universalists or multilateralists. However, their universalism differed in that while Keynes' was an idealism that called for the creation of a new international financial organization as a public organization that would supervise the international financial system, White's placed its trust in the market discipline of the gold exchange standard. Still, these two points of view would undergo substantial changes as a result of the start of competition between the U.S. and Britain to corral allied and quasi-allied states to their side beginning with the publication of both these countries' plans in April 1943. In the process of direct tug-of-war between the U.S. and Britain and the two countries' efforts to get the support of other countries through the signing of the IMF Articles of Agreement in July 1944, both Keynes and White would face situations in which they had to advocate for their own countries' interests. In doing so, the issues they faced included the degree of burden that the U.S. and Britain should bear in formation of the postwar international financial order, the degree of authority that each should possess, the conditions under which the postwar British economy could be rebuilt and recover, and how to reflect the interests of countries other than these two. As their initial universalism and idealism receded into the background, the battle lines of banking principles vs. fund principles and official convertibility vs. market convertibility would emerge from theoretical positions to the forefront of policy choice and consistency.

This work was intended to verify the validity of the coordinate axis of the universal approach vs. the key currency approach, which has served as the main standard even after the collapse of the Keynesian myth after Balogh, in past study of the formative period of the IMF. This is why we have argued for the necessity of introducing the coordinate axes of multilateralism vs. bilateralism, official convertibility vs. market convertibility, and a mechanism for the transitional postwar period vs. a permanent mechanism. However, to get a clear overview of these complex coordinate axes, there is a further need to trace the two major developments of the phase that followed the period discussed herein, the period from the signing of the agreement through the end of 1945 when it was ratified by both the U.S. and Britain, and the period through August 1947 when the Anglo-American Financial Agreement was signed and ratified, the IMF then began operation, and Britain's efforts to recover convertibility ended in failure. These will be the next topics we will examine.

Primary Sources

The Collected Writings of John Maynard Keynes

v.25 Activities 1940–1944: shaping the post-war world: the clearing union/edited by Donald Moggridge, New York: Cambridge University Press, 1980

v.26 Activities 1940–1944: shaping the post-war world: Bretton Woods and reparations/edited by Donald Moggridge, New York: Cambridge University Press, 1980

Bank of England Archives

OV38 INTERNATIONAL MONETARY FUND, 1941–1964, 123 files

ADM14 L. P. Thompson-McCausland's papers, 1941–1965, 91 pieces

IMF Archives

Bretton Woods Collections

Box29 Box30: BWC-Letters & Memorandum 1943

Box36: BWC-MEMORANDA
TREASURY MEETINGS, FUND & BANK, 1942–1944
FEDERAL RESERVE BOARD MEMOS, 1943–1944
Box40, Box41: BWC- BERNSTEIN, E.M.
Princeton University Library Mudd Manuscript Library
Harry Dexter White Papers

References

Akimoto, Eiichi. 1997. Hari dekusta howaito to sengo kokusai tsuka taisei no koso (Harry Dexter White and the design of the postwar international currency system). *Chiba daigaku keizai kenkyu* 12–2.

Balogh, T. 1976. Keynes and the International Monetary Fund. In *Keynes and the international monetary relations work*, ed. Thirlwall. London: Macmillan.

Black, S.W. 1991. *A Levite among the priests – Edward Bernstein and the origin of the Bretton Woods system*. Boulder: Westview Press.

Bordo, M.D., and B. Eichengreen (eds.). 1993. *A retrospective on the Bretton Woods system: Lessons for international monetary reform*. Chicago: The University of Chicago Press.

Bordo, M., and A. Schwartz. 2001. *From the exchange stabilization fund to the international monetary fund*, NBER working paper, vol. 8100. Cambridge, MA: National Bureau of Economic Research.

Boughton, J.M. 2006. *American in the shadows: Harry Dexter White and the design of the international monetary fund*, IMF working paper, vol. 06/6. Washington, D.C: International Monetary Fund, Policy Development and Review Dept.

Dormael, A.V. 1978. *Bretton Woods: Birth of a monetary system*. London: Macmillan.

Gardner, R.N. 1969. *Sterling-dollar diplomacy: the origins and the prospects of our international economic order*. Trans. Takashi Murano et al, Tokyo Toyo Keizai, London: McGraw-Hill.

Harrod, R. 1951. *The life of John Maynard Keynes*. New York: W. W. Norton.

Haynes, J.E., and H. Klehr. 1999. *Venona: Decoding Soviet Espionage in America*. New Haven: Yale University Press.

Honma, Masami. 1991. *Sekai ginko no seiritsu to bureton uzzu taisei* (The formation of the World Bank and the Bretton Woods system). Tokyo: Dobunkan.

Horie, Shigeo. 1962. *Kokusai tsuka kikin no kenkyu* (A study of the IMF). Tokyo: Iwanami Shoten.

Horsefield, J.K. 1969. *The international monetary fund 1945–1965*. Washington: IMF.

Iwamoto, Takekazu. 1999. *Keinzu to sekai keizai* (Keynes and the world economy). Tokyo: Iwanami Shoten.

Kahn, R. 1976. The historical origin of the international monetary fund. In *Keynes and international monetary relations work*, ed. A.P. Thirlwall. London: Macmillan.

Luxembourg Institute for European and International Studies. 2009. *Executive summary; J.M. Keynes and Europe: Memories and prospects*. Trier: University of Trier.

Makino, Hiroshi. 1993. *Reiren no kigen to amerika no haken* (The origins of the cold war and American hegemony). Tokyo: Ochanomizu Shobo.

Mikesell, R.F. 1994. *The Bretton Woods debates: A memoir*, Essays in international finance, vol. 192. Princeton: Princeton University.

Moggridge, D. E. 1986. Keynes and the international monetary system, 1909 – 1946. In *International monetary problem and supply-side economics*, eds. Cohen J. and Harcourt G. C. London: Macmillan.

Moggridge, D.E. 1992. *Maynard Keynes – An economist's biography*. London: Routledge.

Noritake, Yasuo. 1990. Keinzu no kokusai tsuka ron (Keynes's international currency theory). Rissho University *Quarterly Report of Economics* 39–4.

Oliver, R.W. 1975. *International economic co-operation and the World Bank*. London: Macmillan.

Peden, G.C. 2004. *Keynes and his critics – Treasury responses to the Keynesian revolution 1925–1946*. Oxford: Oxford University Press.

Pressnell, L.S. 1986. *External economic policy since the war*. London: HMSO.

Sasaki, Takao. 1986. Sengo kokusai keizai kankei saihensei no koso to genri (2) (Ideas and principles of restructuring postwar international economic relations (2)). Hokkaido University. Sapporo: *Keizaigaku Kenkyu* 35–3.

Shimazaki, Hisaya. 1983. *Kin to kokusai tsuka* (Gold and international currency). Tokyo: Institute of Foreign Exchange and Trade Research.

Shinjo, Hiroshi. 1956. *Sutaringu shokoku oyobi kokusai tsuka kikin to no kankei* (Relations with Sterling Nations and the IMF), Ministry of Finance, Banking Bureau and Financial System Study Group, *Obei shokoku no kinyu seido* (Western Financial Systems), Tokyo: Okura Zaimu Kyokai.

Skidelsky, R. 2002. *John Maynard Keynes: Fighting for Britain, 1937–1946*. London: Macmillan.

Steil, B. 2013. *The battle of Bretton Woods, Jhon Maynard Keynes, Harry Dexter White and the making of a new world order*. Princeton: Princeton University Press.

Tamai, Ryuzo. 1999. *Keinzu seisaku no shiteki tenkai* (Historical development of Keynesian policies). Tokyo: Toyo Keizai.

Yonekura, Shigeru. 2006. *Rakujitsu no shozo Keinzu* (John Maynard Keynes). Tokyo: Upsilon Publishing.

Chapter 2
U.S. International Monetary Policy for the IMF

Isao Suto

1 Introduction

"Everywhere else in the world, though, politicians and businessmen insist that one of the biggest problems with the I.M.F. is that, contrary to the view of Congress, it acts as the United States Treasury's lap dog. Ask in Jakarta or Moscow, and the response is the same: The fund never ventures far without looking back for the approving nod of its master" (Sanger 1998). These joint efforts by the U.S. government and the International Monetary Fund (hereinafter Fund or IMF) are predicated on the idea of Neoliberalism or the Washington Consensus that supports a free and open global market economy (Williamson 1990). On the other hand, international financial institutions such as the IMF and the Bank for International Settlements (BIS) are considered to have taken a position between the market and nation states, and they have comprehensive visions for the world economy. Thus the U.S. could not completely control the Bretton Woods institutions, and the IMF retained considerable autonomy as an international institution.[1]

Even though the U.S. government controlled the Bretton Woods institutions, it was unable to achieve its desired results. Focusing on the National Advisory Council on International Monetary and Financial Problems (NAC), Casey (2011, p. 224) stresses that the U.S. "could eventually aid the transition to and maintenance of a multilateral world monetary system following Europe's recovery." However, we should not underestimate the fact that the U.S. encountered many unexpected difficulties in the early stages of establishing the Bretton Woods system. In 1947, the U.S. government failed in the resumption of the convertibility of sterling, still a

[1] See, Chap. 7 by K. Yago in this book.

I. Suto (✉)
School of Political Science and Economics, Meiji University,
1-1 Kanda-Surugadai, Chiyoda-ku, Tokyo 101-8301, Japan
e-mail: suto@meiji.ac.jp

K. Yago et al. (eds.), *History of the IMF*, Studies in Economic History,
DOI 10.1007/978-4-431-55351-9_2

key international currency,[2] based on the Anglo-American Financial Agreement. While controlled by the U.S. government, however, the Fund was also confronted with the inability to set initial par values, the widespread adoption of multiple currency practices including the floating exchange rate in Canada, and the modification of "the nature of the international monetary system from the adjustable peg intended by the Articles to a fixed rate regime" (Bordo and Eichengreen 1993, p. 46).

In this chapter, we focus on how the U.S., through the NAC, positioned the Fund in relation to its international monetary policy, operated to support it, and coped with difficulties in the transitional period from 1945 to 1952.[3] The U.S. government obtained a critical share of the quotas and influenced the Fund through the use of its "voice and vote" in the Board of Governors as well as in the Executive Board to achieve its desired goals. According to De Vries and Horsefield (1969, p. 11), up to 1952 there was "a tendency for member governments, before submitting a formal proposal or request to the Fund, to ask their Executive Directors to discuss it with their Directors first. Quite frequently the Executive Director for the member concerned went to the Director of the United States—the country with the largest quota. If the U.S. Director concurred with the proposal or request, the member would then continue with the formal procedures of the Fund."

The NAC was an interagency group of executive branch agencies established when the U.S. Congress ratified the Bretton Woods Agreement in 1945, and it took chief responsibility for instructing the U.S. Executive Directors to the Fund and the World Bank until 1965.[4] The NAC was organized by top executives from the Treasury Department, the Board of Governors of the Federal Reserve System (FRB), the State Department, the Commerce Department, the Export–import Bank of Washington (Ex-Im Bank), and the Economic Cooperation Administration, and the Secretary of the Treasury presided at the meetings. The U.S. Executive Director on the Board of the Fund (hereinafter the U.S. Fund Director) and the World Bank attended the NAC meeting regularly, although they did not possess voting rights, and they were guided by NAC policy actions.

We describe in Sect. 2 how the NAC dealt with the governance structure of the Fund from the preparatory period to the failure of sterling convertibility in 1947. Then we explore in Sect. 3 how the NAC coped with the difficulties that the Fund faced and that resulted in malfunctioning between the Marshall Plan and the start of the European Payment Union (EPU) in 1950. The outbreak of the Korean War was

[2] According to Gorski (1945, p. 24), the key currency [stabilization] approach advanced "by the well-known economist John H. Williams is that the economic behavior of key countries largely determines conditions in other countries. If stabilization is achieved between the key countries, others will make workable adjustments to them." This approach, however, "comes dangerously close to a system of monetary blocs or even to bilateralism."

[3] Article 14 of the Fund Agreement provided "transitional period" that member countries were allowed exchange restrictions within 3 or 5 years after the date on which the Fund begins operations in March 1947. Here we cover the period from 1945, when the Anglo-American Financial Agreement was concluded, to 1952, when the Truman administration was practically finished.

[4] In 1966, the Johnson administration deputed the responsibility to direct the U.S. representatives at the Fund and the World Bank to the Treasury Department. See, Weiss (2013), pp. 15–16.

followed by the enactment of the Mutual Security Act in 1951. Following this, the NAC steered Fund policy to be linked to the U.S. national security policy. The focus here is therefore on Sect. 4, which looks at how the NAC would end the Fund's transitional period in relation to the Cold War. Finally, we summarize our analysis.

2 Creation of the Governance Structure

2.1 Executive Board and Managing Director

In the transitional period, the NAC maintained its influence over various aspects of the Fund's business operations. The NAC took leadership, drafting the by-laws and the rules and regulations, before starting on the Fund's business operations. The NAC Technical Committee led by Harry D. White began this work in September 1945. At the NAC meeting on January 22, 1946, White "reported that some difficulty had been encountered in locating a site for the meeting and efforts to this end have been complicated by the fact that the British and others have requested postponement" in the process of the Technical Committee.[5] After discussions between the Technical Committee and the representatives of some 12–15 other countries, on February 2, 1946 the NAC approved the proposed by-laws for the Fund in consultation with the technical representatives of other governments.[6] The by-laws of the Fund and the World Bank were adopted at the Inaugural Meeting of the Board of Governors in Savannah, Georgia, on March 16, and the rules and regulations were adopted at the first Annual Meeting in Washington on September 25.

Even though only minor amendments were made to the draft of the Fund by-laws at the Inaugural Meeting, convincing arguments were raised by other countries. First of all, John M. Keynes, with the support of France and India, proposed New York, rather than Washington, D.C., as the headquarters of the Fund and the World Bank because "New York, in addition to being a financial and economic world center, would afford a good opportunity for cooperation with the Social and Economic Councils of the United Nations Organization." On the other hand, the U.S. with Canada and Mexico asserted that the "Fund, as an intergovernmental institution, should be free of any possible influence from economic, financial, or commercial private interests."[7] The Washington headquarters was in keeping with the intentions of Marriner S. Eccles, chairman of the FRB. This was because only the FRB put forward an alternative suggestion that the "principal office of the Fund shall be located in Washington, D.C." to the draft of the by-laws provisions that the

[5] NAC, Meeting No. 9, January 22, 1946, p. 5.

[6] NAC, Meeting No. 14, February 2, 1946, p. 6.

[7] "Report of the Committee on Site," in IMF (1946), pp. 29–30; IMF, EBD/46/2. New York bankers also hoped that the Fund would be headquartered in New York. See, Casey (2011), p. 186; Horsefield (1969), pp. 129–130.

Technical Committee adopted on September 12, 1945.[8] Furthermore, at the NAC meeting of February 27, 1946, "Eccles expressed strong opposition to permitting the commercial banks to underwrite securities, pointing out that (…) the Securities Exchange Act of 1934 had been passed to prevent a repetition of the abuses which had then occurred."[9] It was also advantageous for the NAC to have both meetings in an adjacent building.

The role of the Executive Directors and the Executive Board was another controversial issue at the Inaugural Meeting. While the U.S. asserted that the Executive Directors "must devote their full time to the business of the Fund," the U.K. claimed that the Executive Directors might be engaged "part-time in some other occupation and receive remuneration therefrom."[10] This was because the U.K. thought that "members should have virtually automatic access to the IMF's resources within the range determined by their quotas." (Casey 2001, p. 187) Actually, the Executive Board meeting of the Fund was held every weekday morning, and then the NAC had a meeting as necessary in the afternoon. Most Executive Directors attended every meeting of the Fund.[11]

The role and responsibilities of the Board of Executive Directors were closely related to those of the Managing Director. J. Burke Knapp, Special Assistant to Eccles, commented to Eccles, who was the vice-chairman of the NAC, as follows: Unlike the World Bank, in which an American took up the presidency, "it is not feasible to delegate broad authority to the chief executive officer. In the case of the Fund, this would mean vesting excessive power in the Managing Director and would tend to undermine the Fund's essential function of providing a meeting place in which representatives of the member countries can discuss and agree upon cooperative international action in the monetary field."[12] Nevertheless, Eccles did not overlook the role of Managing Director. He wrote to Fred M. Vinson, Secretary of the Treasury, as follows: "It is obvious that a great deal of the success of these Institutions will depend upon the persons chosen as their chief executive officers. I appreciate that these officers will not be elected at the Board of Governors' meeting, but I should be surprised if the subject did not come up for discussion there at least on an informal basis."[13]

While the U.S. government was well aware of the significance of the Executive Director's post, it designated a non-American to the position conventionally.

---

[8] NAC Technical Committee, Document No. 7, September 17, 1945, p. 1.

[9] NAC, Meeting No. 14, February 27, 1946, p. 5; Eccles to Fred M. Vinson, February 13, 1946, Marriner S. Eccles Document Collection (hereinafter Eccles Collection).

[10] "Report of the Committee on Functions and Remuneration," in IMF (1946), p. 31.

[11] "For example, George Bolton and Louis Rasminsky, the British and Canadian Directors in the Fund, have probably spent the majority of their time at home, while the French and Belgian Directors in the Bank have spent very little time in Washington." Knapp to Eccles, "Comments Concerning Certain Policy Matter relating to the International Fund and Bank," August 4, 1947, p. 3, Eccles Collection.

[12] Knapp to Eccles, August 4, 1947, p. 4, Eccles Collection.

[13] Eccles to Vinson, February 13, 1946, Eccles Collection.

Horsefield (1969, p. 135) stated that the U.S. authorities could not propose White for this post, because "they considered that the Bank would have to be headed by a U.S. citizen in order to win the confidence of the banking community, and that it would be impracticable to appoint U.S. citizens to head both the Bank and the Fund." However, until the memorandum for the Inaugural Meeting on February 20, 1946 Casey (2001, p. 188) insisted that the Treasury Department considered White suitable for this post. From the viewpoint of the FRB Chairman, who carried out drastic reform of the Federal Reserve Banks in 1935,[14] even in public financial institutions, the chief executive officer should have a greater degree of authority. The U.S. had secured the dominant voting power in the Executive Board. Therefore, White served as the U.S. Executive Director as well as *de facto* deputy Managing Director in the early transitional period.

2.2 Membership, Quota, and Initial Par Value: On the Eve of the Inauguration

The primary tasks that the NAC faced before the inauguration of the Fund were to determine the initial par values for original member countries and a quota and initial par value for new member countries, and to deal with exchange control. For the most part, the NAC dealt with these related issues from the standpoint of foreign aid. The greatest concern was that new member countries would rely on the Fund resources excessively.[15] The quota was the criteria used for drawing from Fund resources and for voting power, but there was no clear published formula for a new member. The formula developed by the U.S. Treasury Department in 1943 referred to the original members,[16] and a revised version was used for new members, even if the U.S. ultimately employed political considerations in determining the quota.

A request from France for a revision of its quota illustrates a typical example of political influence. In the NAC Staff meeting, Chairman Harold Glasser, NAC Secretary, called attention to the fact that a quota revision of $560 million "would place France above China with respect to the size of quotas, and that the French desired such a position." George Luthringer, the U.S. Fund Director, "expressed doubts as to whether the increase should be sufficiently large to raise the French quota above that of China."[17] In the NAC meeting, White similarly pointed out that "the present country hierarchy of quotas cannot be disturbed without political

[14] Eccles deprived the board of directors of the Federal Reserve Banks of many important powers, and then centralized them to the presidents by the Banking Act of 1935.

[15] NAC Staff Committee, Meeting No. 21, May 6, 1946, No. 29, June 27, 1946; NAC, Meeting No. 33, July 9, 1946, No. 37, September 3, 1946.

[16] A number of calculations were made by the U.S. Treasury before the Bretton Woods Conference. See, Horsefield (1969), p. 95; Horie (1964), p. 126.

[17] NAC Staff Committee, Meeting No. 40, September 16, 1946, pp. 3–4.

repercussions." The NAC took his opinion on the matter seriously and recommended a quota of $525 million for France.[18]

After the determination of the quota, member countries had to set their initial par values to borrow or draw from the Fund. It was, however, one of the most difficult problems the NAC faced in the chaotic exchange market after World War II. This was because most members other than the U.S. desired not only a higher par value to draw U.S. Dollars from the Fund, but also a lower exchange rate to have a trade surplus with the U.S.

Although most original member countries established their initial par values on December 18, 1946, the NAC was confronted with a governance question related to the Managing Director. The Fund could provide for a 90-day period of negotiation with member countries on initial par value before the Fund exchange operations. At the NAC meeting of September 26, White reported that "the Board of Executive Directors had decided to drop for the time being the matter of secrecy provisions."[19] This meant such a regulation would prohibit White from consulting with the NAC. Furthermore, White "indicated that there is also a move, which was disapproved by the Board of Executive Directors, to give the Managing Director power to discuss confidential matters with other governments without informing the Board. The Managing Director could not take action without consulting the Board but prior to that stage the Staff might be informed but not the Board of Directors." Therefore, White complained that "this is a frontal attack on the United States position."[20]

However, the Board of Executive Directors did not take any positive decision on the secrecy provisions after all. It was on December 18, 1947, that the NAC put the secrecy issue on the agenda, when Poland communicated its desire for a change in its provisional rate for the zloty from the present 100 to the dollar to a suggested 400 to the dollar. At the meeting, FRB Chairman "Eccles commented that in the past when the Council had considered matters of this kind it had been established procedure to refer the question first to the Staff Committee, have it on the agenda of the Council and act on the basis of a recommendation of the Staff Committee." Andrew N. Overby, who was the second U.S. Executive Director for the Fund, argued that he had not learned of the matter until the preceding Monday and therefore had no opportunity to put the matter through the usual staff channels. Then he added that the "Articles of Agreement provide that agreement on change in exchange rates have to be reached within a very short period of time and under the secrecy provisions agree to by the Fund the Managing Director might not disclose a request until the day on which decision had to be reached." Frank A. Southard, Jr., Director of the Office of International Finance in the Treasury Department, suggested that the NAC

[18] NAC, Meeting No. 39, September 17, 1946, pp. 5–7, No. 40, September 26, 1946, pp. 5–6.

[19] According to a Knapp's letter to Eccles, the Fund Executive Directors other than White "were anxious to adopt an internal Fund regulation providing that any notification of a proposed change in the exchange rate of member country would be made available only to the Executive Directors themselves and to a few selected members of the Fund's staff." Knapp to Eccles, September 6, 1946, p. 3, Eccles Collection.

[20] NAC, Meeting No. 40, September 26, 1946, p. 6.

Staff Committee should study the matter, but he added that "he did not think it would always be necessary for the Council to feel obliged to pass judgment on each exchange rate that is considered." Eccles also commented that "questions of general policy were more important than decisions with respect to certain rates. The Council should not make it its business to establish individual rates. The Council should know what the objectives are and establish certain criteria and standard so that United States Executive Director would know what action should be taken under given conditions."[21] The NAC has rarely placed it on its agenda since that meeting.

Even though the U.S. had utilized its voting power in a key situation, it was not an easy task to establish and maintain the par value system. The U.S. had to allow a few member countries to delay setting the initial par value, to let broken cross rates emerge in several markets, and to introduce a free or fluctuating exchange market.[22] These deviations resulted not only from the limits of U.S. power but also from its flexible response to the international economic and political situation. The NAC policy action in the face of the French exchange policy "was designed to encourage thorough discussion of the problem by the Fund's Executive Directors without suggesting that the U.S. Executive Director use his voting strength to achieve a solution."[23] Southard (1979, pp. 5–6), the third Fund Executive Director for the U.S., also recollected that "a practical problem faced by the U.S. Executive Director was how to exercise his power without convincing the rest of the Directors that discussion was futile because the U.S. view would prevail."

2.3 Failure of Sterling Convertibility and the NAC

The U.S. government concluded the Anglo-American Financial Agreement in 1945 so that the Fund could shorten "the transitional period" through restoration of pound sterling convertibility after July 15, 1947. However, the U.K. lost most of the $3.75 billion it borrowed from the U.S. in exchange for ratification of the Bretton Woods Agreement and suspended sterling convertibility for current account transactions on August 20, 1947. The reason the U.K. had depleted its reserves was that 43.5 % ($1.63 billion) of the U.S. loan had already been used to pay for imports from the U.S. before June 1947, and some of the loan was transferred to dollar areas through capital transactions.[24]

Leading studies have stressed that unlike the time of signing the Agreement, the U.S. maintained an attitude of passivity toward the depletion of U.K. dollar

---

[21] NAC, Meeting No. 78, December 18, 1947, pp. 6–7.

[22] Canada, Mexico, and Peru introduced fluctuating rates, and France set up a limited free market before 1950. See, De Vries and Horsefield (1969), pp. 43–45.

[23] NAC Staff Committee, Meeting No. 48, November 7, 1946, pp. 3–4.

[24] See Kamikawa (2009), and Kanai (2010). Bordo and Eichengreen (1993), pp. 43–44.

reserves.[25] Casey (2001, p. 195) recently stressed that the NAC "did not consider a more flexible position until it became apparent to all observers that Britain's short-lived experiment with sterling convertibility had fail miserably." It was typically thought that the NAC members, in the early stages, became nervous about bilateral agreements with the sterling countries because the Anglo-Argentine Financial and Trade Agreement of September 17, 1946, for example, allowed paying 1/2 % interest on Argentine blocked sterling balances.[26]

However, the NAC documents showed a different attitude. On February 14, 1947, the NAC Staff Committee designated the U.S. – U.K. Financial Agreement Working Group to follow the implementation of the Agreement, and reported to the NAC on April 17.[27] Responding to the recommendations of the Staff Committee, the NAC decided that, "The Secretary of the Treasury should at the earliest possible date explore fully with the appropriate officials of the British Government the nature and progress of British plans for implementation … of the Financial Agreement." In particular, "in the event the British propose to make temporary settlements of the sterling balances; (i) express, if it appears appropriate, his confidence that the decision to reach temporary settlements will be made only after every possible effort has been exerted to reach satisfactory permanent settlement; (ii) express his confidence that, should temporary settlements prove necessary, the U.K. will at the earliest favorable opportunity endeavor to obtain the completion of final settlements consistent with the principle of non-discriminatory use of accumulated sterling balances."[28] The NAC action indicated that the U.S. not only admitted that the U.K. should take the initiative in restoring sterling convertibility but also assumed that there would be difficulty in the permanent settlement of the accumulated sterling balances.

Therefore, it was not a surprise for the NAC to receive a cable from William L. Clayton, Under Secretary of State, stating that "the British will request extensions of time in introducing full sterling convertibility in the case of a few specified countries" on June 23, 1947.[29] The Secretary of the Treasury Snyder received a formal letter from Chancellor Hugh Dalton concerning the postponement of some British obligations on July 7. The next day, the NAC Working Group estimated that Britain's overall balance of payments deficit would be $450 million for the 4th quarter of 1947, $250 million for the 1st quarter of 1948, and $75 million for the 2nd quarter of 1948.[30] Finally, the NAC took the action of "granting the British

[25] For example, Gardner (1969), pp. 313, 320.

[26] The NAC Staff Committee Chairman, Harold Glasser of Treasury Department, questioned this provision of interest payment, and the FRB representative, J. Burke Knapp, pointed "at the time of the U.S. – U.K. financial discussions this government had been unable to obtain from the British any commitment on this matter," and added "the British had expressed the hope that there would be no interest payments on their blocked sterling accounts." NAC Staff Committee, Meeting No. 42, September 27, 1946, pp. 2–3; IMF, RD/46/48, October 15, 1946.

[27] NAC Staff Committee, Meeting No. 62, February 14, 1947.

[28] NAC, Meeting No. 60, April 17, 1947, pp. 7–9.

[29] Knapp to Eccles, July 1, 1947, pp. 2–3, Eccles Collection.

[30] Knapp to Eccles, July 8, 1947, Appendix I, Eccles Collection.

request of a maximum of 2 months' postponement of the July 15, 1947, deadline in those cases where it is impossible for the British to complete technical arrangements with the particular countries before July 15."[31]

The U.K., therefore, resumed sterling convertibility without 14 countries[32] on July 15, and then suspended it on August 20. In the negotiation with the NAC from August 18–22, Sir Wilfrid Eady who headed the British Delegation explained that the recent "run" on the sterling had left the British Government with no other choice. As Eady also appealed to Snyder regarding borrowing dollars from the Fund, the NAC instructed the U.S. Executive Director for the Fund to support liberal treatment of the U.K. application.[33] Furthermore, the failure of the resumption of sterling convertibility led to a change in policy so that the NAC permitted adopting a free or fluctuating exchange market in France, Italy, and Canada, and the resumption of currency convertibility through the EPU, a sub-system of the Fund.

3 Impacts of the Marshall Plan

3.1 A Central Bank for Intra-European Settlements?

The failure of the resumption of sterling convertibility to the dollar meant a limitation of the key-currency [stabilization] approach. In the spring of 1947 when the NAC was concerned about the resumption of sterling convertibility, the Truman administration started planning for the European Recovery Program (ERP), or the Marshall Plan. The EPU plan under the ERP had a great impact on the NAC and Fund policy.

Firstly, the Fund resources came to include a substantial element of "relief" for "reconstruction" on June 7, 1947. This extended beyond the current monetary stabilization operations provided for by Article XIV, Section 1 of the Fund Agreement, that "considerable flexibility in the Fund's operations is required because of the changing circumstances of particular countries or of the general international situation."[34] France bought $25 million for francs on May 8, and $25 million for guilders on June 23, and the Netherlands bought $6.0 million and 1.5 million pounds on May 16 (IMF 1947, p. 62).

The Fund, however, made a decision ("ERP Decision") in April 1948 to limit the access of countries participating in the ERP to Fund resources during the course of

[31] NAC, Meeting No. 68, July 10, 1947, pp. 9–10.

[32] These countries were France, Denmark, Austria, Bulgaria, Greece, Hungary, Poland, Rumania, Turkey, Yugoslavia, the USSR, China, Siam, and Paraguay. Knapp to Eccles, July 22, 1947, Eccles Collection.

[33] Knapp to Eccles, Knapp to Eccles, July 8, 1947; August 19, 1947, p. 2, Eccles Collection. The U. K. purchased/borrowed $60 million for £14,888,337 on September 15, 1947. IMF, EBD/47/219, September 15, 1947.

[34] NAC (1948a), pp. 806–807.

the Program, so that the Fund could make easier to preserve resources for the post-transitional period. This second policy change was approved by the NAC, even though there were some differing views in the Staff Committee. State Department representatives, in particular, pointed out that the decision "was a change in emphasis in administration of the Fund from a negative approach to a more positive approach," and "suggested that there should be a formulation as to the conditions under which countries would obtain access to the use of the resources of the Fund." On the other hand, the Fund Executive Director "questioned the advisability of setting forth certain of the suggested restrictions on the use of the Fund's resources, such as making sales of dollars conditional upon the elimination of harmful exchange practices." Also the Chairman John W. Gunter, of Office of International Finance in the Treasury Department, stated that the "ERP Decision" would serve to protect the Fund's resources.[35]

The third and the most important effect of the ERP on the Fund policy was the EPU, which was signed into existence on September 19, 1950. The Fund and the NAC were faced with the decision as to whether or not they should abandon the "ERP Decision", and whether or not they should be actively involved in the EPU. This decision aroused criticism that the Fund, by failing to organize under its own aegis a multilateral system of European settlements, "missed the bus" (Triffin 1966, p. 406), and the EPU rather than the Fund "formed the nucleus of the Group of Ten".[36]

The EPU intended to facilitate gradual liberalization of intra-European trades and payments. It was established on July 1, 1950 and completed its responsibilities in 1958, when the major European currencies restored their external convertibility. The EPU's membership consisted of the 16 ERP aid-receiving countries including the sterling and the franc zone, and not the Fund but the Bank for International Settlements (BIS) acted as a clearing agent for the Union.

An intra-European clearing union became a fact in early 1948. At the meeting of the Board of Directors of the Fund on June 2, however, Overby (U.S.) raised many questions about the effect of the plan, and lastly "he questioned whether the Fund could go beyond the limits it had set on the use of its resources." The Board also discussed the staff memorandum on whether "the Committee working on a plan in Paris could take the Fund's position into account", but some reservations were expressed.[37] The next day, in the NAC meeting the Secretary, John W. Gunter, introduced a Staff Committee's document that recommended "the Council should favor the Fund's participation in rendering technical and administrative assistance, leaving aside any definite determination of whether the Fund should participate in a financial way in any particular scheme." In a plan proposed by the ECA a month earlier, "the Fund would be asked to perform a function corresponding to that of a

[35] NAC Staff Committee, Meeting No. 122, April 22, 1948, pp. 3–4. There was no statement for this topic in the NAC, Meeting No. 94, May 5, 1948.

[36] De Vries and Horsefield (1969), p. 317. See also, Suto (2008, Chapter 6).

[37] IMF, EBM/48/322, June 2, 1948, p. 9. This memorandum (SM/48/225) was prepared by staffs E. M. Bernstein based on Robert Triffin's memorandum SM/48/225.

central bank."[38] However, Overby insisted again that "this country would not want to make the mistake of getting into increased planning and state intervention". The NAC advised the Administrator of ECA and the Fund Executive Director that "they should favor the active participation of the Fund" to facilitate European multilateral trade without the Fund's resources.[39]

France proposed a reduction of the par value of the franc by around 44 % and a partial floating exchange system for their foreign trade with the U.S. dollar area in early 1948, when many member countries still maintained multiple currency practices. The NAC and the Fund had tried to achieve the relaxation of exchange controls and the exclusion of floating exchange through orderly cross rates. The French plan, however, confronted the Fund with the problem of cross rates, especially in the intra-European clearing union scheme.

The Fund staff members, Bernstein and Triffin, prepared a memorandum entitled "Economic Aspects of the Problem of Cross-Rates" on January 20, 1948. In this memorandum they concluded that the "establishment of free markets in countries with inconvertible currency (...) would of necessity result in a disorderly pattern of cross rates," and that the "danger of disorderly cross rates are greatly increased with the present shortage of dollars." Thus, they recommended that it "must be met through cooperative action on the part of all countries with the same problem."[40] In another memorandum, entitled "A Fluctuating Franc Rate with Orderly Cross Rate," on October 7, Bernstein described that the French proposal "represents a step backward in the establishment of a stable and orderly pattern of exchange rates in Europe."[41]

To achieve stable cross rates, the participating countries in the intra-European clearing union had to adjust the existing exchange rates. Because sterling was particularly over-appreciated, both the U.S. and the Fund began serious consideration of subject of "European exchange rates" in March 1949, when the NAC concluded that the subject should be reviewed with the European countries in the next year.[42] The U.S. government arranged tripartite economic talks with the representatives of the U.K. and Canada from September 8–12, so that they were confident that there was a "prospect of reaching a satisfactory equilibrium between the sterling and dollar areas."[43] On September 18, Sir Stafford Cripps announced the devaluation of sterling by 30.5 % after privately informing the Fund Managing Director. Then other European countries consulted with the Fund and devaluated their currencies up to the end of September. France also consulted with the Fund on a proposal to unify its exchange system on the basis of the free market dollar rate.[44] These

[38] NAC Staff Committee, Meeting No. 139, July 8, 1948, p. 5.

[39] NAC, Meeting No. 96, June 3, 1948, pp. 6–9.

[40] IMF, SM/48/169, January 20, 1948.

[41] IMF, EBS/48/3, October 7, 1948.

[42] Horsefield (1969), pp. 234–235.

[43] See, "Joint Communiqué," Tripartite Meeting, September 12, 1949, *Foreign Relations of the United Sates (FRUS)*, Vol. IV, (1949), p. 839.

[44] See, IMF, *Annual Report for 1950*, pp. 28–41 and Appendix I; IMF, EBM/49/479, September 19, 1949; Horsefield (1969), pp. 236–241.

exchange rate adjustments by the European countries and the unification of the French exchange system contributed to the establishment of the EPU.

3.2 Relationship Between the Fund and the EPU

Even though the Fund rejected the idea of functioning as a clearing agent for the EPU, the U.S. Treasury Department and FRB were still expecting that the Fund would lead to relaxation of trade and payments restrictions within Europe. In the U.S. Ambassadors meeting in Paris held on October 21–22, 1949, William A. Harriman, U.S. Special Representative in Europe for ECA, stated that it was an option since "the establishment of a European branch of the International Monetary Fund to take over the European payments scheme now appears to be the most workable."[45] However, the NAC finally took the following action on January 23, 1950, "In order to avoid any possible U.S. involvement in conflict of recommendations made by the clearing union on monetary policy and those of the IMF, the U.S. should not participate in the management of the clearing union. This would not preclude a U.S. observer in the union for the duration of the ERP period only; nor would it preclude U.S. veto power on any use of funds contributed by the U.S."[46]

There was still serious controversy in the NAC on June 29, 1950, because it had to decide on the policy towards the EPU after the termination of the ERP. Southard, the Fund Executive Director, raised the question of whether the NAC should move in the opposite way in Europe towards a permanent regional organization, which it had opposed in Latin America and other places. He added that there "was no practicable way of keeping the great colonial areas of England, France, and Belgium outside of the EPU." M.S. Szymezak, a Member of the FRB, claimed that there was a weakness from the monetary and credit standpoint, and Thomas C Blaisdell, Jr., Assistant Secretary of Commerce, raised a question regarding proposals for discrimination by Belgium against the dollar area. On the other hand, Richard M. Bissell, Jr., Acting Administrator of ECA, emphasized that "this was not an ideal outcome for the United States but in terms of the negotiations it seemed to be the best it was possible to get. (…) There was a possibility that after 1952 this institution would continue as a clearing house through which not only would settlements be made but credits would be extended." The NAC finally accepted the EPU, subject to a periodic review.[47]

A staff committee of the Fund presented a memorandum entitled "Fund Relations with EPU" to the Executive Board on August 8, 1950.[48] Camille Gutt, the Fund

---

[45] "Summary Record of a Meeting of United States Ambassadors at Paris, October 21–22," *FRUS*, 1949, Vol. IV, p. 490.

[46] NAC, Meeting No. 147, January 23, 1950, p. 11.

[47] NAC, Meeting No. 158, June 29, 1950, pp. 2–12.

[48] IMF SM/50/506, August 8, 1950.

Managing Director, some Executive Directors, and most staff members supported a stronger role for the Fund in the EPU. The staff committee most interested in the EPU was the Managing Committee, which was responsible for the business operations. The Managing Committee consisted of seven members appointed by the Council of the Organization for European Economic Cooperation (OEEC) after nomination by their governments, and was empowered to invite observers. The staff committee concluded that the Fund must be in close communication with the EPU and make its views known to its Western European members, because the "physical distance between the two organizations and the speed with which on occasion decisions may be taken raise the very serious danger that unless a very close relationship is established at the beginning unfortunate situations will arise." The staff committee recommended, therefore, that the "Management Committee should invite an observer for the Fund to attend its meetings and all meetings of any subordinate organs which it may create." In the Executive Board meeting on the August 16, 1950, the Fund postponed the decision until informal exploration in Paris, because the Executive Directors of Europe suggested only informal consultations between both institutions, and Southard also stated that "much more exploration of the factors involved was necessary before the Fund could take any decisions."[49]

However, the OEEC and the EPU did not invite a representative from the Fund until 1952. They felt that the Fund was controlled by the U.S. government and considered the EPU as primarily a European organization. In addition, the ECA and the U.S. State Department "had become committed to an independent EPU as an essential means of promoting European political integration".[50] The relationship with the EPU reflected the fact that the Fund was entering a new period different from the chaotic aftermath of World War II.

4 Policy Change in the Early Stages of the Cold War

4.1 Payments Restrictions for Security

The outbreak of the Korean War in June 1950 hastened the global spread of the Cold War and the rearmament of countries. Four months later, the U.S. government enacted the Mutual Security Act in advance of the termination of the ERP at the end of December 1951. The ECA was integrated into the Mutual Security Agency, and the NAC also had to change its policy towards the Fund.

First of all, the U.S. government imposed payments and transfer restrictions for security reasons on China and North Korea on December 17, 1950. On December 16, the U.S. Director Southard explained the restrictions to the Executive Board of

[49] IMF, EBM/50/599, August 16, 1950.

[50] De Vries and Horsefield (1969), pp. 328–329.

the Fund.[51] He said that these were "not for economic of financial reasons but to assist the United Nations forces in their struggle against aggression", and he added that they were "aware that the Articles, including Article VIII, are not explicit on this point." Chairman Gutt personally supported this as follows: The U.S. proposal "was a restriction and discrimination on current payments which normally would fall under Art. VIII, Sec. 3", therefore, the Fund should "approve the measure inasmuch as is necessary." Ernest de Selliers (Belgium) supported Gutt's proposal, and the General Counsel said that his preliminary view that, in a purely legal sense, that this case would not fall under Art. VIII. Another Director noted that "other areas of the Fund's authority might similarly be imperiled by a doctrine that members were free to act for 'emergency' reasons". The Directors for the Australia, India, and the U.K. abstained from any decision since they had not had the opportunity to consult their governments. For this result, the Executive Board concluded that the Fund took note of the U.S. proposal, but took "no other decision pending study of the question of the jurisdiction of the Fund respecting such actions."

It was after the truce agreement of the Korean War that the Fund Executive Board came to a conclusion on exchange restrictions for security reasons.[52] Firstly, the Executive Board took up a draft of a general decision prepared by the staff, then considered the case of the restrictions that the U.S. and Cuba had imposed on China in December 1950 and July 1951. Some Directors expressed their view that the Fund "was not equipped to decide whether the particular political or military circumstances justified the restrictions." On the other hand, the Directors for Belgium, China, and the UAR gave their full support to the U.S. De Selliers (Belgium) stressed that "Art. VIII had been drafted with no exceptions", and that because mainland China was not under the effective control of the Government of China on the Fund, "it should be treated as non-member territory". However, the Legal Department of the Fund demonstrated that legally mainland China was still the territory of a Fund member.

Despite the existence of opposing views, the Executive Board passed the following resolution with the abstention of the French: (1) Whenever possible, the Fund should be notified of exchange restrictions for security reasons before they are imposed; (2) Unless the Fund informs the member within 30 days after receiving such a notice from the member that it is not satisfied that such restrictions are proposed solely to preserve such security, the member may assume that the Fund has no objection to the imposition of the restrictions; (3) The Fund will review the operation of this decision periodically. The Executive Board finally passed the proposed restrictions that the U.S. and Cuba had imposed on China with the abstention of France and India.

Secondly, the rearmament of countries gave an increasingly political aspect and military sense to Fund resources and U.S. foreign aid. The U.S. rearmament program stimulated a rapidly increasing demand for stockpiling of military and strategic materials, which resulted in a sharp rise in the import prices of raw materials

---

[51] IMF, EBM50/625, December 16, 1950.

[52] IMF, EBM/52/51, August 14, 1952.

and a structural change in world trade. It brought about a noticeable decrease in the "dollar gap" during a few months of the year ending in March 1951.[53]

The NAC turned this change in circumstances into the goal of Bretton Woods. Since June 1949, the World Bank had already sold in the U.S. markets a total of $300 million of its bonds, and it authorized the use of the 18 % of local currency that leading European countries had subscripted to the World Bank's capital.[54] The NAC concluded in 1951 that "where a country is making a satisfactory contribution to mutual defense, an unanticipated accumulation of reserve resulting from the vigorous application of appropriate economic and financial policies should not automatically result in a reduction of aid."[55] In the Third Special Report to the Congress, moreover, the NAC presented a new policy on membership by which "all of the countries outside of the Iron Curtain except a few which for varying reasons have not agreed" should be included as members.[56] The emergence of the Cold War structure forced the NAC and the Fund to admit the former enemy countries.

4.2 *Membership for the Former Enemy Countries*

To admit a former enemy country as a member meant not only the end of the beginning but the start of a new stage for the Fund, because the joining of West Germany (Germany) and Japan required important changes in the Fund's governance and policy. It was on January 26, 1951 that the NAC Staff Committee dealt with this subject in the agenda for an "Increase in Italian Quota", where Germany was indicated as a prospective member.[57]

Konrad Adenauer, Prime Minister of Germany, formally applied for membership of the Fund in February 1951. The committee on membership in the Fund Executive Board held its first meeting on May 15. However, the committee had to deliberate for a long time, since committee members and staff pointed out many complex questions regarding the eligibility of Germany as follows: The territory of the Germany was still under occupation; Germany's authority in domestic and foreign affairs was subject to the regulations of the Occupation Powers; the Occupation Authorities reserved the power to control Germany's exchange rate even after Germany had been accepted for membership in the Fund.[58]

---

[53] NAC (1951b), pp. 543–547.

[54] NAC (1952a), p. 368; NAC (1952b), p. 410.

[55] NAC (1951b), p. 341.

[56] NAC (1952a), p. 365.

[57] NAC Staff Committee, Meeting No. 268, January 26, 1951, p. 1.

[58] IMF, EB/CM/GERMANY/51/1, March 28 1951. In the first meeting it was pointed that the committee did not require the solution of such problems as whether West Germany is the general successor of Hitler Germany, whether the occupation of Germany is based on the Hague Convention, and whether the Potsdam Agreement is still in force. IMF, EB/CM/GERMANY/MTG/51/1, May 14 1951.

These questions were in conjunction with the size of the quota for Germany. In the committee on membership on January 31, 1952, when the qualifications for German membership had been resolved, "the Germans had gone over the staff calculations", and they urged that "$360 million would be more appropriate than $330 million." Because the acting chairman Southard expressed the view that since this was "a larger quota the Committee would have to give it serious consideration", the conclusion was postponed until April.[59] The Directors for France and Mexico preferred a larger quota and the Directors for the U.S. and the U.K. agreed on $3.3 billion for both sides to avoid protracted negotiations.

Five months later, on August 1951, the Japanese government submitted an application for membership to the Fund. On October 12, 1951, the legal department of the Fund reported in a memorandum that, "Japan possesses legal capacity to accept membership," in which the staff calculated three different quotas, $262.9 million, $225.6 million, and $221.1 million, on the basis of pre-war economic indicators.[60] The NAC Staff Committee also discussed the admission of Japan on October 17. In the committee, the U.S. Fund Director expressed dissatisfaction with the calculation by the Fund staff, and he reported that "the British had suggested a figure of $1.9 billion, probably in deference to the Australians." The Treasury Department noted that the Supreme Commander for the Allied Powers (SCAP) "suggested quota ranging from $325 to $350 million." Finally, the Staff Committee agreed to the recommendation made by the representative of the State Department advising the U.S. Fund Director to negotiate within a range of $240 to $270 million.[61] Since Germany had set a precedent, the committee on membership of the Fund decided on the membership and quota at the second meeting on January 14, 1952.[62] Because Arthur M. Stamp (U.K.) expressed no objection, the committee recommended a quota of $250 million Table 2.1.

The Executive Board approved the admission of Germany and Japan, and their quotas, on April 24, 1952. As the following table shows, these admissions did not strain the quota hierarchy of the Big Five, but they did change the underlying hierarchy of the quotas. The admission of former enemy countries also reflected the Cold War. In the voting by all member countries, Czechoslovakia voted against the admission of Germany and Japan by cablegram. It argued that the West German Bonn Government was "in contradiction with the international arrangement set up by the common agreement of the four powers" and did not "have the character of an independent state and the authorities set up there do not have the right to act in the name of Germany as a whole". As regards to Japan, "the situation created by the so

[59] IMF, EB/CM/GERMANY/MTG/52/2, January 31, 1952.

[60] IMF, EB/CM/JAPAN/51/2, October 15, 1951; EB/CM/JAPAN/51/1, October 9, 1951.

[61] NAC Staff Committee, Meeting No. 307, October 17, 1951, p. 1.

[62] IMF, EB/CM/Japan/MTG/52/1, January 14, 1952. In the NAC Staff Committee, the U.S. Executive Director explained that "a more recent communication from the British indicated a willingness to go along with the United States on the basis of such a quota", so that the committee advised him that the $250 million figure appeared appropriate for Japan." NAC Staff Committee, Meeting No. 317, December 20, 1951, p. 1.

Table 2.1 Quotas of members at selected dates (in millions of U.S. dollars)

Country	Dec. 31, 1945	Dec. 31, 1950	Dec. 31, 1955
United States	2,750	2,750	2,750
United Kingdom	1,300	1,300	1,300
China	550	550	550
France	450	450	450
India	400	400	400
Germany	–	–	*330*
Canada	300	300	300
Netherlands	275	275	275
Japan	–	–	*250*
Belgium	225	225	225
Australia	200	200	200
Italy	–	180	180
Other	1,150.0	1,406.5	1,540.5
Totals	7,600.0	8,036.5	8,750.5

Source: De Vries and Horsefield (1969), Table 14, pp. 378–380

called Peace Treaty with Japan of September 8, 1951 is in flagrant contradiction with the declaration of the United Nations organisation of January 1, 1942, the Cairo Declaration of December 1, 1943, the Potsdam Agreement of August 2, 1945 and the Resolution of the Far Eastern Commission of June 19, 1947 on the principles of policy towards Japan."[63]

The adverse relationship between the Fund and Czechoslovakia started when the U.S. imposed exchange restrictions on China and North Korea in December 1950.[64] B. Sucharda, the Governor of Czechoslovakia, sent Gutt a letter of protest concerning the decision of the Executive Board with respect to the U.S. exchange restrictions on December 21, 1950. Gutt answered him with the resolutions adopted by the Executive Board on August 14, 1952. Referring to the reply from Gutt, Sucharda again criticized the resolution as being "contrary to principles of the Articles of Agreement with regard to the protection of the members legitimate interests." Later, Czechoslovakia withdrew from the Fund at the end of 1954 because it refused to provide information on its balance of payments and national income under Article VIII, Section 5 and to hold consultations with the Fund under Article XIV. In the Executive Board meeting on July 26, 1954, a representative of Czechoslovakia referred to the U.S. exchange restrictions for security reasons and contended that the withholding of required information and the rejection of consultations were justified for reasons of national security and self-defense against measures directed against the political independence and sovereignty of Czechoslovakia.[65]

[63] IMF, EBD/52/93, May 29, 1952.

[64] See, cablegrams in IMF, EBD/51/824, January 23, 1951.

[65] IMF, EBM/54/41, July 26, 1954. See also, Horsefield (1969, pp. 359–364).

4.3 *Article XIV Consultations and Stand-by Credits*

Article XIV of the Fund Agreement provided that in the post-war transitional period members could maintain restrictions on payments and transfers for current international transactions. Members still retaining such restrictions after a period of 5 years from when the Fund began operations had to consult with the Fund on these restrictions. There were only six members excluded from the Article XIV consultations at the end of January 1952.[66]

The consultation report with Belgium-Luxembourg (hereafter Belgium) that the staff prepared on July 11, 1952, had an important impact on Fund governance and policy after the transitional period. This was not only because the consultations with Belgium were closely linked to the stand-by arrangements with Belgium, but also because both the consultations and the stand-by arrangements with Belgium became a touchstone for close cooperation between the Fund and the EPU. On June 19, 1952, the Executive Board had practically already assured Belgium of the stand-by credits of $50 million for the first time. The Executive Board took into consideration the facts that Belgium had extended substantial credits to the EPU and had received insufficient dollars from the EPU to cover its deficit. In the meeting, Johan W. Beyen (Netherlands) "hoped that the proposed transaction would help to bring about closer relations between the Fund and EPU", and Southard also said that the requested transactions from Belgium "should help get the Fund forward in the field of stand-by credits for member countries."[67]

Soon after, the bright prospect of a closer relationship between the Fund and EPU was faced with a crisis due to consultations with Belgium. The Executive Board considered the consultation report on Belgium on August 15, 1952. The staff originally drafted the report on July 11. The report examined the fact that while the gross reserves of Belgium had increased since September 1951, loan operations in the EPU had been a factor behind the payments surplus and a number of uncertainties. In conclusion, the report recommended that "it should not suggest to Belgium and Luxembourg the withdrawal or relaxation of those transitional arrangement at this time."[68] For this reason, the NAC Staff Committee held on the previous day criticized the report severely as follows: "the recommendations of the Fund Staff (…) should be opposed because the uncertainties were not sufficiently imminent to justify continuation of such restrictions and because the Fund analysis of the Belgian situation was inadequate." The Staff Committee, therefore, agreed that the U.S. Executive Director "should endeavor to obtain adequate support for this position before the issue comes to a final veto in the Fund."[69]

---

[66] They were El Salvador, Guatemala, Honduras, Mexico, Panama, and the U.S. Canada joined this group on March 25, 1952. See, Horsefield (1969), pp. 312–313.

[67] IMF, EBM/52/34, June 19, 1952.

[68] IMF, SM/5239, July 11, 1952, p. 9.

[69] NAC Staff Committee, Meeting No. 350, July 14, 1952.

The Fund Executive Board on July 15 was divided over the recommendations prepared by the staff. Belgium and the U.S. were in conflict regarding the purpose of the consultations. De Selliers declared that "the Fund was not acting in a judicial capacity, but in an advisory capacity." Therefore, "the consultation did not give the Fund any power to require the removal of restrictions." On the other hand, Southard argued that the Fund "could terminate the period for a particular member", and "it could also, if it wished, declare the period to be ended for all members and, where necessary, grant special exceptions under Art. VIII." The Executive Board continued discussions on the Belgian balance of payments position and the extension of its exchange restrictions on July 16, and August 13. Finally, Southard proposed a draft decision at the Executive Board on August 15.[70] The decision called for Belgium to consult with the Fund under Article XIV, Sect. 4 concerning the further retention of its transitional arrangements, for the Fund to request that Belgium reconsider the necessity of the present level of restrictions affecting dollar imports, and for the Fund to consult with Belgium regarding the free market in EPU currency, discriminatory export taxes, and partial blocking of proceeds arising from transactions with EPU countries.

After voting, the decision was adopted even though the Executive Directors for Belgium, India, Italy, the Netherlands, and the U.K. voted against it, and the Executive Director for Australia abstained. Here we should take notice of the statements of De Selliers after the voting. He stated that the decision should not be taken as a test of the Fund's attitude to the EPU, and that there "had been an appropriate opportunity for the expression of any views on relations with EPU at the time of the opening of the line of credit for Belgium." As his statement suggested, on July 11, 1952 the OEEC Council already had acknowledged the stand-by credit with Belgium, and had hoped "that it may also be possible to have fruitful collaboration in future between Fund and Organization in connection with problems of mutual concern."[71]

The stand-by credits and consultations with Belgium were "the biggest test" for the improvement of relations between the Fund and the EPU. Subsequently, the Fund members in the OEEC resumed the use of the Fund's resources, and the OEEC suggested that "a joint examination of countries which are members of both organizations be undertaken by the two institutions."[72] Since 1953, the Paris Office of the Fund had been invited regularly to attend the meetings of the EPU Managing Board.[73] On the other hand, after Ivar Rooth, the Fund Managing Director, expressed regret that the consultations with Belgium had been put to a vote in the Executive Board, the Managing Director and staff had to restore the strained relations with the U.S. Executive Director

[70] IMF, EBM/52/53, August 15, 1952.

[71] See, Cable from Mladek to Member of the Executive Board. IMF, EBD/52/116, July 11, 1952.

[72] IMF, SM/53/28, April 9, 1953,

[73] See, IMF, EBD/53/71, June 2, 1963.

5 Conclusion

We have examined the governance and policy of the Fund during the transitional period by comparing the arguments and policy actions of the NAC or the U.S. government. At the start of the Fund's operation, the NAC had controlled the Fund as a whole, including the Board of Directors and the Managing Director. As this governance system came to an end and Executive Directors other than the U.S. Director began to share responsibility for its operations, the role and responsibility of the U.S. in the Fund gradually decreased. Another important factor was the fact that a Managing Director without U.S. citizenship had exerted power. When the U.S. was confronted with the failure of sterling convertibility based on the key-currency approach and the continuation of multiple currency practices by many member countries, the NAC allowed the establishment of the EPU, which the Fund regarded as a sub-system. Afterwards, the Fund attempted to realize orderly cross rates and the relaxation of exchange regulations through means such as a float system through the EPU.

The NAC and the Fund Executive Director could not dogmatically control the Fund's governance and policy. They not only gave the leading member countries that constituted the Executive Board most careful consideration but also permitted other members to adopt flexible trade and exchange policies. As we saw in "the ERP decision," the U.S. Fund Director disrupted the relationship between the Fund and the EPU when he urged the protection of Fund resources in the NAC meeting. In the Article XIV consultations with Belgium in 1952, the NAC and the U.S. Fund Director also used their voting power to reject the recommendations of Fund staff. Nonetheless, the U.S. maintained a stance of supporting the relaxation of exchange restrictions, subject to extension of stand-by arrangements to Belgium and other members. Although the Fund gradually came to function as an international institution, NAC policy regarding the Fund was influenced by U.S. national-security concerns, and the NAC's responsibility as a statutory committee was not abolished until 1965.

References

Bordo, Michael D., and Barry Eichengreen (eds.). 1993. *A retrospective on the Bretton Woods system: Lessons for international monetary reform*. Chicago: University of Chicago Press.

Casey, Kevin M. 2001. *Saving international capitalism during the early Truman presidency: The National Advisory Council on International Monetary and Financial Problems*. New York: Routledge.

De Vries, Margaret, and J. Keith Horsefield. 1969. *The International Monetary Fund, 1945–1965*, vol. II. Washington: IMF.

Eccles, Marriner S. Document Collection. Various years. University of Utah, J. Willard Marriott Library, Special Collections Department, Available from FRASER Website: http://fraser.stlouisfed.org/eccles/.

Gardner, Richard N. 1969. *Sterling-dollar diplomacy: The origins and the prospects of our international economic order*. New York: McGraw-Hill.

Gorski, R.S. 1945. Summary report on Bretton Woods monetary conference. William McChesney Martin Jr. Collection, Federal Reserve Bank of St. Louis, FRASER Website.

Horie, Shigeo. 1964. *The International Monetary Fund: Retrospect and prospect*. London: Macmillan.

Horsefield, J. Keith. 1969. *The International Monetary Fund, 1945–1965*, vol. I. Washington: IMF.

International Monetary Fund. 1946. *Selected documents – Board of governors inaugural meeting, Savannah, Ga., March 8 to 18, 1946*. Washington: IMF.

International Monetary Fund. 1947–1952. *Annual report of the executive directors for 1947–1952*. Washington: IMF.

International Monetary Fund (IMF). Various years. *Central files*, Washington, DC. Available from http://www.imf.org/external/np/arc/eng/archive.htm.

Kamikawa, Takao. 2009. Sterling balance problem in war and postwar period. *Economia* 60(1) (in Japanese). Yokohama National University

Knai, Yuichi. 2010. The Anglo-American financial agreement and the crisis of sterling convertibility in 1947. *Economic Science* 57(4) (in Japanese). Nagoya University

Sanger, David E. 1998. A fund of trouble: A special report. *New York Times*, October.

Southard Jr., Frank A. 1979. *The evolution of the International Monetary Fund*, Essays in international finance, vol. 135. Princeton: Princeton University.

Suto, Isao. 2008. *Shaping of the post-war federal reserve policy: From the new deal to the accord*. Nagoya: Nagoya University Press (in Japanese).

Triffin, Robert. 1966. *The world money maze: National currencies in international payments*. New Haven: Yale University Press.

U. S. State Department. 1949. *Foreign relations of the United States (FRUS)*, vol. IV. Washington, DC: GPO.

U. S. NAC. 1948a, 1950a, 1952a. Special report of the National Advisory Council. In *Federal Reserve Bulletin*, July 1948, June 1950; In U.S. Treasury Department, *Annual Report for 1952*. Washington: GPO.

U. S. NAC. 1951b, 1952b. *Report of activities*, in: U.S. Treasury Department, *Annual Report for 1951, 1952*, Washington: GPO.

U. S. NAC. Various years. National Advisory Council on International Monetary and Financial Problems, National Archives and Records Administration (NARA), College Park, Maryland, RG56.

Weiss, Martin A. 2013. International Monetary Fund: Background and issues for congress. *U.S CRS Report*, R42019.

Williamson, John. 1990. What Washington means by policy reform. In *Latin American adjustment: How much has happened?* ed. J. Williamson. Washington, D.C: Institute for International Economics.

Chapter 3
Shaping the Fund's Policy for Exchange Liberalization

Teru Nishikawa

1 Introduction

The transition of the Western Europeans to Article VIII status in 1961 was the end of the postwar transitional period. The 1950s was the period when major countries gradually attained stability of their exchange rates against the U.S. dollar and exchange liberalization; in other words, the gap between the U.S. as an outstanding creditor and Europeans—the dollar shortage—disappeared. As the supply of dollars became excessive in the late 1950s, the stability of the international monetary system was gradually undermined and the world entered into the decade of a dollar crisis.

So far, a bitter appraisal has been given to the performance of the International Monetary Fund (IMF) in this period. For instance, Bordo and Eichengreen concluded that little was done by the IMF (the Fund) to establish multilateralism. Actually, the drawing from the Fund was somehow sluggish and the Article XIV status of major countries lasted much longer than was anticipated (Bordo 1993, pp. 45–47). However, the issue to be considered seems to remain. The commonly held view has been shaped based on a presumption that the Fund is subordinate to the largest industrial countries and so it has overlooked the Fund's own perspective. Considering the governance structure and the founders of the Fund, it is certainly natural that many scholars should describe the Fund as a subordinate body to the major countries. While the Fund has a vast staff division that is headed by the Management and is engaged in policy making and research, the decision maker of the Fund has been the Board of Governors and the Executive Board, which is composed of the delegations from members' monetary authorities. In addition, as is

Part of this chapter was originally published in Japanese as Nishikawa (2014), pp. 90–113.

T. Nishikawa (✉)
Faculty of International Social Sciences, Yokohama National University,
79-3 Tokiwadai, Hodogaya-ku, Yokohama 240-8501, Japan
e-mail: tel-aurora@ynu.ac.jp

K. Yago et al. (eds.), *History of the IMF*, Studies in Economic History,
DOI 10.1007/978-4-431-55351-9_3

well known, the Fund was founded through Anglo-American negotiations, especially under the influence of the United States.

So, I would hardly deny the prevailing understanding that the Fund was governed by certain powers. However, the issue would still remain even if the Fund is a dependent organization. How did the Fund itself perceive such an uncomfortable situation in the postwar transitional period? Did it not really attempt to take the stage? Actually, interesting facts can easily be found in the chronology of the Fund. It was in the 1950s that the basic and major framework of the Fund's policy was created and then the Fund evolved institutionally (Horsefield and De Vries 1969). Then, how should we explain these contradictory events in the 1950s—"the Fund in dormancy" and the Fund's institutional development? What was the missing link connecting them? To answer these questions, it is useful to shed light on the Fund's "institutional autonomy", especially the autonomy of the staff division that seems to be subject to the Fund's interests.

So far, a few studies have described the Fund's autonomy (James 1996). For instance, James successfully modified the negative image of the Fund by showing the initiative of Mr. Jacobsson, the third Managing Director of the Fund. On the other hand, in this chapter, not the initiative but the autonomy of the Fund's staff will be examined. On the assumption that the Fund is an organization that is subordinate to the major countries, the following topics will be examined; How did the staff try to establish multilateralism? How did such autonomous attempts make the "Fund's Policy" create and evolve?

2 Creation of the Fund's Initial Policies

2.1 Postwar Disturbances and the Fund

In July 1944, at the International Monetary and Financial Conference held in Bretton Woods, representatives of 44 governments signed the Fund's Articles of Agreement and agreed on the establishment of multilateralism. It is true that this international monetary plan was an outcome of the "battle" between the Keynes plan and the White plan, but both of them were based on the common perception that the tragedies in the 1930s must never be repeated.

First, both plans were framed to restore the system of exchange stability and liberalization—convertibility of currencies into gold and dollars—reflecting the view that monetary disturbances—competitive depreciation, exchange control and turbulent hot money—had brought about the destruction of the international financial system and thereby the shrinkage of world trade. The scope of convertibility was however limited to the balance on current account, since the movement of short-term capital was thought to be destructive.

Secondly, the plans designed a monetary system that facilitated countries' achievement of full employment through "Keynesian fine tuning" and balance of payments equilibrium, and thereby expanded world trade. The real threat to the postwar world economy was assumed to be not severe inflation but deflationary pressure in the U.S.—an outstanding creditor—and its international transmission. Thirdly, to achieve these objectives, an international body—the IMF—was to be founded. The Fund was supposed to encourage its members to restore current account convertibility, giving them short-term finance that facilitated a conflict caused by the concurrent pursuit of full employment and balance of payments equilibrium.

On the other hand, "Bretton Woods" itself hardly reached consensus and was attacked both in the United States and the United Kingdom. In the U.S., professor Williams of Harvard University argued that it was premature to adopt Bretton Woods before a solution to postwar disturbances was in sight and proposed a "key currency plan" as a constructive alternative way to multilateralism. This plan criticized the ideal of Bretton Woods, noting that close collaboration on solutions to transitional problems between the U.S. and the U.K. was needed prior to international monetary cooperation on the Fund. In the U.K., Bretton Woods was not thought to be useful for bringing the urgent problem—the dollar shortage and accumulated sterling balance—under control.

In March 1947, the Fund began financial operation. Soon after that, however, it turned out that reconstruction was unavoidable before the Fund took the stage. After the declaration of the Truman Doctrine, the Cold War had broken out and the "Marshall speech" in June called for the U.S. government to help European recovery. Moreover, although sterling convertibility was restored in July as promised in the Anglo-American Loan agreement, a run on sterling crushed the trial, causing it to fail after just a month. The dollar gap was so serious that the severe inflation resulting from large reconstruction demand hit major countries, contrary to the assumption of the founders of the Fund, and world trade was taking place not on a multilateral basis but under numerous bilateral arrangements.

In April 1948, Marshal Aid (European Recovery Program; ERP), began and inspired the European recovery. The Organization for European Economic Cooperation (OEEC) organized in response to the Aid led to financial cooperation on establishing an intra-European multilateral payment scheme and, in September 1950, the European Payments Union (EPU), which covered most of the non-dollar area, was established. Moreover, the OEEC took the initiative in intra-European trade liberalization, applying a "Code of Liberalization."

By contrast, by the U.S. Director the Board of Directors made an "ERP Decision" that discouraged the ERP participants—European members of the Fund—from accessing the Fund's resources. Despite the enthusiastic efforts of the Fund's staff,[1] the Board was unwilling to associate with the OEEC and only sent an observer to

[1] At the Board on November 1948, Mr. Gutt—the First Managing Director of the Fund— made a speech and showed intense interest at this development in Europe, saying "The Paris plan is much concerned with multilateralization; e.g., convertibility. Well, on a limited but nevertheless substantial scale, the Fund agreement is an attempt at convertibility. Therefore, nothing of what passes in Paris can leave us indifferent." Furthermore, he advocated that the Fund should lead the OEEC, insisting "There is *one* international monetary policy-making body in the world, and *only one*: the Fund. It should therefore be associated with any movement, any organization having a connection with international monetary policy." IMF Archives (hereafter IMFA), EBM48/382, European Payments Arrangement, November 12, 1948.

the meeting on the establishment of the EPU. In the reconstruction period, the Fund lapsed into dormancy.

Meanwhile, from the outset the Fund was not expected to play a leading role in the reconstruction and was not equipped with effective means to solve the problem. In fact, Article XIV—the Article on the transitional period—allowed members to maintain exchange restrictions due to "balance of payments reasons" till March 1952. In addition, Article VIII—the Article on general obligations of members—set forth that the obligation of convertibility was limited to foreign-held balances that had been acquired "recently," in consideration of the enormous sterling balance. Taking these Articles into consideration, the bitter experience of the Fund is not inconsistent with the Fund's Articles of Agreement.

Nevertheless, it would be too shallow to conclude that the Fund put up with the disappointing situation of being a "Fund with no customer." Were the Fund's staff members really confident that the process of European recovery set the stage for the Fund's prosperity or that the OEEC and the EPU were just sub systems of Bretton Woods? How did they perceive the fact that progress on exchange liberalization—the mandate of the Fund—was led by the OEEC? Consideration of the Fund's autonomy readily raises these questions.

The conclusions will show that the Fund's staff was far from an idle spectator. The staff, headed by the Managing Director, took the situation seriously as a process undermining the Fund's prestige. As early as the early 1950s, they began devising methods to lead members' exchange liberalization.

2.2 *Formulation of the Fund's Adjustment Policies*

2.2.1 Publication of "Annual Report on Exchange Restrictions"

In March 1950, the Fund started to publish the "*Annual Report on Exchange Restrictions*." Article XIV, Section 4 set forth "Not later than 3 years after the date on which the Fund begins operations and in each year thereafter, the Fund shall report on the restrictions still in forth." This report, published based on this prescription, covered the exchange restrictions of all members and reported the policy the Fund should apply in the year.

In the first report, the staff pointed out the instability of members' balance of payments, especially current account vis-à-vis the U.S., and attributed it to residual inflationary pressure and a serious dollar shortage.[2] Then, the staff mentioned the efficacy of tightening policies against inflationary pressures and the significance of international cooperation to overcome the dollar shortage, noting that "Every country must observe restraints in its credit and fiscal policies if its par value is to remain realistic for any length of time [...] the Fund continues, therefore, to urge its member countries to practice the restraints in their domestic policies which are

[2] IMFA, SM50/436, First Annual Report on Exchange Restrictions, February 6, 1950.

necessary to avoid inflation and its adverse effects on their payments position. [...] Some factors which have a bearing on the payments position of members are clearly of external origin, and no country can by itself control them."

In addition, the staff emphasized the importance of the Fund's leading role in resolving members' payments problems and in relaxing exchange restrictions, as follows; "In Article I of the Articles of Agreement, member countries have signified their intention to work together toward the multilateralization of international payments and the elimination of exchange restrictions which hamper world trade. They have established and recognized the Fund as the instrument for coordination and cooperation in the monetary field. [...] The Fund expects also to contribute to the progress toward the relaxation of restrictions by initiating, encouraging and coordinating appropriate concerted action among its members."

Thus, as early as 1950, the Fund's staff had already started to challenge the postwar disturbances in order to recover the Fund's prestige. The policy designed in the report was consequently different from the one that had been expected at the Bretton Woods conference—to realize both full employment and balance of payment equilibrium for its members. Instead, the staff began to pursue a policy which was "balance of payments-oriented," and therefore one of tightening.

2.2.2 Formulation of the Adjustment Theory—Absorption Approach

Then, what was the theoretical background of the policy that emphasized the effectiveness of tightening macroeconomic policy for balance of payments adjustment? The Articles of Agreement did not specify the role of macroeconomic policy. Instead, it envisioned financial assistance from the Fund against short-term deficits and an adjustable peg system against fundamental disequilibrium. In fact, the approach was a brand-new one because under the gold standard a self-correcting mechanism was thought to adjust balance of payments and since the 1930s the elasticity approach had prevailed. It was the theory named the absorption approach that shaped the Fund's policy at that time (Alexander 1952).

Under this approach, current account (CA) represents a gap between national product (Y) and national expenditure (absorption = consumption and investment: A) ($CA = Y - A$, $\Delta CA = \Delta Y - \Delta A$). Based on this theory, although improvements in current account are to be attained by increasing Y and/or restraining A, Y cannot be increased under conditions of full employment. The implication of the absorption approach would be concluded that to improve the current account government restrained absorption, by applying a tightening policy.

The approach was formulated by the Fund's Research Department staff through their efforts to bring inflationary pressure under control, thereby correcting the balance of payments imbalance. At the outset of the Fund's operation, the staff headed by Mr. Bernstein—the Director of the Department—recognized that the imbalance was brought about by inflation. By 1950, through missions, they had formulated the basic idea of the absorption approach—no matter how much par value may be depreciated, it would be impossible to correct the imbalance without curtailing excess national expenditure, which causes inflation.

For instance, devaluation of an exchange rate caused declines in export prices, thereby increasing foreign demand for the goods of the devaluing country. The country needs to cover the increasing demand by expanding national product and/or restraining domestic demand for the goods. However, national product cannot be increased under conditions of full employment. Thus, under severe inflationary conditions, still more, devaluation does not recover a current account balance until national expenditure is restrained. The formulation of the absorption approach must be explained in the postwar historical context.

2.2.3 Formulating the Criteria on Use of the Fund's Resources

In addition to the theory, the method by which the Fund intervened in members' policymaking and adjusted their economies also was established in this period. Two managing directors, Mr. Gutt and Mr. Rooth, developed the Fund's policy on drawing. Article V prescribed the principle of transactions with the Fund, as follows; "The member desiring to purchase the currency represents that it is presently needed for making in that currency payments which are consistent with the provisions of this Agreement." However, the criteria on use of the Fund's resources were still open to some interpretation and at the outset of the Fund's operation, the Directors had discussed the interpretation of Article V. The U.S. insisted that "present need" should be strictly scrutinized while the U.K. expected that members could freely access the Fund by only representing "present need." The prolonged disputes on "automaticity" consequently prevented members from accessing the Fund and resulted in the loss of the Fund's prestige.

It was Mr. Gutt who attempted to break the deadlock. At an informal session of the Board in November 1950,[3] Mr. Gutt advocated that the Fund should be an active and useful adviser to the members and insisted "the Fund's resources could be made available to give confidence to members to undertake practical programs of action designed to help achieve the purposes of the Fund Agreement." It is noteworthy that he described the "practical program" that members were expected to apply as follows: "The activities for which availability of the Fund's assistance would be regarded as appropriate would include the achievement of monetary stability, the adoption of realistic rates of exchange, the relaxation and removal of restrictions and discrimination, the simplification of multiple currency practices."

As his statement "Do you not think this would be a really constructive attitude of the Fund, would give the Fund a useful initiative, an activity, and restore some of the prestige it has—justly or unjustly—lost?" showed, his idea skillfully pursued not only overcoming the immobility of the Fund's resources but also realizing the purpose of the Fund—monetary stability and exchange liberalization for members.

[3]IMFA, EBD51/828, Use of the Fund's Resources-Managing Director, February 5, 1951.

In May 1951, the tenure of Mr. Gutt ended and the work on the formulation of the Fund drawing policy was taken over by Mr. Rooth, the second Managing Director. On arriving at the Fund, Mr. Rooth began to give shape to the general policy proposed by his predecessor and worked out the "Rooth plan" that was designed to make the Fund's resources circulate over the short term.

To ensure the revolving character of the Fund, at a series of Board meetings in autumn Mr. Rooth proposed that (1) the interest rate schedule should be changed so as to lower the interest costs for short-term transactions but graduate them more steeply for longer-term uses, (2) the repurchase period should generally be limited to within 3–5 years and (3) there should be a special term—giving an automaticity—for drawings within the gold tranche.[4] Through discussion, this "Rooth Plan" received the favorable support of the Directors and finally was approved. Thus, the two Managing Directors formulated the fund facility and enabled the Fund to be involved in the process of members' policy making.

3 Implementing Policies in the Early 1950s

3.1 The Fund's Concentration on Sterling Convertibility

3.1.1 Emphasis on International Cooperation

In March 1952, the Article XIV consultation started. The Fund's staff launched into the members' exchange liberalization. As shown below, it was the U.K. and pound sterling that had the key position in this process.

In the "*Third Annual Report on Exchange Restrictions*" published in May, the staff emphasized the importance of international cooperation, noting that "The purpose of many of the restrictions employed is to cope with balance of payments difficulties of the country imposing them. Some of the difficulties, however, are the result of measures in important export markets. Limitations on imports by one country, through exchange or trade restrictions or other devices, restrict the earnings of other countries and consequently may result in the latter restricting their payments. Similarly, the inconvertibility of a country's earnings may lead it to discriminate in order to use its earnings in those areas where such use is possible and to avoid accumulation of inconvertible surpluses." (IMF 1952a, p. 5). They started to collect the members' "prerequisites for exchange liberalization" so that the cooperation would work well.

At the Consultation held in July 1952, the Fund's staff asked the British representatives about the prerequisites for sterling convertibility. Mr. Stamp, the U.K. representative, explained that though the existing gold and dollar reserves at the disposal of the U.K. were completely inadequate to meet any large conversion of

[4] IMFA, EBM51/710, Use of Fund Resources-Charges, October 26, 1951.
IMFA, EBM51/717, Use of Fund Resources-Charges, November 19, 1951.

sterling balances, the pressure to convert existing sterling balances could be restrained in a number of ways—(1) the U.K. might develop sufficient surpluses in its balance of payments by being provided dollars or by increasing its exports vis-à-vis the dollar area, or (2) the U.K. might draw on the Fund or raise loans in the U.S. or Canada and acquire thereby the dollars needed to ensure convertibility.[5]

After the 1952 Consultations, the U.K. requirements were applied as a pivot of the Fund's liberalization policy. At the Annual meeting held in September, Mr. Rooth proclaimed a policy that conformed to the U.K. "prerequisite." He indicated the key role the government of the U.S.—a large creditor—should play and stated that "the deficit countries do not wish to become dependent on the bounty of the United States. I believe that they can pay their way if they are able to expand their exports. The tariffs of the United States have been reduced in the past two decades, but for many goods they are still high." Then, he encouraged members to use the Fund's resources to make progress on their exchange liberalization, saying that "We are interested in having our members establish convertibility of their currencies. [...] a country can risk bold use of reserves which at times may be necessary with convertibility. After all, the Fund's resources are intended to help members to accept the risks and to gain the benefits of a convertible currency." (IMF 1952b, pp. 14–18).

Why did Mr. Rooth apply that policy? We can find a clue in the "*Fourth Annual Report on Exchange Restrictions*" issued in May 1953, as follows: "In many of the consultations, the Fund discussed with member countries the problems which they faced in making their currencies convertible. It recognized the fact that, for a number of them, the extent to which they could make progress depended [...] on what was done by their trading partners, with sterling occupying key position. The Fund, therefore, recorded its view that the interest of all member countries would be much advanced by the convertibility of sterling." (IMF 1953, pp. 16–17). This passage implied that most members mentioned sterling convertibility as their "prerequisites" at the First Consultations. Thus, for the Fund, sterling convertibility was the first step towards the early establishment of a multilateral payments system.

3.1.2 Controversy on Sterling Convertibility

On the other hand, the U.K. authority had conceived the plan for sterling convertibility named "ROBOT" by the end of 1951 and after autumn 1952, a "Collective Approach" was under contemplation. The dilemma of the authority was that the serious dollar shortage caused the need for exchange restrictions or suspension of convertibility, which hampered the position of sterling as an international currency. That made the way to the full convertibility of sterling a peculiar one. For instance, the "ROBOT" involved the application of a managed float as a means of reducing the balance of payments burden generated by convertibility. Moreover, in the "Collective Approach" that was designed so that both the U.K. and the Continental

[5] IMFA, CF C/U.K./420, Exchange Restrictions Consultations in 1952—Record of Third Meeting with U.K. Representative, July 2, 1952, pp. 2–3.

European states would undertake external convertibility together, the U.K. was supposed to maintain import restrictions against its creditor countries such as the U.S. after the achievement of external convertibility (Schenk 1994, pp. 113–128).

Such an approach that explicitly reflected U.K. interests would not possibly be accepted by the Continental Europeans. Especially, some of them were concerned that the floating pound might dissolve the EPU that required a fixed rate system in its operation and strongly resisted it. In addition, in January 1954 the Commission on the U.S. Foreign Economic Policy—the Randall Commission—reported a doubtful view and chilled the U.K.'s ambitions.

3.1.3 Stand-by Arrangement with the United Kingdom

What did the Fund's staff think of the controversial U.K. plan with import restrictions and a managed float? In fact, since the summer of 1953, they had begun preparing to provide the U.K. with financial support and thereby to compel the U.K. authorities to undertake the Collective Approach. In the spring of 1954, among the main staff—Mr. Rooth and the main staff of the Exchange Restrictions Department and the Research Department—a program to conclude a stand-by arrangement with the U.K. had begun to be progressed. Table 3.1 shows the draft design of the program prepared by the staff.

As this table shows, the Fund's staff did not immediately deny the problematic ingredients of the Collective Approach. Mr. Rooth and the other staff were eager for and gave first priority to sterling convertibility. However, they could not figure out a clear solution on how to settle the matter of remaining import restrictions and the managed float, leaving everything to secret consultations between Mr. Rooth and the U.K. Chancellor of the Exchequer.

Furthermore, the insufficient scale of the Fund placed fetters on realizing the stand-by arrangement. In a memorandum,[6] Mr. Bernstein—the Director of the Research Department—examined the feasibility of the stand-by arrangement in terms of the Fund's resources, as follows; "The present gold and dollar holdings of the United Kingdom or those likely to be reached by the end of this year are not adequate to enable the United Kingdom to undertake sterling convertibility. By a very restrictive credit policy, by close supervision of credit to foreign companies, and by making agreements on the drawing down of sterling balances, the magnitude of the capital outflow after the establishment of convertibility can to some extent be kept down. A significant capital outflow will, nevertheless, still take place. [...] To have adequate resources for convertibility, the United Kingdom must have dollar credits of not less than $2 billion and preferably as much as $3 billion." In the early 1950s, the U.K. gold and dollar reserves continued to be around $2 ~ 3 billion, while the sterling balances held by non-dollar area also amounted to about $2 billion.

[6] IMFA, Research Department Immediate Office/Department Director Edward M. Bernstein Subject Files/1, Notes on Sterling Convertibility, April 2, 1954, pp. 23–24.

Table 3.1 Draft design of a stand-by arrangement with the United Kingdom

After full discussion between the Fund and the United Kingdom concerning the program for convertibility of sterling, the following stand-by arrangement has been agreed:
Purpose: The exchange available to the United Kingdom under this arrangement is to be used to support the convertibility program which the U.K. has informed the Fund includes the following major features: (a) The immediate rendering of sterling earned by Fund members on current account convertible into any member currency. (b) The progressive relaxation of remaining restrictions on the making of payments and transfers for current international transactions and restrictions on imports as rapidly as circumstances permit. (c) The adoption and maintenance of fiscal, monetary and credit policies in the United Kingdom that will promote the purposes of the Fund. (d) Possibly a reference to the fluctuation of sterling, if any, in appropriate form.
Remaining Exchange Restrictions: The United Kingdom does not intend to take advantage for any further period of time of the transitional arrangements set forth in Article XIV of the Fund Agreement and has notified the Fund that it is prepared to accept the obligations of Article VIII, Section 2, 3 and 4. The Fund has approved the maintenance of the restrictions on the making of payments and transfers for current international transactions now in effect, provided that the impact of these restrictions will not be intensified without prior consultations and approval of the Fund. The United Kingdom will relax and remove these restrictions as rapidly as circumstances permit and will consult with the Fund not less than every six months regarding such relaxation and removal.
Rates of Exchange: The United Kingdom intends to pursue an exchange rate policy consistent with Article IV, Section 3 and 4 of the Fund Agreement. If it should become necessary to allow movements in the exchange rates, the United Kingdom will before doing so consult the Managing Director of the Fund, inform him of the limits within which the value of sterling will be permitted to move and agree with him the conditions under which the United Kingdom will be prepared to stabilize the value of sterling at the existing par value or propose a new par value to the Fund. During any period when the exchange value of sterling is permitted to fluctuate the United Kingdom will remain in close consultation with the Managing Director and keep him fully informed on all matters affecting the movements of the rates of exchange.

Source: IMFA, CF C/United Kingdom/1760, Secret (Stand-by arrangement with U.K-Draft), May 26, 1954
This table was originally published in Japanese in Nishikawa (2014), p. 102

The sterling balances, directed to be converted into gold and dollars, easily could have drained the U.K. reserves.

Mr. Bernstein concluded that "It would be ideal if the Fund had the resources to provide the United Kingdom with all of the dollar credits required for convertibility. In fact, however, it cannot." At that time, though the Fund's total resources amounted to about \$9 billion, the Fund's total holdings of gold, U.S. dollars and Canadian dollars amounted to only about \$3 billion, and \$400 million of this had already been drawn by the other members. In addition, Mr. Bernstein recognized that the uncommitted gold, U.S. dollars and Canadian dollars ought not to be much below \$1.5 billion after concluding the U.K. stand-by arrangement in preparation for the needs of the other members. It turned out that the maximum amount the Fund could provide for the U.K. was less than \$1.5 billion. Until now, many scholars have described the IMF as a "Fund with no customer" in the early 1950s based on the fact that the drawings were leveling off in that period. On the contrary, however, Fund staff keenly felt a shortage of resources.

In the United Kingdom, Mr. Butler—Chancellor of the Exchequer—and only a few high officials seemed to be involved in the plan. While they fully understood that some financial support was indispensable for undertaking the Collective Approach, they began to hesitate over reliance on the Fund. Without the consent to the Collective Approach among the major countries, they might not restore external convertibility even if they concluded the stand-by arrangement. If they did not take steps within the period of stand-by arrangement, however, it would lead to lack of confidence in the U.K. authorities (Kaplan and Schleiminger 1989, pp. 206–209).

In the early 1950s, Western Europe enjoyed favorable economic conditions. Inflation had gradually been brought under control and gold and dollar reserves favorably increased. Then, in 1954, hope for the end of the transitional period arose inside the Fund. So long as the Fund could not support the U.K. without its request, however, the realization of the stand-by arrangement would depend on the behavior of the U.K. authorities—whether they requested or not, and ultimately whether they could carry out the Collective Approach or not.

3.2 *The Fund's Policy for Balance of Payments Adjustments*

While the Fund's staff emphasized the effect of international cooperation on mitigating the dollar shortage, how did they understand the role of tightened economic policy on balance of payment adjustments? The U.K. government assigned priority to full employment against balance of payment equilibrium. As early as in wartime, the government had proclaimed that it would seek to maintain high and stable employment, which continued to be a common object of both the Labour and Conservative parties. Even if it was inevitable to correct the balance of payments for exchange liberalization, for the U.K. it should be attained by the effort and/or cooperation of creditor countries.

Faced with this policy in the 1953–1954 consultations, the Fund's staff repeatedly were concerned that the U.K.'s full employment policy caused inflation and wage increases and finally deteriorated its balance of payments. However, they did not strongly compel the U.K. to amend its economic policy.[7]

Why was it that the staff did not strictly argue against U.K. domestic policy? It seems to have been related to the fact that the staff gave first priority to restoring sterling convertibility. In the autumn of 1954, when the Fund's staff were working on the stand-by arrangement, Mr. Rooth made an impressive speech at the Annual Meeting, as follows: "In making its currency convertible, a country indicates its willingness to expose its trade to world-wide competition. Such a country should

[7] IMFA, C/U.K./420.1., Exchange Restrictions Consultations in 1953, Minutes of Second Meeting with U.K. Representative, July 18, 1953, pp. 7–9.

buy its import, regardless of origin and of the currency in which payments are made, exclusively on a price and quality basis. [...] The need to sell in all markets under competitive conditions will compel it to maintain productive efficiency and to avoid an inflation of costs." (IMF 1954, pp. 12–16).

In this speech, we can find his view that "after restoring convertibility, control of inflation and thereby attainment of external balance will be unavoidable to maintain the convertibility," which was different from the former view that "before restoring convertibility, control of inflation and thereby attainment of external balance are unavoidable." These remarks implied that the Fund's staff might have the view that once sterling were make convertible, then the U.K. authorities consequently would implement anti-inflationary policies in order to maintain convertibility." Mr. Rooth and the other staff must have resolved to realize sterling convertibility and end the transitional period by themselves. That shaped the Fund's policy that gave priority to sterling convertibility.

4 Implementing the Policies of the Late 1950s

4.1 The Fund's Emphasis on Strong Anti-inflationary Policies

However, the U.K.'s expansionary policy, as far as the Fund's staff were concerned, brought about a serious deterioration of its current account in early 1955. Moreover, in mid-1955, the rumor that the U.K. authorities would let sterling fluctuate to alleviate the persistent current account crisis caused a severe run on sterling.

The U.K. crisis influenced the prospects of the plan for a stand-by arrangement with the U.K. as the Collective Approach became harder to realize amid the repeated crises. In August 1955, the Western Europeans agreed to the foundation the European Monetary Agreement (EMA) as a successor to the EPU. The EPU would be transited to the EMA when the countries holding 50 % of the EPU quota restored their currencies' convertibility. The 50 % level implied that the roadmap of liberalization in Europe would be a collective process among the major three countries—the U.K. (25.5 %), France (12.5 %) and Germany (12 %)—whose holdings amount to 50 %. The agreement on the EMA discouraged the U.K. authorities from carrying out an ambitious Collective Approach (Kaplan and Schleiminger 1989, pp. 210–226).

Ultimately, the Fund's efforts to conclude a stand-by arrangement with the U.K. came to an unavoidable halt. However, as a condition of the transition to the EMA shows, it was obvious that sterling convertibility continued to be a key issue in the whole European liberalization process. For the Fund's staff, sterling convertibility remained a keen interest.

Then, what did they recognize as the cause of the U.K. crisis and how did they promote its liberalization? The answers were shown in the "*Sixth Annual Report on Exchange Restrictions*" published in May 1955. In the report, the staff clearly indicated that the balance of payment disequilibrium was caused by the wrong macroeconomic policies and the members couldn't attribute it to postwar international circumstances—dollar shortage—any more, as follows; "As the effects of the destruction and disruption caused by the war increasingly disappear, the time is coming much closer when the postwar transitional period may end for all other members. […] the use of restrictions as a means of coping with balance of payments difficulties was at best a temporary expedient, and that a sound external position could not be achieved without internal stability." (IMF 1955, pp. 1–13).

The policy requirement for the U.K. also was changed. In the 1955 consultation, Mr. Friedman, the chairman of the Fund's mission, requested that the U.K. should commit to tightened policies, stating "it was important to watch the situation closely and to continue an anti-inflationary policy […] On the problem of wages which were of interest to the Fund since they bore on the United Kingdom's competitive position, the team felt that, under conditions of overfull employment, pressures for wage increases were almost inevitable. Such pressures could constitute a threat to the United Kingdom's competitive position. As to credit policy the team hoped that the tighter monetary policy was working as to be particularly helpful in strengthening the United Kingdom's balance of payments position. The team urged that the aim of achieving and maintaining internal equilibrium as a basic pre-requisite of balance of payments strength be kept."[8] He concluded the consultation by emphasizing that the U.K. should progress exchange liberalization as soon as the balance of payments and foreign reserves had recovered. Thus, the Fund's stress was shifted from mitigating the dollar shortage through international cooperation and/or promoting convertibility using the Fund's resources to exchange liberalization with external balance using tightened policies.

4.2 Management of the U.K. Crisis

Although in 1956 the U.K. external balances recovered, the economic stability never lasted. Through the late 1950s, the U.K. again faced two speculation and foreign-reserve crises. With the end of the transitional period in sight, the Fund staff were pressed to take measures to respond to the U.K. crises. The first crisis occurred later in 1956. The U.K. incursion into Egypt in the Suez Affair undermined confidence among holders of sterling. Severe speculation on sterling was brought about and U.K. foreign reserves were lost sharply.

In December, the U.K. authorities requested the purchase of $561.47 million and a stand-by arrangement for $738.53 million for the duration of 12 months. The Fund's staff immediately recommended to the Board of Directors that the Fund should agree to the request, noting "Unless the decline in the gold and dollar reserves is checked, the U.K. will be faced with serious difficulties in re-establishing a surplus in its current balance of payments with detrimental consequences to the volume of world trade […] This would seriously jeopardize the present freedom from

[8] IMFA, CF C/U.K./420, Exchange Restrictions Consultations 1955, Minutes of the Sixth Meeting, December 7, 1955, pp. 5–6.

restriction on trade and payments with the consequent loss of the progress thus far achieved in the attainment of the Fund's objectives."[9]

At the Board meeting on December 10, Mr. Jacobsson, the third Managing Director, conferred with the Directors as to whether to approve the request. At the meeting, though some voices expressed disappointment that the Fund's resources wouldn't be used for sterling convertibility, the Directors unanimously approved the financial support to the United Kingdom.[10] With this funding, the speculation was quickly alleviated.

However, in the summer of 1957 a speculative run on sterling was brought about again. The widening of the EPU account imbalance among the U.K., France and Germany lay behind this crisis. While Germany became a large creditor, France widened its deficit with the EPU, which sharply expanded the regional imbalance in 1956. At this juncture, in Europe the discussion toward European integration—the European Common Market and Free Trade Area—was enhanced, and thereby the exchange market was filled with rumors of exchange adjustment—revaluation of the deutschemark, devaluation of the franc and sterling—to correct the imbalance before the integration.

Faced with the outflow of gold and dollars, the U.K. authorities showed their intention to stabilize currency, taking measures of strictly tightened policies including a raise of the discount rate from 5 to 7 %. Furthermore, at the Annual Meeting in the autumn Mr. Jacobsson praised the U.K.'s action and completely denied the possibility of exchange adjustment (IMF 1957, pp. 27–28). A series of measures quickly suppressed the speculation in late September. After the crisis, the Fund continued to support the U.K. authorities, approving the request for renewal of the stand-by arrangement in November.

Thus, the crises were brought under control without the application of beggar-thy-neighbor policies by the United Kingdom. Some previous studies have argued that this crisis management helped the Fund recover from its reputation as "the Bank with no customer" or a "white elephant" (James 1996, pp. 102–103). Meanwhile, such a large support, at the same time, threatened the Fund's ability to support its members.

Then, at the 1957 Annual Meeting, Mr. Jacobsson showed his concern that the increasing support would cause a shortage of the Fund's resources and mentioned the necessity of increasing the quota (IMF 1957, pp. 21–22). In fact, the shortage reflected the progress of the exchange liberalization and the expansion of world trade. However, the U.K. crises manifested the danger of an occurrence of sudden capital movement. In such a circumstance, the Fund needed more than the existing framework—adjustment of policy toward an individual member—to maintain the stability of the international monetary system.

---

[9] IMFA, EBS56/44supplement1, Use of the Fund's Resources-United Kingdom, December 7, 1956, pp. 4–5.

[10] IMFA, EBM56/59, Use of the Fund's Resources- United Kingdom, December 10, 1956.

5 Exchange Liberalization and Instability Surges to the Fore

5.1 End of the Postwar Transitional Period

In 1958, the economic position between the U.S. and the Western Europeans was reversed. As Figs. 3.1 and 3.2 show, the Western Europeans recorded current surpluses vis-à-vis the U.S. and gradually accumulated foreign reserves. In contrast to that development, the U.S. ran a current deficit vis-à-vis the Western Europeans and its foreign reserves peaked in late 1957, starting to decrease. Perceiving the change in the situation, at the 1958 Annual Meeting Mr. Jacobsson proclaimed the resolution of the dollar shortage and that the time had come to realize a convertible world. In addition, he proposed the increase of the Fund's quota that came up for discussion at the last Meeting (IMF 1958, pp. 23–36). The proposal was adopted at the 1958 Meeting, and in September 1959 the Fund's scale enlarged from about $9 billion to $14.5 billion.

Thus, in the late 1950s, conditions favorable to the establishment of the multilateral payment system—the end of the dollar shortage and a quota increase—were arranged one after another. The momentum toward worldwide liberalization was gradually growing. At this juncture, in the U.S. and Canada complaints grew against the dollar discrimination Western Europeans still maintained.

In the 1958 consultation, the Fund's staff urged early convertibility of sterling and the abolishment of the U.K.'s remaining discrimination. In response, Mr. Symons, the U.K. representative, said the U.K. expected the Fund's financial support, stating "It was necessary that adequate support should be assured. In this connection

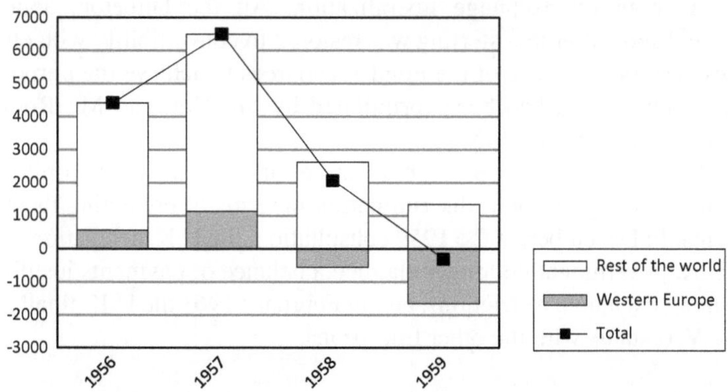

Fig. 3.1 The U.S. current account in the late 1950s (in millions of US$). *Source*: IMF (1957–1960). Notes: Donations and grants were excluded. This figure was originally published in Japanese in Nishikawa (2014), p. 109

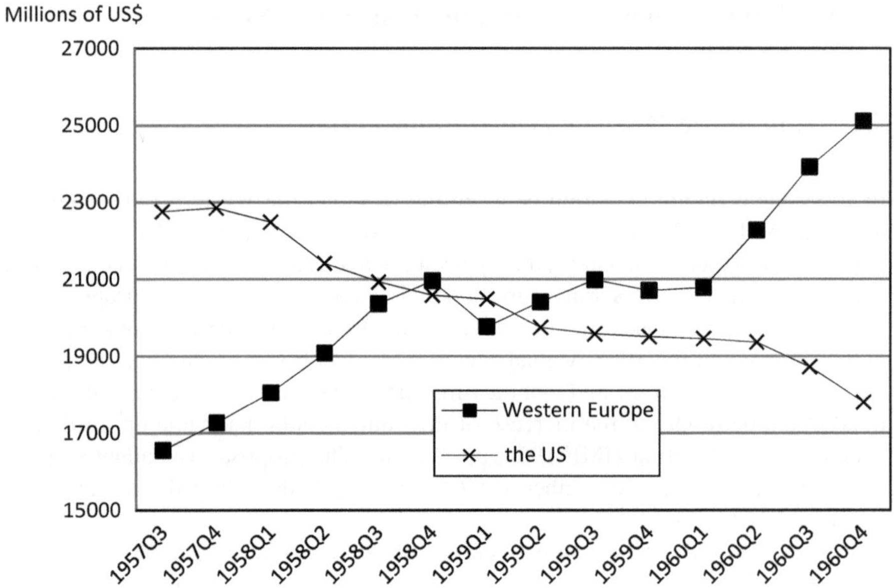

Fig. 3.2 Gold and foreign reserves of major countries in the late 1950s. *Source*: IMF (1959–1961). This figure was originally published in Japanese in Nishikawa (2014), p. 109

the stand-by arrangement was important and the proposal for an increase in the Fund's resources was also relevant."[11]

In December, after the consultation, the Fund received a request for a renewal of the standby arrangement from the U.K. authorities. The aim of this request was to prepare a buffer against the pressure on its balance of payments that possibly would be brought about by exchange liberalization. All the Directors approved the request,[12] and soon after that sterling was restored to convertibility with other major currencies. The policy—use of the Fund's resources to achieve the purposes of the Fund Agreement—that had been formulated by Mr. Gutt and Mr. Rooth finally supported sterling convertibility.

Thus, for Western Europeans, realization of external convertibility greatly reduced the meaning of dollar discrimination in terms of protecting their balances of payments. In December, at the 1959 consultation, the U.K. delegation announced that the U.K. government no longer claimed a balance of payments justification for the remaining exchange restrictions, and in February 1961 the U.K. finally transited to Article VIII status with the other Europeans.

[11] IMFA, CF C/U.K./420, Exchange Restrictions Consultations–1958, Minutes of the Fourth Meeting, November 24, 1958, pp. 6–11.

[12] IMFA, EBM58/59, United Kingdom-1958 Consultations, Repurchase and Stand-by Arrangement, December 19, 1958.

5.2 *Emergence of Speculative Capital Flows*

For the Fund, the resolution of the dollar shortage was a prerequisite to compelling its members to abandon restrictions. However, in 1960, the resolution of the dollar shortage immediately produced extra dollars in the exchange market. In addition, exchange liberalization gradually gave rise to short-term and unstable capital movements (Horsefield and De Vries 1969, Vol. 1, p. 503). Combined with these two changes, in the autumn of 1960 a Gold Rush was brought about.

Soon after the transition of major members to Article VIII status, Mr. Jacobsson started to take steps against the destabilization of the international monetary system. In a Board meeting in February 1961, he presented a paper titled "Future Activities of the Fund" and proposed that the Fund should (1) permit members to rely on the Fund's resources for capital transfer and (2) conclude standby arrangements with major members, thereby strengthening its crisis-response capability.[13]

Actually, the first issue—financing of capital outflow—was prohibited in Article VI, Section 1, which set forth, "A member may not make net use of the Fund's resources to meet a large or sustained outflow of capital." In May 1961, Fund staff in the Legal Department, headed by Mr. Gold the Director of the Department, reinterpreted this to mean that the Fund could assist in cases with no "large and sustained" capital outflows, which was approved at the Board in July 1961.[14] Then, the second subject, through strenuous disputes, led to the General Agreement to Borrow (GAB) in October 1962. The GAB enabled the Fund to borrow at most $6 billion from ten major countries in cases of urgent necessity.

Furthermore, Mr. Jacobsson promoted monetary cooperation among major countries. In March 1961, a run on sterling broke out after the appreciation of the deutschmark and the Netherland guilder. To support the U.K., major countries agreed to the "Basel Agreement." In July, the U.K. government requested the Fund to purchase $1.5 billion in order to repay the borrowing under the "Basel Agreement." Mr. Jacobsson permitted the request and called for the support of the United Kingdom. In fact, the nine supporters together with the U.K. comprised the ten participants in the GAB, and the G10 grew out of these GAB participants.

At the 1961 Annual Meeting, Mr. Jacobsson described the dollar and sterling crisis as a brand-new affair, as follows: "The growing freedom for the international movement of funds, as a result of the increased convertibility of currencies, and the greater stability of prices—so welcome in themselves—have, however, created new problems which the world has not had to face since the start of the Second World War." Meanwhile, the response to the crisis was different from the conspicuous and brand-new one—international monetary reform like "Triffin's dilemma"—indicated. Contrary to such a drastic method, Mr. Jacobsson advocated a policy to buttress the current system, remarking "a number of suggestions have been put forward advocating more or less radical changes in the existing monetary arrangements.

[13] IMFA, EBD61/18., Future Activities of the Fund, February 10, 1961.

[14] IMFA, SM61/45., Use of the Fund's Resources for Capital Transfers, May 24, 1961.

It has been valuable that these matters have been so vigorously discussed, and the first question we have to ask ourselves is whether the present system can be regarded as operating in a manner sufficiently satisfactory to be worth maintaining. […] On the whole, I believe the system has worked well. […] In some quarters, doubts have been expressed whether the system under which countries hold part of their international reserves in currencies (which is known as "the gold exchange standard") will work satisfactorily in the longer run, and whether this system might not break down as it did in the interwar period. I do not think we need draw that conclusion" (IMF 1961, pp. 15, 23–24). Actually, a series of his measures, from quota increase to GAB, was just an ad hoc response.

On the other hand, it was noteworthy that a series of policies didn't restrict but assumed capital movement. Chwieroth stated that as liberalization progressed the Fund gradually perceived that speculation wasn't an abnormal transaction but rather an ordinary one and therefore that regulation wasn't a fundamental solution but only a temporary measure (Chwieroth 2009, pp. 121–137). The Fund's view on capital movement had differed from the founders' one that short-term capital would cause destructive results and restriction was needed. The change was reflected in the formulation of the "Mundell-Fleming model," which incorporated the effect of capital movement into the IS-LM model, inside the Fund at the same juncture (Boughton 2002).

6 Conclusion

Examined from the point of view of the shaping process, actual working of the postwar monetary system cannot be simply described as a combination of an adjustable peg system, discretionary macroeconomic policy and current account convertibility. The Fund's role was not subordinate to its expected one—to promote its members' restoration of convertibility while providing them with short-term finance—which facilitated a conflict caused by the concurrent pursuit of full employment and balance of payments equilibrium.

Undermined in its position as an international monetary policy-making body, the Fund had to cope with the problems in the reconstruction period in order to establish a multilateral payment system. The problem was balance of payments imbalances among major countries that resulted from inflation and the dollar shortage. The expected rule—Fund financial assistance against short-term deficits and an adjustable peg system against fundamental disequilibrium—couldn't automatically resolve the imbalances.

Then, the Fund shaped a policy of macroeconomic adjustment with involvement in members' policy-making processes. Since the balance of payments disequilibrium resulted from inflation and the dollar shortage impeded exchange liberalization, the Fund's adjustment policy wasn't one that primarily encouraged members to attain economic growth and full employment.

It was in the late 1950s that the policy framework alone no longer could maintain the stability of the international monetary system. Exchange liberalization gradually exceeded the expected level and caused short-term capital transfers. The Fund didn't restrict capital movement. On the contrary, it reinforced international liquidity, recognizing short-term capital movement as a given condition.

As described above, in the Bretton Woods era, the Fund wasn't necessarily subordinate to the "rule of games" set by major countries. It steadily formulated "the Fund's policy" impelled by its institutional autonomy.

Primary Sources

Executive Board Documents Collection
- Executive Board Documents (EBD), 1946–1965
- Executive Board Minutes (EBM), 1946–1965
- Executive Board Specials (EBS), 1948–1965
- Staff Memoranda (SM), 1946–1965

Research Department Records
- Research Department Immediate Office Records
  - RESAI Director Edward M. Bernstein Subject Files, 1949–1957

Central Files Collection
- Country Files/United Kingdom/420 Exchange Controls and Restrictions, 1952–1961
- Country Files/United Kingdom/1760 Stand-By Arrangement, 1952–1960

References

Alexander, Sydney. 1952. Effects of a devaluation on trade balance. *IMF Staff Papers* 2(2): 263–278.

Bordo, Michael D. 1993. The Bretton Woods international system: A historical overview. In *A retrospective on the Bretton Woods system: Lessons for international monetary reform*, ed. M.D. Bordo and B. Eichengreen. Chicago: University of Chicago Press.

Boughton, James M. 2002. On the origins of the Fleming-Mundell model. *IMF Working Paper* 2(107): 1–12.

Chwieroth, Jeffrey M. 2009. *Capital ideas: The IMF and the rise of financial liberalization*. Princeton: Princeton University Press.

Horsefield John, K., and M.G. De Vries. 1969. *The International Monetary Fund 1945–1965: Twenty years of international monetary cooperation*, vol. I–III. Washington, D.C.: International Monetary Fund.

IMF. 1952a. Third annual report on exchange restrictions. Washington, D.C.: International Monetary Fund.

IMF. 1952b. Summary proceedings of the seventh annual meeting of the Board of Governors. Washington, D.C.: International Monetary Fund.

IMF. 1953. Fourth annual report on exchange restrictions. Washington, D.C.: International Monetary Fund.

IMF. 1954. Summary proceedings of the ninth annual meeting of the Board of Governors. Washington, D.C.: International Monetary Fund.

IMF. 1955. Sixth annual report on exchange restrictions. Washington, D.C.: International Monetary Fund.

IMF. 1957. Summary proceedings of the twelfth annual meeting of the Board of Governors. Washington, D.C.: International Monetary Fund.

IMF. 1957–1960. *Balance of payments yearbook*, vol. 9–12. Washington, D.C.: International Monetary Fund.

IMF. 1958. Summary proceedings of the thirteenth annual meeting of the Board of Governors. Washington, D.C.: International Monetary Fund.

IMF. 1959–1961. *International Financial Statistics*, vol. 12–14. Washington, D.C.: International Monetary Fund.

IMF. 1961. Summary proceedings of the sixteenth annual meeting of the Board of Governors. Washington, D.C.: International Monetary Fund.

James, Harold. 1996. *International monetary cooperation since Bretton Woods*. Washington, D.C.: International Monetary Fund.

Kaplan, Jacob J., and Gunther Schleiminger. 1989. *The European Payments Union: Financial diplomacy in the 1950s*. New York: Oxford University Press.

Nishikawa, Teru. 2014. IMF policy on the convertible currency system: Toward sterling convertibility. In *IMF history: Foundation and evolution*, eds. Ito Masanao and Asai Yoshio. Nagoya: The University of Nagoya Press.

Schenk, Catherin. 1994. *Britain and the sterling area: From devaluation to convertibility in the 1950s*. London: Routledge.

Chapter 4
"Maybe the Fund needs something else." Per Jacobsson, from the Bank for International Settlements to the International Monetary Fund, 1931–1963

Piet Clement

1 Introduction: Per Jacobsson at the IMF, 1956–1963

On 7 September 1956, the IMF Executive Board offered the position of IMF Managing Director to Per Jacobsson (Horsefield 1969, p. 387). Jacobsson, a Swedish economist, had been Economic Adviser at the Bank for International Settlements in Basel, Switzerland, since 1931. The offer came as a surprise to many, but in spite of the negative advice of some of his close colleagues and friends, Jacobsson decided to accept it (Jacobsson 1979, pp. 283–284). He would remain the Fund's Managing Director until his sudden death from an heart attack on 5 May 1963, at the age of 69.

Created in 1946, as the direct outcome of the 1944 Bretton Woods conference, the International Monetary Fund's primary objective was to restore the international monetary system after the convulsions of the Great Depression and the Second World War. A stable, but flexible, global exchange rate regime of freely convertible currencies was thought to be essential to facilitate the expansion and balanced growth of international trade. Installing such a regime presupposed the abolition of exchange controls, bilateral clearing agreements and trade discriminations that were ubiquitious in the immediate postwar period. Certain forms of capital controls, on the other hand, were permitted under the IMF charter, to allow member countries to curb speculative cross-border capital flows. Implementing the Bretton Woods blueprint required each IMF member country to collaborate through the Fund in order to maintain exchange stability at agreed rates. These rates were only to be changed

The views expressed are those of the author and not necessarily those of the Bank for International Settlements.

P. Clement (✉)
Information & Collaboration Unit, Bank for International Settlements,
CH-4002 Basel, Switzerland
e-mail: piet.clement@bis.org

K. Yago et al. (eds.), *History of the IMF*, Studies in Economic History,
DOI 10.1007/978-4-431-55351-9_4

significantly to correct a fundamental disequilibrium, and in agreement with the Fund (to avoid a mutually harmful descent into competitive devaluations). In the 1950s, the Bretton Woods system would develop into a de facto fixed exchange rate regime, in which most currencies were pegged to the world's key reserve currency, the US dollar, which in turn was fixed to gold (at US$ 35 per ounce of fine gold). Each member country was invited to subscribe its membership quota in the Fund, partly in gold and partly in its own domestic currency. In case of need, these quotas could be drawn down by the respective member, for the first part simply on demand, but for further tranches only after deliberation with the Fund.

The Bretton Woods system relied on a combination of automaticity and supranational controls ("multilateral surveillance"). IMF members were expected to respect certain ground rules – currency convertibility, non-discrimination – and not to adopt any domestic policies that would contradict them. In other words, a certain restriction of national sovereignty for those countries that adopted the IMF Articles of Agreement was implicit. However, at the outset, not many countries were ready to accept such external discipline. Their priority was to rebuild their war-torn economies and to keep unemployment levels as low as possible. To that end they kept many of the war-time controls and restrictions in place, preferring to eliminate them only gradually, as and when their economies gained strength and when their reserves position had improved sufficiently. The need for a relatively long transition phase before the Bretton Woods system could be fully implemented was accepted at the international level, particularly with respect to Europe. This meant that the potential clash between the external commitments imposed by the IMF Articles of Agreement and contradictory domestic policy objectives was, to a large extent, postponed until the European countries attained full compliance with the IMF free currency convertibility requirement (this happened only at the end of 1958).

Per Jacobsson was the Fund's third Managing Director. During the tenure of his predecessors, Camille Gutt (1946–1951) and Ivar Rooth (1951–1956), the Fund had played only a subordinated role in international monetary cooperation. This was partly because the highly regulated environment of the 1940s and early 1950s left relatively little scope for meaningful cooperation, partly because the IMF's own resources were very limited (James 1996, p. 101). It was telling that the Europeans did not look to the IMF for help when they started the tortuous process towards achieving currency convertibility. Rather they created their own organisation, the European Payments Union (EPU, 1950–1958) to help them multilateralise their balance of payments surpluses and deficits, thereby creating the necessary precondition to current account convertibility (Kaplan and Schleiminger 1989). In those rare cases that the IMF offered its services or was called on to intervene directly, it had to walk a fine line: countries were easily irritated when the Fund proposed to intensify surveillance or to dispatch a mission to study local conditions, as they often saw such examples of IMF activism as limiting their domestic policy freedom and generally resented being chastised by an international organisation (James 1996, pp. 99–103). These factors combined to curtail the field of action and influence of the IMF. Indeed, by the mid-1950s it looked to many observers that the Fund was gently sinking into irrelevance (Polak 1994, p. 102).

Per Jacobsson came to the IMF at a critical juncture. The Suez crisis of October–November 1956, and the speculation against the French franc and sterling that ensued, prompted both France and the UK to request IMF assistance. They quickly obtained several US$ 100 millions in drawings and standby arrangements. In the course of 1957 other countries – e.g. India, Argentina and Japan – made substantial drawings, with the result that during the fiscal year 1956–1957 – the first under Jacobsson's direction – nearly US$ 1.5 billion were drawn from the Fund, more than the total of drawings made during the 10 years up to September 1956 (Horsefield 1969, p. 426). All of a sudden, the IMF was in demand. Of course, as Jacobsson himself pointed out, this flurry of activity was in the first place an indication of mounting problems in the international financial system, and therefore not in itself a good thing (Jacobsson 1979, p. 299). But such problems were not likely to go away either. In Europe, the collective move towards free currency convertibility, prepared by the EPU, had stalled, not least because of the political and financial instability in one of its largest members, France. The IMF, and its Managing Director, played a significant role in facilitating the stabilization programme of December 1957 that put France firmly back on track (Feiertag 2006, pp. 536–546). The achievement of currency convertibility in Europe at the end of 1958 meant that the Bretton Woods system, as it had been intended in 1944, came fully into its own. This led to a freer but also potentially more unstable international monetary system, in which the scope for IMF activism was to expand even further. On top of that, with the end of colonial rule in most of Asia and Africa, the membership of the IMF swelled from 59 countries in 1956 to 102 in 1963.

In the face of these challenges, the IMF underwent a rapid evolution that would set the organisation's course for the next 15 years and beyond.[1] The developments that took place in three key areas were particularly significant.

First, the IMF's resources were greatly expanded. The inadequacy of the IMF's resources had become a major cause for concern in view of the Fund's increased lending operations after October 1956. This was tackled by a substantial increase in the quotas assigned to the IMF member countries, which took effect in 1959 and almost doubled the available resources (from US$ 8 billion to more than US$ 14 billion) (De Vries and Horsefield 1969, pp. 349–373). On top of this, the IMF expanded its capacity to borrow significantly through the General Arrangements to Borrow (GAB), a commitment undertaken by the Group of Ten countries to lend the IMF in case of need up to US$ 6 billion "to forestall and cope with an impairment of the international monetary system". The adoption of the GAB in 1962 owed a lot to Jacobsson's persistent diplomacy (James 1996, pp. 161–165).

Secondly, during the late 1950s and early 1960s IMF lending and support procedures became more formalised, crystallising into a template that would be applied over and over again during the following decades (Horsefield 1969, pp. 429–433). The main advantage of using mutually agreed procedures, including standard clauses and provisions, was that it made it easier for the countries receiving IMF support to accept the often demanding conditionality attached to it. IMF

[1] For a broader perspective, see also: Boughton 2004.

conditionality – very much like the practice of "multilateral surveillance" – would remain controversial by nature, so there was every interest in formalising and depoliticizing the related procedures as much as possible.

Thirdly and finally, under Jacobsson's guidance the IMF's role in international financial diplomacy was greatly enhanced. This owed a lot to Jacobsson's personality. By all accounts he was a towering, ebullient man, who possessed considerable charm. He was a compulsive diplomat, who, through the force of plain logic and argumentation could be very persuasive, particularly in private, bilateral talks. He savoured his personal interventions with the powers that be, for instance when he met with French President Charles De Gaulle in June 1958 to press the case for stabilisation. His energy, self-confidence and missionary zeal were certainly assets for the IMF, although on occasion they also provoked disapproval and even aversion. Some in the IMF thought him overbearing, even to the point of being a megalomaniac (James 1996, p. 106). Edward Bernstein, the Director of Research at the IMF took a dislike to Jacobsson and resigned in 1958, making way for Jacques Polak.[2] Also his message was not always liked. As earlier in his career, Jacobsson put great store in the virtues of financial and monetary stability, and hardly ever missed an occasion to speak out against deficit spending and inflation (Garritsen De Vries 1987, pp. 64–68). As a result, he was often criticised for being inflexible, particularly when trying to force developing countries that sought IMF support to swallow the medicine of IMF conditionality (e.g. James 1996, p. 142). Jacobsson's commitment to 'sound' (i.e. orthodox) policy principles, his steadfast belief in the benefits of international cooperation and his active diplomacy and straight talking were, however, very well-suited for an era in which the Bretton Woods system became more consensual and cooperative, as the United States sought to share the burden of supporting it with its western European partners. Jacobsson had always felt that although the United States undoubtedly occupied the central position in the post-war international system—and would continue to do so for the foreseeable future—it would be of great benefit to all involved, and to the IMF itself, if the United States and the handful of other economically and financially important countries in the western world—West Germany, the United Kingdom, France, Japan—were to cooperate closely and make sure to speak and act in unison (James 1996, p. 162). The *General Arrangements to Borrow* negotiated in 1961–1962 were a point in fact, as they gave rise to the institutionalisation, within the IMF and beyond, of the Group of Ten (G10) main industrialised countries of the day. Thus, two longer-term effects of the increased activism of the IMF and of its Managing Director's conspicuous diplomacy after 1956 were, first, a power shift away from the IMF Board of Directors to the benefit of the IMF management, and, secondly, an increased focus on a small group of what today would be called "systemically important" players.

In this contribution, we argue that Per Jacobsson's action as IMF Managing Director owed a lot to his previous experience as the long-standing Economic

[2]Black 1991, pp. 71–76. Charles Kindleberger, who had worked with Jacobsson at the BIS in 1939–1940, felt he suffered from egomania: Kindleberger 1980.

Adviser of the BIS. In fact, more than anything else, it was the postwar reconstruction of Europe during the years 1946–1951 that played a decisive role in preparing Jacobsson for his future role as Managing Director of the IMF. In what follows, the first section provides a brief overview of Per Jacobsson's career at the BIS between 1931 and 1946, with a focus on his intellectual influences. Section two analyses his close involvement with European postwar reconstruction, with a particular focus on the stabilisation in Italy in 1947 and in France in 1948–1949, and on the German balance of payments crisis of 1950–1951. The research for this section is based on Per Jacobsson's written legacy as well as on archival records kept at the Bank for International Settlements in Basel and in the Per Jacobsson collection at the Basel University archive. The third section concludes.

2 Per Jacobsson at the BIS, 1931–1946

Per Jacobsson was born in 1894 in Tanum, Sweden.[3] He studied law and economics at the University of Uppsala. Towards the end of the First World War and in subsequent years he was active in the Economic Club in Stockholm, in which he met renowned Swedish economists such as Gustav Cassel, Knut Wicksell and Bertil Ohlin, and wrote extensively on international and monetary issues in a variety of newspapers and journals. Such connections were certainly helpful in landing him the job as a researcher assigned to the League of Nations office in London to help prepare the International Financial Conference which was to take place in Brussels in September 1920. From London, Jacobsson moved to Geneva, where the League of Nations had its seat, as a member of the League's Financial Committee. His assigned field of expertise was public finance, and in that capacity he was closely involved in the League-sponsored stabilisation programmes in Central Europe. In the summer of 1925 he spent some time in Vienna, to assist in the writing of the report on Austria's economic situation (the report was officially authored by Walter Layton and Charles Rist). Jacobsson was to remain with the League of Nations Financial Committee until 1928. The experience left a deep imprint on his further career, not only because of the people he worked with—many of whom would cross his path again later on[4]—but also because it taught him to quickly analyse a multitude of quantitative and qualitative data at an aggregated and comparative level, and to formulate conclusions and recommendations in a diplomatic but nevertheless pertinent and precise style.

In late 1928, Jacobsson returned to his native Sweden to take up the job of Secretary General of the Economic Defence Commission in Stockholm, a government body set up to review the measures Sweden ought to take to protect itself in

[3] See Per Jacobsson's biography, written by his daughter: Jacobsson 1979. Per Jacobsson himself wrote a semi-autobiographical essay: Jacobsson 1958a.

[4] Among them Otto Niemeyer (1883–1971), then of the UK Treasury and later of the Bank of England; and Pierre Quesnay (1895–1937), later the first General Manager of the BIS.

the event of a war. In July 1930, he moved on to become Economic Adviser at the Swedish multinational Kreuger and Toll, working directly for Ivar Kreuger, the legendary *Match King*, whose suicide in March 1932, and the revelations of financial malpractices that followed it, would bring the firm down. Per Jacobsson, it would seem, was mainly used as "a respectable front" by the company (Jacobsson 1979, pp. 84–92). He spent most of the 14 months he was in Kreuger's employ as an international financial expert advising the League of Nations in Geneva. This work brought him in close contact with the newly established Bank for International Settlements (BIS) in Basel.

The BIS had been created following the January 1930 Hague Conference, to administer the First World War reparation payments due by Germany to the so-called creditor nations (primarily France, Belgium, Italy and the United Kingdom), and to act as trustee for the Young Loan, which was intended to help Germany meet its reparations obligations and would turn out to be one of the last big international loans being floated after the onset of the Great Depression.[5] Even more importantly, the BIS had the statutory aim to promote general cooperation between central banks. The brilliant French economist Pierre Quesnay, an acquantaince of Jacobsson's from his time in Geneva, had been appointed General Manager of the BIS. The BIS's Board of Directors consisted of the Governors of the main European central banks of the day. Naturally, from the outset, the work of the BIS was greatly affected by the Great Depression, not only because of its repercussions on the contentious reparations issue (reparation payments were soon abandoned), but also because of the unorthodox monetary and financial policies taking hold in many of its member countries as the crisis spread and persisted. The collapse of the Austrian Credit-Anstalt in May 1931, the financial crisis and banking panic in Germany that summer, and the British decision to take the pound sterling off gold in September 1931, were severe blows against the open international financial system, based on freely convertible, gold-based currencies, that had been so painstakingly re-built during the 1920s.

In July 1931, Jacobsson was called to Berlin to work with the Swedish banker Marcus Wallenberg on the German banking crisis, which had taken on alarming proportions. His frequent contacts with central bankers and with BIS staff on this occasion landed him an invitation to join the newly created Central Banking Department (soon to be renamed to Monetary and Economic Department) of the BIS in Basel, as its chief Economic Adviser. The job, eminently international in outlook and with its main focus on the key monetary problems of the day, appealed to him enormously. He left Kreuger and Toll and took up his new position in Basel in mid-September 1931, days before the pound left the gold standard.

Jacobsson would remain the Economic Adviser of the BIS for 25 years, until he accepted the position of IMF Managing Director in September 1956. In 1946, he was promoted to Head of the BIS Monetary and Economic Department, a hierarchical administrative title that formalised his permanent membership of the BIS top management group. In his role as Economic Adviser, he not only advised the Bank's

[5] On the history of the BIS, see in particular: Toniolo 2005. Also: Yago 2013.

senior management but also, and more importantly, the BIS Board of Directors, that is to say, the central bank Governors. He excelled so much in this role, that soon the opportunity to discuss domestic and international monetary and economic problems with the Economic Adviser became one of the drawing factors of the BIS's monthly Board meeting weekends. Montagu Norman, Governor of the Bank of England, was one of those who greatly appreciated Jacobsson's breadth of knowledge, analytical clarity and candour (Jacobsson 1979, pp. 99–103). Jacobsson clearly felt at ease among the high-ranking officials that regularly gathered in Basel. By all witnessed accounts he was an impassioned and very persuasive debater.[6] During the 1930s, Jacobsson was very much involved in the ongoing discussions concerning the economic and financial crisis, the need to restore global monetary order following the collapse of the gold exchange standard and the role of the central banks in all of this; without, however, taking active part in the parallel academic debate, nor in the reformulation of economic theory, as would be done, for instance, by John Maynard Keynes in his 1936 classic *The General Theory of Employment, Interest and Money*. Jacobsson was a practical economist, not a theoretical one.

After the disastrous summer of 1931, the League of Nations undertook what would prove to be a last-ditch attempt to salvage the world economy and the international monetary system from further wreckage. Under its aegis, a World Monetary and Economic Conference, bringing together 66 sovereign nations, gathered in London in June–July 1933, with the aim of reviving the international economy and of agreeing on a coordinated stabilisation of exchange rates (Clavin 1996). The BIS was closely involved in the preparation of the Conference (Toniolo 2005, pp. 136–149). Per Jacobsson and other BIS staff spent considerable time in Geneva, drafting the agenda and technical documentation. In two internal BIS notes, Jacobsson expounded the orthodox central bankers' view, making the case for international monetary stability as the best guarantee for economic prosperity.[7] The restoration of the gold standard (in the meantime both the pound sterling and the US dollar had been taken off gold) was still the central banks' preferred way to achieve such stability. However, Jacobsson conceded that stability could in theory also be reached by "a system of international paper money managed by a single international body", but the time seemed not yet ripe for this. Together with BIS President Leon Fraser, Jacobsson headed the BIS delegation that participated in the London Conference, and more particularly in the Conference's subcommittee dealing with the necessary

[6] See for instance the testimony from Rudolf Pfenninger, a later General Manager of Swiss Bank Corporation: "He would listen and was always liberal in his approach, imaginative and generous with his ideas. I never met anyone who was so generous with his ideas" (quoted in: Jacobsson 1979, p. 99). Also – albeit somewhat more pejorative – Charles Kindleberger's memory, who worked with Jacobsson at the BIS in 1939–1940: "[Per Jacobsson] was an overwhelming personality. One might start talking to him in the center of a room, and find oneself after a time backed into a corner with his large frame and thick glasses still in attack" (Kindleberger 1991, p. 55).

[7] BISA, 9.1.002 – Monetary and Economic Department (19 Oct 1932), *General problems of a return to a common international standard* (CB 58), Basel: BIS. And: BISA, 9.1.002 – Monetary and Economic Department (20 Oct 1932), *General problems of the gold standard* (CB 59), Basel: BIS.

measures for the re-establishment of an international monetary system. In pressing for a reestablishment of the international gold standard, the BIS found itself on one line with the central banks of continental Europe, also as regards their belief in sound public finances and their opposition to reflation as a means to combat the crisis. However, Jacobsson and his colleagues were not entirely dogmatic with regard to the gold standard, and suggested various technical measures to increase its flexibility. The London Conference ended in failure, not least because of President Roosevelt's refusal to stabilize the US dollar. In more than one way the debates at the 1933 London Conference foreshadowed those of the 1944 Bretton Woods Conference.

After London, Jacobsson's direct involvement in international financial diplomacy waned (although he still sat, as one of two foreign members, on the Irish Banking Commission between 1934 and 1938). So did that of the BIS, in a world where multilateralism and international cooperation increasingly made way for bilateralism and autarky. Jacobsson's main focus shifted to research, and most significantly to turning the BIS Annual Report into a reference publication with regard to international monetary and economic developments (Toniolo 2005, pp. 193–195). Not only did the Report expand considerably in size and coverage, it also based its analysis on increasingly sophisticated statistical data. These efforts were not in vain, as testified by John Maynard Keynes' opinion that the BIS Annual Report had become "the leading authority for certain statistics, not easily obtainable" and was generally "of high interest" (Keynes 1934). The Annual Report was the main public vehicle through which the BIS articulated its view on the world. A view determined by a strong belief in the self-adjusting forces of the market, in the benefits of monetary stability and budgetary orthodoxy, and in the importance of international cooperation to reduce the impact of negative externalities and spillover effects – all of this without losing sight of particular circumstances and of political necessities that might call for a good dose of pragmatism when applying these policy principles. In short, the BIS view came down to what Enders and Fleming have characterised a "special brand of practical, liberal international political economy" (Enders and Fleming 2002, p. 233 and p. 249).

The outbreak of the Second World War in September 1939 threw the BIS off balance. The regular meetings of the Governors—and thus of the Bank's Board of Directors—were suspended indefinitely. And while the BIS continued to operate, the scope for meaningful central bank cooperation had practically disappeared overnight. Per Jacobsson spent most of the war in Basel, where he continued to work, with the MED staff, on the BIS Annual Report, in spite of the difficulties in war-time communications and in obtaining reliable information. Anxious that the BIS risked being cut off entirely from developments in the Anglo-Saxon world, BIS President Thomas McKittrick encouraged Jacobsson to travel to the United States in the winter of 1941–1942 (Jacobsson 1979, pp. 158–162). The journey there and back was not without danger, given the raging Battle of the Atlantic (Jacobsson was at sea on an American ship on 7 December 1941, when the Japanese attack on Pearl Harbor brought the USA into the war). From Jacobsson's perspective the 4-month long visit did pay off, as he came into contact with the leading economists and government officials of the time, and was directly exposed to the new direction economic thinking had taken in the USA since the beginning of Roosevelt's New Deal in 1933–1934. At a young age, Jacobsson's main intellectual influences had been the non-conformist monetary economist Knut Wicksell (1851–1926), and the neo-classical mathematical economist Gustav Cassel (1866–1945), founding members of the Swedish School of Economics (Yago 2006; Jacobsson 1958b). Jacobsson had of course closely followed the academic revolution in economics following the Great Depression. Although he claimed to admire John Maynard Keynes as "the most gifted and most artistic man of his generation",[8] he never fully subscribed to his ideas.[9] In the USA, Jacobsson now entered into debate with Alvin Hansen (1887–1975), who was a key figure in popularizing Keynesian economics in the USA. He was also keen to exchange views with Jacob Viner (1892–1970), who was more critical of Keynes and was one of the mentors of the early Chicago School of Economics. One of the stated goals of his trip was to try to exert an influence on the New Deal economists to temper their belief in deficit spending. Whether he was successful in this respect is rather doubtful. In any case, Jacobsson strongly opposed the Keynesian idea of deficit spending as a useful means of creating employment: "Deficit spending is dangerous not only because it aggravates the debt situation but because it diverts attention from the real problems to be solved".[10] Jacobsson believed that the war would be followed by an economic boom period – not a depression as many predicted – which threatened to release a lot of pent-up inflation. In that context, deficit spending would only succeed in making the necessary adjustment more difficult.

The experience of his trip to the USA strongly influenced Jacobsson's reaction to the Anglo-Saxon plans for a new post-war international monetary order, that became known in the spring of 1943. From the outset, he saw more merit in the so-called White Plan as opposed to the Keynes Plan, which he believed was too complex in conception and would inevitably lead to excessive credit creation.[11] One thing was absolutely clear, though. Jacobsson fully recognised – and even favoured – that after the war the world would have to accept the paramount economic and monetary position of the United States. The position of the United States and of the US dollar would therefore be key to the proper functioning of the international financial system.[12] In the end, the White Plan did carry the day and decisively influenced the outcome of the July 1944 Bretton Woods Conference.

---

[8] UNIBAS-HAN, Basel, NL 324, A/63 – *Nachlass Per Jacobsson, Diary 63*, entry 22 April 1946.

[9] Jacobsson argued that Keynes' theories, and in particular the demand-side policies he proposed, disregarded the often delicate balance of payments situation of many countries, other than the UK and the USA, and paid little or no attention to the importance of currency stability and credibility (Jacobsson 1958a, p. 43).

[10] UNIBAS-HAN, Basel, NL 324, A/41 – *Nachlass Per Jacobsson, Diary 41*, entry 23 February 1942.

[11] BISA, 9.1.003 – Monetary and Economic Department (April 1943), *Proposal for an International Clearing Union ('Keynes Plan')* (HS 87), Basel: BIS. Also: BISA, 9.1.003 – Monetary and Economic Department (June 1943), *Unitas and Bancor, Two Plans of International Payment* (HS 91), Basel: BIS. And BISA, 9.1.003 – Monetary and Economic Department (10.07.1943), *Proposal for a United and Associated Nations Stabilization Fund ('White Plan')* (HS 89), Basel: BIS.

[12] BISA, 9.1.003 – Monetary and Economic Department (01.09.1943), *The Place of the United States in the post-war Economy* (HS 96), Basel: BIS.

3 Per Jacobsson and Europe's Postwar Reconstruction, 1946–1951

At the end of the war in Europe, Jacobsson found himself in Basel without a lot to do. The Bank for International Settlements had suffered opprobrium because of its alleged less-than-neutral attitude vis-à-vis the German Reichsbank during the hostilities (Toniolo 2005, pp. 201–82). In fact, the July 1944 Bretton Woods had adopted a resolution calling for the abolition of the BIS. Nevertheless, the European central banks were keen to maintain "their" institution in the heart of Europe. Accepting that the fulcrum of global monetary and financial cooperation had moved to Washington, they believed that the BIS could and should continue to play its role as a regional meeting place for European central banks, particularly to assist in Europe's postwar financial reconstruction. It took some time to turn the BIS into a going concern once again. The first postwar meeting of its Board of Directors (on which the main European central bank Governors sat) did not take place until December 1946. In the meantime, the BIS did what it had done best before the war: rebuilding a network among European central banks, collecting and analysing financial and economic data from across the continent, and encouraging research. In other words: leveraging the expertise accumulated and nurtured within the BIS Monetary and Economic Department (MED) under the dynamic leadership of its Economic Adviser, Per Jacobsson. This soon led to the BIS becoming actively engaged in the debates concerning the financial and economic reconstruction efforts underway in most European countries, starting with Italy in 1946–1947.

3.1 The Italian Stabilisation, 1946–1949

The Italian economy had suffered greatly from the war, particularly between the Allied landings in Sicily in July 1943 and the armistice in Northern Italy in April 1945, during which time the country witnessed heavy fighting and was effectively split, causing additional dislocations.[13] Infrastructure and communications were gravely disrupted, and in spite of the industrial centres in the North having escaped large-scale damage, industrial production had plummeted, largely through a lack of energy and raw materials. Industrial output in 1946 reached barely 40 % of the level of the last pre-war boom year in 1938. Agricultural production had dropped by a quarter, in spite of a steadily rising population. War time food rationing and price controls remained in force and the black market thrived. Reconstruction was seriously hampered by a lack of resources and monetary reserves, a highly negative balance of payments and rampant inflation. During the second half of 1946, inflation rose by 9 % per month on average. Over the following year, prices would shoot up

[13] An excellent recent overview of Italy's economic history can be found in: Toniolo 2013. For the immediate postwar period see also: Cotula 2000.

to over 60 times their pre-war levels. Meanwhile, the Italian lira exchange rate against the dollar dropped continuously: in 1946 the official rate was adjusted from 100 lira to the dollar to 225 lira, but by the end of 1946 the daily free rate stood close to 600 (Hildebrand 1965, pp. 15–23). On top of this, Italy faced political and administrative uncertainty, if not chaos, caused by the violent collapse of the fascist regime, the abolition of the monarchy (June 1946) and the growing antagonism between communist and Christian-democratic forces, who had struck a tenuous power-sharing deal in a coalition government that had been in charge since June 1944.

In these circumstances, Italy's central bank was called upon to play an important stabilising role. The Bank of Italy's Governor, Luigi Einaudi (1874–1961), was a fervent believer in free market reforms and in the necessity to restore monetary and financial stability as an essential precondition to recovery.[14] This belief was shared by Alcide De Gasperi, the Christian democratic prime minister, who felt increasingly frustrated by the concessions he had to make to his left-wing coalition partners, including the introduction of index-linked wages (*scala mobile*) and the reinstatement of bread subsidies that had been abolished shortly after the war. In order to make a more convincing case for policy reforms and to obtain new foreign credits and loans for Italy, the government and the Bank of Italy considered inviting an Anglo-American mission to Italy to draft a comprehensive report on the country's situation and prospects. When Luigi Einaudi attended the first post-war meeting of the BIS Board of Directors in Basel in December 1946, he discussed this idea with the Vice-Chairman of the Board, Sir Otto Niemeyer of the Bank of England (Baffi 1990, pp. 103–106). Niemeyer recommended that it would be preferable that the Bank of Italy should itself select a sympathetic and trustworthy external expert to write such a report. Einaudi seized upon the idea and immediately invited the BIS Economic Adviser Per Jacobsson, whom he had known since 1928, to pay a visit to Italy and to write a report about the country's economic and financial position. Jacobsson accepted on the spot. He went to Rome, where on 20 January 1947 he had a long meeting with Einaudi, whom he held in great esteem.[15] Einaudi showed Jacobsson the magnificent Bank of Italy rooms, while Jacobsson went on about the importance of balancing Italy's budget. He was preaching to the converted: "Einaudi agreed of course". During the following weeks Jacobsson spent most of his time in Rome, as well as a few days in Milan, collecting information and talking to Italian experts, government officials and businessmen. Throughout the spring of 1947 he worked closely with the Bank of Italy research department, led by Paolo Baffi, whom he liked instantly.[16] Finally, Baffi himself came to Basel in the summer of

[14] On Luigi Einaudi's stance as a liberal economist and his view on society and social justice see: Gigliobianco 2010.

[15] UNIBAS-HAN, Basel, NL 324, A/66 – *Nachlass Per Jacobsson, Diary 66*, entry 20 January 1947. Jacobsson was impressed by Einaudi's "moral strength". He found him to be "maybe somewhat oldfashioned liberal in his economics, but (..) transparently honest, without deceit or malice. As a liberal he has a sense for equilibrium: he won't believe that control (often ineffective in the bargain) does away with the need of establishing an equilibrium".

[16] Baffi reciprocated the appreciation in writing to Jacobsson, shortly after the latter had left Rome: "I have learnt much from you. I often had the impression of being the inhabitant of a provincial

1947, to complete the report together with Jacobsson. It was published in the BIS's internal central banking studies series and distributed in a limited edition to the Bank of Italy and other central banks, who passed it on to interested policy makers and commercial banks.[17] According to Baffi, the report was well received, particularly among American commercial bankers, as it provided them with a rare detailed insight in the situation in Italy and with the first (preliminary) assessment of the monetary reforms that had just been initiated (Baffi 1990, p. 106).

In the report, Jacobsson came out squarely in favour of stability-oriented policies, aimed at fighting inflation, reducing the balance of payments deficit, balancing the budget and halting the downward slide of the Italian lira on the foreign exchange markets. To achieve this, he recommended, among other things, reorganising and thereby improving tax collection, cutting non-essential government expenditure and reducing the number of civil servants, stopping monetary funding of the Treasury's financing needs and giving priority to re-constituting the central bank's monetary reserves. If this policy prescription were to be pursued vigorously, Jacobsson argued, Italy should be able to stop inflation in its tracks and restore confidence in the Italian currency. This was essential to put Italy on a sustainable growth path. Rampant inflation and currency depreciation had only served to stimulate hoarding—farmers and even manufacturers withholding their produce from the market—and to discourage commercial credit and in particular foreign direct investment. Thus, in Jacobsson's view, monetary stabilisation had to be the central tenet of government policy, even if it meant temporarily slowing down the pace of reconstruction by means of a reduction in public spending for reconstruction purposes as well as a stricter regulation of private credits granted by the banks.[18] Foreign (mainly US) aid, of which Italy was to receive substantial amounts through the European Recovery Program (Marshall Plan), ought to serve primarily to add to Italy's depleted foreign exchange reserves. Such stability-oriented policies might bring additional hardship in the short term but were, in Jacobsson's view, the only way that in the end would allow Italy to "modernise its industrial equipment and to reconstruct its economic life more speedily and more effectively than would otherwise be possible".[19]

In essence, Jacobsson's report came out as a strong and carefully argued endorsement of the policy propagated by the Bank of Italy and by the Christian Democrat and conservative elements in the Italian government. This was all the more important as it came from an international expert, an outsider to Italian politics, who, moreover, enjoyed excellent contacts in the central bank world generally and with

town who through you came in touch with the great currents of interests and ideas of the capitals of the world". UNIBAS-HAN, Basel, NL 324, B 140 – *Nachlass Per Jacobsson, Correspondence Paolo Baffi*, letter Baffi to Jacobsson, 21 February 1947.

[17] BISA, 9.1.002 – BIS, Monetary and Economic Department (1947), *Italy's Economic and Financial Position in the Summer of 1947* (CB 200), Basel: Bank for International Settlements, 79 p.

[18] BISA, 9.1.002 – *Italy's Position*, p. 75.

[19] BISA, 9.1.002 – *Italy's Position*, p. 79.

the United States monetary authorities—Italy's main external creditor—in particular. As Donato Menichella, the Director General and later Governor of the Bank of Italy, testified: "[Per Jacobsson] stood by us with advice and encouragement and was ready to vouch for the successful outcome of our attempts to re-establish monetary stability. He spoke in our support to the many prominent financial personalities on both sides of the Atlantic whom he met in his capacity as Economic Adviser and Head of the Monetary and Economic Department of the Bank for International Settlements, and thus his attitude did much to secure for us the understanding and confidence of the various international credit institutions with which we subsequently had important and cordial dealings" (Menichella 1966, p. 6).

Luigi Einaudi would be instrumental in implementing the proposed stability-oriented policies.[20] In January 1947 prime minister De Gasperi and Bank of Italy Director General Donato Menichella had travelled to the USA, where they obtained a politically important US$ 100 million loan from the US Export-Import Bank. On the occasion, the Italian delegation was also made aware of the impending change of policy of the Truman administration, promising increased financial assistance to those countries whose stability was seen to be threatened by growing communist and Soviet influence (Truman doctrine). Upon his return to Italy, prime minister De Gasperi pushed through a cabinet reshuffle, in which the left lost control over the key ministries dealing with economic and financial affairs. In February 1947, Bank of Italy Governor Einaudi wrote a letter to the new minister of the Treasury, the Christian Democrat Campilli, in which he pleaded for a new system of imposing minimum reserve requirements on banks, so that the Bank of Italy would dispose of a more efficient instrument to regulate the volume of credit granted through the banking system (Ricossa 2003, pp. 403–404). Bank of Italy experts had been working on the details of such a scheme under the guidance of Donato Menichella since December 1946. However, the government was increasingly paralysed by internal antagonism and with inflation out of control and the lira sliding further, a crisis of confidence took hold (Mershon 2002, pp. 41–42). De Gasperi let things come to a head, provoking a cabinet crisis in May 1947. He tried to leverage the crisis and the threat of a new left-wing government to obtain additional financial support from the USA, but the Americans were reluctant to commit unless a new government were to take decisive action to stabilise the Italian economy and finances. On 31 May, De Gasperi took the leap of faith and announced the formation of a new Christian Democrat-dominated cabinet, from which the socialists and communists were ousted and to a large extent replaced by liberal-minded technocrats, the most important of whom was central bank Governor Luigi Einaudi as the new Minister of the Budget and Deputy Prime Minister.

In spite of this, additional American aid was not immediately forthcoming, as the US administration was not convinced that the new government would be able to hold its line under pressure from the left-wing opposition. However, on 5 June 1947, less than a week after the formation of the new government, US Secretary of State Georges Marshall announced a far-reaching multilateral European Recovery

[20] A very lucid analysis of the 1947 crisis in: Martinez Oliva 2005.

Program (Marshall Plan), from which Italy would benefit as of the beginning of 1948. This, together with a new-found dynamism and unity of purpose within the government produced a favourable psychological effect. For the first time in a long time the lira's exchange rate began to strengthen. The new De Gasperi government announced its stabilisation programme in August 1947 and implementation was forced through in September, despite fierce opposition from the left. The most important measures included the application by the Bank of Italy of the new system for imposing minimum reserve requirements on banks (used actively to curtail the granting of non-productive credits), spending cuts and the raising of the discount rate from 4 % to 5.5 %. The new, stabilisation-oriented policy produced a shock-effect. As of October, the cost of living and wholesale price indices began to drop. The disinflation process would continue until the end of 1948 and price increases would remain moderate thereafter throughout the 1950s. Returning confidence expressed itself in the strengthening of the currency and an increase in savings. Martinez Oliva credits the 1947 stabilisation with setting "..Italy on the virtuous path that led it within a decade to hold a prominent position among the European economies" (Martinez Oliva 2005, p. 3).

It would seem then, that the stabilisation policies advocated by experts in the Bank of Italy and endorsed by external experts such as Per Jacobsson were fully vindicated. Luigi Einaudi, who was rightly seen as the main architect of Italy's restored financial and monetary stability, was elected President of the Italian Republic on 11 May 1948. However, the battle was not yet entirely won. Throughout 1948–1949, the Christian Democratic government, which reinforced its position in the bitterly fought elections of 18 April 1948, maintained its stability-oriented, anti-inflationary stance. Fierce opposition came, as was to be expected from the left-wing parties and labour unions, but also from a much less expected quarter, the Economic Cooperation Administration (ECA), the US government agency set up in 1948 to administer the Marshall Plan aid. In their country study on Italy, published in February 1949, the ECA experts criticised the Italian government for its "exaggerated fear" of inflationary pressures and called for expansionary measures ("aggressive action"), particularly through the launching of a huge public investments programme (ECA 1949, p. 2 and p. 21). The Italian economy, they argued, was being held back by a lack of private investment, under-utilisation of existing industrial capacity, and low productivity—particularly in the dominant agricultural sector. The ECA experts were not impressed by the Italian government's economic programme for 1949 and beyond, which entailed only a relatively moderate increase in investment expenditure (ECA 1949, pp. 45–53). They were of the opinion that in view of the high unemployment rates in the cities and on the countryside – with a lot of hidden unemployment in agriculture – economic expansion and job creation ought to be the Italian government's top priorities.[21] And since private finance was not forthcoming, the state had to step in on a much more significant scale than had hitherto been the case.

[21] "Clearly, the continued under-utilization of a considerable part of industrial capacity is inconsistent with the objectives of the recovery program and will not contribute to a solution of Italy's fundamental employment problem". ECA 1949, p. 35.

The criticism stung, particularly because it came from Italy's foremost donor and ally. The Italian government and the Bank of Italy felt it important to refute the arguments put forward by the ECA report, if only to justify why they thought it essential to stick to an orthodox policy stance. In this context, the Bank of Italy, now headed by Donato Menichella who had succeeded Einaudi as Governor, approached Per Jacobsson once more, asking him to update his 1947 report on Italy's economy and finances. Jacobsson was happy to oblige. The updated and much extended BIS report *Economic and Financial Problems of Italy in the summer of 1949* was distributed, in a limited edition, on 1 September 1949.[22] In it Jacobsson, not surprisingly, sang the praise of the policy change initiated in May 1947 under the guidance of Einaudi. Part of the success in restoring monetary stability, he wrote, had been the psychological factor: "the knowledge that the economic and financial policy was being firmly directed and applied".[23] But more remained to be done: "Considerable results have been attained by the politics thus adopted, as is borne out by the statistics and is, moreover, manifest to any regular visitor to Italy. But the undeniable success, of which the country can be proud, does not mean that all is well".[24] Jacobsson listed four key weaknesses that required "unremitting thought and action": the persistent high level of unemployment, the budget deficit, a lack of rationalisation in certain industries (e.g. electricity production), and weak savings and distortions in the credit policy.

Significantly, Jacobsson devoted considerable attention in the report to the issue of unemployment, with the aim of demonstrating that a sudden expansion of credit and public investment was not the right solution to the problem. While he recognised that the acute situation in Southern Italy warranted "some altogether extraordinary form of financing" to boost investment, he strongly cautioned against a general credit expansion with the aim of absorbing under-utilised resources. The arguments he developed were completely counter to the earlier advice from the ECA experts to do exactly that, by trying to disprove their Keynesian premises and by stressing the danger of overly expansionist policies igniting a renewed bout of inflation. Jacobsson's main argument was that much of the Italian unemployment was structural rather than cyclical, given the shortfall of productive capacity. As a result, increased public spending would not necessarily increase productive investment, but would most definitely lead to an increase in consumption spending, which at the current state of the Italian recovery could not possibly be met by domestic production of consumption goods and would therefore inevitably boost imports, thus upsetting the balance of payments and creating dangerous inflationary pressures. In essence, the BIS report held that the Italian budget for 1949–1950 was already mildly expansionist and that this was about as much as could be safely done in the prevailing circumstances.[25] Projected investment expenditure from both the

[22] BISA, 9.1.002 – BIS, Monetary and Economic Department (1949), *Economic and Financial Problems of Italy in the summer of 1949*, Basel: Bank for International Settlements.

[23] BISA, 9.1.002 – *Economic and Financial Problems of Italy*, p. A5.

[24] BISA, 9.1.002 – *Economic and Financial Problems of Italy*, p. A17.

[25] BISA, 9.1.002 – *Economic and Financial Problems of Italy*, pp. F1-F22.

state and private enterprises would likely absorb all resources available from domestic savings and foreign aid. Any expansion of investment and of bank credit beyond this level would endanger monetary and financial stability and would, moreover, interfere with the necessary process of industry rationalisation and reorganisation. For some time still, Italy would have to rely on foreign aid (mainly through the Marshall Plan), while giving priority to rebuilding its monetary reserves and stimulating domestic savings. The argumentation developed in the BIS report fitted in perfectly well with the "Italian economic policy makers' [mobilisation] of conservative foreign economists … who agreed with the Italian government's set of priorities and policy sequencing" in response to the publication of the ECA report.[26]

The passionate debates in the years immediately following the war subsided in the 1950s, when Italy embarked on a genuine economic expansion cycle. The Korean war (1950–1953) boosted demand for industrial products, but also led to a rapid rise in commodity prices. Italy avoided major balance of payments problems thanks to its monetary reserves that had been prudently accumulated from the late 1940s onward. A stable base for economic growth was thus maintained. The Italian economic miracle during the 1950s and 1960s was the result of a strong catch-up process facilitated by a huge unused labour supply (and hence moderate wage pressures), with an increasingly strong export sector benefiting from an undervalued currency (Di Nino et al. 2013, pp. 372 ff.). Public investment, particularly in utilities and in motorway construction, played an important role. Thus, in the end, during the 1950s, Italian policy makers followed both the central bank's call for continued orthodoxy and the Keynesian advice to increase public spending put forward in the ECA report (De Cecco 2013, pp. 143–147). It would seem they managed to get the best of both worlds.

3.2 *More 'Sound Policies': Denmark, Austria, The Netherlands, France, 1947–1949*

Over the next few years, Per Jacobsson and the BIS Monetary and Economic Department (MED) made the type of country study Jacobsson had done for Italy their trademark. There were good reasons for this. The IMF was as yet not ready to perform this kind of detailed analysis, which was informed to a large extent by personal visits and close contacts with local experts. Most importantly, the prospect of Marshall Plan aid—first announced in June 1947—acted as a powerful external incentive for European countries to put their house in order.[27] Individual countries

[26] De Cecco 2013, p. 143. Paolo Baffi of the Bank of Italy explicitly congratulated Jacobsson on those pages in the report that dealt with the refutation of the Keynesian arguments for credit expansion: UNIBAS-HAN, Basel, NL 324, B 140 – *Nachlass Per Jacobsson, Correspondence Paolo Baffi*, letter Baffi to Jacobsson, 26 September 1949.

[27] As Per Jacobsson wrote: "The receipt of aid under the European Recovery Program imposes upon each country not only a legal, but even more a moral, duty to put its own house in order".

were keen to prove that they were not basket cases, and were deserving of the maximum amount of US aid. A detailed survey, undertaken by an independent expert, of the financial and economic recovery efforts that were already underway was certainly helpful in getting the point across.

Practically simultaneously with Jacobsson's work on Italy, MED completed a survey of the Danish economy and finances.[28] The focus was on Denmark's postwar problems, particularly with regard to restoring productive capacity, reestablishing trade relations and the relative overvaluation of the Danish krone. Later in 1947, Jacobsson was invited by the Governor of the Austrian National Bank to visit Austria. Jacobsson was in Vienna in November 1947, and again, with other MED colleagues, in January 1948. This resulted in a report on Austria, distributed internally and to the Austrian National Bank on 1 March 1948. It focused on the by then habitual issues: postwar reconstruction, the budget, currency and credit, price structure and inflation, international economic relations.[29] The BIS report found a lot to commend in the reconstruction policies embarked upon by the Austrian authorities, for instance with regard to the currency reform of November 1947. At the same time, the discrepancy in prices between the official and black market, the continued division of the country into four occupation zones and Austria's disappointing export performance remained causes for concern and pointed to a continued need for foreign aid for some time to come.

The report on Austria had barely been finished, when Jacobsson was invited by the President of the Netherlands Bank, Marius Holtrop, who was also a member of the BIS Board of Directors, to visit the Netherlands and shed light on its postwar economic and financial problems. Jacobsson spent some time in Amsterdam, The Hague and Rotterdam at the end of June 1948, just after the BIS's Annual General Meeting had taken place in Basel. He summarised his views in a long letter to Holtrop, which was subsequently published as a report for internal distribution.[30] In the Netherlands, Jacobsson found a somewhat different atmosphere from that prevailing in Italy or Austria. The country had suffered greatly during the final stages of the war (it was not fully liberated until the German capitulation on 8 May 1945), which had not only caused substantial human suffering (the "hunger winter" of 1944/1945) but had in turn created a strong sense of solidarity and national cohesion. This, in a way, had made it easier for the Dutch population to accept the immediate postwar policy of austerity as well as the continuation of stringent price controls, regulations, and government subsidies supporting basic consumption.

BISA 9.1.002 – BIS, Monetary and Economic Department (20 July 1948), *Letter from Per Jacobsson to Marius Holtrop* (CB 207), Basel: Bank for International Settlements, p. 17.

[28] BISA, 9.1.002 – BIS, Monetary and Economic Department (6 January 1947), *Some Economic and Financial Problems in Denmark* (CB 195), Basel: Bank for International Settlements, 41 p.

[29] BISA, 9.1.002 – BIS, Monetary and Economic Department (1 March 1948), *The Economic and Financial Position in Austria at the beginning of 1948* (CB 205), Basel: Bank for International Settlements, 84 p.

[30] BISA, 9.1.002 – BIS, Monetary and Economic Department (20 July 1948), *Letter from Per Jacobsson to Marius Holtrop* (CB 207), Basel: Bank for International Settlements, 27 p.

Jacobsson was somewhat surprised to find that "… in the Netherlands even people with liberal views thought that control had been necessary and still was so in many fields".[31] In order to alleviate the burden on the budget, Jacobsson – in line with the Netherlands Bank itself – recommended that food subsidies be reduced, but only gradually. In view of the large budget deficit, further aggravated by the costly colonial war fought in the Dutch East Indies (Indonesia), the Netherlands would be well advised to adopt immediate policy measures aimed at reducing government spending, tightening the money market and increasing earning capacities through international trade. Given its history and economic orientation, the country's true interest, surely, was "bound up with a return to a system of free multilateral trade".[32]

The last of these country studies concerned western Europe's second-biggest economy, France. In the autumn of 1948, Per Jacobsson had been invited by the Bank of France to write a detailed report on the financial and economic situation of France after the war. Abundant statistical data were provided by the French monetary authorities, and Jacobsson and his staff in Basel worked on the report throughout the winter of 1948–1949 (Jacobsson 1979, pp. 233–235). Running up to 264 pages, the report was distributed in a few hundred copies to BIS member central banks and other interested parties in March 1949.[33] It was quite critical of French policies pursued during the immediate postwar years. Huge budget deficits had been covered in part by printing more money. The balance of payments deficit had drawn down France's gold and foreign exchange reserves. Rising prices had been offset by corresponding abrupt increases in money wages. In general, there had been very little resistance against the ensuing and highly detrimental wage-price inflation cycle, which led Jacobsson to blame excessive government deficit spending as the main "root of the trouble".[34] The result was a complete lack of confidence in the French franc, and hence very little propensity towards saving. Jacobsson was naturally not enamoured with France's complex foreign exchange regulations, allowing for multiple official exchange rates. On top of that, import restrictions on consumer goods had tended to shield French production from foreign competition, thereby eroding its own external competitiveness. The report warned against "a mistaken belief in the adequacy of controls" of prices and exchanges to address France's current problems.[35] In his conclusions, however, Jacobsson, true to his own nature, sounded an optimistic tone. The problems may have been serious and manifold, but "the task is certainly not impossible".[36] The first priority had to be restoring the balance in France's public finances, because "…the primary problem of France today is the monetary problem, and the monetary problem is largely, though, of course,

[31] BISA 9.1.002 – *Letter Jacobsson to Holtrop*, p. 5.

[32] BISA 9.1.002 – *Letter Jacobsson to Holtrop*, p. 15.

[33] BISA 9.1.002 – BIS, Monetary and Economic Department (March 1949), *The post-war Economic and Financial Position of France, from the Liberation to the Beginning of 1949* (CB 210), Basel: Bank for International Settlements.

[34] BISA 9.1.002 – BIS (1949), *The post-war Position of France*, p. F3–F4.

[35] BISA 9.1.002 – BIS (1949), *The post-war Position of France*, p. F7–F8.

[36] BISA 9.1.002 – BIS (1949), *The post-war Position of France*, p. A31.

not wholly, a reflection of the budget problem".[37] Reforms initiated from late 1948 onward were promising in this context. The continued US aid provided through the Marshall Plan was important because it gave France the necessary breathing space to push through further necessary reforms.

The common theme in these different reports was that currency stabilisation and budgetary balance (or at least something approaching budgetary balance) were the essential prerequisites to setting these countries on a sustainable growth path. In other words: first monetary and financial stability had to be guaranteed; then it would be possible to get rid of the ubiquitious regulations, restrictions, subsidies and price controls inherited from the war that created distortions in the market place and weighed too heavily on the state budget; and only then economic (and social) expansion could really take a hold. Within this ideal sequence, it was of paramount importance to bring down inflationary pressures as quickly as possible. This can be typified as an orthodox, neo-liberal (a word often used by Jacobsson himself) policy stance, as opposed to the demand-management policies in Keynesian style applied at various times in many western countries after the Second World War. Quite obviously, Jacobsson felt more sympathy – and admiration – for those countries that, by drastic measures, had achieved early stabilisation after the war, such as Belgium, Denmark and Italy, than for those that seemed to drag their feet or maintained tight controls in support of different policy priorities – cheap credit, full employment – such as the United Kingdom, Sweden, and, at least for a while, France.[38]

However, this opposition should not be turned into a caricature. Jacobsson and his MED colleagues were not blind to the pressing social (and political) expediency of government subsidies, price controls (for instance for basic foodstuffs) and foreign exchange restrictions in postwar Europe. If their policy advice to individual countries was very straightforward and consistent as regards its ultimate goals (reestablishment of monetary and financial stability; budgetary and balance of payments balance; cutting back of restrictions and controls in favour of free market forces; restoring currency convertibility and multilateral trade), there was nonetheless considerable leeway in how best to reach these goals. In the case of the Netherlands, Jacobsson recognised that there was merit in maintaining certain price controls for somewhat longer than was strictly speaking necessary. In the case of France, the application of multiple exchange rates, though in contradiction with IMF policy, was deemed tolerable, at least for as long as prices did not converge sufficiently and controls could not be relaxed without further endangering France's already strained balance of payments. In the case of Italy, the BIS report came out squarely in favour of a state-sponsored development programme to stimulate the economy in Southern Italy. The specific circumstances of each country always had to be taken into account, and determined how rigid or flexible the application of the

[37] BISA 9.1.002 – BIS (1949), *The post-war Position of France*, p. B1.

[38] "..those countries that have pursued flexible interest policies in the period since the Second World War have been able to expand their production just as much as – or even more – than those which have stuck obstinately to cheap money, and (..) the former countries have, in fact, been more successful than the other countries in avoiding harmful monetary disturbances" (Jacobsson 1958a, p. 15).

policy principles had to be (Jacobsson 1958a, pp. 36–37). Importantly, Jacobsson emphasised again and again the international element: the need to restore mutlilateral trade, and to lower prices and increase efficiency through international competition. He was a great believer in the discipline imposed by open markets and in the benefits of genuine international exchange. He saw great advantages in a closer cooperation between European countries, as stimulated by the US Economic Cooperation Administration, distributing and supervising the Marshall Plan aid, and later by the OEEC. These were, in short, the policy principles Jacobsson always tried to stick to, also later as Managing Director of the IMF.

3.3 The West German Balance of Payments Crisis, 1950–1951

The economic analysis and policy advice provided in the BIS country studies was in demand with European central banks during the critical reconstruction phase following the Second World War. This is hardly surprising: the BIS provided an independent view, it came for free, and did not commit the recipient country to anything. That would be quite different for the next piece of country advice Per Jacobsson was called upon to deliver. This time it concerned West Germany.[39]

In 1947, the BIS had become involved in the intra-European *Agreement on Multilateral Monetary Compensation*, aimed at restoring multilateral payments between European economies and thereby preparing the way for the return to full currency convertibility as envisaged by the Bretton Woods agreements. The BIS was designated as the agent to whom the participating countries had to report their bilateral payment balances each month with the aim of offsetting deficits against surpluses. However, it was only with the establishment of the European Payments Union (EPU) in September 1950, under the aegis of the OEEC, that a truly multilateral system was inaugurated, in which countries settled their cumulative payment surpluses and deficits with the Union as a whole rather than with each individual country bilaterally (Kaplan and Schleiminger 1989). Any country that ran a trade balance deficit with its EPU partners was required to settle only part of it in gold or convertible dollars; the largest part could be converted into longer-term credits. This allowed deficit countries to save on their scarce foreign exchange and gold reserves. However, the total amount of credit available to any given country was capped by a system of country quotas. Also, to avoid placing the burden of adjustment too heavily on the surplus countries, the deficit countries were committed to gradually liberalise their trade with all EPU partners. Thus, in exchange for accepting the temporary immobilisation of their surpluses through credits, the countries running surpluses avoided the risk of trade discrimination by deficit countries seeking to reduce their deficits. Finally, it was planned that, as time went by and the European economies gained strength, the debtor countries would increasingly settle their deficits vis-à-vis the EPU in gold and convertible currencies, relying less and less on credits. This

[39] This section reproduces parts of Clement 2006.

was indeed what happened, and by 1958 almost all deficits were settled 100 % in gold or cash, whereupon the EPU was wound up, and full current account currency convertibility was achieved throughout Europe.

The BIS was called upon to act as the agent for the EPU, assembling all bilateral trade balances and calculating the net position of each EPU member on a monthly basis. In its capacity as agent, the BIS reported to the EPU Managing Board, based at the OEEC in Paris. Soon, a close network was woven between Paris and Basel, with BIS experts attending the EPU meetings in Paris and the central bank Governors, on the occasion of their regular meetings in Basel, informally discussing the operations of the EPU.[40]

Barely established, the EPU was faced with its first crisis.[41] By 1949–1950, the West German economy, spurred on by the successful currency reform of June 1948, had finally launched headlong into a frenzied postwar reconstruction boom. In the autumn of 1950, however, the inexorable rise in imports at a time of rising commodity prices caused by the Korean War, combined with Germany's still weak reserves position, had produced a severe payments imbalance. Under the EPU rules, West Germany was able to offset its trade deficit with some EPU countries through surpluses with others, while the residual deficit had to be settled only partly in gold and dollars, with the largest part being automatically transformed into an EPU credit. Such credit, however, was only granted up to the maximum of a given country's quota with the EPU. Once the quota was exceeded, the entire deficit had to be settled in gold or dollars. From the start of the EPU in July 1950 until the end of October, West Germany's net cumulative deficit reached US$ 289 million. It was predicted that if deficits continued at the same rate, the country's US$ 320 million quota with the EPU would be exhausted by mid-November.

The very first meeting of the EPU Managing Board, held in Paris on 20–22 October 1950, tried to tackle the crisis, but participants were not able to reach a consensus on the appropriate method. Some felt that Germany should bear the consequences of its predicament as it had failed to take timely corrective action. Others argued that trade liberalisation in Germany ought to be reversed in order to restrict imports, while still others believed that there was a case for making additional foreign exchange available to Germany through a special EPU loan. In the knowledge that this was the first major test case for the EPU's authority and resolve in addressing serious payments imbalances, the EPU Board eagerly sought to break the deadlock and therefore called on the opinion of two experts: Alec Cairncross (1911–1998), who was economic adviser to the OEEC, and Per Jacobsson, who held the same position at the BIS.

---

[40] Hubert Ansiaux of the National Bank of Belgium, who attended the meetings of the EPU Managing Board as Chairman of the OEEC Intra-European Payments Committee, was at the same time alternate member of the BIS Board of Directors. Two of the nine initial voting members of the EPU Board – Carli for Italy and Calvet for France – would later also become members of the BIS Board of Directors.

[41] On this episode, see in particular: Kaplan and Schleiminger 1989, pp. 97–117; Jacobsson 1979, pp. 236–245; Holtfrerich 1999, pp. 333–341. Also: Alec Cairncross, "Report on visit to Germany 28 October to 3 November 1950", DBHA, N2/K3 – *Europäische Zahlungsunion, Cairncross-Jacobsson Mission 1950.*

Time was of the essence. The choice of Jacobsson as an expert proved particularly fortuitous as he had already, through the BIS network, established a close relationship with one of the main interlocutors of the EPU experts, Dr Wilhelm Vocke (1886–1973), the President of West Germany's new central bank (*Bank deutscher Länder*). Indeed, Vocke himself took the initiative to call Jacobsson in Basel the day after the EPU Board had invited the two experts to report on the German situation. The very next day, Jacobsson travelled to Frankfurt for a series of meetings with Vocke and other officials from the German central bank as well as members of the Allied Banking Commission.[42] Quickly assessing that the situation was less dramatic than feared, Jacobsson joined a small chorus of voices urging the Germans, and the central bank in particular, to resist calls for a suspension of trade liberalisation and to instead tackle the situation through monetary and fiscal means. In his talks with Vocke, Jacobsson was emphatic that the central bank should decide on an "… impressive increase in the discount rate" and should do this immediately, as otherwise it would make "… a lamentable impression". Fortified by Jacobsson's firm opinions, Vocke participated the following day in a marathon session of the central bank council in which, exceptionally, Chancellor Adenauer and several cabinet ministers also took part. Finally, the council, overruling Adenauer's strong objections, increased the discount rate from 4 % to 6 %.

All of this had taken place even before Alec Cairncross reached Frankfurt to embark with Jacobsson on the EPU experts' official consultations on the German situation. Cairncross may have been somewhat irked by Jacobsson's swift action, but this did not prevent the two men from developing an excellent working relationship. They presented their oral report to the EPU Managing Board scarcely 1 week later, arguing that, given the right policy mix, Germany's payments position was bound to improve dramatically over the months to come.[43] The diagnosis of the experts was the basis for the Managing Board's recommendation of 6 November 1950 – adopted by the OEEC Council on 13 December – to grant a first ever EPU special credit of US$ 120 million to West Germany.

The EPU Board was swayed to support a special credit with some difficulty, and there were strings attached. First, the policy recommendations to the German government contained in the experts' report were taken over by the EPU Board. These recommendations included the maintenance of the DM exchange rate (no devaluation); an increase in German income and turnover taxes; the avoidance of deficit spending in favour of a balanced budget, not just at the Federal but also at the regional and local levels; and a centralisation of power and strengthening of the authority of the *Bank deutscher Länder*. Germany was also expected to better pace the granting of import licenses, without, however, going back on its commitment to

[42] Among them was Otmar Emminger, later President of the Bundesbank, then economic adviser to the Bank deutscher Länder, for whom these talks were the start of a "close and trusted friendship" with Jacobsson and the basis for their future cooperation at the IMF (Emminger 1986, p. 52).

[43] The written report of the experts was submitted 2 weeks later: Organisation for European Economic Co-ordination, MBC(50)13, *European Payments Union: Consideration of Germany's Position*, 20 November 1950.

trade liberalisation.[44] The release of the US$ 120 million credit was made subject to the submission by Germany of a detailed programme outlining the implementation of policy measures compatible with these recommendations in a way that was acceptable to the EPU Board and OEEC Council. The German government delegation duly submitted such a programme. It was accepted by the OEEC Council on 13 December 1950, freeing the way for the release of the US$ 120 million credit. In order to monitor the implementation of this programme, the EPU Board was empowered to "… keep under review the economic and financial situation in Germany and the implementation of the … programme", while the German government was required to "supply the Managing Board with all the information required for this purpose".[45]

In other words, there was a lot of conditionality attached to the granting of the EPU credit to Germany. To put this into a broader perspective, what Germany received in return for agreeing to EPU monitoring was an additional US$ 120 million that it could draw on to cover its trade deficit with its EPU partners. These US$ 120 million (or DM 504 million), represented only 18 % of the total deficit incurred on Germany's current account over the whole of 1950 (US$ 673 million), and just a little over 0.5 % of West German GDP at the time.[46] Significantly, though, it represented no less than 55 % of West Germany's total gold and dollar reserves at the end of 1950. It is very likely that without the credit Germany probably would have been forced to halt trade liberalisation altogether and leave the EPU.[47]

Once the credit had been granted, the outcome of the crisis was by no means self-evident. When during the first 2 months of 1951 Germany's position seemed to deteriorate further and the government – with the approval of the EPU Board – was forced to suspend trade liberalisation after all, the experts' opinion was increasingly questioned. Jacobsson even felt ostracised at the February Board meeting of the BIS. Soon, however, the experts were fully vindicated. In March 1951, West Germany, for the first time, showed a surplus in its EPU accounts. The surpluses grew over the next months. By the end of May, the EPU special credit was reimbursed in full, ahead of schedule. This successful outcome had the welcome side-effect of putting the EPU firmly on the map and strengthening the authority and independence of the German central bank vis-à-vis its government. Jacobsson, for his part, felt that the German episode confirmed once more the soundness of an essentially orthodox monetary and fiscal approach to any cyclical balance of pay-

[44] OEEC Council, *The position of Germany in EPU, Report by the Managing Board of the EPU*, C(50)315, Paris, 13 November 1950.

[45] OEEC Council, *Decision on the settlement of the deficits of Germany within EPU (adopted by the Council at its 117th meeting)*, C(50)342, Paris, 13 December 1950, p. 4.

[46] Figures taken from: OEEC, *European Payments Union, Consideration of Germany's Position* (experts' report submitted by Per Jacobsson and Alec Cairncross), MBC(50)13, 20 November 1950, p. 46. West Germany's current account balance: Kaplan and Schleiminger 1989, p. 101. West Germany's GDP: Mitchell 2003, p. 916.

[47] West Germany's official gold and dollar reserves stood at a mere US$ 222 million at the end of 1950. Bank for International Settlements, *Twenty-first Annual Report*, Basel, 1951, p. 163.

ments problems (Jacobsson 1979, pp. 243–245). In the years that followed, Jacobsson continued to make the case for such reforms, and more generally for policies that should allow European countries to get rid of excessive controls and achieve free currency convertibility at the earliest possible date.[48]

4 Concluding Remarks

Per Jacobsson's nomination as the IMF Managing Director in September 1956 came like a bolt from the blue. The idea was first floated by Randolph Burgess (1889–1978) in a private letter to Jacobsson dated 28 May 1956: "This is just to tell you very confidentially and informally that I have been playing a little with the idea of suggesting your name to the Directors of the Monetary Fund to succeed Rooth. My belief is that what they need more than anything else is a personality who can talk to people in a way that will carry influence, and I know of nobody who can provide that sort of leadership better than you can. I know this is a little shocking and perhaps a disturbing idea to you, but I hope you will just hold your mind open".[49] Jacobsson noted in his diary: "Coming back from Paris I found a letter from Randolph Burgess. … I was just astonished – it had never occurred to me that I should be thought of for that position".[50] Burgess and Jacobsson had been good friends since the early 1930s, when Burgess was Deputy Governor at the Federal Reserve Bank of New York and Jacobsson had just entered the BIS Monetary and Economic Department. They visited whenever possible, exchanged letters, sent each other publications, and always remained in contact, also after 1938, when Burgess had left the Federal Reserve for a vice-chairmanship at the National City Bank of New York. In 1946, they jointly wrote a report for the International Chamber of Commerce, in which they argued for the flexible use of interest rates as a monetary policy instrument (and thus against the dogma of cheap money).[51] In 1953, during the Eisenhower administration, Burgess had joined the US Treasury, where he rose to Undersecretary rank in 1955. He was now in a position to put forward Jacobsson's name for the IMF job: "Personally, it would mean a great deal to me to see you in this position and my enthusiasm is shared by my associates in the Treasury".[52] Without even waiting for Jacobsson's reply, Burgess started canvassing support for his idea with those people

[48] See for instance: BISA 9.1.002 – BIS, Monetary and Economic Department (1954), *Problems of the Return to Convertibility, Lecture by Per Jacobsson given at the University of Iceland, Reykjavik, on 8 September 1954*, Basel: Bank for International Settlements.

[49] UNIBAS-HAN, Basel, NL 324, B 562 – *Nachlass Per Jacobsson, Correspondence Randolph Burgess,* letter Burgess to Jacobsson, 28 May 1956.

[50] UNIBAS-HAN, Basel, NL 324, A/110 – *Nachlass Per Jacobsson, Diary 110,* entry 19 June 1956.

[51] International Chamber of Commerce (December 1946), *Monetary Problems in the World of Today*, brochure n° 104.

[52] UNIBAS-HAN, Basel, NL 324, B 562 – *Nachlass Per Jacobsson, Correspondence Randolph Burgess,* letter Burgess to Jacobsson 1 June 1956.

that mattered: through Cobbold and Bolton of the Bank of England, he got the UK Treasury on board. The matter was soon taken up by the BIS Board of Directors. On 8 June 1956, just days before the BIS Annual General Meeting, Cameron Cobbold, Governor of the Bank of England, told Jacobsson that he had at first been incredulous when Burgess had approached him – "One sees from the papers on your table that you are not an administrator", he added – but that he had changed his opinion: "We had looked in vain for the name of a candidate on which we all would agree. After all there are others who can help to administer. Maybe the Fund needs something else. ... the [UK] Treasury agreed".[53]

The other Governors, and particularly the long-standing vice-Chairman of the BIS Board of Directors Otto Niemeyer, were as yet unconvinced. Jacobsson noted: "Frère and Niemeyer said the Governors of the BIS wanted unanimously that I should remain in Basel, and also that I might not succeed at the IMF – a very difficult task".[54] Nevertheless, throughout the summer support for Jacobsson's candidacy gained momentum, while he himself quickly decided that the honour and the challenge were impossible to resist. By mid-September he was in Washington to sign the contract, and at the beginning of December 1956 he officially took up the position of Managing Director of the IMF, which he would retain until he died on 5 May 1963.

When Jacobsson moved from Basel to Washington in the autumn of 1956, he was 62 years old and full of energy. He came to the IMF with a broad experience in both financial and economic policy analysis and in international negotiations, two traits that must have made him seem cut out for the IMF job. These qualities and skills had been honed during over 30 years of international experience, first at the League of Nations and then at the BIS. But it was arguably Jacobsson's close involvement with Europe's financial reconstruction efforts during the years 1946–1951 that proved to be the most relevant preparation for his role at the IMF. His views, and in particular his steadfast commitment to monetary and financial stability were well known to, and shared by, those that put him in that position. He would play his part as IMF Managing Director with gusto.

As argued earlier, during his tenure in Washington the IMF expanded its role and its activities significantly. Through a quota increase and through the successful negotiation of the General Arrangements to Borrow (GAB), the IMF increased its available resources. With a greatly increased membership after decolonisation, the IMF lending and support procedures became firmly established. And, finally the

---

[53] UNIBAS-HAN, Basel, NL 324, A/110 – *Nachlass Per Jacobsson, Diary 110,* entry 19 June 1956 ff.

[54] UNIBAS-HAN, Basel, NL 324, A/110 – *Nachlass Per Jacobsson, Diary 110,* entry 19 June 1956 ff. The Governors apparently nurtured some doubt about Jacobsson's capacity to successfully steer a big administration like the IMF. As Governor Frère of the National Bank of Belgium put in a note to Burgess: "Jac[obsson] is certainly wonderful as an economist but he has absolutely no administrative capacity and no interest for administrative problems", BISA, 7.16(3) – *BIS Foundation and History, Baffi papers*, Box RBL/B3, copy from National Bank of Belgium files, letter Maurice Frère to Randolph Burgess, 28 June 1956.

IMF fully claimed its intended pivotal role in international financial diplomacy, which during the 1950s and 1960s was particularly strong between the United States, Japan and the main western European countries – a small circle in which Jacobsson moved with ease. This last achievement was probably the one closest to Per Jacobsson's heart, given that he was a great communicator (he delivered over 100 public speeches during the 6 years and a half he was at the IMF – Horsefield 1969, p. 521), and a consummate – albeit somewhat self-righteous and vain – diplomat (it had been exactly for those qualities that Randolph Burgess had put forward Jacobsson's name for the IMF job in the first place).

These were important developments, which had longer-lasting effects. The liquidity issue would continue to dominate the international debate until the creation of the Special Drawing Rights (SDR) in 1967–1969 and beyond. The IMF lending and support arrangements became a mainstay of the international financial system, particularly after the collapse of the Bretton Woods system in the early 1970s, and followed to a large extent the template that had first been created in the 1950s and early 1960s. Financial diplomacy through the 1960s, 1970s and 1980s focused primarily on a small inner circle of western, developed countries: the G10, soon to be even further limited to the G5/G7. One unintended result was an increased reliance on regional forums and solutions to bypass the extreme concentration of decision making power into only a few hands (James 1996, pp. 594–599). Repeated attempts to broaden the basis of the international financial system by including the systemically important emerging market economies only really bore fruit in the 1990s–2000s, when the G20 superseded the G10.

The years 1957–1963, when Per Jacobsson was the Fund's Managing Director, can thus be said to have been a pivotal period in the history of the IMF. Of course similar developments would no doubt have taken place regardless of who was at the helm in Washington. Indeed, Jacobsson's successor, Pierre-Paul Schweitzer, played an equally important role in strengthening the IMF's role in international monetary affairs. Nevertheless, in many instances, Per Jacobsson, in his own indefatigable way, was a catalyst and active promotor of these changes. In that respect, and certainly from the IMF's own point of view, he was the right man in the right place at the right time. After all, people make history, albeit not in the circumstances of their own choosing.

Primary Sources

BISA	Bank for International Settlements Archive. BIS, Centralbahnplatz 2, CH-4051 Basel, Switzerland. Information: www.bis.org/about/archive.htm; contact: archive@bis.org
DBHA	Deutsche Bundesbank Historisches Archiv Wilhelm-Epstein-Strasse 14, D-60431 Frankfurt am Main, Germany Information: www.bundesbank.de
UNIBAS-HAN	Universitätsbibliothek Basel Handschriften. Address: Schönbeinstrasse 18–20, CH-4056 Basel, Switzerland. Information: www.ub.unibas.ch; contact: info-ub@unibas.ch

References

Baffi, Paolo. 1990. *Testimonianze e ricordi*. Milan: Libri Scheiwiller.

Bank for International Settlements. 1951. *Twenty-first annual report*. Basel: BIS.

Black, Stanley W. 1991. *A Levite among the priests, Edward M. Bernstein and the origins of the Bretton Woods system*. Boulder: Westview Press.

Boughton, James M. 2004. *The IMF and the force of history: Ten events and ten ideas that have shaped the institution*. IMF Working Paper, WP/04/75. Washington: IMF.

Clavin, Patricia. 1996. *The failure of economic diplomacy: Britain, Germany, France and the United States, 1931–36*. Basingstoke: Macmillan.

Clement, Piet. 2006. The BIS and Central Bank Cooperation in the 1950s and the 1960s: Two Tales. In *European Central Banks and Monetary Cooperation after 1945*, ed. Piet Clement and Juan Carlos Martinez Oliva, 27–38. Frankfurt am Main: EABH-Adelmann.

Cotula, Franco. 2000. La riconquista della stabilità. Tra sviluppo e vincolo esterno (1946–1963). In *Stabilità e sviluppo negli anni cinquanta*, Vol. 1, ed. Cotula Franco, 3–73. Collana Storica della Banca d'Italia, Roma-Bari: Editore Laterza.

De Cecco, Marcello. 2013. The Italian Economy seen from Abroad. In *The Oxford handbook of the Italian Economy since unification*, ed. Gianni Toniolo, 134–154. Oxford: Oxford University Press.

De Vries, Margaret G., and J. Keith Horsefield. 1969. *The International Monetary Fund 1945–1965*, Analysis, vol. II. Washington, DC: IMF.

Di Nino, Virginia, Barry Eichengreen, and Massimo Sbracia. 2013. Real exchange rates, trade, and growth. In *The Oxford handbook of the Italian Economy since unification*, ed. Gianni Toniolo, 351–377. Oxford: Oxford University Press.

ECA Economic Cooperation Administration. 1949. *Italy, country study, European recovery program*. Washington, DC: US Government Printing Office.

Emminger, Otmar. 1986. *D-Mark, Dollar, Währungskrisen, Erinnerungen eines ehemaligen Bundesbankpräsidenten*. Stuttgart: Deutsche Verlags-Anstalt.

Enders, A.M., and G.A. Fleming. 2002. *International organizations and the analysis of economic policy*. Cambridge: Cambridge University Press.

Feiertag, Olivier. 2006. *Wilfrid Baumgartner, Un grand commis des finances à la croisée des pouvoirs (1902–1978)*. Paris: Ministère de l'Economie, des Finances et de l'Industrie.

Garritsen De Vries, Margaret. 1987. *Balance of payments adjustment, 1945 to 1986, the IMF experience*. Washington, DC: IMF.

Gigliobianco, Alfredo, ed. 2010. *Luigi Einaudi: libertà economica e coesione sociale*. Collana Storica della Banca d'Italia, Roma-Bari: Editore Laterza.

Hildebrand, Georges. 1965. *Growth and structure in the economy of modern Italy*. Harvard: Harvard University Press.

Holtfrerich, Carl-Ludwig. 1999. Monetary policy under fixed exchange rates (1948–1970). In *Fifty years of the Deutsche mark, Central Bank and the currency in Germany since 1948*, 333–341. Oxford: University Press.

Horsefield, J. Keith. 1969. *The International Monetary Fund 1945–1965*, Twenty years of International Monetary Cooperation, vol. I. Washington, DC: IMF.

Jacobsson, Per. 1958a. Background 1917–1958. In *Some monetary problems, international and national, by Per Jacobsson*, ed. Erin E. Jucker-Fleetwood, 5–59. Oxford/Basel: Oxford University Press.

Jacobsson, Per. 1958b. Theory and practice: Knut Wicksell and Sweden's monetary policy. In *Some monetary problems, international and national, by Per Jacobsson*, ed. Erin E. Jucker-Fleetwood, 227–254. Oxford/Basel: Oxford University Press.

Jacobsson, Erin E. 1979. *A life for sound money, Per Jacobsson, his biography*. Oxford: Clarendon.

James, Harold. 1996. *International Monetary Cooperation since Bretton Woods*. Washington, DC/New York/Oxford: International Monetary Fund/Oxford University Press.

Kaplan, Jacob J., and Günther Schleiminger. 1989. *The European payments union, financial diplomacy in the 1950s*. Oxford: Clarendon.

Keynes, J.M. 1934. The Bank for International Settlements: Fourth annual report. *Economic Journal* 44(175): 514–518.
Kindleberger, Charles P. 1980. A life for sound money: Per Jacobsson, his biography by Erin E. Jacobsson, review. *Journal of Money, Credit and Banking* 12(2-I May): 235–237.
Kindleberger, Charles P. 1991. *The life of an economist, an autobiography*. Cambridge: Basil Blackwell.
Martinez Oliva, Juan Carlos. 2005. *The Italian stabilization of 1947: Domestic and international factors*. Berkeley: University of California, Institute of European Studies.
Menichella, Donato. 1966. Per Jacobsson and monetary developments in Italy, 1946–1947. In *The role of the Central Banker today*, ed. Louis Rasminsky. Washington, DC: IMF/The Per Jacobsson Foundation.
Mershon, Carol. 2002. *The costs of coalition*. Stanford: Stanford University Press.
Mitchell, B.R. 2003. *International historical statistics, Europe 1750–2000*. Basingstoke/New York: Palgrave Macmillan.
Polak, Jacques J. 1994. *Economic theory and financial policy, the selected essays of Jacques J. Polak*, vol. 1. Aldershot: Edward Elgar.
Ricossa, Sergio. 2003. La Banca d'Italia e il risanamento postbellico, 1945–1948. In *La Banca d'Italia, Sintesi della ricerca storica 1893–1960*, ed. Franco Cotula, Marcello de Cecco, and Gianni Toniolo. Collana Storica della Banca d'Italia, Roma-Bari: Editore Laterza.
Toniolo, Gianni (ed.). 2013. *The Oxford handbook of the Italian economy since unification*. Oxford: Oxford University Press.
Toniolo, Gianni, with the assistance of Piet Clement. 2005. *Central Bank Cooperation at the Bank for International Settlements, 1930–1973*. Cambridge: Cambridge University Press.
Yago, Kazuhiko. 2013. *The financial history of the Bank for International Settlements*. London/New York: Routledge.
Yago, Kazuhiko. 2006. Wicksellian tradition at the Bank for International Settlements: Per Jacobsson on money and credit. *Keizaigakushi-kenkyu* (The Japanese Society for the History of Economic Thought) 48(2): 1–18.

Chapter 5
International Liquidity Problems in the 1960s: The Examination of the Minutes of the Executive Board of the International Monetary Fund

Yasutoshi Noshita

1 Introduction

One of the features of the international monetary system after World War II has been the establishment of international financial organizations (Bretton Woods Institutions) as an integral part of the governance structure to manage the international monetary system. However, the views about the role of the international financial organizations, especially the International Monetary Fund (IMF), have been largely divided into two approaches.

The first approach is that international financial cooperation among the main industrialized countries has managed the postwar international monetary system. Charles Kindleberger argued that the stability of the international monetary system during the Bretton Woods era (1945–1971) had been supported by the hegemony of the United States (1970). On the other hand, Susan Strange argued that the hegemony of the United States during the Bretton Woods era had led to financial instability due to the asymmetry of the international monetary system (1971). Although both are contra-positions on the role of the United States, they had the same position that the international financial cooperation of the main industrialized countries had managed the postwar international monetary system.

Since 1971, this approach has been carried forward to the after-hegemony theory and brought forth the various arguments such as international political economics and the international relation theories. These theories have analyzed the governance structure of the international monetary system as the problem of the relationship between the political and economic interests of the main industrialized countries (Cohen 2008, p. 24).

Y. Noshita (✉)
Faculty of Political Science and Economics, Kokushikan University,
4-28-1, Setagaya, Tokyo 154-8515, Japan
e-mail: noshita@kokushikan.ac.jp

K. Yago et al. (eds.), *History of the IMF*, Studies in Economic History,
DOI 10.1007/978-4-431-55351-9_5

Whether under U.S. hegemony or under the international cooperation of main industrialized countries, these studies have focused on the international cooperation of the main industrialized countries. As a result, these studies have overlooked the significance of international financial organizations in the postwar international monetary system. However, the various international financial organizations have been founded since the 1970s. These international financial organizations have come to play an important role in managing the international monetary system after the 1970s. Therefore, it has become insufficient to regard the international financial organizations as conference rooms to promote international cooperation among the main industrialized countries (Wilki 2012, p. 132). In the face of the growing importance of the international financial organizations, to focus only on the main industrialized countries in analyzing the postwar international monetary system is a limited approach.

The second approach is that the international financial organizations newly established after World War II have played essential roles in managing the postwar international monetary system. According to this approach, the international financial organizations could not be ignored in the policy formation of the postwar international monetary system. In fact, in recent years, there were studies that have identified the role of international financial organizations in the policy formation of the postwar international monetary system (Keohan and Nye 1977; Keohane 1989; Chwieroth 2010; Yago 2010). However, these studies also have following problems.

Firstly, these studies have mainly focused on the development of international financial organizations since the 1970s. Secondly, these studies have overestimated the individual characters, on which policy makers are basing the policy formation of the international monetary system. Thirdly, these studies have not analyzed the relationship between the main industrialized countries, the developing countries, and the international financial organizations before 1971. As a result, these studies have not analyzed why international financial organizations would be necessary for the postwar international monetary system. Therefore, this approach has been forced to base the role of the international financial organizations on the personal characteristics of the policy makers.

Whether the approach to focus on the international cooperation of the main industrialized countries or the approach to emphasize the role of international financial organizations, both approaches have overlooked the fact that the formation of international cooperation in the postwar international monetary system has a unique characteristic, which differs from other areas of international cooperation. The international monetary system has to be supported by the private clearing and settlement networks of commercial banks. That fact means that the countries other than the main industrialized countries have been playing some part in the international monetary system. The postwar international monetary system has not included only the main industrialized countries, but also many other countries, especially the developing countries that became independent from European colonies powers after World War II. Therefore, only the main industrialized countries and the international financial organizations have not been able to form the international cooperation to manage the postwar international monetary system. The international financial organizations, especially the IMF have been necessary to fill the gap between the main industrialized countries and the other countries.

In the face of the speculative increase of the price of gold and the disturbance of the foreign exchange markets, the reform of the International Monetary System emerged as an urgent issue in the early 1960s. The issue had been discussed without a drastic solution but had resulted in the establishment of the Special Drawing Rights (SDRs) in 1968. There are also the two kinds of approaches in the studies about the establishment of SDRs.

The first approach is that the establishment of SDRs was determined as a result of negotiations between the Finance Ministers and Central Bank Governors of the Group of Ten (G10) and the IMF under the initiative of the United States (Solomon 1982, pp. 66–67). The second approach is that the establishment of SDRs was determined mainly by the political dynamics between the United States and the United Kingdom, although the IMF played a unique role (Wilki 2012, p. 11). Although both approaches appear different, they have the same position that the establishment of SDRs had been determined by the cooperation among the main industrialized countries. As a result, neither approach has recognized that non-G10 countries, especially the developing countries, had proactively been involved in the discussions about the establishment of SDRs.

The purpose of this chapter is to examine the Minutes of the Executive Board of the IMF on the process of the establishment of SDRs. In the studies so far, it has not been adequately evaluated the fact that the Executive Board of the IMF won some concessions from the G10. Due to the failure to evaluate the significance of the concession gained by the Executive Board, the role of the IMF has still not been defined in the international cooperation of the international monetary system in the 1960s. The examination of the Minutes of the Executive Board will reveal the relationship between the international cooperation and the role of the IMF in the international monetary system in the 1960s.

2 Controversy on the International Monetary Reform and International Liquidity Problem

In the late 1950s, when Western Europe had recovered currency convertibility in the current account, the networks of foreign exchange banks began to expand, although some exchange controls had still been left in place in most countries.

In the international monetary system in the Bretton Woods era, member countries of the Fund other than the United States had to intervene in the foreign exchange markets in order to maintain the official exchange rate of their currencies to the dollar. Whether by the increase of foreign trade or by the expansion of foreign aid, the dollar-denominated foreign lending by U.S. foreign exchange banks resulted in increases in foreign exchange reserves through the intervention of each country's monetary authority in the foreign exchange markets.

As big U.S. companies increasingly transformed into multinational companies and U.S. investors increased their foreign securities investments, the Western European countries experienced revaluation pressure due to current account surpluses and capital account deficits. Therefore, their monetary authorities bought dollars and supplied their own currencies at home in order to maintain the official exchange rates of their own currencies to the dollar. Further, the international activities of U.S. financial institutions made it easy to raise dollars for speculators to trade in the foreign exchange markets and the London gold market. Under these financial circumstances, the increase of speculation in currency and gold had made it difficult for countries other than U.S. to maintain the official exchange rates of their currencies to the dollar.

As the speculations in currency and gold intensified and began to threaten the stability of the foreign exchange system beginning in the late 1950s, the main industrialized countries were forced to deal with such situations by international cooperation and by reevaluating their currencies. In fact, West Germany decided to revalue the Deutsche Mark up by 5 % in March 1961. The Netherlands and several countries followed this revaluation with their own.

A currency revaluation, however, often gave birth to conjecture concerning other currency revaluations and led to currency speculation. Therefore, international cooperation had become indispensable to manage speculation in currency and gold. The currency speculation in the Deutsche Mark was tranquilized by the conclusion of the Basel Accord in March 1961. In November 1961, the United States and seven central banks of major industrialized countries decided to join the London gold pool to stabilize the market price of gold in the London gold market.

The swap agreement between the central banks of main industrialized countries was another example of international cooperation. The first swap agreement among the central banks of main industrialized countries was the agreement between the Bank of France and the U.S. Federal Reserve Board of Governors in March 1962. By the end of 1964, the U.S. Federal Reserve Board had signed swap agreements one after another with the central banks of main industrialized countries, such as the Bank of England and the central banks of major Western European countries, the Swiss National Bank and the Bank of Japan. The U.S. Federal Reserve Board even entered into a swap agreement with the Bank for International Settlements.

The swap agreement was a short-term means to defend the official exchange rates. In contrast, the issuance of foreign-currency-denominated securities such as the Rosa Bond was supposed to be used as a means to maintain the official exchange rate over the medium to long term. In 1962, when Italy had accumulated dollar-denominated reserves, both the Italian and U.S. governments issued lira-denominated Treasury bonds. By replacing the dollar with the lira through issuing such bonds, the United States absorbed the dollars held by Italian government. Thereafter, such bonds also were issued in West Germany and Austria. However, this type of international cooperation was not enough to ensure the stability of the international monetary system.

The United States had not made the resolute radical measures to address the problem of dollar overhang. Rather, the United States was preoccupied with half-hearted measures. For example, the United States required Western European countries to refrain from exchanging dollars for gold. Such measures led to a sharp rise in the gold price and the further worsening of the dollar overhang problem.

At the Joint Annual Meeting of the IMF and the World Bank (the Annual Meeting) in 1961, high-ranking officials from each country admitted for the first time that the international monetary system had not been operating soundly (Machlup 1964, p. 3). The reform of the international monetary system had become a problem to be solved urgently. However, as long as the United States hesitated over reform of the international monetary system, the reform of the international monetary system did not advance an inch.

In the early 1960s, the United States balance of payments had improved. However, this improvement was only temporary due to intergovernmental special deals for the defense of the dollar. In fact, in the first half of 1963, the United States recorded a huge deficit of 5 billion dollars by subtracting intergovernmental special deals for the defense of the dollar from the surplus of the balance of payments.

In response to this situation, shortly after his inauguration as President of the United States Kennedy began to think seriously about international monetary reform.[1] Overseas gold purchases by Americans already had been banned by the Eisenhower administration in 1961. However, in February 1962 the Kennedy administration considered bold measures to defend the dollar, such as tax reform to encourage the repatriation of profits earned by foreign private investments. In 1963, President Kennedy gave a special message on the balance of payments. In this presidential message, it was stated for the first time that the United States would prepare to discuss the improvement of the international monetary system. Thanks to this change in the U.S. attitude, the momentum toward international monetary reform accelerated.

Famous scholars, policy makers, and practitioners had made various proposals for the reform of the international monetary system.[2] In confronting the shaking of the dollar following the pound sterling crisis, various arguments about international

[1] President Kennedy took an intense and sustained personal interest in the balance of payments (Odell 1982, p. 96). In May 1962, US Treasury Secretary Robert Roosa said at the International Monetary Conference in Rome that it was the time to examine the international monetary system of the future and proposed measures to strength the gold exchange standard system, such as credit arrangements between countries (Wilki 2012, p. 18). In addition, US Secretary of the Treasury Clarence Douglas Dillon also expressed in the Annual Meeting in 1963 that it was necessary to examine the long-term issues of the international monetary system.

[2] The proposals from academia were directed mainly to the reduction of the dollar balance outstanding against the holdings of gold. These included (1) Harrod's plan to reduce the outstanding balances of the pound sterling and the dollar and to abolish the fixed gold price, (2) Jacques Rueff's proposal to make the Bretton Woods system approximate the gold standard, (3) the Composite Reserve Unit (CRU) plan to use as an equivalent of gold the composite reserve unit (CRU) received in exchange for the pool (deposit) of the major countries' currencies. On the other hand, dollar standard theorists argued that since the US balance of payments deficit was a result of the dollar-denominated liquidity demand, U.S. deficits would not cause any problem (Eichengreen 1996, p. 114). Practitioners such as the Brookings Institution and four countries' central bankers (those of the United States, West Germany, Switzerland, and Italy) had also presented reform proposals.

monetary reform had gradually resolved into the three topics of: (1) the problem of international liquidity, (2) the problem of balance of payments adjustment, and (3) the confidence problem of the dollar.[3]

1. The problem of international liquidity was that international liquidity might not be enough to sustain world economic growth in the postwar international monetary system as long as gold production was limited.
2. The problem of balance of payments adjustment was that the international monetary system had no longer been adjusting the balance of payments between the United States and other member countries by changing official exchange rates flexibly. The international monetary system had transformed practically into a fixed exchange system different from the adjustable exchange system originally designed at the Bretton Woods Conference.
3. The confidence problem of the dollar was that the balance of payments of the United States had been deteriorating and the outstanding U.S. dollar-denominated debt held by other countries had been increasing against the U.S.'s holding of gold, leading to a loss of confidence in the dollar, which increased the possibility to run on the dollar.

The problem of international liquidity, the problem of balance of payments adjustment and the confidence problem of the dollar were closely related to each other. At the same time, the three problems also involved conflicting interests between the G10 countries and the non-G10 countries and also between the IMF member countries and the IMF.

The United States had become concerned that international monetary reform would lead to the necessity for adjustment of its balance of payments. Therefore, the United States had previously refused any plans for international monetary reform. Western European countries observed that balance-of-payment imbalances underlay the international monetary instability. Therefore, they considered the U.S. balance of payments deficit to be the cause of the dollar confidence problem. On the other hand, they were concerned that the revaluation of their currencies would lead to an overall review of official exchange rates and a fixed exchange rate system.

The non-G10 countries, especially developing countries, and the IMF joined in the conflict of interests around international monetary reform. The developing countries had feared that the supply of international liquidity would be reduced by the tightening of U.S. monetary policy brought about by international monetary reform. IMF officials were concerned that the IMF would be excluded from the international monetary reform. It was Triffin's Dilemma that offered a solution to the problem of international monetary reform, which included three complicated problems and the conflicting interests of member countries and the IMF.[4]

---

[3]At the Bellagio Group conferences in 1964, the reform of international monetary system was sorted mainly into the problems of payments adjustment, liquidity and confidence (Machlup 1964; Bordo 1993, p. 50). At these conferences, 32 economists participated, who were most influential at that time. However, the issue of the relationship between economic development and the supply of international liquidity was avoided from a political point of view (Wilki 2012, p. 30).

[4]Maxwell Stamp proposed the plan that securities exchangeable with convertible currencies the IMF held would be issued and such securities would be allocated to central banks (de Vries 1976,

Already in 1947, Robert Triffin had warned of the vulnerability of the Bretton Woods international monetary system. According to him, the main cause of the instability of the postwar international monetary system was the shortage of gold reserves. On one hand, the decreasing real price of gold had reduced gold production since the end of World War II. On the other hand, the decline in the real price of gold had increased gold demand. Consequently, the relative decrease of the gold supply should be filled by increasing foreign exchange of both the pound sterling and the dollar. However, as the outstanding balance of pound sterling had not increased, the shortage of international liquidity had to be filled by increasing the supply of dollars through the U.S. current account deficit.

Based on this understanding, he argued that as long as the supply of international liquidity necessary to the development of the world economy depended on U.S. current account deficit, the confidence problem of the dollar would necessarily occur. On the contrary, the resolution of the confidence problem of the dollar by reducing the U.S. current account deficit would give rise to a shortage of international liquidity. As long as the supply of international liquidity was based on the U.S. current account deficit, the confidence problem of the dollar and the shortage of international liquidity would present a trade-off that could not be resolved.

The plan for international monetary reform that was proposed by Triffin was to create a new source of international liquidity like the Bancor, which Keynes had previously proposed at the Bretton Woods Conference. According to his plan, the confidence problem of the dollar could be resolved by absorbing the surplus liquidity of each country in exchange for a new reserve. Furthermore, if a new reserve would be lent to the deficit countries, the supply of international liquidity could increase with the growth of world trade and the world economy.[5]

Triffin's plan could not only resolve the problem of international liquidity but also make it possible to disconnect the problem of the balance of payments adjustment from the confidence problem of the dollar by the creation of liquidity that would not be in any national currency. In addition to these benefits, transforming the problem of international monetary reform into a problem of new liquidity creation gave the U.S. government more time to improve its balance of payments. Therefore, Triffin's theory won the support of not only academia but also policy makers, including the U.S. Treasury, the financial authorities of many countries, and IMF officials (Wilki 2012, p. 16).[6]

---

p. 19). Stamp's plan was the first proposal that linked the creation of reserves with development finance for developing countries (Williamson 1973, p. 716).

[5] Under conditions in which the foreign exchange activities of private commercial banks are the major suppliers of international liquidity, the vision of Triffin would not be realized unless the world's central banks could put private foreign exchange banks under its umbrella. Triffin tried to find the optimal international liquidity by using the ratio of international liquidity reserves to imports (Williamson 1973, pp. 688–689). In this regard, his reform proposals had a problem when the ratio of international liquidity reserves to imports was decreasing as the international capital movements became increasingly active.

[6] In particular, the US Treasury under the Kennedy administration supported Triffin's theory (Odell 1982, p. 130). The Influence of Triffin theory to the US policy makers can be confirmed in the other literatures (Bergsten 1975, p. 210; Gowa 1983, p. 43; Nau 1990, p. 138).

At that time, the revaluation of the gold price for official transactions and the devaluation of the dollar vs. other currencies had been considered an important means to solve the current situation of the international monetary system. However, there were fears that the rise of the gold price and the devaluation of the dollar would bring about significant pressure on the currencies of all member countries of the IMF. Therefore, many member countries opposed the rise of the gold price and the devaluation of the dollar. On the other hand, the United States, other member countries and the IMF opposed adopting a floating exchange rate system.

There were conflicts of interests between the United States and Western European countries, non-G10 countries, and the IMF. Under these conflicts of interest, the matter of international monetary reform had resolved into three problems, namely, the international liquidity problem, the dollar confidence problem and the problem of balance of payments adjustment. Moreover, then, the problem of international liquidity becomes the center of international monetary reform. Further, the problem of international liquidity had been transformed into the issue of creation of reserves. Finally, the creation of reserves gradually converged on the establishment of SDRs (Wilki 2012, p. 18).[7]

The establishment of SDRs was favorable not only for member countries but also for the IMF. For the United States, it provided more time to adjust its balance of payments as well as to relieve the dollar confidence problem. For Western European countries, it made it possible to avoid the responsibility of surplus countries and currency reevaluations. On the other hand, it might provide to Western European countries the means to correct the asymmetry of the Bretton Woods system. For the developing countries, the establishment of SDRs might bring the possibility of expanding the supply of international liquidity, which would be essential to their development. For the IMF, the establishment of SDRs had the benefit of expanding the business areas of the IMF as long as the reserves would be created as an extension of Drawing Rights.

The Executive Board in the 1960s was only a multilateral international financial forum at that time. At the same time, the Executive Board was also a decision-making body on policy for the international monetary system in the 1960s. Before examining the minutes of the Executive Board, the role and the personnel composition of the Executive Board have to be confirmed.

The Executive Board was composed of 20 Executive Directors in total, namely five appointed Executive Directors and 15 elected Executive Directors, in the period during which the international liquidity problems had been discussed. The five appointed Executive Directors were appointed from the five largest fund countries. The 15 elected Executive Directors were elected from the 15 electoral districts classified by the weighted voting of member countries. The electoral districts had not been specified in the Articles of Agreement of the IMF. The electoral districts were mostly classified according to regions but not always so. As a result, in addition to

[7] Strange criticized the creation of SDR as the product of compromise putting off the essential problems such as the adjustment problem of balance of payments, and the roles of gold and dollar (Strange 1976, p. 258).

five appointed Executive Directors (U.S., U.K., West Germany, France, and India), five Executive Directors were elected from the ten main industrialized countries. On the other hand, the Executive Directors of developing countries consisted of an appointed Executive Director (India) and nine elected Executive Directors.

The governance structure of the IMF consisted of the Annual Meeting, the Board of Governors, the Executive Board, and the Managing Director and the IMF Secretariat. The Annual Meeting was held once a year in the fall, jointly with the World Bank.

The Board of Governors was the highest decision-making body and was composed of two representatives of the member countries, namely, the finance ministers and central bank governors. The Board of Governors was held once a year. The voting rights of the Board of Governors were given in accordance with the ratio of fund contribution (quota) to the IMF.

The Executive board was the executive agency for the ordinary course of business of the IMF. The resolutions discussed at the Board of Governors were first subjected to deliberation by the Executive Board and were then sent to the Board of Governors to resolve.

The Managing Director served as the representative of the IMF and the chairman of the Executive Board. He also controlled the IMF Secretariat. The Managing Director played a decisive role as the chairman of the Executive Board and as the coordinator of interests between Executive Directors.

The voting at the Executive Board meeting adopted the weighted voting system. However, most decisions in the Executive Board were usually made unanimously. As a result, most discussions at the Executive Board meeting had been carried out thoroughly until some agreement had been obtained. In the 1960s, the Executive Board had functioned as a global forum and a world discussion and decision-making body for the international monetary system. Therefore, the Managing Director (who was the chairman and the coordinator of the Executive Board) had great influence on policy making for the international monetary system in the 1960s.

3 The International Liquidity Problem in the Minutes of the Executive Board

3.1 The G10 Plan of Reserve Creation Had the Following Characteristics

1. The G10 plan was a so-called "dual approach." Firstly, reserves would be created and allocated only to a limited group of about 15 countries. Then, these countries would make resources such as credit lines available to the IMF in accordance with their allocated amounts of the reserves. On the basis of these resources, the IMF would establish a new facility or enlarge drawing rights to finance the other member countries. As a result, all member countries would be supplied reserves.

2. As for the decision-making on the creation of reserves, the G10 had proposed a two-tier method of decision-making. The timing and the amount of reserve creation would first be determined by a limited group of countries that had the ability to take responsibility for the management of reserves. After that, the IMF would make the final decision.

The G10 countries claimed that the role of creating reserves should be left to the main industrialized countries that would have the responsibility and capacity to support the creation of reserves. In opposition to the G10, the Executive Directors argued that the creation of reserves would affect not only the G10 countries but also all member countries and that managing international liquidity was the IMF's most important role.

The discussions about the problem of international liquidity at the Executive Board meetings can be divided into three phases.

The first phase was from the Executive Board meeting on 23rd September 1963 until the Executive Board meeting on 11th May 1966. In this phase, the Executive Board had been negotiating with the G10 on how to proceed with the creation of reserves. The second phase was from the Executive Board meeting on 12th May 1966 until the Executive Board meeting on 7th September 1967. In this phase, the G10 was forced to make some concessions on the procedures for decision-making on the creation of reserves at the request of the Executive Board. The third phase was from the Executive Board meeting on 6th December 1967 to the Executive Board meeting on 16th August 1971. The previous day, on 15th August 1971, U.S. President Nixon had announced the suspension of dollar-gold conversion. In this phase, amendments to the Articles of Agreement had been completed at the Executive Board meeting on 22nd April 1968.

3.2 Phase 1: The Executive Board and the Creation of Reserves

In response to the sudden death of the ex-Managing Director Per Jacobson, Pierre-Paul Schweitzer was appointed as the Managing Director on 1st September 1963.

With the change of the Managing Director, the problem of international liquidity began to be actively discussed by the Executive Directors.[8] In a meeting on 23rd September, the Managing Director arranged the discussion of a proposal to issue a statement about the problem of international liquidity. He thought to use the

[8]At the Annual Meeting of the previous year, the draft for expanding the functionality of the IMF proposed by the former Managing Director Jacobson has been approved. In spite of it, Schweitzer felt a sense of danger that the IMF might be excluded from the issue of international monetary reform. Therefore, 18 days was after being appointed the Managing Director, he remarked that there was a problem in how to proceed with the international liquidity problem (Wilki 2012, p. 21). Schweitzer was very popular in the IMF and won the support of the developing countries in particular. This helped to adjust the relationship between the IMF and the United States (*ibid.*, p. 63).

opportunity for a meeting of the G10, which would discuss the problem of international liquidity during its Annual Meeting.

The Managing Director welcomed the discussion about the problem of international liquidity in an institution outside of the IMF. On the contrary, despite agreeing to the proposal of the Managing Director, Executive Director Ahmed Zaki Saad (United Arab Republic) asserted the need for the leadership and the initiative of the IMF, since the problem of international liquidity was related to the interests of all member countries.[9] Also, Executive Director J. J. Anjaria (India) added that developing countries were seeking an increase in international liquidity.

The G10 held a meeting just before the Annual Meeting. At the meeting, the G10 decided to launch the Meeting of the Deputies of the Group of Ten (the Deputies). The Deputies were established to examine the long-term problems of the international monetary system on the condition that the fixed exchange rate system and the official price of gold would not be changed.

The United States held the position that there were not any international liquidity problems (Horsefield 1969, p. 541). In addition, since agreeing to the London gold pool and establishing the General Arrangements to Borrow (the GAB) in 1961, the United Kingdom and the United States had lost the initiative in the G10 (Weatherford 1988, p. 613). Rather, Western European countries, especially West Germany, had led the discussion of international monetary reform in the G10.

At the Annual Meeting in 1963, the Managing Director reported that the IMF would conduct research on international liquidity over the next year.[10] The problem of international liquidity was taken up by the Executive Board meeting on 16th October, promptly after the end of the Annual Meeting. Executive Director Karl Skjaevelan (Norway) pointed out that the problem of international liquidity had not been mentioned in any reports. He suggested that any reform plan should be proposed at the next Annual Meeting.[11] He also criticized the remark by the U. S. Treasury Secretary C. Douglas Dillon at a press conference during the Annual Meeting as disuniting the IMF. At a press conference, Secretary Dillon had said that the work of the IMF should be to protect the interests of the 92 countries other than the G10.

In 1964, short-term capital outflows from the United States showed a tendency to increase. During this time, short-term capital movements had increased as dollar-denominated bank deposits in place of bank acceptance and loans. In contrast to the United States, West Germany adopted a variety of measures to prevent capital outflows and inflows in the spring of 1964. Thereby, West Germany was able to return its current account to a balanced state.

In the meeting on 8th January, the Managing Director reported on the discussions of the meeting of the G10 in December of the previous year. After his report, he emphasized his assertion that the problem of international liquidity should be considered from the viewpoint of the IMF as well as the G10 at the meeting of the

[9] IMF EBM/63/56, September 23, 1963, pp. 14–16.

[10] IMF 1963, p. 29.

[11] IMF EBM/63/58, October 16, 1963, p. 1.

G10.[12] On the other hand, at the Executive Board meeting on 10th January, the Managing Director said that the views on the problem of international liquidity did not converge among member countries.[13]

At the Executive Board meeting on 22nd April, the discussions at the meeting of the Deputies in April 1964 were reported on as the fifth agenda item, by Jacques J. Polak (Director General, Research and Statistics of the IBM). At the same meeting, the current state of the balance of payments was discussed as the sixth item on the agenda.

Executive Director Jean de Largentaye (France) emphasized that the structural changes in international financial markets, such as the integration of foreign exchange markets, should be taken into consideration in examining the balance of payments problem. Executive Director Ulrich Beelitz (West Germany) said that the current account of West Germany was influenced mainly by the capital movements. Executive Director J.M. Garland (Australia) and others agreed with his view. Executive Director van der Valk (Netherlands, alternate) claimed that the study of capital movement should be strengthened. On the other hand, Luis Escobar (Chile) and other Executive Directors of developing countries were concerned that the enforcement of U.S. deficit reduction measures would reduce the growth rate in Latin America.[14]

The outcome of this meeting and other informal meetings of the Deputies held from the end of 1963 to early 1964 led to the submission of a report to the G10 in June 1964. Regarding the discussions at the meeting of the G10, the Managing Director reported informally to the Executive Board on 17th June 1964.[15]

After the Annual Meeting, the G10 announced a statement in October 1964. A summary of the subjects of the statement is as follows (Group of Ten 1964, p. 8). (1) The Maintenance of a fixed exchange system and the official price of gold. (2) The importance of international cooperation between the monetary authorities of main industrialized countries. (3) The establishment of a Committee chaired by the Italian Minister of Finance Rinaldo Ossola, namely the "Research Group on Reserve Assets Creation," to consider various proposals for new reserve assets. (4) A request to the third Working Group of OECD Economic Policy Committee to research balance-of-payments adjustments. (5) The establishment of a multilateral joint discussion committee to examine the means to mitigate the balance-of-payments imbalances in the OECD. (6) Re-examination of the quotas of the IMF. (7) Instructing the Deputies to update the GAB.

With regard to the increasing need of reserves due to the imbalance of world payments, the IMF also identified measures to increase reserves in its Annual Report. These measures included increasing quotas, enlarging credit tranches, easing conditions of drawing and investment deposit accounts.[16]

[12] IMF EBM/64/1, January 8, 1964.

[13] IMF EBM/64/2, January 10, 1964, p. 19.

[14] IMF EBM/64/22, April 22, 1964, pp. 17–18.

[15] IMF EBM/64/32, June 17, 1964, p. 35.

[16] IMF 1964a, pp. 30–39.

The G10 and the IMF had prepared for the creation of reserves. On the other hand, the view that priority should be given to the problem of balance of payments adjustments was still strong in the G10, especially in Western European countries. Therefore, Deutsche Bundesbank manager Otmar Eminger was appointed to the chairman of the Deputies in place of U.S. Treasury Undersecretary Robert Vincent Roosa.[17]

Since short-term capital had shifted to outflows from the U.K. in the second half of 1964, the ninth pound sterling crisis after World War II broke out in November of the same year. In the United States, under the record-breaking surplus of the trade balance, the deficit of the capital account increased, since capital outflows from the U.S. did not stop. For this reason, in February 1965, the U.S. government announced self-regulation concerning foreign loans by U.S. banks and investments by U.S. corporations as dollar defensive measures.

Primary commodity-exporting countries experienced exacerbated difficulties in raising foreign funds due to the U.S. policy of dollar defense. Amid such circumstances, a conflict of views in the Executive Board became apparent. While some Executive Directors supported the G10 plan, other Executive Directors criticized it.

At the Executive Board meeting on 6 January 1965, Executive Director A.F.W. Plumptre (Canada) pointed out that Latin American countries had requested a long-term increase of the international liquidity, unlike Western European countries and the United States.[18] Furthermore, in the meeting on 19 February 1965, where the Annual Report was discussed, Executive Director Ulrich Beelitz (West Germany) and Executive Director Rene Larre (France) asserted that it would be too early to publish the view of the IMF concerning the problem of international liquidity in the Annual Report.[19] Against their assertions, Executive Director J.M. Garland (Australia) and Executive Director J. J. Anjaria (India) argued that the IMF should express their position on the problem of international liquidity.

The Executive Directors representing the developing countries often had meetings with the Indian Executive Director, who was the only appointed Executive Director of the developing countries (Reserve Bank of India 2005, p. 578). Therefore, on behalf of the developing countries, the Indian Executive Director would have to make a positive utterance about the creation of reserves.

Discussion on the international capital movements became active in the Executive Board meetings on 12th March and 10th May. In the meeting on 10th March, Executive Director William B. Dale (U.S.) remarked that there were huge private capital outflows from the United States, while the U.S. current account had improved. In response to this remark, Executive Director Sergio Siglienti (Italy) argued that the main causes of U.S. deficits against EEC countries were the export of private capital and the financing of private capital exports.[20]

[17] At the Annual Meeting, the Managing Director warned of a conflict between governors of developing countries and governors of the G10 (IMF 1964b, p. 200).

[18] IMF EBM/65/1. January 6, 1965.

[19] IMF EBM/65/9, February 19, 1965, pp. 6–11.

[20] IMF EBM/65/12, March 10, 1965, pp. 7–12.

Executive Director Beelitz (West Germany) also argued that capital inflows from the United States and the United Kingdom were the primary cause of the current account surpluses and the increasing foreign exchange reserves in Western European countries. According to him, the imbalance of the balance of payments between Western European countries and the United States was caused by international capital movements rather than the international trade between the two areas.

At the Executive Board meeting on 12th May, consultation about the U.K. was on the agenda. The Executive Director J. M. Stevens (U.K.) reported on the U.K.'s current situation. After that, Executive Director Larre (France) argued that as the process of relief for the pound sterling crisis at this time made clear the limits of the IMF's ability to deal with such a crisis. He also emphasized that it would be necessary to cooperate internationally, criticizing the reluctant attitude of the United States toward international cooperation.[21]

However, Executive Director Enrique Tejera-Paris (Venezuela) said that the problem in this pound sterling crisis had not been the limit of the financial resources of the IMF. He added that it was a problem that the activation of the GAB had been determined only by some member countries although the pound sterling crisis had affected all member countries. Executive Director A.K. Ghosh (India, alternate) also insisted that the currency crisis could not be solved by only the main industrialized countries and that it was necessary to enhance the IMF's capacity to supply international liquidity. The necessity of reserve creation had come to be recognized even among the Executive Directors. Moreover, some IMF officials had thought that new reserves should be created as an artificial international currency and this could promote the management of international liquidity (Polak 1967, p. 280).

3.3 *Phase 2: Opposition of the Executive Board and Concessions of the G10*

The Ossola Committee submitted a report to the G10 in May 1965 through several meetings held since October 1964. The report primarily compared the three plans, namely, (1) various CRU plans centered on the French plan, (2) the plan of reserve asset creation with the IMF, and (3) the plan to provide alternative currency assets to countries with international reserve currencies.[22]

Support for the plans to create reserves diverged among the G10 countries. At this time, the United States had turned to support the plan to create reserves with the

[21] IMF EBM/65/25, May 12, 1965, pp. 24, 32–34.

[22] France's plan was a kind of composite reserve unit (CRU). In the plan, participating countries would receive the CRU in return for their currencies to contribute according to gold holdings, and the gold and the CRU would circulate in a fixed ratio. Mr. Ossola had early asked the IMF to examine a plan for a new international reserve. The third alternative plan included the Canadian plan to provide the deposit account and the mutual account plan proposed by British Chancellor of the Exchequer Reginald Molding (de Vries 1976, pp. 52, 59–60).

IMF, although not rejecting other plans within the G10. This view was supported by the U.S. government: one of the reasons being that the plan would not create any alternative to the dollar as the international currency and would also mitigate the pressures on the dollar (Wilki 2012, p. 125).

On 10th July, the U.S. Treasury Secretary Henry Fowler of the Johnson Administration proposed to hold an international conference toward the creation of reserves at the Virginia Bar Association (Odell 1982, p. 79). This statement suggested that the U.S. government had turned toward a direction that would actively involve the reform of the international monetary system, including the reform of international liquidity. Also, the U.S. Congress opened public hearings on holding such an international conference.

Aiming to propose his plan at the Annual Meeting in September 1965, Secretary Fowler visited Western European countries but did not observe the agreement of opinion. At the Annual Meeting, the Managing Director emphasized again that it was the task of the IMF to solve the problem of international liquidity. At the same time, he insisted that a comprehensive approach should be taken considering the views of all member countries regarding their reserve needs.[23] Despite some Governors of the IMF supporting the Managing Director, many Governors took the position that it was premature to create reserves.

At the Executive Board meeting on 10th November, the meetings of the Deputies in November were taken up. Mr. Polak (the Director of the Research and Statistics Department) summed up the details discussed at the meeting as follows.[24]

(1) Much attention of country delegations was paid to the question of the need for reserves. (2) Many countries shared the view that reserve creation could not be expected to do much to influence short-term economic conditions in the world and would have to be guided primarily by the secular trend in the need for reserves, with short-term adjustments taken care of by variable use of credit facilities. (3) Many countries expressed the view that the responsibility for such reserve creation should rest principally on a limited group of countries, but not necessarily the G10. (4) All countries were almost certainly in favor of some kind of association of any reserve creation with the IMF, which might range from an arrangement in the IMF to a scheme outside of the IMF but associated with it in some manner to be arranged. (5) There were a wide variety of views as to how wide a group of countries should participate in the distribution of the newly created liquidity, including the suggestion that this participation might be much wider than that of the group of countries that would contribute to the scheme. (6) There seemed to be considerable sympathy for a distribution, among such countries as would be included in any scheme, in proportion to Fund quotas or Fund quotas plus GAB commitments. (7) Most countries did not seem to have a strong preference between the two basic techniques available, automatic drawing rights or an exchange of claims.

[23] IMF 1965, pp. 30–31.

[24] IMF EBM/65/60. November 10, 1965.

At the Executive Board meeting on 22 December, the meeting of the Deputies in December had been discussed. At the meetings, three important questions of policy were discussed. Mr. Polak summed up the discussions at the meeting as follows.[25]

Firstly, any newly created asset would bear a relation to existing reserve assets, especially dollars in countries' reserves. On this subject, two broad views were expressed. One view was that there should be agreement on the future level of dollars in official reserves, particularly in the reserves of the G10 countries. This agreement would strengthen the force of the adjustment mechanism, remove the present instability of the system, and make the total amount of reserves of a determinate magnitude. The other view was that fixing the amount of dollars in reserves would make the whole system insufficiently flexible and that any excess of dollars that might at some time arise could be dealt with ad hoc as part of the process of multilateral surveillance. Secondly, the suggestion that the process of decision-making should be taken in two steps found considerable support. The first step should be a proposal by the Managing Director. Then, as a second step, member countries would vote for the proposal. Thirdly, there was some discussion on a parallel operation for other countries if reserve creation was limited to a small group. Specific suggestions made included the possibility that other countries would receive additional drawing rights in the IMF, automatic or conditional, or that the limited group would make resources available to the IMF. However, the need for parallel operations would not arise if the reserve creation was handled across-the-board in the IMF, with a degree of conditionality applied determined by each country's position in the IMF. In this meeting of the Deputies, signs of the plan later called the two-tier approach emerged.

As overseas long-term investments had been increasing through 1965–1966, the United States and the United Kingdom had strengthened their controls of capital exports. While the role of the Euro-dollar Market had enlarged as a short-term funding market, funding for direct investments had been raised in the securities markets of Western European countries. As a result, even in France and Italy reforms had been carried out to the securities markets and company law. On the other hand, the net capital exports of the main industrialized countries to developing countries had only slightly increased year-on-year, because of shrinkage of official aid from the United States and the United Kingdom.

These changes in the international financial markets were immediately reflected at the Executive Board meeting on 22nd December, where the staff report on the 1965 Article VIII consultations with the United States was discussed. While Executive Director Stevens (U.K.) supported the U.S. capital controls, against his support Executive Director Pieter Lieftinck (Netherlands) noted that a great improvement in the U.S. balance of payments had come from private short-term capital. He argued that the reduction of the U.S. current account deficit was mainly due to short-term private capital surpluses and a considerable decline in U.S. gold holdings in 1965.[26] Executive Director Larre (France) also pointed out that the

[25] IMF EMB/65/66, pp. 3–4.

[26] IMF EBM/65/66, December 22, 1965, pp. 23–24.

improvement in the U.S. current account would be temporary and not of a continuing character.[27] Conversely, Executive Director Mauricio Bicalho (Brazil) said that direct capital controls, even "voluntary" ones, might have some usefulness if properly applied and for a relatively short period.[28]

At this Executive Board meeting, the Executive Directors of developing countries emphasized that U.S. defensive policies for the balance of payments had a serious impact on developing countries. Executive Director Jorge Gonzalez del Valle (Guatemala) said that the Latin American countries had been suffering from the voluntary regulation and that they had welcomed the decision of U.S. authorities to exempt from the limitations imposed by the voluntary foreign credit restraint program those financial operations with developing countries.[29] Executive Director Beue Tann (China) also argued that the export of capital to the developing countries should be promoted to avoid pressure on those developing countries and that industrialized countries with a payment surplus should endeavor to increase their capital flows to less developed nations to the greatest extent possible.[30]

In 1966, the creation of reserves was actively discussed. On the other hand, the opposition of the Executive Directors to the G10 plan became stronger. The original plan of the G10 for the creation of reserves was called the dual approach. The dual approach involved two issues that the Executive Board could not overlook. Firstly, the G10 had initially considered the two-tier system of the decision-making procedure. The amount and timing of reserve creation would first be determined by a limited group of countries (15 countries or so) responsible for the management of reserves and then the final decision would be made by the IMF. Secondly, the distribution of reserves was considered in two stages, or in a dual way.[31] The created reserves would be allocated to the limited group of countries, and then these countries would set credit lines to the IMF in their local currencies in accordance with their allocated amounts of reserves. Finally, on the basis of these credit lines, the IMF would provide lines of credit to member countries other than the limited group.

The opposition to the G10 plan by the Executive Directors, in particularly by the directors of developing countries, was revealed at the Executive meeting on 4th February, which discussed the meeting of the Deputies in January-February 1966.[32]

L. P. Salle (the European Office Director of the IMF) pointed out the following six points that the G10 had agreed on. (1) The new reserves would be created by, and under the responsibility of, a limited group of countries, which would undertake the financial obligations for the assets created. (2) The limited group would not be closed but would accept new members if they met a certain number of qualitative tests and if they had sufficient financial importance at the same time. (3) The distribution

[27] IMF EBM/65/66, December 22, 1965, p. 28.

[28] IMF EBM/65/67, p. 7.

[29] IMF EBM/65/67, p. 9.

[30] *ibid.*, p. 10.

[31] The G10's plan took over Edward Bernstein's CRU plan. However, the decision-making problem that was lost in the CRU plan was introduced following the GAB by Roosa (de Vries 1976, p. 56).

[32] IMF EBM/66/7, February 4, 1966, pp. 3–4, 4–5, 8–10.

of the financial obligations and the allocation of reserves among members of the group would be based on the IMF quota, the quota plus GAB commitments, or similar criteria. (4) The amount of reserves to be created should be based on the basic trend in total reserves, and not on short-term considerations. (5) All of these plans had a common feature in that there should be a so-called "dual approach," which meant that special facilities should be provided to take care of the needs of countries outside the limited group. (6) Close cooperation would be maintained between the limited group and the IMF.

Mr. Salle also pointed out the following seven points the G10 had not agreed on. (1) Although there was a consensus for the dual approach in all the plans, the details of their application were different. (2) The institutional relationship between the new scheme and the IMF were not very clearly explained in all plans. (3) There were differences of emphasis on the desirability and necessity of parallel decisions by the Executive Board. (4) Several members of the Deputies supported the creation of reserves as units while others felt that the form of drawing rights would have the advantage of being already in use. (5) There were differences on whether or not the obligation to accept the new units in payment was limited. (6) Rules against the destruction of liquidity were provided for in some cases, but not in others. (7) The scheme of creating reserves would be agreed upon as a contingency plan. In other words, it would only be put into operation when a certain number of conditions were realized.

Mr. Salle added that although no attempts were made to reconcile these differences of views, some G10 members supported the view that the allocation of reserves should be done in a comprehensive and unconditional manner. He also mentioned that he had stressed as the representative of the Managing Director that the IMF should be the center of reserves.

Executive Directors Amon Nikoi (Ghana), Anjaria (India), and Saad (United Arab Emirates) had expressed their support for the statement of Mr. Salle. Executive Director Saad also argued that it was important that the IMF had the business of creating reserves in order to maintain the unity of the IMF. Finally, Executive Director Paul L. Faber (Guinea) pointed out that there was an impression that the G10 had fixed its views about international liquidity needs by accepting the request of the developing countries.

At the Executive Board meeting on 11th March, Mr. Pollack (the Director of the Research and Statistics Department of the IMF) reported to the Executive Directors on the meeting of the Deputies held in March 1966. He said that the Deputies had for the first time devoted considerable attention to improvements in the international monetary system, as distinguished from mechanisms to add to reserves. According to him, two improvements in particular were discussed, namely, the harmonizing of reserve ratios and strengthening of the reserve character of the gold tranche position in the IMF. However, there was no discussion of these at this Executive Board meeting.

At the Executive Board meeting on 29th April, the meeting of the Deputies in April was discussed. According to Mr. Polak's statement, the Deputies discussed the following three major issues:

1. Contingency Planning

   The G10 assumed that reserves were adequate at the present time but that they would become inadequate at some time in the future unless new reserve assets were created. Therefore, the creation of reserves was seen as contingency planning for the time when it would be necessary to create new reserves.
2. The Role of the Limited Group

   The major decisions on the timing and the amounts of reserve creation should be borne by a limited group consisting of countries with primary responsibility for the functioning of the international monetary system and for the assets that would back any reserve creation.
3. Arrangements to Take Care of the Reserve Needs of all Countries

   The G10 accepted that any scheme for reserve creation must meet the global reserve needs of all countries but that the reserve needs of other countries other than the limited group should be met by equivalent reserve assets in equivalent amounts.

Mr. Polak added that, different from before, the consensus to consider the reserve needs of all member countries was born for the first time at the meeting of the Deputies. He also provided additional information about the G10's dual approach.[33] He said that the creation of reserves under the dual approach would substantially have the same effect on the limited group of countries and other member countries, since a new financing facility would be established for other member countries separate from the creation of reserves. The Executive Directors strongly dissented from the dual approach.

Executive Director Escobar (Chile) claimed that many member countries would not accept leaving major decisions to the limited group of countries in order to give the impression that the IMF would be dependent on some group. Executive Director Ghosh (India) also opposed the G10's dual approach. He argued that even if the Articles of Agreement had given the main industrialized countries preference in decision-making, it did not mean that other member countries were excluded from making decisions.

The conflict of interests between the interested parties around the creation of reserves became clear.[34] The G10 countries wanted to take the initiative in the creation of reserves. The non-G10 countries, especially the developing countries, and the IMF officials were concerned with the G10's dual approach because that approach might exclude them from the major decisions to create reserves. In particular, the developing countries thought that the dual approach would separate the creation of reserves from development finance, but they wanted to connect the creation of reserves to development finance. The developing countries tried to accomplish their aim by both criticizing and supporting the IMF officials through discussions at the Executive Board meetings.

---

[33] IMF EBM/66/28, April 29, 1966, p. 5.

[34] The Expert Group of UNCTAD announced in October 1965 a report that International Monetary reform should reflect the views of developing countries. For this report, Latin American countries expressed support, and the G31 warned that they would oppose a plan that would not include the comprehensiveness principle (Wilki 2012, p. 43).

While there was a conflict of interests between G10 countries, that between the non-G10 countries and the IMF Secretariat was deepening. The statement of the Managing Director during his visit to Western Europe had been a subject to be discussed by the Executive Board on 11th May. In his statement, the Managing Director strongly criticized the dual approach as something that disrupted the member countries.[35] At the opportunity of this statement, the concessions on the side of the G10 became more evident.

The Executive Board meeting on 27th May discussed the meeting of the Deputies in May. Mr. Polak (the Economic Advisor of the IMF) reported that the proposal to distribute new reserves comprehensively had been greeted favorably for the first time. He also said that in order to examine the impact of creating reserves, the G10 had proposed an alternative plan to establish a Special Advisory Committee consisting of some 20 Governors and alternates at the Annual Meeting in September.[36]

Executive Director Leaftink (Netherlands) welcomed Polak's remark and observed the concessions of the G10 in his remarks. Mr. Polak also expressed his satisfaction as a representative of the IMF with the changing attitude of the G10 on the need for and the allocation of new reserves.[37] However, his satisfaction repelled some Executive Directors.[38]

Executive Director Anjaria (India) firstly questioned whether or not the change of attitude in the G10 meant that the creation of new reserves would be under the control of the IMF. Then, Executive Director Larre (France) expressed his concern that establishing a Special Advisory Committee might eliminate the Executive Board from the major decisions to create new reserves, although he appreciated that the Economic Adviser and the IMF staff had been trying to keep the creation of reserves as part of the business of the IMF. Furthermore, Executive Director Farber (Ghana) pointed out the difficulty of reaching an agreement on the appointment of the members and the voting procedures of the Special Advisory Committee. He also claimed that the Executive Board was the only worthy organization to examine the creation of reserves.

These Executive Directors' remarks made clear the difference between the Executive Directors and the IMF officials. The Executive Directors wanted to clarify the involvement of the Executive Board in the major decision-making on reserve creation. On the other hand, the IMF officials were satisfied with the confirmation of Fund involvement in the creation of reserves.

---

[35] IMF EBM/66/30, May 11, 1966, p. 3.

[36] IMF EBM/66/33, pp. 4–5. Originally, this committee was conceived by the Managing Director and the IMF Secretariat, in order to break the bottleneck of Western Europe countries opposed to the new reserve creation by adding the five governors from Australia, India, Middle East, Africa, and Latin America to the governors of G10 countries (de Vries 1976, p. 67).

[37] IMF EBM/66/33, pp. 5–6. In this period, the IMF staff considered that loan amount might be increased significantly if the new reserve creation would be unconditional on the drawer rights (*ibid.*, pp. 48–49).

[38] IMF EBM/66/33, pp. 7–9.

The concessions of the G10 became more apparent than before at the meeting of the Deputies in June. According to Mr. Polak, who had attended the meeting, the following four points had largely been determined.[39] Firstly, reserves would be created on the basis of the reserve needs of the world rather than the deficits in balances of payments. Secondly, reserves would be distributed to all member countries unconditionally. Thirdly, while the interests of all member countries would be reflected in the major decision-making on creating reserves, the special responsibilities of the main industrialized countries should also be emphasized. Fourthly, reserves would not be created until the additional conditions and the reserve needs were confirmed.

The Meeting of the Deputies in July 1966 reached an agreement with the final report addressed to the meeting of the G10. The final report of the Deputies was reported to the Executive Board on 8th July. According to Mr. Salle, who attended the meeting as a representative of the IMF, there was no significant change in the final report, but the Deputies were concerned about the conflict with the Executive Board. Chairman Emminger of the Deputies sent his letter to the Managing Director concerning the procedure for the creation of reserves. The letter was circulated among Executive Directors and was discussed in informal sessions.[40]

In Hague, Finance Ministers and Central Bank Governors of the G10 had three meetings in the afternoon of 25th July and the morning and afternoon of 26th July. The G10 announced in a communiqué that it considered it best for the creation of reserves to be examined by both the limited group of countries and the IMF.

At the Executive Board meeting on 1st August, Mr. Polak explained the subjects discussed in the meetings of the G10. Following his explanation, Executive Director Saad (United Arab Republic) questioned why they would consult the IMF after making the major decisions on the creation of reserves. Mr. Polak replied that even if the limited group of countries had made a decision, the approval of the IMF was essential to establish a new financing facility for other member countries. Furthermore, Executive Director Saad questioned whether or not the IMF's approval would be required in the creation of reserves. In response to this question, Mr. Polak said that he would refrain from commenting on such procedural questions since no specific plans to create reserves had been decided on yet.[41] Executive Director Anjaria (India) refuted Mr. Polak's statement. He said that although Mr. Polak was right that no plans had yet been decided on, it seemed that there was a specific plan already considering that the responsibilities of some countries had been emphasized in the communiqué.

The procedural question was taken up by the Executive Board meeting again on 7th September.[42] Then, the Managing Director said that the G10 had recommended that the joint meetings of the Executive Board and the Deputies should be used to resolve the conflicts between the Executive Board and the Deputies.

---

[39] IMF EBM/66/45. June 27, 1966.

[40] IMF EBM/66/55.

[41] IMF EBM/66/65, August 1, 1966, pp. 8–9.

[42] IMF EBM/66/74.

The procedure to create reserves was also discussed by the Executive Board meeting on 16th September. However, the Managing Director said that he would forgo the submission of a resolution at the Annual Meeting. In response to the Managing Director's remark, Executive Director Dale (U.S.) said that the United States could no longer come to a conclusion.[43] The procedure to create reserves was discussed by the Executive Board meeting on 19th September again. Executive Director Saad argued that it would be unrealistic and unacceptable to grant special responsibilities to the limited group of countries referred to in the communiqué that would put the developing countries in a subordinate position.[44]

At the Executive Board meeting on 19th October, the subject of the Joint Meetings was on the agenda. The Managing Director said that he had consulted with Chairman Emminger of the Deputies about the procedural problem and that the Deputies had proposed a co-chair of the Joint Meetings.[45]

From the first meeting in November 1966 until the fourth meeting in June 1967, Joint Meetings were held four times. In the meantime, the practical issues involved in the creation of reserves had been studied by the IMF staff and the Deputies. The first meeting and the second meeting in January 1967 made significant contributions to achieving a convergence of opinions. In the joint meetings, the concessions of the G10 also became clearer. Although the IMF staff had made a great contribution to putting into practical shape the plan to create reserves[46] and the United States had consented to making the concessions to the G10 in the Executive Board, making the concessions to the G10 was greatly affected by the dissenting opinions on the Executive Board.[47]

The Executive Board started the discussions of the Resolution of the Board of Governors on the Special Drawing Rights, which had been negotiated informally with the meeting of the Deputies, at the Executive Board meeting on 6th September 1967. At this meeting, (1) the final draft of the Special Drawing Rights, (2) the economic advisor's report about the G10 meeting, and (3) the draft Resolution proposed by Executive Director Dale had been discussed.

[43] IMF EBM/66/79, September 7, 1966, p. 3.

[44] IMF EBM/66/80, September 19, 1966, p. 4.

[45] IMF EBM/66/84, October 19, 1966, p. 18. The Executive Board had informal meetings about the joint meetings and discussed various issues such as the purpose and the form of reserve creation (de Vries 1976, pp. 106–119). During this period, nine directors of developing countries had informal meetings called the G7 and tried to reconcile their opinions (*ibid.*, p. 7).

[46] It was a necessary condition of the G10 concessions that the United States shift to supporting the IMF plan. Traditionally, foreign monetary policy of the United States has been done on an ad hoc basis due to confrontations within the government. But, both president Kennedy and President Johnson expected SDRs to maintain the official price of gold (Wilki 2012, p. 145). In addition, the US Treasury, which had wanted to avoid balance of payments adjustments, supported the SDRs, as did the Federal Reserve Bank of New York, which had seen the role of SDRs in limited admitted SDR creation (*ibid.*, pp. 122–123).

[47] If the G10 plan would be forced to be implemented, there was a concern that the developing countries would create a regional settlement mechanism (de Vries 1976, p. 58). The Managing Director had thought that the new reserve currency would be difficult to creation without the agreement of the developing countries (*ibid.*, p. 67).

Executive Director Nadeem Mansour (Egypt) said that he could not agree to the outline of a facility based on Special Drawing Rights in the IMF, because of the requirement in the outline for an 85 % majority of the voting power of participants. He added, in proposing 80 % instead of 85 %, that the required majority for execution should not be tied to specific membership of a group exercising veto powers unrelated to quotas, since all the members had recognized the principle that the liquidity of the international payments system was an international problem and that its solution concerned the membership as a whole. However, he finally abstained, and the outline was approved by the Executive Board.[48] On the other hand, Executive Director Paul Mentre de Loye (France) opposed Executive Director Dale's proposal for the end of February 1968 to be the deadline for submission of the Amendment of the Articles of Agreement.

At the Executive Board meeting on the following 7th September, in the morning the draft of Resolution was modified to avoid a clarification of the terminal date.[49] However, at the Executive Board meeting in the afternoon, "March 31, 1968" was inserted in the draft and deliberation was settled.[50]

At the Annual Meeting in September 1967, the problem of international liquidity, which had been discussed for 4 years, was settled with the establishment of the Special Drawing Rights. Setting the time limit to March 1968, it was decided to proceed with the work on amending the Articles of Agreement and the By-Laws. Thus, the creation and the allocation of new reserves became a part of the business of the IMF.

3.4 Phase 3: The Amendment of the Articles of Agreement and the Suspension of the Convertibility of the Dollar

Starting on the 1st of December 1967, the Executive Board began discussions to amend the Articles of Agreement and the By-laws accompanying the introduction of Special Drawing Rights. Amending the Articles of Agreement continued up to the Executive Board meeting on 12th February 1968. Starting in the Executive Board meeting on 22nd February, the Executive Board began discussions on the draft of the Amendment of the Articles of Agreement required for the special drawing rights facility and the connected amendments. In March of the same year, a meeting of the G10 was held. At this meeting, the G10 countries other than France reached an agreement.[51] Following this, the discussions on the final draft of the

[48] IMF EBM/67/72. September 6, 1967.

[49] IMF EBM/67/73. September 7, 1967.

[50] IMF EBM/67/74. September 7, 1967.

[51] The conflict was born between the U.S. Congress and the U. S. government. The U.S. Congress rejected the aggressive support for the SDR. On the other hand, the U.S. government supported the SDR. The SDR had the contradictory effects that it was likely to erode the status of the dollar while it might also alleviate the pressures of balance-of-payments adjustments (Wilki 2012, p. 83).

Amendment of the Articles of Agreement were settled from the Executive Board meeting on 16th April through the Executive Board meeting on 24th March. The Executive Board had 74 meetings to review the draft word for word (de Vries 1976, p. 167).

The summary of the SDRs, first published first in 1968, was as follows.

1. When necessary to supplement reserve assets, the SDRs would be distributed to all member countries.
2. One unit of SDRs would be equal to 0.888671 g of pure gold.
3. The SDRs would be distributed according to IMF quotas.
4. If a member country were to draw the SDRs, it would be possible to acquire currency of equal amounts of SDRs from member countries designated by the IMF.
5. The country using the SDRs would bear the restoration obligation. If the average outstanding balance of the SDRs over the immediately preceding 5 years reached at least 30 % of the average cumulative allocations of SDRs for the same period, member countries would have the obligation to use and restore the SDRs in the first basic period.
6. An 85 % majority of the voting power of participants would be required for the activation of SDRs.

The reason to hasten the establishment of SDRs might be because of the rising price of gold and the growing anxiety affecting confidence in the dollar from the end of 1967 to early 1968. The international financial markets, which had remained relatively smooth until the autumn of 1967, were seriously changed by the outbreak of the Middle East War and the closure of the Suez Canal. As speculation against the pound sterling turned out to be excessive, the United Kingdom government was forced to devalue the official exchange rate of the pound sterling on 18th November 1967. Following the United Kingdom, 23 other countries, such as Denmark and Ireland, which had deep trade ties with the United Kingdom, devalued their currencies against the dollar.

After the devaluation of the pound sterling, President Johnson made a statement promising to adhere to the current official price of gold. Despite this, the exchange rate against the dollars was setting a floor for Western European currencies and the market price of gold soared. When the central bank governors joining the London gold pool announced a statement to maintain the price of gold, the speculation on gold subsided for a time. However, speculation on gold intensified again in December. Although this speculation subsided after the statement by the U.S. government, the gold equivalent of about 1 billion dollars had flowed out from the United States.

In January 1968, President Johnson announced defensive measures to strengthen the U.S. dollar, such as the regulation of foreign investments by U.S. financial institutions and corporations. At the same time, he asked Congress to eliminate the

---

However, the American financial community pressured the government in being afraid that the expansion of U.S. financial institutions in the Eurodollar market might deteriorate the international financial stability as well as increase the role of the dollar (*ibid.*, p. 64).

Gold Reserve Requirements. The Federal Reserve Board also repurchased dollar-denominated debt through currency swap arrangements between central banks. The market price of gold, which had been calmed temporarily by such measures, suffered speculation again in March.

The United States raised the discount rate in March 1968. At the same time, the U.S. Congress passed the Gold Reserves Elimination Act. In addition, on the 15th the United States has requested the closing of the London Gold Market. On 17th March, the United States invited seven central bank governors joining the London gold pool to Washington, D.C. Together, these seven central bank governors and the United States announced the closure of the London gold pool and the introduction of the two-tier gold price system.

In response to this sudden turn of events, amendments to the Articles of Agreement were announced in April 1968. This announcement calmed the international financial markets, though only temporarily. This indicated the strength of market participants' demands for international monetary reform. Furthermore, leading figures of the U.S. financial community, such as the Federal Reserve Chairman and the Chairman of First National City Bank, requested fiscal restraint to relieve the pressure against the dollar devaluation. Due to pressure from both domestic and overseas, the U.S. Congress approved the Revenue and Expenditure Control Act, including spending cuts and tax increases, in June 1968.

Deliberations on the amendment of the Articles of Agreement were still underway at the Executive Board meetings on 10th April and 12th April 1968. In these Executive Board meetings, conflict between the non-G10 countries and the G10 countries became apparent over issues such as the countries participating in the SDRs, the value of gold and the gold tranches. However, at the Executive Board meeting on 12th April, final agreement was reached on international liquidity problems, in the form of the establishment of the SDRs.

At the Executive Board meeting on 1st May, the establishment of SDRs and the By-Laws were agreed upon. At the Executive Board meeting on 17th June, every sentence of the report for the Board of Governors, including the first Amendment of the Articles of Agreement and the By-Laws, was approved.[52]

On 15th July, U.S. Treasury Secretary Fowler announced that the United States had become the first country officially approving the SDRs. The U.S. Congress passed the Special Drawing Rights Act and ratified the First Amendment of the Articles of Agreement in the Senate on 11th May and in the House of Representatives on 6th June.

Amid this progress, the May 1968 events occurred in France, and the Franc became subject to speculation on the foreign exchange markets. The French government had introduced exchange controls and, at the same time, raised the discount rate. However, because the outflow of short-term capital had accelerated together with rumors of a revaluation of the Deutsche Mark in November, the French government was forced to introduce defensive measures for the Franc again. At this time, the West German government had been forced virtually to revalue the Deutsche

[52] IMF EBM/68/99, June 17, 1968.

Mark by adjusting the value-added tax on 19th November. In 1969, the revaluation pressure was increasing on the Deutsche Mark. Following the devaluation of the Franc in August, West Germany was forced to revalue the Deutsche mark in September 1969.

While the prices of raw materials including crude oil were rising, other commodity prices were sluggish. This situation gave a blow to the current accounts of developing countries. After an interruption of about a year, the meeting of the Deputies was resumed in June 1969. At this meeting, attended by the Managing Director, problems such as foreign exchange forward transactions by the GAB, SDRs, and the adjustment of the balance of payments were discussed.

At the Executive Board meeting on 12th September, the outline of the first allocation of SDRs had been proposed by the Managing Director. Many Executive Directors highly praised the first allocation of SDRs. However, the Executive Directors of developing countries such as Mr. Mansour (Egypt) requested that the developing countries also utilize SDRs for their economic development.[53]

At the Annual Meeting (Rio de Janeiro) in September 1969, it was decided that SDRs equivalent to 65 billion dollars would be distributed in January 1970 and January 1972.

In 1970, the instability of the international financial markets was gradually reflected in the discussions of the Executive Board. At the Executive Board meeting on 1st May 1970, concerns about the fixed exchange rate system had been expressed by some Executive Directors. In addition, even though the floating exchange rate system was discussed at the Executive Board meeting on 30th November, many Executive Directors rejected introducing a floating exchange rate system.

At the Executive Board meeting on 7th December, Executive Director De Kock (South Africa, alternate) said that it was regretful that the Executive Board meeting had been neglecting the fundamental problems and taking too long to establish the SDRs.[54]

In 1971, although support for introducing the floating exchange rate system increased all around, the Executive Board confirmed once again that it would reject the adoption of a floating exchange rate system.[55] However, the international financial situation had deteriorated beyond expectations. At the Executive Board meeting on 5th May, a countermeasure to the sudden change in the foreign exchange markets was discussed.

At the Executive Board meeting on 19th May, Executive Director Tom de Vries (Netherlands) proposed examination of short-term capital movements.[56] Under these circumstances, on 13th August U.S. President Nixon announced the suspension of the gold-dollar exchange. At the Executive Board meeting on 16th August, Executive Director Dale (U.S.) reported after the fact on the Nixon announcement.

---

[53] IMF EBM/69/86, September 12, 1969, p. 6.

[54] IMF EBM/70/108, December 7, 1970, p. 21. At the Annual Meeting in September 1970, 77 developing countries asked to reconsider the relationship between the development finance and the SDR (Reserve Bank of India 2005, p. 577).

[55] IMF EBM/71/18, March 12, 1971.

[56] IMF EBM/71/43, May 19, 1971, p. 17.

4 Conclusion

The findings from examining the Minutes of the Executive Board and their implications are summarized in the following two points.

1. Examining the minutes of the Executive Board revealed the following three interconnected facts. Firstly, the G10 countries could not unilaterally lead on the problem of the international liquidity. Conversely, the developing countries had succeeded in bringing out some concessions from G10 countries in the decision-making procedures and the allocation of creating reserves. Secondly, supporting the Managing Director and IMF officials through the discussions at the Executive Board meeting, the Executive Directors of developing countries could realize their requests to a certain extent. Thirdly, the Managing Director and the IMF Secretariat could keep the problem of creating reserves as part of their business, leading the discussions in the Executive Board.

   However, the implications of these findings should not be overestimated. It was also in the United States' interests that the problem of international liquidity had finally been settled by the creation of SDRs. From the very beginning, the United States had hoped that the creation of reserves would be realized as the enlargement of drawer rights. However, it is too easy to regard the management of the postwar international monetary system as unilaterally dominated by the United States or as managed through the international cooperation of the main industrialized countries.

   After World War II, the colonial countries became independent and participated in the international monetary system. Therefore, non-G10 countries, including developing countries, have been playing some part in the international monetary system. For the governance of the international monetary system, it was necessary to incorporate those countries in international cooperation. Non-G10 countries had only limited political and economic influence in the international financial community. In order to fill this gap, the role of the IMF as an international financial organization was indispensable. The Managing Director and the IMF Secretariat were able to position the creation of reserves as part of the business of the IMF by using the opposition of the Executive Directors against the G10-led reform plans.
2. It was confirmed that many Executive Directors recognized the significant impact of the international capital movements that had upset the international monetary system in the 1960s. These international capital movements had reflected the international activities of private financial institutions in the main industrialized countries after restoring the convertibility of Western European currencies in the late 1950s. The large scale of capital movements, more than expected, also had to be recognized by the Managing Director as a new problem in the international monetary system (de Vries 1976, p. 66). The disturbance of the international monetary system in the 1960s was closely related to the postwar development of the international monetary and financial system. Under the relatively stable monetary and financial environment after World War II, private financial institutions in major industrialized countries had been expanding their international activities.

Accompanying the re-establishment of the foreign exchange system after the late 1950s, the activities of asset management had been accelerating in the United States and then spread from the United States to other main industrialized countries.

The unregulated Euro-dollar market had supported foreign exchange and fundraising for international securities trading and buoyed international capital movements. The foreign exchange system in the Bretton Woods era had been designed to support world trade but not to manage international capital movements. Therefore, the international activities of financial institutions had produced a variety of system failures in the foreign exchange system in the 1960s.

The foreign exchange trade deriving from international asset management changed the structure of supply and demand in the foreign exchange markets. As a result, the operation of foreign exchange under the Bretton Woods era experienced increasing interference.

The problem of international liquidity in the 1960s was the reappearance of problems that the Bretton Woods Conference should have discussed in 1944. The Articles of Agreement had left two problems unresolved: the conflict that existed between the international activities of financial institutions and the fixed foreign exchange rate system. Firstly, although managing the international activities of private financial institutions was essential to ensure the stability of the fixed exchange rate system, the Agreement of Articles failed to agree on the international control of such economic entities. Secondly, in the Agreement of Articles, the role and authority of the IMF in international monetary governance was not clarified and left unresolved. Since its establishment, the IMF had the vulnerability of an institution that was not designed to provide international financial governance and to be a firm financial resource.[57]

When international capital movements started increasing remarkably, it was indispensable to introduce a floating exchange rate system or to manage the international activities of financial institutions in order to mitigate the disruption of the foreign exchange system. However, in the debates on international monetary reform in the 1960s, monitoring and regulating the international operations of commercial banks and securities firms were not subjects for discussion. Rather, the establishment of SDRs was presented as the major goal of the international monetary reform, partly due to the narrow view of IMF officials.

At that time, the establishment of SDRs was regarded by many policy makers and IMF officials as the revival of Keynes's idea of stabilizing the international monetary system through the creation of artificial international liquidity. However, the large fluctuations of the foreign exchange market could not be controlled, as long as there was only a minimum mechanism to govern the foreign exchange business of commercial banks.

[57] In a report released by the Economic and Social Committee of the International Union (ECOSOC) in 1952, the need to expand the funding resources of the IMF had already been recommended (Wilki 2012, p. 13).

Placing the creation, the allocation and the operation of SDRs under the business of the IMF seemed to strengthen the authority and capability of the IMF in the international monetary system. However, after the announcement of Nixon's statement, the purpose of managing international liquidity considered in the original scheme of the SDRs could barely be realized in the face of the swelling of private credit with the U.S. easy monetary policy and the expansion of the Eurodollar market (Cohen 1970; Machlup 1982). As a result, managing the international activities of private financial institutions emerged, again, as a problem for stabilizing the international monetary system (Triffin 1964; Kessler 1980). The IMF had departed from the main stage of policy formation on these issues. The primary roles of policy formation have been left to the multilateral regulatory and supervisory committees such as the Basel Committee.

Primary Sources

IMF. 1963. Opening address by the Managing Director. *Summary Proceeding of the Eighteenth Annual Meeting of the Board of Governors*, Washington, DC: International Monetary Fund.

IMF. 1964a. *Annual report of the Executive Directors for the first fiscal year ended April 30, 1963*. Washington. DC: International Monetary Fund.

IMF. 1964b. Closing address by the Managing Director. *Summary Proceeding of the Nineteenth Annual Meeting of the Board of Governors*. Washington, DC: International Monetary Fund.

IMF. 1965. Opening address by the Managing Director. *Summary Proceeding of the Twentieth Annual Meeting of the Board of Governors*. Washington, DC: International Monetary Fund.

References

Bergsten, Fred. 1975. *The dilemma of the dollar—The economics and politics of United States international monetary policy*. New York: New York University Press, for Council on Foreign Relations, reprinted by M. E. Sharpe, 1996.

Bordo, Michael D. 1993. The Bretton Woods international monetary system: "A historical overview". In *A retrospective on the Bretton Woods System: Lessons for international monetary reform*, ed. Michael D. Bordo and Eichengreen Barry. Chicago: The University of Chicago Press.

Chwieroth, Jeffrey M. 2010. *Capital ideas: The IMF and the rise of financial liberalization*. Princeton: Princeton University Press.

Cohen, Stephen D. 1970. *International monetary reform 1964–69: The political dimension*. New York: Preager.

Cohen, Benjamin J. 2008. *Global monetary governance*. London: Rutledge.

de Vries, Margaret Garritsen. 1976. *The international monetary system 1966–71, the system under stress, Vol. 1, Narrative; Vol. 2, Documents*. Washington, DC: IMF.

Eichengreen, Barry. 1996. *Globalizing capital*. Princeton: Princeton University Press.

Gowa, Joanne. 1983. *Closing the gold window—Domestic policy and the end of Breton Woods*. Ithaca: Cornell University Press.

Group of Ten. 1964. Ministerial statement of the Group of Ten and annex prepared by their deputies, Board of Governors of the Federal Reserve System. *Federal Reserve Bulletin* 50(8): 975–999

Horsefield, J. Keith. 1969. *The International Monetary Fund 1945–1965, Vol. 1 – Chronicle*. Washington, DC: IMF.

Keohan, Robert O., and Joseph S. Nye. 1977. *Power and independence: World politics in transition*. Boston: Little Brown and Company.

Keohane, Robert O. 1989. *International relations and state power – Essays in international relation theory*. Boulder: Westview Press.

Kessler, Geldolph A. 1980. The need to control international bank lending. *Banca Nationale del Lavoro Quarterly Review* 132(March): 57–81.

Kindlberger, Charles P. 1970. *Power and money: The economics of international politics and the politics of international economics*, Macmillan Student Editions. London/Basingstoke: Macmillan.

Machlup, Fritz. 1964. *Plans for the reform of the international monetary system*. Special Papers in International Economics, No. 3, International Finance Section, Princeton University.

Machlup, Fritz. 1982. *Remarking the international monetary system: the Rio agreement and beyond*. Baltimore: Johns Hopkins Press.

Nau, Henry R. 1990. *The myth of America's decline—Leading the World Economy into the 1990s*. New York: Oxford University Press.

Odell, John. 1982. *US international monetary policy: Markets, power, and ideas as sources of change*. Princeton: Princeton University Press.

Polak, Jacques J. 1967. Special drawing rights: The outline of a new facility in the fund. *Finance and Development* IV(4): 275–280.

Reserve Bank of India. 2005. *The Reserve Bank of India, 1967–1981*. Mumbai: Central Office, Reserve Bank of India, National Government Publication, Distributed by Foundation Books.

Solomon, Robert. 1982. *The international monetary system, 1945–1981*. New York: Harper & Row.

Strange, Susan. 1971. *Sterling and British policy: Political study of an international currency in decline*. London/Toronto: Oxford University Press.

Strange, Susan. 1976. International monetary relations. In *International economic relations of the western world 1959–71, Vol. 2*, ed. Andrew Shonfield, 18–359. London/New York/Toronto: Royal Institute of International Affairs/Oxford University Press.

Triffin, Robert. 1964. The evolution of the international monetary system: Historical reappraisal and future perspectives. In *Princeton Studies in International Finance 12*. Princeton: International Finance Section, Department of Economics, Princeton University Press.

Weatherford, M. Stephen. 1988. The international economy as a constraint on US macroeconomic policy making. *International Organization* 42(4): 605–639.

Wilki, Christopher M.D. 2012. *Special drawing rights (SDRs): The first international money*. New York: Oxford University Press.

Williamson, John. 1973. Surveys in applied economics: International liquidity. *Economic Journal* 83(331): 685–746.

Yago, Kazuhiko. 2010. *Kokusai Kessai Ginkou no 20 Seiki (20 Century of the Bank for International Settlements)*. Tokyo: Sotensha.

Chapter 6
Restoration of European Currency Convertibility and Securing International Liquidity: The IMF and Key Currencies

Masayoshi Tsurumi

1 Introduction

The end of 1958 saw an attempt to restore convertibility of major Western European currencies by shifting from the managed economic system of the war years and the postwar period to a market economic system. Until then, in the world of international finance the free movement of capital had been impeded by strong trade and foreign-exchange controls in each country. These controls had been centered on the closed pound and the Sterling bloc. Despite the fact that the pound shared with the dollar the status of a key currency worldwide, it could not be exchanged freely for dollars outside the bloc of nations using the pound as currency. The restoration of convertibility between the pound and the dollar marks the end of the postwar transitional period. However, the postwar pound was not strong enough to restore convertibility on its own. The obstacle was the large amount of pounds confined within the pound bloc. There were fears of a massive liquidation and outflow of those pounds accompanying the restoration of convertibility. The success or failure of restoration of convertibility depended on whether or not it would be possible to prepare sufficient foreign reserves or liquidity in preparation for currency speculation. Any shortages in these needed to be addressed by relying on international cooperation. This chapter will describe in detail the process of restoration of convertibility of major Western European currencies, particularly the pound, during the 1950s, from the standpoint of securing foreign reserves.

During the 1950s, both the British and American governments embarked on a course toward a market-based system of international finance, under the slogan "Trade not Aid." The breakthrough on this course would be the restoration of convertibility. Its success or failure depended on from where aid for foreign

M. Tsurumi (✉)
Department of Economics, Hosei University, 4342 Aihara, Machida, Tokyo 194-0298, Japan
e-mail: masaturu@hosei.ac.jp

K. Yago et al. (eds.), *History of the IMF*, Studies in Economic History,
DOI 10.1007/978-4-431-55351-9_6

reserves would come. Models for this purpose had been the international financial centers of the 1920s, the Tripartite Monetary Agreement of the 1930s, and the IMF of the 1940s. The problem was the two key currencies under the IMF system, the pound and the dollar. While they both aimed to secure positions as key currencies under free markets, Britain and the U.S. adopted different strategies concerning the IMF.

The British strategy depended on a revival of the pound as a key currency and making progress on liberalization of the pound, centered on the developed financial center of London. A point of contention was whether to implement this strategy as a decisive action or gradually. It was unclear whether the relationship with the IMF would be based on fixed or floating exchange rates. American strategies, on the other hand, was of two minds: whether to focus on the IMF or the dollar. The NAC approach,[1] which sought to secure U.S. interests in coordination with the IMF and the World Bank, was in conflict with the key-currency approach and the dollar-diplomacy approach, both of which prioritized U.S. interests ahead of international cooperation.

Attention turned toward restoration of the pound through the tussle among various strategies and negotiations by related institutions. Calls for support for the pound spread from the British collective approach to the U.S. Randall Committee, the IMF, the Fed, and the Export-import Bank of the United States (EXIM), and in the process a framework for international liquidity support was developed. The aim of this chapter is to reconstruct this chain reaction by bringing the circumstances to light based on primary materials from related institutions.[2] The Sects. 2 and 3 will trace this debate in Britain and the U.S. on the subject of restoring convertibility of the pound. The focal point will be the market-based "Trade not Aid" strategy. The following two Sects. (4 and 5) will trace the spread of calls for supporting the pound from the Randall Committee to the IMF and the Fed. They will look at the responses of the IMF and the Fed to the question of who would support foreign reserves. The discussion will concentrate on restoration of the bankers' acceptance (BA) market. The final Sect. 6 will look in detail at support for the pound during the Suez Crisis, from the handling of the IMF and EXIM.

2 The Collective Approach: Restoration of Convertibility of the Pound

2.1 The Pound Crisis and the Collective Approach

The starting point was Britain's collective approach, and that is where our discussion will begin.

[1] The terms "NAC approach" and "dollar diplomacy approach" are borrowed from the Martin papers (FED Archives (Fraser), Martin Papers, "U.S. Foreign Lending and Dollar Diplomacy," 1950?).

[2] Previous studies using primary materials include Fford (1992), Schenk (2010), and Nishikawa (2012).

In 1952 the attempt to restore convertibility of the British pound entered a new phase.[3] Restoration of convertibility was proposed to the Meeting of Commonwealth Finance Ministers in January, and at the end of February the governor of the Bank of England prepared a draft External Financial Policy as a countermeasure against the pound crisis, calling on the government to institute thoroughgoing reforms.[4] Although limited in nature, this plan was based on self-help through restoring convertibility of the pound for nonresidents and addressing speculative pressure by restricting withdrawals from pound balances in Commonwealth countries and employing floating interest rates.

Chancellor of the Exchequer R.A. Butler submitted this proposal from the governor of the Bank of England to the cabinet, where it met a mostly lukewarm reception. Cabinet members argued that restricting withdrawals of pound balances or restoring convertibility all at once could have the opposite effect of shaking confidence in the pound, leading to an outflow of gold dollar reserves.[5] Troubled by this cautious sentiment in the cabinet, the Bank of England revised its first proposal into the External Sterling Plan, which it submitted again to the cabinet for consideration in May. The revised plan incorporated two changes. First, it removed the proposal to restrict withdrawals of pound balances. Second, it limited restoration of convertibility to new transactions in countries outside the pound bloc. This made it a more realistic plan that would soften the shock of the restoration of convertibility. Based on this second proposal from the Bank of England, in October the Foreign Minister and the Chancellor of the Exchequer proposed a collective approach.[6] An outline of this approach is described below:

1. Restoration of convertibility would be carried out gradually for new transactions by nonresidents, based on floating exchange rates.
2. While quantitative restrictions on imports would be eliminated, the U.S. would bear the responsibility of a country with a surplus in its balance of international payments.
3. A small number of developed countries would create a new foreign-exchange fund to assist the restoration of convertibility.
4. The IMF and the GATT would form a joint committee on issues involved in international trade and finance.

[3] Macmillan later described restoration of convertibility as the logical conclusion of Britain's policies since 1951 (UK National Archives, C.P.(55)111, "Cabinet: Economic Situation" August 31, 1955).

[4] The original text of the Bank of England's proposal could not be located. The summary and process described below is from UK National Archives C.(52)217, "External Financial Policy: Memorandum by the Chancellor of Exchequer," June 28, 1952, pp. 112–118.

[5] UK National Archives C.(52)221, "External Financial Policy: Memorandum by the Paymaster-General," June 30, 1952, pp. 183–186.

[6] UK National Archives C.(53)22, "The Collective Approach to Freer Trade and Currencies," January 21, 1953.

The reserves committee of the Commonwealth Heads of Government Meeting failed to reach agreement on this proposal as a variety of views were brought up.[7] A revised proposal was prepared in light of concern about the scale of the risks that would be involved if the proposal were rejected. This was a substitute proposal to expand existing funding sources such as the IMF instead of setting up a new foreign-exchange fund. This was the first time the IMF had been brought up as part of support for international cooperation.

2.2 *The Issue of Support for Pound Liquidity*

Britain's greatest concern was the issue of liquidity. It was focused on the point of how to secure additional liquidity in response to an outflow of gold-dollar reserves accompanying the restoration of convertibility. As of October 1953, Britain's gold-dollar reserves had fallen below the USD1.7 billion level. The proposal to float the pound was a last resort to relieve the resulting pressure. However, the proposal of a floating system also was recognized as a difficult question relating to the philosophy of the IMF itself. The reserves committee proposed a number of ideas as routes to supplementing liquidity:

1. Creation of a foreign-exchange fund by the U.S., Canada, and a small group of Western European countries (for example, in an amount of USD5 billion)
2. Provision by the IMF of special standby credit to restore convertibility. This would have a term of at least 12 months and be renewable
3. Providing flexible automatic standby credit on a one-day basis
4. Supplementing through bilateral credit agreements when funds become even shorter
5. Obtaining credit from the U.S. Federal Reserve Bank or Stabilization Fund
6. Increasing IMF capital
7. Establishment by the IMF and GATT of a joint committee to serve as a venue for negotiations between lenders and borrowers

Each of these measures would have required the approval of the IMF, and particularly the United States.[8] In mid-November 1952 the Commonwealth Economic Conference approved the proposed collective approach, over the year's end the Foreign Office and the HM Treasury considered a rough draft for the U.S., the "Collective Approach to Freer Trade and Currencies," and in March 1953 they

[7] UK National Archives C.E.C.(O)(H.D.)(52)1(Final), "Commonwealth Economic Conference: Preparatory Meeting of Officials: Report on Finance and Trade," October 15, 1952, pp. 204–220.

[8] In cabinet, Churchill expressed approval for the "collective approach" as multilateral convertibility, but he was not optimistic that the U.S. would accept it (UK National Archives C.M. 92 (52) November 3, 1952, cabinet memo).

proposed it to the Americans.[9] At first, both governments were unified on the point of solving the economic problems of the free world. Under its fundamental policy of "Trade not Aid," the Churchill cabinet argued on a wide range of topics including restoration of convertibility, resolution of trade discrimination, development through international investment, and constructive use of the IMF, GATT, and the World Bank. While in August Prime Minister Eden and Chancellor of the Exchequer Butler both went to the U.S. as a tentative overture on the "collective approach," the U.S. did not accept their proposals for measures to support the pound. At that time the U.S. was undergoing a change of administrations, and it was not able to respond immediately to Britain's urgent proposal. Specific policies would have to wait until the report of the Randall Committee.

3 The Report of the Randall Committee on Foreign Economic Policy

3.1 The Eisenhower Administration's External Financial Policy

Backed by the Commonwealth Heads of Government Meeting, Britain proposed a collective approach to the new U.S. administration, seeking a new international economic order. The theme was "Trade not Aid." Eisenhower and the Secretary of State John Dulles wanted to base the new administration's foreign economic policy on this same principle of "Trade not Aid," and in August 1953 the Committee on Foreign Economic Policy (usually called the Randall Committee) was formed to consider specific policies. There was an urgent need to put together nonpartisan foreign economic policies and move toward their implementation, with the involvement of both the House of Representatives and the Senate.

The Committee first looked at the issue of the "dollar gap," which it considered a fundamental problem faced by American foreign economic policy.[10] While in recent years the U.S. current account balance appeared at first glance to have been approaching a balanced state, its balances of international trade and services excluding military expenditures and aid were in a massive deficit. Such a global trade imbalance should be balanced through private-sector investment, not American foreign aid. The main purpose of the Randall Committee was to propose practical prescriptions for shifting from government aid to private investment, in accordance with the "Trade not Aid" approach. For this reason, the scope of its report was wide ranging, from the military to trade and currency.

The Randall Committee report is a strategy for foreign economic policy put together by the new Eisenhower administration and a nonpartisan group of legisla-

[9] After this, "Role of United States Policies" was delivered to Treasury Secretary Humphrey on April 24 (UK National Archives C. (53)144, "Freer and Currencies: Role of United States Policies," May 1, 1953, pp. 130–148).

[10] *Report to the President and the Congress: Commission on Foreign Economic Policy*, January 23, 1954.

tors. It served as the American proposal in response to Britain's new "collective approach" to foreign economic strategy. Aiming to break out of the postwar transitional period, Britain and the U.S., under the slogan "Trade not Aid," had begun competition between the pound and the dollar for the position of key currency in connection with restoration of convertibility. The following two proposals were made regarding international finance.

1. The EXIM Bank would be act in accordance with specific American interests, while the World Bank would be managed in accordance with banking principles.
2. The Fed would extend credit lines to central banks as a means of financial support for restoration of convertibility of each country's currency.

We will consider each of these points below.

3.2 International Financial Issues

The first concerns the division of roles between the EXIM Bank and the World Bank with regard to development finance. In response to calls from Congress spurred by concern about competition between the EXIM Bank and the World Bank in the area of development finance, the National Advisory Council on International Monetary and Financial Problems (NAC) was established to coordinate the two. However, the EXIM Bank was shaken by being drawn into a bureaucratic dispute on its role. This was the competition between the "NAC approach" and the "dollar diplomacy approach." The NAC approach called for restraining politicization of policies by the U.S. by prioritizing cooperation between the IMF and the World Bank in foreign lending. Supported by the Treasury Department, this approach was suited to its aims by focusing on economic rationality. In contrast, the theme of the dollar diplomacy approach was "friendship and need." Led by the State Department, this approach was one of highly political lending policies focused on U.S. interests, chiefly in Latin America. Under the Eisenhower administration, a bitter struggle for leadership took place between Secretary of State Dulles and Secretary of the Treasury George Humphrey.[11]

While at first President Eisenhower supported Treasury Secretary Humphrey, swayed by the efforts of Senator Homer Capehart, chairman of the Senate's Banking and Currency Committee, he moved toward supporting Dulles' argument. Following a period of unsettled policy, in the summer of 1953 Eisenhower entrusted this issue to the Randall Committee. The Committee's report drew a line between the two banks' roles somewhat reflecting the dollar diplomacy approach, calling for the EXIM Bank to act in accordance with specific U.S. interests and the World Bank to promote economic development overseas in accordance with banking principles.

[11] For the course of events, see Kaufman (1982) and Becker and McClenahan (2003), Chapter 3.

The second point of discussion concerned convertibility of European states' currencies. The report proposed an approach of gradual controls toward full restoration of convertibility. It argued that it would be desirable to restore convertibility of European states' currencies through concerted action in order to ease speculative pressure on the pound. At question was when to take such action. On this point, the report argued that it would be desirable to proceed gradually, waiting for recovery of the interested countries' competitiveness in the global economy and economic balance. In doing so, it would be important to have adequate gold-dollar reserves. In particular, Britain, which held massive pound balances, would need to strengthen its international reserves. Two policies were proposed for this purpose. The first called for using the USD3.3 billion in funds held by the IMF, easing the IMF's lending conditions in order to do so. The second called for international cooperation, through means including use of other countries' foreign reserves. An example would be the conclusion of credit lines between the Fed and other countries' central banks.

The Randall Committee's chapter on this issue of restoration of convertibility was based on a staff paper by John Williams.[12] Seriously concerned about the post-war structural issues faced by Britain, Williams argued for gentle, gradual progress. He also expressed concerns about floating of the pound if movements of capital were to spur a crash in the pound and bring about inflation. He proposed specific numerical figures for supplementing foreign reserves, calling for the IMF to allocate to Britain USD2 billion of its funds on hand of USD3.3 billion and the rest to other countries. He also proposed that the Fed provide stabilization credits to foreign central banks to cover any shortages, avoiding a proposal to increase IMF funding through U.S. government expenditures.

These policies represented ideas already brought up in the collective approach. While Williams proposed specific figures regarding sources of funds for aid, with the IMF playing the main role and the Fed a secondary role, the report removed these specific figures and described an option in which the IMF and the Fed would be parallel. In addition, the report excluded Williams' proposed foreign-reserve measure of increasing funding of the IMF by the U.S. government in accordance with the "Trade not Aid" approach, while incorporating the others.

The Randall Committee report was published and delivered to Congress at the end of January 1954. The Randall Committee advocated gradual progress on restoration of convertibility, rearranging the original idea offered by the collective approach in line with American interests. Neither Britain's demand for a joint IMF-GATT committee nor its call to create a stabilization fund had been accepted, and the call for floating exchange rates proved unable to break through the IMF's call for restoring convertibility of the pound at a fixed exchange rate. At this time, as the position of Prime Minister was handed over from Churchill to Eden, Britain too abandoned the floating exchange rate and switched to a strategy of restoring con-

[12] "Memorandum by John H. Williams of the Commission on Foreign Economic Policy to the Members of the Commission", December 15, 1953, *FRUS, 1952–1954, Vol. 1, Part 1, General: Economic and Political Matters,* Document 107.

vertibility of the pound at a fixed rate.[13] In this way, like a chain reaction of billiard balls the issue of additional liquidity under the collective approach would impact the IMF, the Fed, and the EXIM Bank via the Randall Committee. We will trace the repercussions below.

4 Promotion of Bankers' Acceptance Markets by the IMF

4.1 IMF Standby Credit

The ripples of the Randall Committee report first headed toward the IMF. The IMF was waiting for an opportunity to see how it could contribute to restoration of convertibility of the pound. It would find that opportunity in standby credit.

In May 1951 the IMF decided to use its funds to strengthen the credit of member nations, and in February 1952 it asked the NAC to approve a new form of lending. To strengthen the credit of member states faced with temporary international settlement problems, it would provide support in the form of special loans. They would be repayable in less than 18 months and would be granted in consideration of past loan performance.[14] One of the stated goals was to help achieve the objectives of the IMF, with restoration of convertibility in mind. Concerned about whether the loans would be repaid within the term of 3–5 years, the NAC demanded that each loan be reported to it in advance and the guidance of the American representative director be followed. In August, despite considerable opposition chairman Schneider proposed acceptance of this proposal as a further development of the IMF's policies, and it was approved.

Twenty months later on December 4, 1953, as if following on the heels of the Randall Committee discussions, the IMF developed an execution system after consulting with the NAC on matters such as the terms and interest rates of standby credit.[15] This movement was spurred into action by the Randall Committee. Together with the release of the commission's report in January 1954, the IMF began full-fledged consideration.

---

[13] In July 1955 Prime Minister Eden sent a note to President Eisenhower stating that Britain's objective was stability for the pound as an international currency and that broad fluctuation of the pound would not be desirable (July 23,1955, *FRUS, 1955–1957, Vol. 27, Western Europe and Canada*, Document 214).

[14] "Memorandum by the States Executive Director of the International Monetary Fund (Southard) to the Acting Secretary of the National Advisory Council on the International Monetary and Financial Problems (Willis)", February 11, 1952, *FRUS, 1952–1954, Vol. 1, Part 1, General: Economic and Political Matters,* Document 97.

[15] "Memorandum by the States Executive Director of the International Monetary Fund (Southard) to the Acting Secretary of the National Advisory Council on the International Monetary and Financial Problems (Glendinning)", December 4, 1953, *FRUS, 1952–1954, Vol. 1, Part 1, General: Economic and Political Matters,* Document 97.

First, in April Director of Research E.M. Bernstein prepared a note that would serve as the model for discussions. At issue was the response to massive amounts of standby credit for the pound.[16]

1. While it would be desirable for Britain's gold-dollar reserves to be in an amount of USD3 billion, this amount would vary with economic trends.
2. The amount of reserve credit for restoration of convertibility of the pound would be USD2 billion, the same as the amount Williams proposed.
3. If of the gold-dollar assets of USD3.31 billion held by the IMF, the amount allocated to Britain and members of the pound bloc were to be USD1.26 billion (USD5.036 billion for all members), then the remaining amount available for use being USD2 billion.
4. If USD2 billion were allocated to Britain, then the unused gold tranche would be no more than USD900 million, not enough to meet the gold tranche demand from other countries.
5. For this reason, the amounts directed to Britain would be gold tranche of USD100 million and standby credit of USD1.4 billion, for a combined total of no more than USD1.5 billion.
6. The Federal Reserve Bank of the U.S. would handle the remaining USD500 million.

A meeting led by Managing Director Ivar Rooth was held based on this note by Bernstein, identifying some problems with its implementation. This meeting discussed whether the IMF had sufficient liquidity to meet requests for standby credit involved in restoration of convertibility; if not, then whether additional support should be requested; and what kind of loan conditions would facilitate liquidity. The discussion was extended even to the possibility of suspending convertibility again.[17] Bernstein and the others considered two cases regarding IMF cash flow: a case involving the pound alone and one including other currencies such as the franc. If standby credit to Britain were in the amount of USD1 billion, then there would be no shortage of IMF liquidity for 5 years following the extension of the loan. If the credit were USD1.5 billion, then a prominent problem of a rapid decrease in liquidity would not arise, but if it were to swell to USD2 billion then the severe problem of a shortage of liquidity would appear beginning in the third year. In June 1954, the IMF summarized its principles for large-scale standby credit[18]:

1. The IMF considered maintenance of liquidity to be its top concern.
2. The draw currency for restoration of convertibility of Western European currencies would be the dollar, at a rate of three dollars to one unit of the other currency.

---

[16] IMF Archives Bernstein Papers, 6115–51 "Notes on Sterling Convertibility", April 2, 1954. Access to Bernstein's papers on the restoration of convertibility was through the kind offices of Akira Nishikawa.

[17] IMF Archives Bernstein Papers, 6152–53, "Notes by Mr. Rooth", April 20, 1954.

[18] IMF Archives Bernstein Papers, 6226–43, "Repurchase under a UK Stand-by", Date unknown, and 6271 "The Liquidity of the Funds", March 31, 1954.

3. The period for repayment would be longer than the standard period of 3–5 years in order to maintain liquidity.
4. Flexible management would be employed, so that the period would lengthen when the amount drawn was large.
5. Loans could not be drawn merely for the purpose of strengthening reserves.

Even if lending procedures were handled flexibly, if the amount of loans to Britain exceeded USD1 billion and approached USD2 billion then the IMF would be exposed to a shortage of liquidity. At the time, the limit that the IMF could handle probably was USD1.5 billion. For this reason, there was a need for USD500 million in support from another funding source.

4.2 Possibility of Additional Support: The Fed

In the Ruth meeting in March a variety of options were brought up as sources of such additional support. Bernstein and the others focused only on the IMF and the Fed as sources of additional funds, comparing the costs and discipline of each.

While there were two ways by which Federal Reserve credit could be used—unofficial loans to the Bank of England or additional supply of dollars by the Fed to the IMF or a member nation—there was no major difference between the two in terms of costs (fees plus interest) to the IMF and the Fed. Bernstein decided to make no clear decision regarding whether the facilities of the IMF or the Fed would be preferable, instead arguing for flexible use of both routes. He also concluded that there was a need for prior discussions between both agencies to make sure that the total amount of loans did not swell to the point where it could not be repaid.[19]

After these studies, in the board meeting on June 25, 1954 IMF Managing Director Ruth proposed that the board provide its full moral support to large-scale financial support for restoration of convertibility of the pound, and the board approved this proposal. Half a year after the Randall Committee's report was released, the IMF had completed the operational procedures required to implement a restoration of convertibility of Western European currencies. The ball had passed from the Randall Committee to the Fed's court.

5 The Fed's Policies to Promote the Bankers' Acceptance Market

But how did the Fed respond to the 1954 Randall Committee proposal on standby credit?

[19] IMF Archives Bernstein Papers, 6271, "The Liquidity of the Funds", March 31, 1954.

5.1 The Fed and the Bankers' Assurance Market

There are no indications that the Randall Committee's proposal on standby credit was submitted as-is to the Fed's Open Market Committee. The standby credit proposal was modified in form and discussed as an issue related to development of the bankers' acceptance (BA) market. Because the Eisenhower administration advocated "Trade not Aid" and did not favor supporting the pound with government funds, the Randall Committee recommended support from the Fed rather than public funds. Even so, the Fed did not accept the proposal for credit lines between central banks. Why not? In 1951 the Fed concluded an accord with the Treasury Department, and at the time progress was being made on shifting toward market-based monetary policies.[20] Fed governor Martin adopted a "bills only" policy to avoid intervention of monetary policies in the market, and international cooperation to support the pound took place in accordance with this principle as well. This took the form of policies to nurture the bankers' acceptance market.

The bankers' acceptance market would become a topic of discussion in the Open Market Committee in 1954. It was R.G. Rooth, secretary of the Open Market Committee, who started the discussion. On February 17, 1954 the issues of revisions to the Fed's minimum interest rate for purchase of bankers' acceptances was tabled in the Executive Committee.[21] From 1953 to 1954 market interest rates for bankers' acceptances had fallen, reaching a level below the prime rate. There was a need to lower the Fed's minimum interest rate for purchase of bankers' acceptances to below the prime rate in order to maintain equilibrium between supply and demand. Rooth based his argument on the perspective of promoting trade finance.

After Rooth brought up the issue, the Open Market Committee met on March 3. However, it was unable to reach a conclusion.[22] Following a number of subsequent twists and turns, gradually the committee reached its final conclusions in March 1955. In a meeting of the Fed's Executive Committee on March 30, 1954,[23] Secretary R.G. Rooth submitted a staff paper on promoting the bankers' acceptance market.[24] It included the following points:

1. Restoration of the U.S. bankers' acceptance market would help restore the international money markets.
2. The lack of a bankers' acceptance market was impeding countries' shifts to gold-dollar reserves and convertibility of currency.
3. The Fed's minimum interest rate for rediscounting of bankers' acceptances was impeding the development of the bankers' acceptance market.

---

[20] See Meltzer (2009), Chapter 2 concerning Fed monetary policy in this period.

[21] FRB Archives, FOMC Intermeeting Executive Committee Minutes, January 17, 1954.

[22] FRB Archives, FOMC Intermeeting Executive Committee Minutes, March 3, 1954.

[23] FRB Archives, FOMC Intermeeting Executive Committee Minutes, March 30, 1954.

[24] U.S. Federal Reserve Bank of New York, Sproul Papers, "Current Problem of System Policy with Respect to the Bankers' Acceptance Market", March 25, 1954.

4. It would not be desirable merely to lower the minimum interest rate for bankers' acceptances while retaining the minimum interest rate restriction.
5. It would be desirable to encourage market development through purchases by the Fed of USD200-300 million.
6. The development of international bankers' acceptance markets could contribute to restoration of convertibility.

Rooth envisioned facilitating short-term movements of capital among bankers' acceptance markets in preparation for convertibility of currency. For this purpose, it would be desirable for the Fed to end its interest-rate restrictions on bankers' acceptances that had been in place since 1952. While this was in accordance with the shift toward market-based monetary policy since the 1951 accord, it also was a policy that extended beyond that shift in that it would introduce a quantitative quota. Rooth sought the restoration of the bankers' acceptance market of the 1920s, and he proposed that the Fed support this. This constituted the New York Fed's answer to the Randall Committee report.

The bankers' acceptance market in the U.S. grew during the 1920s under the Fed's stewardship. It then declined after peaking in 1929. For this reason, Fed staff in Washington were not very familiar with the topic of the bankers' acceptance market, and they needed to start by collecting information from the New York market. The report was the Hexter and Youngdahl report of May 14, 1954.[25] His report was quite opposed to nurturing the bankers' acceptance market. In opposing Rooth's proposal, it argued that bankers' acceptance trading practices in New York violated the National Bank Act and that it would be difficult to promote the bankers' acceptance market without restoration of convertibility of Western European currencies.[26]

In response to this negative research report from board staff, an argument arose between board members Robertson, Ruth, and others, which assumed the aspect of a leadership struggle between the New York Fed and the Federal Reserve Board. The Federal Reserve Board took the opportunity of the accord to demand from the New York Fed, which was seeking to restore New York as a financial center, the independence of the FOMC in order to strengthen its financial policies. Chairman Martin entrusted the discussion to a special committee on the overseas activities of U.S. banks. Its findings were submitted to the board at the end of the year, in December. Robert Solomon had been responsible for the subject of bankers' acceptance transactions. As seen by the paper's title, "Bankers' Acceptances and the International Flow of Credit," it proactively argued for the role of the bankers' acceptance markets from the perspective of facilitating international movements of capital.[27] It presented a counterargument to that of Hexter and Youngdahl, arguing

---

[25] NARA RG82 FRB Central Files 1913–1954 Box 1316, "Bank Acceptance: Present Conditions and Practices", by the staff (R.G. Rouse), FRB, May 14, 1954.

[26] NARA RG82 FRB Central Files 1913–1954 Box 1316, "Whether National Banks May Lawfully Endorse Bank Acceptances for Pecuniary—Good Will of Customers", by Hexter and Youngdahl, FRB, July 1, 1954.

[27] NARA RG82 FRB Central Files 1913–1954 Box 1316, "Bankers' Acceptances and the International Flow of Credit" by Robert Solomon (Special Committee on Foreign Operations of American Banks), FRB, December 5, 1954.

for contributing to the restoration of convertibility instead of overvaluing the fetters on nonconvertible currencies such as the pound.

The model behind Solomon's argument was the interwar international financial center, and the related balanced short-term international movements of capital. Looking toward the revitalization of New York as an international financial center, he argued for actively nurturing the bankers' acceptance market as the core of that center. This means that Solomon, a member of the staff of the Federal Reserve Board, was in tune with the argument of the New York Fed.

5.2 *The IMF and the Bankers' Acceptance Market*

Together with the announcement by Solomon of the report of the special committee, in December 1954 the IMF tossed another ball into the Fed's court. This was the plan for the IMF to build a new international bankers' acceptance market. A note by Bernstein making this proposal remains today.[28] Its content is outlined below:

1. Bankers' acceptances are an important source of international credit.
2. The IMF is interested in the revitalization of the bankers' acceptance markets.
3. The IMF would establish a special standby credit facility to enable member nations to access the bankers' acceptance markets.
4. The upper limit would be 50 % of a member nation's IMF quota, subject to approval by the member nation's central bank.
5. The bankers' acceptance markets would be located in London, New York, Brussels, and Amsterdam.
6. A remittance system would be constructed as a step toward restoration of convertibility.
7. The IMF would ask the Federal Reserve Board and the Bank of England about the fundamental cause of the decline of the bankers' acceptance market and the feasibility of its revival.

The Solomon report and Bernstein's bankers' acceptance draft both adopted the same line of seeking revitalization of the bankers' acceptance market as mechanisms for coordination of international balances of payments after restoration of convertibility. The Bernstein proposal sought to back up the Fed's proposal to revive the bankers' acceptance markets through creating a new facility in the IMF. To the IMF, this proposal constituted a revolutionary plan that extended beyond its existing standby credit.

First, it would be a bridge between the IMF and the markets. While the World Bank interacted with the markets through trading in World Bank bonds, the IMF did not interact with the markets directly, instead negotiating only with member nations' currency authorities. Bernstein's plan would link the IMF to international short-term financial markets through bankers' acceptances.

[28] NARA RG82 FRB Central Files 1913–1954 Box 1316, "Fund Encouragement of Bankers' Acceptance Market" by E.M. Bernstein, FRB, December 20, 1954.

Second, it would strengthen the international reserve system. Bridging the gap between the IMF and the bankers' acceptance markets would enhance the reserve buffer by adding a third line of reserve, short-term international capital through bankers' acceptances, to the first line of reserve, gold dollar reserves, and the second, IMF standby credit.

As Fed discussions on promoting the bankers' acceptance market reached a critical phase, Bernstein acted to provide backup support. He proposed that international bankers' acceptance markets be restored for the purposes of restoring convertibility of Western European currencies, and for the development of a system for cooperation with the U.S. Fed for this purpose. While Bernstein already had made this proposal unofficially to the New York Fed and others on the Fed side, there are no signs that it had been discussed by the Fed in public. Only the issue of cooperation with other countries' central banks had been brought up.[29]

On January 11 of the following year, in response to the Solomon report from the special committee and Bernstein's proposal, the Executive Committee met at the Open Market Committee, where the proposal to promote the bankers' acceptance market was discussed. While the majority of members were inclined to support the proposal to promote the bankers' acceptance market, Robertson argued against it from beginning to end, arguing that it ran against the Fed's guiding principles. In response to this opposition, Sproul was forced to give up his insistence on setting monetary limits as argued in the proposal, claiming that by doing so the proposal would not deviate from the guiding principles.[30]

Later, in 1955 trading in the bankers' acceptance market grew, so that the taking of special measures by the Fed decreased in importance. On March 2 a final proposal on policies to promote the bankers' acceptance market was made to the general committee, calling for gentle purchasing of bankers' acceptances in accordance with the Open Market Committee's general credit policies.[31] While Robertson opposed changing the traditional policy stance, the majority accepted Martin's proposal, and the policy of promoting the bankers' acceptance market was approved, about 1 year after Sproul's proposal. This approval had been supported in the background by the strong backing of Solomon's special committee report and the proposal by Bernstein of the IMF. The fact that even so the Fed's policy of promoting the bankers' acceptance market had settled on a policy of gentle nurturing of the market with no special systemic support was due to a wish to avoid deviating greatly from the conservative bills-only principle advocated by Chairman Martin. This stance was made clear in two papers on trade finances published by the Fed in spring 1955, 1 year after Sproul's proposal.[32] They argued that the existence of

[29] FRB Archives, FOMC Intermeeting Executive Committee Minutes, March 2, 1955. It was only confirmed that Britain, France, and Canada had opened central bank accounts with the New York Fed since 1936.

[30] FRB Archives, FOMC Intermeeting Executive Committee Minutes, January 11, 1955.

[31] FRB Archives, FOMC Intermeeting Executive Committee Minutes, March 2, 1955.

[32] Solomon and Tamagna (1955) and Tamagna and Axilrod (1955).

broad-ranging bankers' acceptance markets in two or more international financial centers would contribute to the restoration and maintenance of convertibility by simplifying short-term international movements of capital.

The Fed, led by Martin, responded to Bernstein's plan for IMF-led development of the bankers' acceptance market with a policy for gently nurturing that market. It did not respond to calls for IMF-led international cooperation. In the face of this passive Fed stance, Bernstein did not formally submit this plan for discussion by the IMF board. It is interesting to note here that the new development under which the IMF and the New York Fed, former antagonists, cooperated and the Federal Reserve Board moved toward their point of view. Throughout these negotiations, the Federal Reserve Board had held predominance over the New York Fed.[33]

In this way, the Randall Committee proposal on restoration of convertibility spawned organizational preparations for restoration of convertibility on the IMF side and a policy of gently nurturing the bankers' acceptance market on the Fed side. As a result, preparations were being made for s system of international support for restoration of convertibility of Western European currencies. However, uncertainty still remained on the point of additional liquidity.

6 The Suez Crisis and Liquidity

6.1 The Suez Crisis and the Pound Crisis

The Churchill cabinet's "collective approach" never saw the light of day as an urgent measure. The succeeding Eden and Macmillan cabinets jettisoned the proposal for floating interest rates and shifted to fixed rates, moving forward on preparations for gradual restoration of convertibility. However, this situation did not last long. The outbreak of the Suez Crisis in July 1956 quickly brought with it an opportunity to test the pound's resistance to crisis.[34] The military confrontation that resulted from Egypt's nationalization of the Suez Canal triggered credit uncertainty on the pound, leading to withdrawal of nonresident pound balances and a massive flow of gold-dollar reserves through short-term capital movements reflecting leads and lags. The balance that had been USD3 billion in December 1954 had fallen to nearly USD1.4 billion in December 1956.[35]

---

[33] Axilod (2009) and FRB Archives, Martin Papers, "Management of the System Open Market Account," from J.L. Robertson to Members of Special Committee of the Federal Open Market Committee, July 6, 1955.

[34] See Fford (1992), Chapter 8 and Boughton (2001) concerning the Suez financial crisis.

[35] IMF Archives, DM/57/35, "The United Kingdom and the World Economy," by E.M. Bernstein, July 25 1957.

The Eisenhower administration was critical over the Suez crisis, arguing that British and American colonialism was a thing of the past.[36] Treasury Secretary Humphrey in particular was critical of Britain and France, arguing for waiting to provide support until the two countries had implemented a ceasefire as called for by the United Nations. They saw the problem as disaffection of Middle Eastern countries and an oil crisis in the West due to closure of the canal. Both Britain and France were concerned about petroleum settlement, estimated to total USD600-800 million.[37] Humphrey envisioned an EXIM credit line, which would not require congressional approval. He also envisioned on November 8 that Britain would follow France's lead in applying for an IMF loan up to its maximum limit. On November 20, the British cabinet decided on a gradual withdrawal of British troops from Egypt, and in response Humphrey suggested the provision of EXIM Bank credit of USD600 million in addiction to the IMF loan of USD560 million. The crisis was approaching on December 4. Finance Minister Macmillan needed to indicate a plan for strengthening Britain's gold-dollar reserves prior to announcing the balance of such reserves. On December 3, Macmillan laid out a plan for announcing the three conditions of drawing from the IMF gold tranche, borrowing form the EXIM Bank, and extending payment of interest on loans under the 1948 Anglo-American Financial Agreement.[38]

On December 10 the IMF held an emergency board meeting in which it approved a gold tranche of USD560 million, a standby credit facility of USD738 million, and an extension on payment of interest on loans under the 1948 Anglo-American Financial Agreement.[39] Together these large-scale loans accounted for one-third of the IMF's funds at USD1.3 billion, the maximum under the quota, although USD200 million less than the IMF had anticipated in 1954. The terms of the standby line of credit involved no conditionality, with a term of 12 months and repayment to begin after 3 years, in line with Britain's wishes as expressed in the "collective approach".[40] The reaction of the board members had a strong tinge of supporting the international currency of the pound, and many expected it to serve as aid for restoration of recoverability. It is interesting to note that Secretary Southard indicated a new relationship by touching on the past key currency debate with IMF, describing the approval of this loan as showing that the two rival approaches were not mutually exclusive.[41]

The Fed did not sign on to additional liquidity support. The additional support was provided by the U.S. EXIM Bank. On December 21, with the end of the year

---

[36] "Memorandum of Discussion at the 304th Meeting of the National Security Council", November 15, 1956, *FRUS, 1955–1957, Vol. 10, Foreign Aid and Economic Defense Policy,* Document 233.

[37] "Memorandum of Conference With the President, White House, Washington", October 30, 1956, *FRUS, 1955–1957, Vol. 16, Suez Crisis, July 26-December 31, 1956,* Document 419.

[38] "Editorial Note", *FRUS, 1955–1957, Vol. 16, Suez Crisis, July 26-December 31, 1956,* Document 51.

[39] IMF Archives, Executive Board Meeting 56/59, December 10, 1956.

[40] The Eden cabinet considered the IMF to have received the proposal in a "friendly" way (UK National Archives C.M.(98)56, "Cabinet Conclusion" December 11,1956).

[41] IMF support for the pound as a key currency had continued from Jacobsson's predecessor Rooth.

imminent, the EXIM Bank resolved to provide a 4.5-year, 4.5 %-interest loan of USD500 million against collateral of USD264 million in U.S. treasuries held by Britain, nominally to increase Britain's dollars for purchasing petroleum.

Why did the EXIM Bank provide the aid instead of the Fed? While the British government had considered both either the Fed or the EXIM Bank as an additional source of aid, at the urgent stage reached in December it needed a fig leaf to support trust in the pound. It sought direct support from the U.S. government under the fig leaf of withdrawal of troops from the Suez.[42] However, under its "Trade not Aid" policy the U.S. government did not favor direct lending of government funds, and under its bills-only policy the Fed did not want to participate in foreign aid. The only means remaining was aid from the EXIM Bank as a countermeasure against an oil crisis. Probably neither Treasury Secretary Humphrey nor State Secretary Dulles, fierce rivals for leadership, objected to the reason of countering an oil crisis arising in the Suez.[43]

At that time France faced an outflow of USD600 million in gold and required urgent supports. Here too the government had envisioned a loan from the EXIM Bank rather than direct aid, but since it was unable to invoke an oil crisis as Britain had done a new reason was needed.[44] France sought a credit line for purchase of consumer goods, but Treasury Secretary Humphrey opposed this as being counter to the EXIM Bank's principle of lending for capital goods. In response the French government switched to a proposal for USD100 million in aid for purchase of aircraft for Air France, approaching the State Department with this proposal. However, did not desire to go over the head of the Treasury Department to place political pressure on the EXIM Bank.[45] The Treasury Department was lukewarm toward France because the Franc was not a key currency.

6.2 Toward Restoration of Convertibility

During the Suez Crisis the British government succeeded in curbing a pound crisis with the support of the IMF and the U.S. EXIM Bank. An issue that pressed down on the British government after it had overcome the Suez Crisis was that of

[42] According to a statement by Treasury Secretary Humphrey. Participants in British-American negotiations were of the same view ("Memorandum of Conference With the President," November 20, 1956, *FRUS, 1955–1957, Vol. 16, Suez Crisis, July 26-December 31, 1956*, Document 596).

[43] The complete series of materials on this IMF policy to promote the bankers' acceptance market remains in the U.S. Archives in connection with export/import finance. These documents show that the request for pound support went from the Fed to the EXIM Bank.

[44] Already in October 1956 France had received from the IMF an ordinary standby credit (50 % of its quota, with a term of 1 year) (IMF Archives, Executive Board Minutes, October 17, 1956). See Klug and Smith (1999) concerning the differences between Britain and France.

[45] "Memorandum of Conversation Between the Secretary of State and the French Ambassador(Alphand)", January 22, 1957, January 28, 1957, *FRUS, 1955–1957, Vol. 17, Western Europe and Canada,*, Document 34, 35.

restoring convertibility of the pound. In 1957, IMF standby credit stood at USD740 million, EXIM loans at USD500 million, and gold-dollar reserves at USD 2.14 billion. Conditions were improving as total foreign reserves had risen to USD3.38 billion.[46] An issue of concern was whether the two aid loans would be extended.

At the end of 1958, the first steps were taken toward full restoration of convertibility of the pound together with other key currencies of Western Europe. For this purpose, repayment of IMF standby credit and EXIM loans would need to be extended. The Macmillan cabinet remained doubtful and suspicious even in December.[47] No matter what, the gold tranche of USD560 million needed to be repaid on time. They dealt with this by planning to repay USD200 million by April of the following year and then make monthly payments from 1960 through 1961. In response, on December 10 the IMF board approved a further 12-month extension. While describing Britain's foreign reserves as having improved in preparation for restoration of convertibility, IMF staff also added that a failure to approve the rollover would shake the pound's position as a key currency.[48]

7 Conclusion

Attempts to restore convertibility of Western European currencies began in 1952 and ended at the end of 1958. A framework for supporting international liquidity had taken definite form through tough negotiations. We will conclude by summarizing the significance of this framework and its prospects.

First, the IMF would now play a central role in supporting international liquidity. While at the time of the starting point of the collective approach and the Randall Committee the roles of the IMF and the Fed had not been finalized, ultimately the IMF would play a central role in supporting international liquidity by beginning to provide standby credit.

Second, although the Fed and the EXIM Bank had vied to serve as an additional route for support to supplement the IMF, in the end it would be the EXIM Bank that would fill that gap. It would play a fig-leaf role to back international cooperation. Later, it established a firm position by providing means separate from those of the IMF, in areas such as international cooperation and the central-bank swap network.

Third, together with the move toward market economies the roles of international financial centers were reassessed. The role of the bankers' acceptance market, pivotal for this purpose, again attracted attention, and efforts were made to promote that market, albeit gently.

[46] Bank of England Archives, OV44/10, "Sterling Part 1: The Present Position," *United Kingdom Sterling Policy 12,* September 3, 1957.

[47] UK National Archives, C.C.(58), "Cabinet: Conclusions," December 4, 1958.

[48] IMF Archives, EBS/57/68 Supplement 1, "United Kingdom: Renewal of Stand-by Arrangement," December 6, 1957.

Fourth, a system was formed to support international liquidity during an age of market economies, with gold foreign reserves serving as the first line of reserve and IMF loans as the second.[49] With the further addition of the international cooperation credit network and short-term movement of capital, international reserve coordination would become multilayered.

Fifth, while during the 1940s the rival approaches were the IMF approach and the key-currency approach, together with the shift toward market economies during the 1950s these converged on the international financial center approach.

Sixth, while as a result of restoration of convertibility both the pound and the dollar stood together at the starting line, due to competitive pressure in the market the pound later would slip out of this position, in less than a few years.

The waves of the shift toward market economies, which began in domestic finance, had reached international finance, which had been freed from the yokes of controls. This was not the terminus but a new starting point. While the bankers' acceptance markets grew in London and New York, at the same time the new Euro markets were born as well. Free short-term movement of capital would advance beyond the Bretton Woods system, with liberalization of current account balances from exchange-exchange controls and furthermore liberalization of capital and financial accounts as well. In this sense, the restoration of convertibility at the end of 1958 can be described as the starting point of the shift toward market economies.

References

Axilod, Stephan H. 2009. *Inside the Fed: Monetary policy and its management, Martin through Geenspan to Bernanke*. Cambridge, MA: The MIT Press.

Becker, William H., and William M. McClenahan. 2003. *The market, the state, and the Export-import Bank of the United States, 1934–2000*. Cambridge: Cambridge University Press.

Black, Stanley W. 1991. *A Levite among the priests: Edward Bernstein and the origins of the Bretton Woods system*. Boulder: Westview Press.

Boughton, James M. 2001. Northwest of Suez: The 1956 Crisis and the IMF. *IMF Staff Papers* 48(3): 425–446.

Casey, Kevin M. 2001. *Saving international capitalism during the early Truman presidency: The National Advisory Council on International Monetary and Financial Problems*. New York: Routledge.

Fford, John. 1992. *The Bank of England and public policy 1941–1958*. Cambridge: Cambridge University Press.

Gold, Joseph. 1970. *The stand-by arrangements of the International Monetary Fund: A commentary on the formal, legal, and financial aspects*. Washington, DC: International Monetary Fund.

Horsefield, J. Keith (ed.). 1969. *International Monetary Fund 1945–1965: Twenty years of international monetary cooperation*, vol. 1, 2. Washington, DC: International Monetary Fund.

Johnson, Arthur M. 1968. *Winthrop W. Aldrich: Lawyer, banker, diplomat*. Boston: Graduate School of Business Administration Harvard University.

[49] UK National Archives C.(57)65, "Cabinet: Economic Survey, 1957," March 12, 1957, pp. 39.

Kaufman, Burton I. 1982. *Trade and aid: Eisenhower's foreign economic policy 1953–1961*. Baltimore: The John Hopkins University Press.

Klug, Adam, and Gregor W. Smith. 1999. Suez and Sterling, 1956. *Queen's Economic Department Working Paper* No. 1256.

Meltzer, Allan H. 2009. *A history of the Federal Reserve, Vol. 2, Book One, 1951–1969*. Chicago: University of Chicago Press.

Nishikawa, Akira. 2012. *Sengo kokusaitsuka shisutemu no keisei to IMF* (Formation of the postwar international currency system and the IMF), Doctoral Thesis, Graduate School of Economics, University of Tokyo.

Schenk, Catherine R. 2010. *The decline of sterling: Managing the retreat of an international currency, 1945–1992*, Chapter three. Cambridge: Cambridge University Press.

Solomon, Robert, and Frank M. Tamagna. 1955. Bankers' acceptance financing in the United States. *Federal Reserve Bulletin*, May.

Tamagna, Frank M., and Stephen H. Axilrod. 1955. United States banks and foreign trade financing. *Federal Reserve Bulletin*, April.

Williams, John. 1949. *Post-war monetary plans and other essays*. Oxford: Basil Blackwell.

Part II
IMF in Relation to National Economies and International Organizations

Chapter 7
The IMF and France (1944–1960): A "Cooperative Game" in the Bretton Woods System

Kazuhiko Yago

1 Introduction

No other member of the IMF has experienced such a peculiar relationship with the institution as France has had. On the one hand, France, as a major signatory nation of the Bretton Woods Agreement, has been one of the most important members of the IMF, sending several high-ranking officials to the Fund, including Managing Directors. On the other hand, the position of France often has been contrary to the IMF's views and it has proposed distinctively alternative plans for an international monetary system. France has in fact been a "watchdog" of the Bretton Woods System (Bordo et al. 1994, p. 10).

Although such particular actions by France are well known, the explanation for them varies among scholars, as follows. (1) Conventional views explain this independent French behavior as coming from its "anti-Americanism" and "self-reliance reconstruction policy" as represented by stance of Charles de Gaulle, or even from "independent imperialism" standing upon a "gold standard" view (Kuisel 1993). (2) Another view emphasizes the French domestic political situation, with the strong presence of the Communist Party. This explanation focuses on the weak side of the particular French stance, represented by the devaluation of the franc: "between the Liberation and the stabilization of the franc under de Gaulle, the currency was, in one way or another, devalued seven times". Owing to its complex political situation, "France did not try to maintain an unrealistic par value of its currency" (Gilbert 1980, p. 76). (3) Contrary to the explanations above, Michael Bordo and co-authors regarded the apparent "anti-American" policy conducted by de Gaulle as being "a weapon to further a French gold policy that was an extension of earlier politics

---

K. Yago (✉)
School of Commerce, Waseda University, Shinjuku-ku, Tokyo, Japan
e-mail: yago@waseda.jp

K. Yago et al. (eds.), *History of the IMF*, Studies in Economic History,
DOI 10.1007/978-4-431-55351-9_7

dating back to the interwar period", and that the real goal for the French authorities was "a revision of the international monetary system along the lines of the gold exchange standard of the 1920s and of the Tripartite Agreement of 1936". According to their view, the French response was therefore "a consistent, rational long-term policy" (Bordo et al. 1995, pp. 153–180). Developing this idea, Bordo et al. proposed the hypothesis that French–American relations under the Bretton Woods System constituted a "non-cooperative game" with the French gold–dollar exchange system as a "rational threat" (Bordo et al. 1994, pp. 28–33). (4) French economic historians emphasize the antagonism within the French camp, unlike the coincidence of international policy presented by Bordo et al. According to the distinction made by French historians, the market-friendly "neo-liberalists" and their appraisal of the gold standard stood on one side, with the state-oriented Keynesians, putting the priority on reconstruction and tolerating the expansion of fiscal policy, on the other (Bossuat 1992). This antagonism is expressed in various ways, for example "*austéro-liberaux*" versus "*expanso-atlantisme*" (Margairaz 1991), theorists versus pragmatists (Gonjo 1999), or the "overdraft economy" and efforts to overcome it (Feiertag 2006).

However, the foregoing interpretations regarding French behavior under the Bretton Woods System seem to have common weaknesses. First, all these views presuppose a dichotomy, namely, "France versus the United States" or "France versus the IMF", which seems too simplistic. The studies depending upon French archives, for instance, while precisely describing various interests on the French side, often ignore a variety of opinions and motives within the IMF or the United States authorities. Second, these views depend on another dualism, "expansion versus austerity" or "Keynesians versus neo-liberals". These schemas, often referred to in explaining the contemporary international monetary system or domestic macroeconomic policy, seem too narrow to interpret complex historical processes. The "neo-liberals" did not always insist on budget austerity and sound money. Instead, they often changed their opinion depending on political circumstances. Or some actors even expressed the same policy in a different manner, namely, referring to "stabilization" as a domestic explanation and "devaluation" as a foreign excuse, as we shall examine in this chapter.

In order to overcome the weaknesses of the previous studies, this chapter focuses on the relationship between France, the United States, and the IMF, paying special attention to conflicts within each camp. The archives of the IMF as well as French and American authorities are referred to, especially the documents of the National Advisory Council on International Monetary and Financial Problems (hereafter NAC). This chapter, based on those historical records, aims to examine the relationship between France and the IMF (and also with the United States), from the Bretton Woods Conference to 1960. The end point of 1960 has been chosen because the final consultation regarding France under Article XIV was conducted that year, and France became a country under Article VIII from 1961 on.

2 Bretton Woods Agreement and France: Quota and the IMF Parity

At the beginning of the Bretton Woods Conference, under the French Provisional Government representing France, de Gaulle sent a delegation headed by Pierre Mendès-France, but the role of the French delegation at the Conference was less important than that played by the US and the UK (Lepage 1994; Frank 1994, pp. 9–14; James 1996, p. 43). However, by the time the Conference came to decide the IMF quotas of the member countries, France started to display its aggressive attitude. Following the initial quota proposal, France was supposed to be the fourth member, after the US, the UK and the Republic of China. France then required the IMF to raise its quota, right after ratification of the Bretton Woods Agreement on 26 December 1945. The French requirement had been put on the agenda of the Executive Board Meeting on 10 September 1946, to be approved on 24 September.[1]

Who decided this quota change, and how? One of the most important arenas of the decision was the NAC of the United States. In fact, the NAC took note of the French request on 10 September 1946, simultaneously with the IMF Executive Board.[2] The NAC Staff Committee took up the case on 16 September, more promptly than the IMF.[3] Finally, the NAC on 17 September also discussed the French quota request in detail, and the Chairman John Snyder, US Secretary of Treasury, summed up the discussion in the following action statement: in view of the preceding action, the NAC "advices the U.S. Executive Director on the Fund [IMF] that the request of France for a revision of her quota be considered on its merits, provided that the French subscription to the Bank [IBRD] be revised to equal any new quota established"[4] [underline original, parenthesis by the author]. However, China also required a quota rise following France, and so did India. Facing this confusion, the NAC meeting held on 26 September again took up the matter. At the meeting Harry White reported that "if France were not allotted a quota of more than $525 million the Chinese would withdraw their request", and that White "told the French representative that the U.S. government was willing to make a concession".[5] Finally, the NAC maintained its approval for France to raise the quota. France also agreed to the proposal of White, to raise the quota only up to 525 million dollars and not more.[6] France and the United States represented by the NAC were thus friendly towards each other. After the US-France negotiations, the IMF officially approved the French request on 12 February 1947, which made the French quota the third largest in the IMF.[7]

---

[1] IMF EBM46/53, September 10, 1946; EBM46/65, September 23, 1946.

[2] NARA, NAC Documents, Meeting No. 38, September 10, 1946.

[3] NARA, NAC Documents, Staff Committee, Minutes, Meeting No. 40, September 16, 1946.

[4] NARA, NAC Documents, Meeting No. 39, September 17, 1946.

[5] NARA, NAC Documents, Meeting No. 40, September 26, 1946.

[6] IMF EBM46/72, September 30, 1946.

[7] IMF EBM47/135, February 12, 1947.

As for the initial franc par value, the negotiations were more confused. Graph 1 below represents the evolution of the franc exchange rate, of which the historical background was as follows. According to the decree of 26 December 1945, the franc rate was fixed at 1 dollar=119.10669 francs and 1 lb sterling=480 francs. During the period, the Exchange Equalization Account concentrated the foreign exchange operations with this decreed rate.[8] Along with this official rate, unofficial black markets were active in France, rating 1 dollar=350 francs in November 1945 and 1 dollar=295 francs in December 1945 according to the stipulation of the official rate. The black markets were supplied with hoarded money under the German occupation period (Gilbert 1980, p. 77): the French government under occupation issued a huge amount of banknotes in order to pay the occupation costs of the German authorities, but due to strict price controls by the German occupiers, the sum supplied to the market resulted in hoarding.[9]

The franc rate thus decreed, the question for the IMF was whether to officially approve this rate as an initial par value. It was Robert Triffin in the Research Department of the IMF who was in charge of the decision making. Triffin's view was expressed in a report addressed to the IMF Board dated 30 October 1946.[10] Beginning his explanation by referring to the interwar period French economic history, Triffin warned "considerable deficits in her international accounts over the period 1946-49". As for the decreed franc rate of 1 dollar=119.10669 francs, he says that "its maintenance in the future is predicated on the checking of the inflationary forces inherent in the present situation and which, if allowed to develop further, will soon make the proposed parity untenable", predicting more devaluations to come due to harsh inflation in France. On the other hand, Triffin was optimistic about the dollar shortage, on which France had been presenting a pessimistic view. He estimated that France, after paying the quota and capital to the IMF and the World Bank, would still keep a gold-dollar reserve of 1 billion dollars equivalent.[11] Nevertheless Triffin criticized the French modernization program, the *Plan Monnet*, as "based on rather ambitious investment goal, which may well overestimate the absorptive capacity of the economy".[12] Triffin concluded that the IMF could approve the decreed rate as par value, but sooner or later it would have to be revised.

[8] IMF SM35, Foreign Exchange Transactions in France, January 27, 1946.

[9] IMF SM35, Foreign Exchange Transactions in France, January 27, 1946. This report was written by Raymond Bertrand, approved by Edward Bernstein, before its proposal to the Board.

[10] IMF EBD99, Initial Par Values, France, prepared by Robert Triffin, October 30, 1946.

[11] Triffin's estimation was based on the sum of aid granted to France, i.e. "500 million from the International Bank, $300 to $400 million from other sources, especially the British Dominions and Latin America, and $100 to $200 million of private loans and investments, in the latter part of 1946–49, mostly from the United States". This sum makes "a gap of about $300 million between estimated needs and resources. Such a gap", however, represents "only 7 per cent of the total contemplated deficit". Ibid.

[12] Ibid. According to Philippe Mioche, Monnet held the view that execution of the Plan would be a prerequisite for American aid supply. Cf. Mioche (1987), pp. 201–202.

Just a week after the Triffin report, France officially proposed the initial par value to the Executive Board Meeting of the IMF on 8 November 1946.[13] The proposed value was equal to the decreed rate of 1945, namely 1 dollar = 119.10669 francs. In the proposal, Jean de Largentaye, the French representative Director to the IMF, stated as follows[14]: "For more than two centuries the gold equivalent of the French monetary unit had not varied" before WWI; the decreed par value in 1945 was the one which devalued the previous rate by 58 %; "a moderate devaluation at that time could have made necessary a further devaluation when the initial par value would be fixed, and it was felt that a succession of devaluations would have lessened the confidence in the currency"; according to de Largentaye, "that is why the French Government has deemed it advisable, [...] to devaluate the francs to a level which allowed participation in the International Monetary Fund without the need for further readjustment". The IMF Board approved this proposal without further debate. The approved initial rate, however, would be devalued a year later.

Unlike the silent decision process in the IMF Board, the NAC took time to discuss the franc par value. Four days before the IMF Board Meeting on the franc par value, the NAC gathered a Staff Meeting on 4 November 1946. In the meeting, no one except a representative of the Export–Import Bank of America (hereafter EXIM) agreed to the franc's devaluation.[15] Three days later, on 7 November, i.e. a day before the IMF Board Meeting on the issue, the NAC could not reach a conclusion,[16] and finally the NAC action was amended on 26 November, after the official decision made by the IMF Board.[17] In this NAC Meeting, Harry White, the US representative to the IMF, stated that "it would be a mistake to object to the suggested rate for the French franc at this time", since refusing the French proposal and further demanding devaluation would lead to higher dollar demand in the black market, and that additional devaluation after a 60 % franc devaluation in 10 months might incite hyper-inflation. The NAC, after discussion, adopted an "action" that the United States would not oppose the French proposal "with great reluctance".

The initial par value setting, stipulated in the Bretton Woods Agreement, was a criterion for the fixed rate system, and was not supposed to be changed easily. The French proposal has been criticized for its optimism, and the fear of re-devaluation came true. Nevertheless, the process of decision making was not as simple as "French optimism" versus "IMF pessimism". The relationship between the IMF and France would become more complicated by the French proposal after the initial value setting.

[13] IMF EBM46/88, November 8, 1946.

[14] De Largentaye was a first translator of Keynes' *General Theory* into French, and served as the IMF Director from 1946 to 1964.

[15] NARA, NAC Documents, Staff Committee, Minutes, Meeting No. 47, November 4, 1946.

[16] NARA, NAC Documents, Staff Committee, Minutes, Meeting No. 48, November 7, 1946.

[17] NARA, NAC Documents, Meeting No. 45, November 26, 1946.

3 Franc Devaluation: French Unique Strategy and the IMF/ NAC

By the time the IMF started its daily activities, France would insist on its proper demands and strategy. The franc devaluation is the most typical issue.

In January 1947, after the quota revision and initial par value setting, France paid up its quota equivalent to the IMF, not in gold and francs, but in Treasury Bonds bearing no interest. Simultaneously on 22 January, a cabinet decision was made on the *Plan Monnet*, an ambitious reconstruction program. In May 1947, on the other hand, France signed a World Bank loan of 250 million dollars, which was the first loan by the Bank to a member country. France also made the first drawing from the IMF in May, up to 125 million dollars (Horsefield 1969, pp. 169, 190 et passim). France signed the above borrowings one after another, since the year 1947 was a critical period for the French economy, known as "the 1947 crisis" year (Bossuat 1992, pp. 99–139). Overcoming this "1947 crisis" with Marshall Plan Aid, France then made new proposals to the IMF: introduction of the floating rate system under the name of a "free market" on the one hand, and the franc devaluation on the other.

The first proposal for a "free market" was made at the beginning of 1948. The proposal was so firm that France would have withdrawn from the IMF if the proposal had been rejected.

It was the NAC that responded quickly to the proposition: the NAC Meeting on 6 January 1948 discussed the practices of several IMF member countries regarding a floating rate system, including France. The focus was on whether the IMF should approve drawing requests made by those countries violating the IMF Agreement.[18] As for the French case, the opinion was divided among the meeting participants. Andrew Overby, the IMF Governor representing the United States, criticized the French proposal since France, unlike Italy or Greece, had already fixed a parity officially approved by the IMF. The floating of this already fixed rate, according to Overby, would "tend to undermine the purposes of the Fund". Marriner Eccles, the FRB Governor, followed with a comment that "if other countries follow France in adopting a floating exchange rate system and there is no time limit, the Fund might well be wrecked". Eccles added bluntly that he "did not think that the Fund gained strength and prestige by continuously compromising and retreating from its original purposes". Contrarily, Frank Southard Jr., the US representative member of the IMF Board replied that he "would not feel to establish this policy was a retreat". Southard's opinion was that the IMF should be more realistic in fixing the parity of the member countries, and that for France, a temporary floating was also effective in managing the exchange rate. Thus, the FRB Governor stood with the IMF's principle, and the IMF official was more conciliatory towards France. The State Department representative Willard Thorp also supported the latter's opinion regarding a compromise.[19] Finally

[18] NARA, NAC Documents, Meeting No. 79, January 6, 1948.

[19] Thorp was Deputy Assistant Secretary of State for Economic Affairs (later Assistant Secretary), representing the Department at the NAC. In an interview in a later year, Thorp testified about the

the NAC Meeting concluded an "action" that the United States would not oppose the French proposal of floating "during the transitional period" and would propose that the IMF not approve drawings by member countries adopting a floating system.

Two weeks later, however, the situation changed dramatically: on 19 January 1948, the NAC Meeting was informed that France was seeking not only to introduce the "free market" floating system, but also to immediately devalue the franc.[20] The opinion presented at the Meeting was divided into two: Thorp, representing the State Department, insisted on not intervening in European and French affairs, while Overby and Eccles objected to the French proposal. The NAC finally decided to adopt the compromise program proposed by Overby, to admit the devalued plural parities of 1 dollar = 250–272 francs or a single parity of 1 dollar = 214 francs, and to limit the use of the "free market" for non-trade transactions.

The French proposal for floating and devaluation was, from the French side, a part of the stabilization program *Plan Mayer*, named after the Finance Minister René Mayer. This plan consisted of the following policies: (1) Establish "free markets" for the exchange of hard currencies (dollar, Swiss franc and Portuguese escudo), outside the official exchange market managed by the Exchange Equalization Account, (2) Devalue the IMF parity from 1 dollar = 119,20 francs to 214.39 francs. According to economic historian Michel Margairaz, *Plan Mayer* exercised the "triple logic of liberal adjustment", i.e. Government fiscal equilibrium, a balance between prices and costs, and parity stabilization. In other words, the franc devaluation aimed to achieve a rapid return to convertibility (Margairaz 1991, tome 2, pp. 999–1000, 1077–1083; Caron 1982, pp. 423–437). According to Margairaz's view, to which we agree from our point of view, the devaluation was a tool, not an objective.

How did the IMF respond to this *Plan Mayer*? Five days before the start of the Plan, the French Governor to the IMF Mendès-France and the IMF Managing Director Camille Gutt conferred in Washington. Gutt proposed a considerable compromise to the French representative: the IMF would approve the devalued parity of 1 dollar = 250–280 francs, but would require France to limit the use of the "free market" to capital transactions and tourist accounts only, which meant use of the fixed IMF parity for trade. But the French side rejected Gutt's proposal, after the Finance Minister Mayer insisted on making use of the floating rate for trade (Bossuat 1994, p. 27).

At the NAC Board Meeting held on 22 January 1948, three days before the devaluation, Overby reported the most recent trends of the IMF Board.[21] The NAC Meetings of this period put the French issue at the top of agenda. Overby reported the IMF's position as follows: (1) the IMF would approve the French devaluation, (2) the IMF also approves of the introduction of a "free market" exchange rate for non-trade transactions, (3) but it does not agree to a floating rate system for trading goods. However the NAC members response was negative:

conflict between the Treasury and the State Department of the period, particularly with Snyder at the Treasury. Harry Truman Library, Oral History Interview with Willard L. Thorp (Amherst, Massachusetts, July 10, 1971), http://www.trumanlibrary.org/oralhist/thorpw.htm#52

[20] NARA, NAC Documents, Meeting No.80, January 19, 1948.

[21] NARA, NAC Documents, Meeting No. 83, January 22, 1948.

Eccles stated that the "French proposals represent a serious departure from the Fund's basic principles and philosophy". Eccles also summed up the discussions in the NAC that most members were "not convinced that a retreat by the French government to some more compromise position would have such serious political consequences in France as have been alleged". Finally, the NAC unanimously concluded that it agreed to the French proposal but would "vote to reject the proposal that French have a free market for 50 percent of the export proceeds to convertible currency areas".

Against these negative opinions, France devalued the franc on 25 January 1948, setting the exchange rate of 1 dollar=214.39 francs and 1 lb=864 francs. In the "free market" the real franc rate had been devalued to become 1 dollar=305 francs (Bossuat 1994, p. 27).

Although the devaluation was carried out under severely antagonistic circumstances, the NAC finally tolerated the French policy after the new parity. For example, the NAC decided an action on 27 January 1948, 3 days after the devaluation, that "endeavors be made to meet temporary French financial needs through expedition of the payment of vouchers for reimbursement of Interim Aid expenditures or through commercial bank financing". This action was based on an aid request from the French Ministry of Finance to the United States: right after the devaluation, France was suffering from speculators selling francs and buying dollars, since they expected further depreciation of the franc.[22] At the NAC Meeting held the following week, Southard Jr., the US representative member of the IMF Board reported that the franc rate in a "free market" moved from 1 dollar=311 to 309 francs, while the black market rate was 304 francs, which meant that "developments were as predicted by the French": the franc rates of the two markets were approaching each other due to the return of the hoarded dollars back into the "free market".[23] The "liberal logic" of *Plan Mayer* was thus appreciated in the NAC.

The IMF Board, on the other hand, sanctioned the franc devaluation as being against the IMF Agreement, and administered a suspension of drawing rights against France. This punishment, however, was not well-grounded, and nor was the lifting of the punishment either: at the same time, the IMF adopted its so called "ERP decision", which stopped drawings by the member countries receiving Marshall Plan Aid, but the French case was not clear as to whether France was the only country being "punished" due to the devaluation, or France came under the ERP decision as well as other member countries (Lepage 1994, p. 55). The franc rate was further devalued, to become 1 dollar=350 francs in September 1949, while the "floating system" was abandoned at the end of 1948. It was under these obscurities that the IMF Article XIV consultations with regard to France started in 1952.

[22] NARA, NAC Documents, Meeting No. 84, January 27, 1948.

[23] NARA, NAC Documents, Meeting No. 86, February 4, 1948.

4 Article XIV Consultations with Regard to France

The franc exchange rate had been fixed at 1 dollar = 350 francs from the 1949 devaluation until the next devaluation in 1957. During this 8-year period, the franc rate stayed stable. However, France experienced successive foreign reserve crises during this period: an austerity policy followed the reserve crisis, and when the crisis was over, the policy returned to relaxed spending. Thus a repeated "stop-go" policy characterized the period, during which the IMF Article XIV Consultation had been exercised with regard to France. The following Table 7.1 represents the main economic indicators of the period.

In this section, the consultation debate is described by time series, depending mainly upon the IMF archives.

4.1 Consultation Under Punishment (1952–1953): Evaluating the "Pinay Experiment"

The first consultation took place during 11–20 June 1952.[24] The consultation consisted of two hearings with the French Ministry of Finance's Exchange Control Division (represented by Pierre Calvet) and three hearings with the Ministry of Finance's Foreign Finances Division (represented by Guillaume Guindey).[25] The IMF delegation was headed by Jan Mladek, an IMF Director of Czech origin. What was happening in France during the year was a political debate between the Premier Antoine Pinay, a champion of anti-inflation measures, and Guindey, who as mentioned above insisted on the franc devaluation with the expectation of worldwide deflation. The debate ended with victory for Pinay, followed by austerity measures called the "Pinay experiment". Guindey, who was defeated, was later sent to the Bank for International Settlements to become the General Manager of the Bank.[26] Although both Pinay and Guindey were "neo-liberalists" in European terms, their opinions were divided between "stabilization at once" versus "temporary stabilization", or "price regulation" versus "exchange rate regulation".

In the course of the consultation, the IMF delegates questioned the regulatory measures taken by the French side. The French idea was that (1) the primary goal was to improve the trade balance deficit. In order to achieve this goal, France would first of all liberalize trade between OEEC member countries, (2) trade liberalization with the dollar area would follow the improvement of the dollar account, (3) the

[24] On the first consultation, cf. IMF SM/52/56, "France—Restrictive System", August 8, 1952; ERD/52/16, "France—Restrictive System", August 6, 1952; ENA/52/20, "France—1952 Consultations", August 7, 1952.

[25] On the career background of Guindey, Cf. Yago (2013), pp. 130–131.

[26] Cf. Rimbaud (1990), pp. 150–226 for the political aspect of *Plan Pinay*. For the relationship between Pinay's program and the Banque de France relief to the French Treasury, cf. Feiertag (2006), pp. 415–419. See also de Lattre (1999), p. 73.

Table 7.1 Major indicators on French economy (1950–1960)

	1950	1951	1952	1953	1954	1955	1956	1957	1958	1959	1960
GNP growth (%)	8.3	5.9	2.6	2.9	4.8	5.8	5	6	2.6	2.8	7.1
Balance of payment (1 billion francs)	−27.4	−269.6	−216.5	−118.5	−62.8	30.3	−283.1	−323.3	−103.4	2.1	0.5
Balance of service trade (1 billion francs)	−12.8	−69.9	−206.9	−41	91.7	210.8	−293.4	−421.3	−120.1	3.6	3.1
Wholesale price rise (%)	8.3	27.8	4.7	−4.5	−7.8	−0.1	4.3	5.7	11.5	4.8	2.6
Retail price rise (%)	10	16.2	11.9	−1.7	0.4	0.9	4.2	3	15	6.1	3.6
Banque de France discount rate (annual average: %)	2.72	2.79	4	3.8	3.3	3	3	4.1	4.9	4	3.5

Source: Annuaire Statistique de la France, exercices 1950–1960; Jean Pierr Patat et Michel Lufalla, Histoire Monétaire de la France au XXe siècle, Economica, Paris, 1986

Note: GNP growth after 1960 indicates GDP growth; balance of service trade after 1952 indicates invisible balance

restrictions on capital movements would be lifted after the above liberalization. The French representative rejected the IMF's request for deregulation, with the excuse that France aimed first to improve its foreign exchange position among the European Payments Union member countries, and that by that time the roadmap to deregulation was not ready. Surprisingly, the IMF delegate accepted the French excuses: "it was necessary for the Fund staff to survey the French restrictive system against the background of the existing acute difficulties of the present stabilization effort".[27]

How could France, under punishment measures, persuade the IMF delegate in the consultation? It was the United States that supported the French side vis-à-vis the IMF. In fact, the NAC approved in January 1951 that France could use 95 % of the amount of the counterpart fund of the Marshall Plan Aid.[28] Moreover, the NAC gave consent to extend EXIM credit to France of up to 45 million dollars for cotton imports (February 1952) plus 200 million dollars guaranteed by military expenses (June 1952). These credits, decided by the NAC during the period between the first consultation in 1951 and the second one in 1952, helped France to reject the IMF demands that were on the table of the consultation.

The second consultation proceeded in a similar way.[29] The IMF appreciated the stability of wages and prices in France brought about by the "Pinay experiment". As for the budget deficit and rise in the money supply, the consultation delegate only requested further efforts. The French side, contrary to IMF advice, stated that they would continue the export subsidy measures in order to balance the rise in wages and prices that started in 1950–1951. The IMF expressed anxiety that this measure could lead to irregular interference in trade patterns, but no further sanctions were applied since France was already under punitive measures.

The French logic was unique for insisting on the need for regulation and intervention with regard to the market simultaneously with the liberal "Pinay experiment". In other words, the French priority was put on "price tuning", so that the exchange rate would be managed after price stability was achieved. The French statement, however, included the somewhat contradictory and circular logic that the regulation of dealings with regard to exchange rates may be continued as a prerequisite for price stability. The "Pinay experiment", on the basis of their logic, was a "stabilization" measure at the domestic level but a "regulatory" measure at the international level.

4.2 "Regulation for Price Stability" Versus "Price Stability Without Regulation": Debate Over Import Liberalization

France took initiatives during the first two consultations, backed by American support aid. In the following consultations held in the mid-1950s, however, the IMF side strengthened its counter-proposals. International turmoil such as the wars in

[27] IMF ENA/52/20, "France— 1952 Consultations", August 7, 1952.

[28] NARA, NAC Documents, Meeting No. 267, January 11, 1951.

[29] IMF SM/54/20, March 17, 1954.

Algeria and Indochina as well as the Suez crisis would also change the power balance among the United States, France and the IMF.

The third consultation was held during 12–22 February 1955.[30] The French representative gathered important figures such as Jean Sadrin, head of the Division of Foreign Finances of the French Ministry of Finance after Guindey; Pierre-Paul Schweitzer, Director of the Treasury and later IMF Managing Director; Calvet who became Vice Governor of the Banque de France. It was the first consultation after the sanction measure regarding France was lifted on 15 October 1954.

The consultation opened with the French presentation of an optimistic trade cycle forecast. The IMF delegation agreed with the French view, though the IMF criticized the rise in wages, budget deficit and inflation. The IMF, on the other hand, severely criticized the discriminatory trade regulation imposed by France, i.e. trade liberalization for the dollar area but restrictions on the OEEC area. The IMF appraised the French policy on price stability, but blamed France for continuing trade restrictions, using the need for price stability as an excuse for these restrictions. French logic was that to maintain the price stability after the "Pinay experiment", trade must be regulated: the IMF's logic was, contrary to that adopted by the French, that prices had already become stable, so France could lift its regulation. The French reply was somewhat confused, that the deregulation on imports in dollars "should not be understood and be conducted in a way which might be an obstacle to the intra-European liberalization" (Lepage 1994, pp. 59–60). France proposed postponing deregulation, but the pressure from the IMF side was augmented.

The fourth consultation was held during July and August 1956.[31] This was a period of serious international disputes, from the Independence War in Algeria to the Suez Crisis, to be followed by the Second Middle East War. Under these tensions, the IMF changed its previous optimist view: "The French economy which in the period 1953–55 had managed to achieve rapid growth without inflation, but had not yet remedied all of its structural weaknesses, has been confronted in the recent past with two serious contingencies. There were the development of a situation in Algeria which necessitated diverting considerable resources from normal use, and the occurrence of severe frost in early 1956 which caused a large reduction in agricultural output. Under the circumstances, these adverse developments exert a heavy strain on internal stability as well as the balance of payments". The IMF, however, only expected France to improve its inflation trend and trade deficit, but did not present any strong requests.

4.3 Deepening Crisis: Trade Deficit and Inflation

The fifth consultation took place during 1–10 July 1957.[32] This was the consultation that was held just before the franc returned to convertibility. By this time France had already drawn all of its standby credit and the franc counterpart in the IMF amounted

[30] IMF SM/55/25, April 25, 1955.

[31] IMF SM/56/61, October 17,1956.

[32] IMF SM/57/69, August 9, 1957.

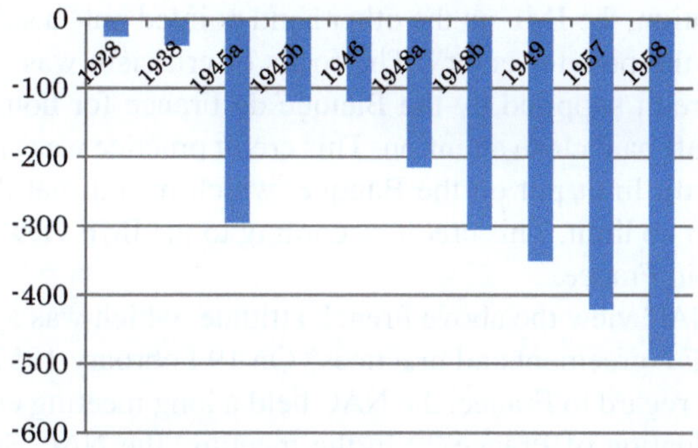

Fig. 7.1 Franc/dollar par value (1928–1958). 1928: legal franc as of 25 June 1928 (le franc Poincaré). 1938: real franc in April 1938. 1945a: real franc in December 1945. 1945b: legal franc as of 25 December 1945. 1946: IMF parity approved on 8 November 1946. 1948a: legal franc as of 25 January 1948 (le Plan Mayer). 1948b: real franc in the "free market" in January 1948. 1949: legal franc rate in September 1949. 1957: legal franc in October 1957. 1958: legal franc as of 27 December 1948 (convertible franc) (*Source*: INSEE, Annuaire Statistique de la France, exercices 1928–1959. Note: The *vertical diagram* represents the franc rate per 1 dollar, displayed in minus figures)

to 125 % of the French quota. Under the Suez crisis, Franco-American diplomacy was no longer going smoothly. The French position faced difficulties, both with the IMF and the United States.

The IMF, in the course of the consultation, bluntly commented on the French macro-economic policy: "The Fund considers that firm measures are required to counter growing inflationary tendencies and to restore the balance of payments equilibrium". The inflation was due to military expenses caused by the Suez Crisis and rapid economic growth led by the strong demand pull. In fact, inflation galloped ahead and price controls did not function and failed, as shown in Fig. 7.1 above. The net foreign reserve availability fell to 360 million dollars, of which 50 million was financed temporarily by an American commercial bank as a petroleum purchase fund. The IMF commented on this situation as follows: "there are serious dangers in the present situation", "It is apparent that the steps taken by the French Government to stem the drain on reserves were too late to prevent the latter from falling substantially".

Contrary to the IMF's suggestion to limit rising wages, the French government introduced consumer price index sliding of minimum wage. France also introduced an Import Restriction Measure in March, which consisted mainly of temporary additional taxation on imports. The IMF, however, could not present a strong position against these irregular measures. Regarding the weak stance of the IMF delegates, France introduced an Export Subsidy System in August 1957, less than one month after the consultation. The Export Subsidy, which encourages exports through government aid, was a de facto currency devaluation, but was not included in the consultation agenda focusing on currency matters.[33]

[33] As for the process from the 1957 devaluation to the return to convertibility, cf. IMF, France: Establishment of Par Value, prepared by the European Department in consultation with the Legal and Exchange Restrictions Departments, December 26, 1958, confidential.

In the consultation, the IMF on the other hand pointed out "a substantial increase in bank credit to the private sector". The focus of criticism was the Medium-term Rediscounting Credit supplied by the Banque de France for housing purposes, to which the IMF staff paid close attention. This credit practice was an exception to the rediscounting credit limit put on the Banque, which meant that the Banque could supply credit with no limit. This credit, according to the IMF view, was a key factor causing inflation in France.

How did the NAC view the above French attitude, which was aggressive enough to violate the IMF Agreement and practices? On 19 February 1957, before the fifth consultation with regard to France, the NAC held a long meeting entitled "Financial and economic situation of France".[34] In the meeting, the NAC Secretary Georges Willis, presenting the report, criticized the French policy as follows: "The French had resorted to a flood of imports as a means of sopping up purchasing power, but had made no attack on the inflationary forces at work in their economy". Against this statement, a new argument was presented by H. McClellan representing the Secretary of Commerce: he questioned "whether, if the United States should consider major aid to France, it could successfully to bring pressure to bear on France to deal with its problems". The Chairman Randolph-Burgess promptly replied "this represented the key problem" and said that "past aid to France had been conditional on French undertaking of anti-inflation measures", but "the French had taken no steps". Randolph-Burgess's proposal was to reexamine the aid given to France, which had been too easy from the US point of view. However, Christian Herter, representing the Department of State, stood by the traditional policy of compromise, saying that the European Common Market Agreement and the Euratom Agreement were expected to be ratified soon by France, and the State Department "would be concerned if financial difficulties should interfere with this". Herter also raised a point that "the French were making very large payments for budget support to Morocco and Tunisia as well as for military operations in North Africa, a situation which raised the question of whether pressure on the French to reduce expenditures might result in either difficulties for our base negotiations" in the concerned areas. In reply to this statement, the chairman of the NAC meeting Randolph-Burgess, stated in an exceptionally harsh manner that France had already exhausted its standby credit; "the franc is not a major world currency like the pound sterling"; "the French had the capacity to solve their financial problems, if they would only face up to them"; "this view should be made clear to the French". Here the NAC and the IMF finally agreed to deal with France on the basis of further austerity.

Right after the above 1957 consultation, on 12 November 1957, three French high ranking officials met with the American government agent confidentially at the Banque de France. The French members were the Central bank governor Wilfrid Baumgartner, vice-governor Calvet and Treasury Director Pierre-Paul Schweitzer. The meeting aimed to explain the French crisis of its foreign reserves, which were almost depleted, and to ask for a rescue package. The American agent at this secret meeting was Randolph-Burgess, the NAC president who had previously insisted on the hardline measures with

[34]NARA, NAC Documents, Meeting no. 256, February 19, 1957, "Financial and Economic Situation of France".

regard to France. Just after the above consultation, Randolph-Burgess was named Ambassador to NATO and was to stay in Paris, thus he could stay in direct contact with the French government. France continued with its requests for foreign reserve relief to the EPU and West Germany, adding that France was asking for help from several institutions and countries so that there would be no major risk by concentrating the burden on a few particular agents (Feiertag 1995, pp. 15–22).

The discussions were hard during these negotiations, but nothing changed after all: the IMF consultation could not alter the French policy; the NAC criticized France but with no results; France postponed its domestic policy reforms and just asked for relief.

This deadlock was resolved through the intervention of Per Jacobsson, the newly named IMF Managing Director. Jacobsson visited France in December 1957 and, surprisingly, occupied an office in the Banque de France to observe and comment on French financial and monetary policy.[35] After hard talks with the French government, Jacobsson at last succeeded in putting an upper limit on the budget deficit, suspended the supply of medium-term credit by the Banque de France, and established a longer term program for the 1959 budget (James 1996, p. 105). The most important of these interventions was the medium-term credit issue, which was deeply related to the traditional practices of the Banque de France (Gonjo 1999, pp. 417–432). During the above IMF consultation, the IMF staff had commented on this type of credit: "There is undoubtedly a need to make drastic reductions in public expenditures as part of any program to bring about a sound recovery in the balance of payments. In the absence of cuts in military expenditure such a move would entail reductions in public investment and price subsidies, admittedly highly sensitive areas. The conscious avoidance of appreciable reductions in these sectors in the past has greatly contributed to the present difficulties".[36] Finally, these medium-term credit practices, which were the incarnation of the "overdraft economy" in France, would be limited in return for the IMF standby credit supply to France, following the intentions of Jacobsson. The view of Jacobsson, to get rid of the French-American compromise and to reestablish the Bretton Woods System, would also lead to domestic reform in France, to be planned by Jacques Rueff.

4.4 Neo-Liberal Stabilization: Plan Rueff and the IMF Consultation

French policy changed considerably in 1958 with the *Plan Rueff*. This plan, officially named the "New Stabilization Program", was prepared under the de Gaulle government in power from June 1958 by Rueff, who was invited by the Minister of

[35] It was Wilfrid Baumgartner who confronted Per Jacobsson this time at the Banque de France. In fact, Baumgartner had been a candidate for the position of Managing Director of the IMF instead of Jacobsson, but this French high-ranking official refused the offer. Feiertag (2006), p. 537. As for Jacobsson's visit to France, cf. Jacobsson (1979), pp. 291–296.

[36] IMF SM/57/69, August 9, 1957.

Finance Pinay. The plan consisted of tax rises, subsidy cuts and trade liberalization, all of which were aimed at coping with the foreign reserve crisis (Gonjo 1999, pp. 445–450). De Gaulle himself was anxious about the plan which seemed to him to be too relentless. It was Jacobsson who persuaded de Gaulle, referring to Napoleon, to step into the austerity policy of the *Plan Rueff* (Jacobsson 1979, pp. 295–296).

The sixth IMF consultation was held during 20–30 October 1958, just before the publication of the *Plan Rueff* in December 1958.[37] This was just after France had drawn on the standby credit approved by Jacobsson, and just before the French return to convertibility. The consultation started with the IMFs comment on the austerity policy in 1958. The IMF delegates welcomed the outcome of the policy in the areas of budget spending, bank lending and medium-term credit. The IMF however asked if the Banque de France would grant whatever credit within the credit ceiling. The French side replied that the Banque would be selective with the loan requests, which meant to introduce not only a "quantitative" but also a "qualitative" credit policy. No special comment was presented at the seventh and final consultation held during 1–14 March 1960: The *Plan Rueff* had already been put into effect and the franc had returned to convertibility.[38]

It should be noted however that the franc exchange rate, fixed after the *Plan Rueff* and the return to convertibility, was a "realistic" one, which approved the existing devalued rate. The monetary policy also was kept easy and medium-term credit was not abolished as previously planned. The NAC discussion of the period reveals why.

The NAC held a long meeting on 28 January 1958 regarding the "French financial situation". The chairman of the session Julian Baird and Tom Coughran, both representing the Treasury Department, presented a report stating that "while the stabilization program envisaged by the French was perhaps not everything that could be desired, it represented a substantial and serious effort toward financial stabilization".[39] After the report, the chairman proposed the French aid program, consisting of (1) $250 million of EPU credit and (2) $131.25 million of IMF standby credit, and to examine (3) $274 million in US government lending. The NAC meeting members gave consent to the proposal one after another: "there had been excellent cooperation among the agencies involved in the negotiations with the French" (Samuel Waugh representing the EXIM), "French negotiations had been very well coordinated, both within the Government and with the international agencies involved" (Arthur Marget of the FRB). The French aid was thus approved in full. The NAC, in spite of its harsh comments regarding France, finally agreed to give aid and supported the French return to convertibility. France could cope with its foreign reserve crisis, not only due to Reuff's austerity policy, but also thanks to the US aid.

[37] IMF SM/59/20, March 27, 1959.

[38] IMF SM/60/37, May 20, 1960.

[39] NARA, NAC Documents, Meeting No. 264, January 28, 1958, "French Financial Situation".

5 Conclusion

The IMF and the United States seemingly criticized France and proposed harsh measures, but in fact gave consent to credit and lending, ignoring the delayed reforms. France also seemed to protest against the IMF and the NAC views, but cooperated with them in the course of negotiations. The IMF, the United States and France were playing a "cooperative game", depending on each other and tolerating the others' defects. The conventional view, which indicates there was a "non-cooperative game" between the above actors, seems to be too simple in just viewing the antagonism on the surface of the Franco-American negotiations.

From our point of view, the austerity policy of Mayer, Pinay and Rueff, or even the severe intervention of Jacobsson, may have been "conditions" or "performance" targets in order to enable approval of the devaluation of the franc and the drawing of standby credit. In fact, new aid was given by the United States to France after these strict policies.

Why was this? Several hypotheses can be drawn from the situation: in the Cold War context, special attention was given to France as the third largest IMF quota member, or there was a strategy to govern Europe via France as a leading nation. Precise studies on the subject, however, are to be examined in future. It should be noted that the IMF of the period was quite different from the 1970s, with a still powerful dollar and abundant standby resources. The United States was also in its heyday: as expressed by the EXIM representative in the NAC, the US aid of the period contributed to certain domestic industries in America via the European purchases of American products. Under these conditions, France could rely on the IMF and the United States playing a "cooperative game", which is the incarnation of the plural character of the Bretton Woods System.

References

Bordo, Michael, Dominique Simiard, and Eugene White. 1994. *France and the breakdown of the Bretton Woods international monetary system*. IMF Working Paper, no. 94/128, October 1994.

Bordo, Michael, Dominique Simiard, and Eugene White. 1995. France and the Bretton Woods international monetary system, 1960 to 1968. In *International monetary systems in historical perspective*, ed. Jaime Reis. New York: Macmillan Press/St. Martin's Press.

Bossuat. Gérard. 1992. *La France, l'aide américaine et la construction européenne, 1944–1954,* 2 tomes. Paris: Comité pour l'Histoire Economique et Financière de la France.

Bossuat, Gérard. 1994. La France et le FMI au lendemain de la Seconde Guerre Mondiale: les raisons de la tension. in Comité pour l'Histoire Economique et Financière de la France, *La France et les institutions de Bretton Woods, Colloque tenu à Bercy les 30 juin et 1er juillet*. Paris: Comité pour l'Histoire Economique et Financière de la France.

Caron, François. 1982. Le Plan Mayer: un retour aux réalités. *Histoire, Economie et Société* 3.

de Lattre, André. 1999. *Servir aux finances, mémoire*. Paris: Comité pour l'Histoire Economique et Financière de la France.

Feiertag, Olivier. 1995. La Banque de France et son gouverneur face à la sanction des finances extérieures sous la IVe République. *Matériaux pour l'histoire de notre temps* 37–38.

Feiertag, Olivier. 2006. *Wilfrid Baumgartner, un grand commis des finances à la croisée des pouvoirs (1902–1978)*. Paris: Comité pour l'Histoire Economique et Financière de la France.

Frank, Robert. 1994. Bretton Woods, un esprit plus qu'un système. in Comité pour l'Histoire Economique et Financière de la France. *La France et les institutions de Bretton Woods, Colloque tenu à Bercy les 30 juin et 1er juillet*. Paris: Comité pour l'Histoire Economique et Financière de la France.

Gilbert, Milton. 1980. *Quest for world monetary order, the gold-dollar system and its aftermath*. New York: Wiley.

Gonjo, Yasuo. 1999. *Huransu Shihonshugi to Chuo Ginkou* [French Capitalism and the Central Bank]. Tokyo: University of Tokyo Press (in Japanese).

Horsefield, John Keith. 1969. *The international monetary fund 1945–1965, Vol. 1: Chronicle*. Washington D.C.: IMF.

Jacobsson, Erin. 1979. *A life for sound money, Per Jacobsson, his biography*. Oxford: Clarendon.

James, Harold. 1996. *International monetary cooperation since Bretton Woods*. Washington D.C. IMF/New York: Oxford University Press.

Kuisel, Richard. 1993. *Seducing the French, the Dilemma of Americanization*. Berkeley: University of California Press.

Lepage, Solenne. 1994. Chroniques d'un malentendu: la direction des Finances extérieures et le Fonds monétaire international, 1944–1958. in Comité pour l'Histoire Economique et Financière de la France. *La France et les institutions de Bretton Woods, Colloque tenu à Bercy les 30 juin et 1er juillet*. Paris: Comité pour l'Histoire Economique et Financière de la France.

Margairaz, Michel. 1991. *L'Etat, les finances et l'économie, histoire d'une conversion, 1932–1952*, 2 tomes. Paris: Comité pour l'Histoire Economique et Financière de la France.

Mioche, Philippe. 1987. *Le Plan Monnet, genèse et élaboration, 1941–1947*. Paris: Publications de la Sorbonne.

Rimbaud, Christiane. 1990. *Pinay*. Paris: Perrin.

Yago, Kazuhiko. 2013. *Financial history of the Bank for International Settlements*. London: Routledge.

Chapter 8
The IMF and Germany: Currency Crisis and Exchange Rate Policy

Ayako Ishizaka

1 Introduction

This chapter will focus on the relationship between the International Monetary Fund (IMF) and the Federal Republic of Germany (Germany hereinafter) from the 1950s through the start of the 1960s.[1] During this period, Germany rapidly advanced liberalization of trade and foreign exchange as it accumulated gold and foreign reserve through its current account surplus. Despite the fact that Germany had joined the IMF in August 1952, since by that point in time Germany already had a current account surplus it did not have the opportunity to receive financial support from the IMF, and already by 1956 its liberalization of trade and foreign exchange largely was complete.

Although 5 years had passed since the IMF's establishment when Germany joined, over that period the IMF's operations had been rather inactive. For this reason, the actual state of the Bretton Woods system reflected a drawing back from the initial ideal as of the time of the signing of the IMF Articles of Agreement, moving in the direction of deployment in settlement within Western Europe (Yago 2007, pp. 326–328). Under these conditions, Germany had joined the Organization for European Economic Cooperation (OEEC) and the European Payments Union (EPU), so that even before joining the IMF it had been involved deeply in regional frameworks among Western European states. The fact that use of such regional settlement systems contributed greatly to Germany's rapid economic growth has been pointed out in past studies. Germany first built up a current account surplus by promoting trade and foreign exchange liberalization in the OEEC region, and then

[1] Also see Ishizaka (2006) and Ishizaka (2012), as works by the author discussing the IMF and Germany.

A. Ishizaka (✉)
Aichi Shukutoku University, Faculty of Business, 23 Sakuragaoka, Chikusa-ku, Nagoya, Aichi 464-8671, Japan
e-mail: iayako@asu.aasa.ac.jp

K. Yago et al. (eds.), *History of the IMF*, Studies in Economic History,
DOI 10.1007/978-4-431-55351-9_8

it achieved reintegration into the global economy (Buchheim 1990; Bührer 1997; Neebe 2004). Germany's role in the EPU was to provide credit to member states as a country with a surplus, and it also helped to strengthen the EPU (Dickhaus 1996). However, a current account imbalance arose within the EPU—between Germany with its surplus and France with its deficit—and this imbalance continued to grow (Kaplan and Schleiminger 1989; Tanaka 2000). As a result, Germany's buildup of its current account surplus came to be the subject of severe criticism internationally.

What kind of initiative did the IMF demonstrate with regard to Germany's current account surplus? In discussing the relationship between the IMF and Germany the topic most deserving of attention is that of policies intended to regulate this surplus, in particular the 5 % revaluation of the Deutschemark (mark) in March 1961. Through this revaluation Germany showed the priority it gave to domestic currency value stability.[2] Otmar Emminger, then the director responsible for international finance at Bank deutscher Länder (Länderbank) and IMF representative director from Germany, recalls that Germany revalued the mark to protect domestic stability from external economic factors, employing foreign exchange market policies as the means of doing so (Emminger 1976, S. 485–554; 1986). Since November 1956 Emminger had argued that revaluation of the mark was inevitable.[3] The foreign exchange markets in 1957 saw currency speculation in anticipation of a revaluation of the mark. This speculation was the first sign of the rise of the mark in contrast to the decline of the pound (Furuuchi 2007, pp. 128–133; Zimmermann 2008, pp. 155–176, in particular p. 176).[4]

Germany's rise to the status of a country with a surplus and the revaluation of the mark also are discussed in Harold James' study of the history of the IMF, as "German Surpluses" (James 1996, pp. 110–115).[5] That study makes it clear that Per Jacobsson, the IMF's third Managing Director, did not support the revaluation of the mark and encouraged Germany to capital exports, chiefly in the form of aid to developing countries.[6]

[2] See Holtfrerich (1998), concerning Germany's monetary policy under the fixed exchange rate system. Also see Lindenlaub (2013), a recent study on postwar Germany's monetary policy.

[3] See James (1996), pp. 110–115, and Holtfrerich (1998), S. 400–413, concerning Emminger's proposal and the revaluation of the mark.

[4] Zimmermann has pointed out the following concerning the relationship between the Bretton Woods system and Germany's monetary policy, including the subsequent collapse of the Bretton Woods system and the timing of progress on European currency integration: "Developments within the Bretton Woods system had sharply constrained the autonomy of both the FRG government and the Bundesbank, … German policy remained consistent with the central principles of the larger Bretton Woods order in which the commitment to fixed exchange rates had been embedded – namely, the pursuit of national economic autonomy within a framework of expanding international trade. What had changed was the monetary regime within which these fundamental goals were pursued".

[5] Also see Schmidt (2003), S. 155–195, concerning the German position in the International monetary system.

[6] James (1996) and Holtfrerich (1998) also make it clear that IMF Director of Research Jacques J. Polak considered it appropriate to revalue the mark by at least 10 % or 15 % if possible. See Erin

But what kind of relationship formed between the IMF and Germany after it joined the organization, and how did Germany interact with the IMF? This chapter will examine the following topics. First, focusing on Germany at the time it first joined the IMF, it will describe how Germany saw IMF membership and the kinds of issues it faced in trade and foreign exchange liberalization. While Germany had accumulated gold and foreign reserves through its current account surplus, by the mid-1950s this situation was reflected in an increasing sense that the mark was undervalued, resulting in pressure toward revaluation. Just before the 1957 IMF general meeting, pressure to revalue the mark developed into currency speculation including pressure to devalue the pound and the franc. Second, this chapter will describe the debate concerning Germany's judgement to the IMF's response to it. Third, focusing on Germany at the time of restoration of convertibility, it will look at why it conducted capital exports proactively and describe Germany's political considerations, including those concerning its shifting to IMF Article VIII status. Lastly, after elucidating the above topics, it will summarize the kind of impact the IMF had on Germany's policy choices and how Germany interacted with the IMF.

In the following section, the above-mentioned issues are examined using Article XIV consultation materials and minutes of the Executive Board from the IMF archives, to make clear the process of discussions between the IMF and Germany. In addition, to look at Germany's interaction with the IMF, we will carry out an analysis using materials from the Deutsche Bundesbank Historical Archive (Historisches Archiv der Deutschen Bundesbank) and the German Federal Archive (Bundesarchiv).

2 Germany as a New IMF Member Country

2.1 From a Foreign Exchange Crisis to a Pioneer in OEEC Liberalization of Imports

This section will look at Germany's joining the IMF. At the end of 1949 the German government was unofficially approached by the IMF about joining, and in September 1950 its membership was approved in talks among the foreign ministers of the U.S., Britain, and France. While the U.S. government took a proactive approach to Germany joining the IMF, Germany's entry involved a diverse range of difficulties of a political, economic, and technical nature.[7] In these talks, the three foreign ministers confirmed that the Allies would continue to control trade and foreign exchange policies in order to enable compliance with the IMF Articles of Agreement.

E. Jacobsson (1979) regarding Managing Director Jacobsson, including his views on this revaluation rate.

[7] NAC Working Group-Fund Problems to The NAC Staff Committee, Admission of Germany to the Fund and Bank, November 9, 1950. RG56. Box 49. National Archives and Records Administration (hereafter NARA).

Negotiations on Germany joining the IMF took place in the midst of a foreign exchange crisis. This crisis, which began in autumn 1950, intensified at the start of 1951, and Germany was forced to suspend liberalization of imports from the OEEC region.[8] Fear of reigniting this foreign exchange crisis led Germany to be as cautious as it was about trade and foreign exchange liberalization after joining the IMF.

The start of the 1950s, when Germany's entry to the IMF was imminent, also was a time in which the country faced the need to become independent from postwar aid, and there were concerns about whether Germany would be able to contribute its quota with its meager gold and foreign reserves.[9] Originally, the U.S. assumed that Germany would join the IMF with a pocket-vote. Furthermore, while the nations of Western Europe had been IMF members from the organization's start, they later came into conflict with the IMF, and Germany tried to ascertain the details of this development. As Marshall Plan aid came into full implementation, the IMF had withdrawn from the field of aid for European recovery, and cooperation between the IMF and the EPU had not been established sufficiently (James 1996, p. 92). In a meeting at the BIS, Länderbank President Wilhelm Vocke acknowledged the relationship between the IMF and the Western European states. Britain was in opposition to the IMF on the subject of measures to devalue the pound, while in countries such as France and Belgium there even were movements to consider withdrawal.[10] While the EPU board also sought ways of cooperating with the IMF, in general it was unable to reach a positive conclusion.[11] Arguing that if the IMF demanded devaluation of the mark as it had in the case of the pound even though there were no problems at all with Germany's ability to export it would lead to wage and price inflation, Vocke had strong concerns about joining the IMF (Dickhaus 1996, S. 97–98). Vocke feared that by joining the IMF Germany would lose its currency sovereignty and its ability to export would decrease as prices rose.

Germany was the 53rd country to join the IMF, with a quota of USD330 million, the sixth largest among member states. In addition, in January 1953 the exchange rate was set at 4.20 marks to the dollar.[12] At first, the NAC and IMF staff considered a quota in the range of USD280-400 million.[13] While the U.S. Department of the Treasury desired a figure even higher than the quota ultimately decided on, Britain

---

[8] See, for example, Dickhaus (1996), S. 49–116, concerning responses to this foreign exchange crisis.

[9] Wilhelm Vocke an den Bundesminister für Finanzen, Fritz Schäffer, 20. März 1951. B136 (Bundeskanzleramt)/3339, Bundesarchiv (hereafter BArch).

[10] Wilhelm Vocke an den Bundesminister für Finanzen, Fritz Schäffer, 20. März 1951. B136/3339. BArch.

[11] Otto Pfleiderer an Wilhelm Vocke, Betr.: Beziehungen zwischen der europäischen Zahlungsunion und dem Internationalen Währungsfonds, 2. Mai 1951. B330/44758. Historisches Archiv der Deutschen Bundesbank (hereafter HADBB).

[12] Par Value-Federal Republic of Germany, January 21, 1953. EBS/53/3. IMFA.

[13] James E. Wood (Chief, European Division) to Brown M. Weir (U. S. Treasury Representative), March 14, 1952. RG56. Box 49. NARA.

desired a lower figure in light of the quota assigned to Japan (USD250 million), which joined at around the same time as Germany, and of Australia's opposition to setting a higher quota for Japan. The final quota was a compromise.

2.2 *The Restrictive, Discriminatory "Import Rights System": IMF Article XIV Consultation (FY1952)*

As noted in the Introduction to this chapter, Germany's economic growth was driven by exports to the OEEC region. In January 1952, liberalization of imports resumed for the OEEC region at a rate of 56.8 % (51.3 % for agricultural produce, 60.0 % for raw materials, and 59.8 % for finished products).[14] Earlier, in July 1951, the Bundesverband für Deutschen Industrie (BDI) had called for a liberalization rate of at least roughly 60 % the pre-suspension level (Neebe 2004, S. 166–168). In light of a shortage of stores of raw materials the BDI was concerned that if suspension of liberalization continued unchanged then over the long term industrial production would be restricted and German industry would lose opportunities for exports. While the Federal Economics Ministry and the Länderbank both agreed with the BDI's call for resumption of liberalization, they were cool to the proposal of resumption at a level even higher than the pre-suspension one, arguing that Germany needed to accumulate solid gold and foreign reserves in order to avoid another currency crisis. However, after the resumption of liberalization of imports the liberalization rate rose in August 1952 to 80.9 % (71.5 % for agricultural produce, 90.7 % for raw materials, and 80.0 % for finished products). Thus, when Germany joined the IMF its liberalization rate for imports from the OEEC region already was more than 80 %.

The IMF's first Article XIV consultation regarding Germany took place in December 1952. During this consultation, Germany told the IMF that a current account surplus with the OEEC region and a deficit with the dollar zone had emerged as structural characteristics.[15] Germany maintained a cautious stance, having estimated in summer 1952 its surplus with the OEEC region during the period from mid-1952 to mid-1953 to be roughly USD400 million. However, the scale of transactions grew more than expected with the progress of import liberalization, so that Germany's surplus quickly rose to USD443 million by September 1952.[16] With this building current account surplus in the background, in April 1953 the liberalization rate for imports from the OEEC region rose further to 90.1 % (79.4 % for agricultural produce, 97.8 % for raw materials, and 93.7 % for finished products).

[14] See Bührer (1997), S. 287, concerning the figures on liberalization rates for imports from the OEEC region (January 1952-April 1953) discussed in this section.

[15] IMF, Federal Republic of Germany-1952 Consultations, Part I, Staff Report and Recommendations, February 16, 1953. SM/53/11. IMFA, p. 4.

[16] IMF, Federal Republic of Germany-1952 Consultations, February 16, 1953, SM/53/11, IMFA, pp. 5–6.

Federal Minister of Economics Ludwig Erhard expressed to IMF staff a strong desire for restoration of currency convertibility of the mark. However, one issue Germany faced in restoring currency convertibility of the mark was the need to advance the liberalization of imports with the dollar zone and repeal its bilateral agreements. The current account surplus was limited to the OEEC region, and liberalization of imports from the dollar zone had not yet begun. Also, Germany had concluded bilateral agreements with nations in Eastern Europe and South America.

The IMF assessed Germany's situation at the time as follows: "during 1952 gold and dollar holdings increased substantially at the same time that aid from the United States and hoped that the Federal Republic of Germany will continue to pursue such policies as will enable it to make further progress toward convertibility."[17] Thus, it pointed out a gap between the level of restrictive and discriminatory measures and actual circumstances. In response, Germany pointed to differences from its prewar position and argued that "there are still a number of inherent weakness in the German position in world trade."[18]

Germany described the reasons for this assessment as follows: "German exports (by volumes) in 1951 were only 126 per cent of the 1936 level, whereas in the United Kingdom, France and the United States they were 173, 226 and 293 per cent, respectively. During 1951 United Kingdom exports of machinery and electrical equipment were 1.5 to 2 times those of Germany, while in the prewar period they were only one-half to three-fourths those of Germany....Germany's share in world exports is now 4.6 per cent, against 6.6 per cent before the war."[19] In this way, Germany continued to maintain a cautious stance even after establishing a stable surplus.

Promoting exports to the dollar zone was a pressing issue. Germany had been implementing restrictive and discriminatory measures such as an import license system and a retention quota (foreign currency to stimulate exports) system (Devisenbetriebsfonds). The retention quota system gave exporters preferential treatment in using for imports of some of the foreign currency they earned from exports, as a means of stimulating exports.[20] A system of free foreign-currency quotas (Devisenfreibetrag) was introduced from July 1950 to March 1951, allocating to exporters 20 % of the value of their exports. This was followed by the import rights system (Einfuhranrechte) implemented beginning in April 1952. Under this system, exporters could retain 40 % of the value of exports when they involved the securing of dollars or Swiss francs, using these import rights to import certain products within 3 months or else selling them to others.[21] In mid-April 1952 the premium on import

---

[17] IMF, Federal Republic of Germany-1952 Consultations, February 16, 1953, SM/53/11. IMFA, p. 26.

[18] IMF, Federal Republic of Germany-1952 Consultations, February 16, 1953, SM/53/11. IMFA, p. 7.

[19] IMF, Federal Republic of Germany-1952 Consultations, February 16, 1953, SM/53/11. IMFA, pp. 6–7.

[20] See Asai (2005), pp. 52–55, concerning the system of foreign currency allocation to promote exports and the case of Japan.

[21] IMF, Federal Republic of Germany-1952 Consultations, February 16, 1953, SM/53/11, IMFA, p. 14, Table 1; also see Dickhaus (1996), S. 136, in particular note no. 82.

rights reached 20–20.75 %, and exporters received them at an exchange rate of 4.54 marks to the dollar, which fell to 4.41 marks to the dollar in May. However, the premium later fell massively to 13–14.5 % in mid-May, 4.60–5.25 % in December 1952, and 2 % in February 1952 (Dickhaus 1996, S. 136). This drop was due to the progress of import liberalization policies and decreasing demand for imports.

Minister of Economics Erhard told IMF staff that Germany intended to abolish this system of import rights to the extent that it could.[22] To Germany, these import rights were merely a temporary, emergency measure to secure markets for exports. Another reason for the desire to abandon the system was the fact that as the price differential between dollar and non-dollar markets disappeared and the premium decreased, its direct effects were limited. The IMF saw it as problematic that these import rights were traded at a premium, resulting in dual exchange rates, but it was uncertain whether Germany actually would move to abolish the system.[23] This is because although Germany had stated its intention to abolish the system it also had made this conditional on countries such as France and the Netherlands abolishing their own such systems at the same time.

3 The IMF and Revaluation of the Deutschmark

3.1 IMF Executive Board Discussions (June 1957)

While the liberalization rate for imports from the OEEC region already exceeded 80 % at the time Germany joined the IMF, liberalization for imports from the dollar zone did not start until February 1954 (at a rate of 51.9 %: 29.8 % for agricultural produce, 61.0 % for raw materials, and 70.5 % for finished products).[24] The start of this liberalization brought about major changes to Germany's trade transactions. The liberalization rate for imports from the dollar zone increased further in November 1954 (to 56.9 %: 30.0 % for agricultural produce, 68.7 % for raw materials, and 75.8 % for finished products) and May 1955 (to 68.1 %: 49.6 % for agricultural produce, 75.6 % for raw materials, and 78.2 % for finished products). Due to the effects of these increases in the liberalization rate and the benefits of supplies of imported raw materials, in 1955 Germany's imports from the dollar zone rose by 68 % and its exports to that same zone grew by 30 %.[25]

[22] IMF, Federal Republic of Germany-1952 Consultations, February 16, 1953. SM/53/11. IMFA, pp. 11–16.

[23] Mission 1953 (Friedman and Staff), Barend A. de Vries, Germany: Staff Visit on Retention Quotas, May 20, 1953. CF C/Germany/810. IMFA.

[24] See Neebe (2004), S. 384, concerning the figures on liberalization rates for imports from the dollar zone (February 1954-June 1956) discussed in this section.

[25] IMF, Federal Republic of Germany-1955 Consultations, March 20, 1956. SM/56/26. IMFA, pp. 8–9.

The IMF saw this increase in imports as having made a major contribution to Germany's domestic price stability.[26] In June 1956, the liberalization rate for imports from the dollar zone reached 92.7 % (88.4 % for agricultural produce, 96.0 % for raw materials, and 82.7 % for finished products), roughly the same level as the liberalization rate for the OEEC region. Also, since limited convertibility mark (beschränkt Konvertierbare Mark: Beko-Mark) accounts were opened in April 1954, Germany no longer was dependent on bilateral settlement, and the diversification of settlement advanced (Buchheim 1990, S. 154–155; Dickhaus 1996, S. 187–189). Under this system, through the creation of these accounts EPU member states and countries that were parties to bilateral agreements were handled for transaction purposes as the same region. As is clear from the above, in 1956 it appeared that Germany would succeed in liberalization of trade and foreign exchange. In response, in its Article XIV consultation (FY1956) the IMF regarded highly Germany's moves toward easing of restrictions and abolition of discriminatory practices. Recommended to Germany that restrictions on imports were no longer necessary in order to safeguard Germany's monetary reserves and balance of payments.[27]

On June 11, 1957, the IMF Executive Board met and discussed the FY1956 Article XIV consultation regarding Germany. In response to this consultation, the main topic of discussion in the Executive Board was Germany's extreme surplus position, and a succession of representatives of Western European states including Britain, France, and Denmark expressed criticisms of Germany.[28] This is because in contrast to Germany's current account deficit with the dollar zone, its surplus with the OEEC region increased rapidly, so that the regional imbalance had grown further. Also, as pointed out in the IMF Executive Board, in 1956 Germany's gold and foreign reserves grew rapidly to USD1.213 billion.[29] The current account surplus was a new contributing factor to domestic inflation, and the risk increased that no matter how hard Germany tried to stabilize domestic prices inflation would be imported to the country through an inflow of foreign currency. For this reason, Germany's financial policies also were a subject of discussion. Germany's anti-inflationary measures were understood to have had the effect of intensifying the deficits of Western European states. As discussed below, the OEEC Council of Ministers was unable to bring a conclusion to the difference of opinions between Germany and Britain on the former's monetary policies, so that the IMF Executive Board was charged with resolving this conflict.

The IMF Executive Board did not consider Germany's extreme surplus position to be desirable, to the extent that its stance gave the impression of recommending policies of intentional inflation in order to regulate Germany's current account sur-

---

[26] IMF, Federal Republic of Germany-1955 Consultations, March 20, 1956. SM/56/26. IMFA, p. 18.

[27] IMF, Federal Republic of Germany-1956 Consultations, May 27, 1957. SM/57/46. IMFA, pp. 28–29.

[28] IMF, Minutes of Executive Board Meeting, June 11, 1957. EBM/57/25. IMFA, pp. 8–9.

[29] IMF, Minutes of Executive Board Meeting, June 11, 1957. EBM/57/25. IMFA, p. 8.

plus.[30] Canadian representative Louis Rasminsky observed: “the conflict between the policies Germany felt necessary for its domestic situation and those it pursued on the external side had been obvious for some time and that the consequences of this conflict were serious for other countries, in addition to being unwelcome in Germany. He thought Mr. Thorold had accurately described the situation: either the surplus Germany had achieved had to be dealt with in a way which did not impose pressure on other countries or steps had to be taken in Germany or elsewhere to reduce it to acceptable levels.”[31]

In response to the criticisms of Germany, IMF representative director Emminger argued that Germany was most interested in striving to maintain domestic equilibrium in the future as well. This was because over the preceding 2 years Germany's wage level had risen by 15 % and its price level by 4–5 %. Emminger offered the following argument: “In a country whose population was very sensitive to inflation, this was certainly sufficient justification for taking anti-inflationary measures. Germany had also made sizable attempts at cutting down trade barriers, the over-all effect of which was a much larger increase in imports than in domestic expenditure over the last three years. From 1953-56 total demand in Germany increased by about 34 per cent, while demand for imports rose by 56 per cent. That this big expansion in internal demand and especially in demand for imports did not lead to a better external balance, could only be explained by the fact that, at the same time, demand, wages and prices in other countries were rising even more.”[32]

Germany's gold and foreign reserves were increasing, and this led to expansion of domestic liquidity. Growing demand from Western European states combined with their inflationary growth policies to accelerate Germany's imported inflation. This would continue until the 1970s as what was called Germany's lonely international struggle to achieve domestic stability (Einzelgang in Stabilität) (Emminger 1986, S. 30–33). This was because the fixed exchange rate system did not have a mechanism for immediate adjustment of differences in inflation. In the IMF Executive Board, Emminger rejected the possibility of revaluation of the mark, citing as the reason “such action would tend to increase the German dollar deficit and, thus, the over-all European dollar deficit.”[33] However, as noted in the Introduction to this chapter Emminger himself was a central figure in proposing the revaluation of the mark. At root, Emminger's favored argument was that this situation could be resolved by employing flexible foreign exchange market policies to avoid domestic inflationary effects in Germany and maintain stability in the value of German currency (Emminger 1976, S. 513; Holtfrerich 1998, S. 400–413; James 1996, pp. 112–113).

[30] IMF, Minutes of Executive Board Meeting, June 11, 1957. EBM/57/25. IMFA, pp. 9–11; also see James (1996), pp. 111–112, concerning U. K. representative's demand.

[31] IMF, Minutes of Executive Board Meeting, June 11, 1957. EBM/57/25. IMFA, p. 10.

[32] IMF, Minutes of Executive Board Meeting, June 11, 1957. EBM/57/25. IMFA, pp. 3–4; Otmar Emminger an Herrn Bundesminister für Wirtschaft, 12. Juni 1957, Betr. Deutschland-Konsultation 1956. B330/1087. HADBB.

[33] IMF, Minutes of Executive Board Meeting, June 11, 1957. EBM/57/25. IMFA, p. 14.

Even so, Emminger could not obtain sufficient understanding of this argument within the Länderbank, where it was considered a peculiar view. As a result, Emminger refrained from making his favored argument on revaluation of the mark in the IMF Executive Board as well.

Cautionary, conservative views were stronger within the Länderbank. It was expected that the current account surplus would decrease with the advancement of foreign exchange liberalization and promotion of investment in Germany (Schlesinger 1976, S. 595). On the other hand, it retained the liberalized capital mark (liberalisierte Kapitalmark: Libka-Mark) accounts established in September 1954 as the sole means of investment in marks, attempting to control capital inflows through these accounts (Buchheim 1990, S. 165; Dickhaus 1996, S. 189–192). Under these circumstances, from the IMF's point of view Germany did not appear to be attempting to implement any measures at all, instead simply accumulating foreign reserves and avoiding drastic measures such as a revaluation of the mark.[34]

3.2 Currency Speculation and the IMF Annual Meeting (September 1957)

In July 1957, the foreign exchange markets saw fierce currency speculation in anticipation of a revaluation of the mark and devaluation of the franc. This development put strong devaluationary pressure on the pound as well. In the foreign exchange markets the impression that the mark was undervalued steadily grew stronger.[35] Figure 8.1 shows Germany's gold and foreign reserves in 1957. Speculative currency flowed from Britain and France to Germany at the start of July. Later, even the effective devaluation of the franc (by 16.75 %) was unable to curb this speculation, and new inflows from the Netherlands began in August.[36] The inflow of foreign exchange contributed significantly to Germany's accumulation of gold and foreign reserves, which peaked in September (Emminger 1976, S. 493).

These inflows had been spurred by the anti-inflationary policies of the Central Bank of Germany (Deutsche Bundesbank; Bundesbank hereinafter). This led to full discussion of how to regulate Germany's current account surplus and how to prevent imported inflation. As already noted, Germany's current account imbalance began in its balances with OEEC member states, and the currency speculation began with its currency ties to OEEC member states. IMF Director of Research Jacques J. Polak focused on the way Germany's exports were affected broadly by the Western European states.[37] In 1956 Germany's net surplus with the EPU was more than

[34] The German Balance of Payments Situation and the Question of Revaluation, 24. August 1956. CF C/Germany. Box 11. IMFA.

[35] See Tüngeler (1982), S. 35, concerning the foreign exchange markets in 1957.

[36] Jacques J. Polak, Balance of Payments 1954–1957, Germany's Balance of Payments Surplus -A Statistical Analysis, September 18, 1957. CF C/Germany/1430. IMFA, p. 5.

[37] Jacques J. Polak, Balance of Payments 1954–1957, September 18, 1957. CF C/Germany/1430. IMFA, pp. 13–15.

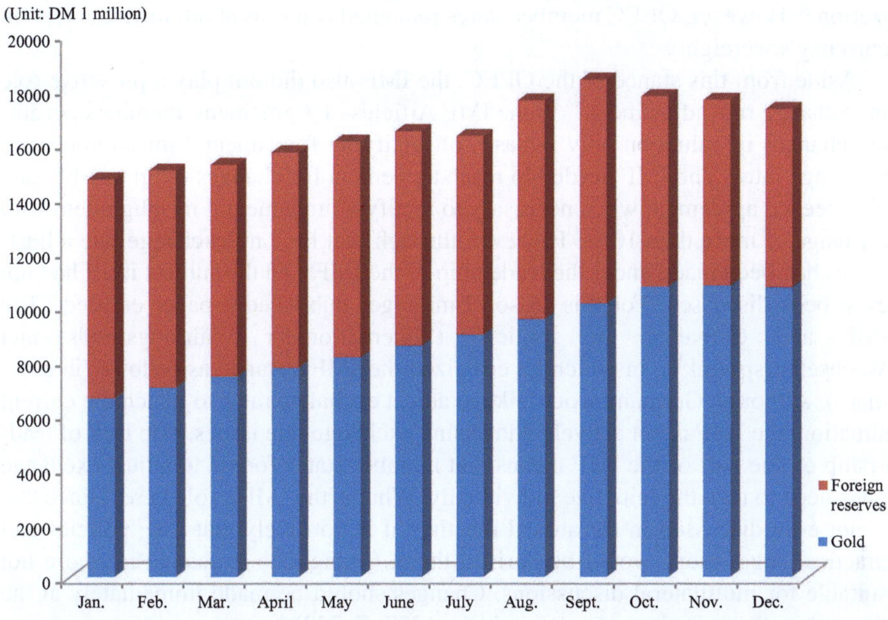

Fig. 8.1 Germany's gold and foreign reserves (1957) (*Source*: Based on statistics from the Deutsche Bundesbank website. http://www.bundesbank.de/Navigation/DE/Statistiken/Zeitreihen_Datenbanken Außenwirtschaft, Auslandsposition der Deutschen Bundesbank bis zum Jahresende 1998)

USD1 billion. This surplus was roughly equal to the total amount of the deficits of France (–USD654 million) and Britain (–USD269 million) combined. Polak's analysis led him to the conclusion that the main factors behind Germany's current account surplus were growth in exports and a lack of pure credit creation by financial institutions. These two factors were inextricably linked. If Germany's exports increased together with credit expansion, then imports would increase at an even faster pace and the surplus should have shrunk. However, in 1956 credit creation by German financial institutions was in a decreasing trend. Within the framework of this analysis Polak determined that the Bundesbank needed to relax monetary policy in order to regulate the surplus.

Multilateral adjustments to exchange rates were one conceivable way of rectifying the currency relationship with OEEC states. However, the OEEC was unlikely to serve as a venue for discussion of such adjustments. This is because ever since the conflict with the IMF Executive Board when it actively supported the devaluation of the pound in September 1949 the OEEC had acknowledged exchange rate adjustments to be within the IMF's sphere (Kaplan and Schleiminger 1989, p. 258, 264; Tanaka 2000, p. 148, in particular note no. 25). Later, relations between the IMF and the OEEC began to improve with the 1952 standby credit provided by the IMF to Belgium (James 1996, p. 97–98). The IMF recognized the need to build a system for cooperation with the OEEC in order to promote trade and foreign exchange liberalization.[38] However, OEEC member states remained cautious about infringement on currency sovereignty.

Aside from this stance of the OEEC, the IMF also did not play a proactive role in exchange rate adjustment.[39] In the IMF Articles of Agreement, members permitted changes in valuation only in cases of rectifying fundamental misalignment of exchange rates. The IMF needed to reach agreement for changes of up to 10 % and also needed agreement when necessary to rectify a fundamental misalignment with a change of more than 10 %. However, through that time no exchange rate adjustments had been made under the leadership of the IMF, and the subject itself had not even been discussed. For this reason Emminger published a paper entitled "The IMF and exchange rate policy" ("Internationaler Währungsfonds und Wechselkurspolitik"), in which he criticized the IMF's stance as follows (in summary): Although Germany would like to adjust exchange rates to match the current situation, the IMF is not actively addressing exchange rate issues. The lack of leadership on the part of the IMF means that member states forced to adjust exchange rates need to take the initiative individually. What is the IMF's role here? Since this is not even discussed in the annual meeting, it is not likely that IMF policies and practical suggestions would be derived there. Changes to exchange rates are not suitable for multilateral discussions. Changes should be made immediately at the time when they are necessary (Emminger 1957, S. 732).[40]

Contrary to Emminger's argument, in its annual meeting (in September 1957) the IMF Board of Governors decided to maintain current exchange rates under the leadership of the IMF and to eradicate currency speculation through cooperation between Britain and Germany.[41] Through the Board of Governors, Germany recognized the activities of the IMF as having secured an influence not seen before in calming the foreign exchange markets and bringing currency speculation under control.[42] In this meeting British Chancellor of the Exchequer and OEEC chair Peter Thorneycroft and German IMF representative and EPU chair Hans-Karl von Mangoldt-Reiboldt issued a joint statement that said, "Current exchange rates will remain unchanged and there is no need to set a floating range."[43] This statement reflected the fact that Britain desired secret bilateral talks with Germany and expected prudent action by Germany with regard to the pound's difficulties. Emminger understood the compromise with Britain in the following terms: "Britain

---

[38] Co-operation with OEEC, July 1, 1953. EBD/53/87. IMFA.

[39] See James (1996), p. 115: "There had been no international discussion at all appropriate exchange rate policy in the event of german changes, either in the OECD or at the IMF."

[40] This article focused on the IMF's role in exchange rate adjustment. Also see James (1996), pp. 101–102, and Holtfrerich (1998), S. 406, in particular note 180, concerning the proposed exchange rate bands discussed in Emminger's article (1957).

[41] See Kaplan and Schleiminger (1989), pp. 262–263; Holtfrerich (1998), S. 406, concerning the 1957 annual IMF general meeting.

[42] Bundesminister für Wirtschaft an Staatssekretär des Bundeskanzleramtes, 6. Dezember 1957. B102/12660. BArch, S. 1–4.

[43] Otmar Emminger an Bundesministerium Abteilung VI, Btr.: Deutsche und Englische Erklärungen auf der IWF-Tagung, 24. September 1957. B102/12660. BArch, S. 1–2.

is desperate to maintain exchange rates, as a devaluation of the pound and loss of credibility would have severe repercussions on the Labour government. Britain is seeking Germany's support to secure international trust in the pound. Under these circumstances, Germany probably would face resentment if it were to spur distrust in the pound."[44] Britain welcomed the decision of Germany, which sought to avoid revaluation of the mark, and it curtailed criticism of Germany after the IMF general meeting. The harmonization of monetary policies implemented prior to the joint statement (in which Britain's official discount rate rose from 5 to 7 % and Germany's decreased from 4.5 to 4 %) also demonstrated results in curbing speculation (Kaplan and Schleiminger 1989, pp. 262–263; Holtfrerich 1998, S. 406). This agreement between Germany and Britain suggested an IMF stance of avoiding adjustments that would lead to new distrust in another country's exchange rate.[45]

Judging the agreement between the two countries to represent an important outcome in political terms as well, not just for purposes of currency policy, Emminger saw this agreement as the first fruits of the OEEC in connection with future currency discussions in Europe. However, at the same time he saw Germany as being able to revalue the mark in an emergency without being bound by this agreement. He was concerned about the extent of Managing Director Jacobsson's influence, which he saw as a "role beyond understanding" ("unverständliche Rolle") (Emminger 1986, S. 85–88). In fact, the conclusion of the annual meeting of the IMF Board of Governors reflected Jacobsson's thinking. Declaring the end of postwar inflation, Jacobsson was opposed to revaluation of the mark. This was because he saw leaving exchange rates alone as the best policy because revaluation would bring about further speculative currency inflows (James 1996, pp. 113–114). Furthermore, he also argued for Germany to adjust the current account surplus through repayment of foreign debts ahead of schedule, shouldering of defense costs, and capital exports in the form of aid to developing countries, and Britain too strongly supported this position.

4 The IMF and Currency Convertibility of the Deutschmark

4.1 Encouragement of Capital Exports: IMF Article XIV Consultation (FY1957)

The declaration in the annual meeting of the IMF that exchange rates would be maintained as they were curbed the currency speculation that had anticipated revaluation of the mark. However, starting at the end of 1957 current account imbalances among OEEC member states grew, so that Germany faced even stronger pressure

[44] Otmar Emminger, Btr.: Konfliktsmöglichkeiten zwischen England und Deutschland in der Währungspolitik, 10. Oktober 1957. B102/12660. BArch, S. 1–5.

[45] Otmar Emminger, Bericht über die Jahrestagung 1957 des Internationalen Währungsfonds (IWF), 30. Oktober 1957. B102 /12660. BArch, S. 1–11.

for measures to adjust its current account surplus. Germany's current account surplus was the subject of criticism at the IMF annual meeting.

In its Article XIV consultation (FY1957), the IMF again recommended Germany, as it had in FY1956, that "restrictions on imports are no longer necessary in order to safeguard Germany's monetary reserves and balance of payments."[46] On the subject of the continuation of Germany's current account surplus, it stated, "Without endangering price stability, the Government may wish to consider policies designed to maintain internal demand and production at high levels, thus ensuring a buoyant market for imports and contributing to the expansion of world trade."[47] The IMF welcomed the stimulation of capital markets and promotion of capital exports, in particular expecting German capital exports to make a major contribution to balanced growth in the global economy. This statement by the IMF overlapped with the November 1956 demands of the OEEC board. The OEEC called for publicly funded capital exports as a short-term measure until the capital markets recovered and the structure of interest rates improved, arguing that Germany's anti-inflationary measures could not be expected to lead to private-sector capital exports.[48] This demand reflected the judgment that imbalances among OEEC states were unlikely to be balanced without future measures on the part of Germany. This would require consideration for debtor countries.

In response, the IMF Article XIV consultation (FY1957) discussed the calls for capital exports as a measure for adjustment of the current account surplus.[49] IMF staff asked the German side for its views on whether it thought there were any prospects for increasing capital exports, either through private or public funds, and on whether it thought it would be possible to adjust the current account surplus through capital exports. The IMF thought that Germany was not likely to implement direct measures to encourage private-sector capital exports since the German government was strongly oriented toward a market economy. Backed by the growth of its competitive strength in global markets, Germany's private-sector capital exports were in an increasing trend, rising rapidly from DM383 million (1956) to DM780 million (1957). Despite this, since demand for domestic capital was high and a unilateral increase in private-sector capital exports could not be expected, the IMF concluded that it would take even more time to adjust the current account surplus. Germany argued that it would be difficult to promote public-sector capital exports due to the tight federal budget situation, and the IMF also fully acknowledged this difficulty. Comprehensive treatment of prewar and postwar debts was finalized and the London Debt Agreement concluded.[50] Decisions also already had been made on large amounts of additional expenditures such as short-term and medium-term loans to

[46] IMF, Federal Republic of Germany-1957 Consultations, June 4, 1958. SM/58/43. IMFA, p. 26.

[47] IMF, Federal Republic of Germany-1957 Consultations, June 4, 1958. SM/58/43. IMFA, p. 26.

[48] Betr. Weltbank: Weitere Freigaben aus der deutschen 18 %-Quote, 14. Dezember 1956. B136/3339. BArch.

[49] IMF, Federal Republic of Germany-1957 Consultations, June 4, 1958. SM/58/43. IMFA, pp. 13–14.

[50] See Nishimuta (2007) pp. 85–93 and Scholtyseck (2013), S. 334–348, concerning the London Debt Agreement.

the International Bank for Reconstruction and Development (IBRD) (in the amount of USD175 million).[51] In connection with the start of the European Economic Community (EEC), Germany also needed to make political considerations for France. For this reason, Germany approved a withdrawal of marks (DM189 million) from the IMF as financial support for the French currency crisis, and it extended a special line of credit (DM420 million) to France through the EPU. It also decided to provide new capital to the European Investment Bank (DM126 million) and capital to the European Development Fund (DM84 million).

As seen above, IMF staff was concerned about the burden of capital exports on Germany. However, in the June 1958 meeting of the IMF Executive Board that discussed this point, U.S. representative director Frank A. Southard and British representative director Thorold strongly pressed Germany to carry out long-term capital exports.[52] This debate greatly interested other representative directors, including Bhaskar N. Adarkar of India who had expectations for Germany playing an active role in development aid as well as the representatives of Canada, Greece, and Finland. Discussing Germany's international contributions, Emminger cited loans to the IBRD and provision of credit overseas.[53] However, Southard pressed further, commenting, "the German authorities had no additional plans to promote private capital exports." And "he wondered why the German authorities had not considered the establishment of an institution along the lines of the U. S. Export-import Bank."[54] Also, while regarding highly the loans to the IBRD, Thorold argued that those alone were not enough. What Britain expected of Germany was an increased shouldering of defense costs and support for the pound through lessening the costs of stationing troops in Germany, payment of external debts ahead of schedule, and prepayment for defense-related imports.[55] Germany responded to these demands because it expected Britain's support for the reunification of East and West Germany and its active support in response to any provocation from the Soviet Union (Zimmermann 2002, p. 81).

4.2 The Shift to IMF Article VIII Nation Status (February 1961)

Germany shifted from IMF Article XIV nation status to Article VIII nation status in February 1961. Germany's political considerations for Britain and France were expressed in the form of a simultaneous shift to IMF Article VIII status (Schmidt 2003, S. 157). Convertibility of the mark was restored in December 1958 for

[51] See Ishizaka (2012), pp. 22–24, concerning the German capital exports through the IBRD in the 1950s.

[52] Otmar Emminger, Bericht über den Abschluss der Konsultation 1957 zwischen dem IWF und der Bundesrepublik, 30. Juni 1958. B330/1087. HADBB.

[53] See Harries (1998), S. 60–62, S. 223–225. Germany's Reconstruction Loan Corporation (Kreditanstalt für Wiederaufbau) accepted a USD10 million line of credit from the EXIM for August-Thyssen-Hütte for import of machinery from the U.S. in 1956 and provided credit to India, Iceland, and the Sudan in 1958.

[54] IMF, Minutes of Executive Board Meeting, June 27, 1958. EBM/58/29. IMFA, p. 4.

[55] IMF, Minutes of Executive Board Meeting, June 27, 1958. EBM/58/29. IMFA, pp. 5–6.

nonresidents and in May 1959 for residents of Germany. In this way, convertibility of the mark had been restored fully at the end of the 1950s, earlier than for the currencies of other Western European nations. Before that, Germany had begun preparations for shifting to Article VIII status in the summer of 1955, expecting an early demand for such a change in status from the IMF.[56] This is because it understood the shift to Article VIII status to reflect the progress of trade and foreign exchange liberalization by individual countries. However, since Britain and France desired to shift to Article VIII status at the same time as Germany, Germany's shift to Article VIII status was put off even though it had satisfied the conditions for the shift.[57] In December 1958, convertibility of Western European currencies was restored for nonresidents. However, there were significant gaps among Western European states in their progress on trade and foreign exchange liberalization.

While Germany had expected the shift to Article VIII status to be discussed in the IMF Executive Board meeting held in July 1959, no specific discussions of the matter took place at that time. Behind this were the concerns of Britain, which was ready to attempt a restoration of the pound.[58] In March 1959, the British government learned through IMF representative director George Cromer that the response of Managing Director Jacobsson would be to permit the postponement of Germany's shift to Article VIII status and to approve a simultaneous shift of the leading Western European powers.[59] In response, when the IMF Article XIV consultation (FY1958) for Germany began in April the British government asked Germany to postpone its shift to Article VIII status until such a time as a simultaneous shift in status of Western European states would be possible.[60] In response to this request, on June 30, 1959, secret talks were held between British Deputy Chancellor of the Exchequer David B. Pitblado and Fritz Stedtfeld, head of the foreign economic bureau in Germany's Federal Ministry of Economics. In this meeting the British side argued again that considerable time still would be needed before a shift to Article VIII status. As a result, Germany was unable to identify the specific time at which such a shift would be possible.

On the other hand, the EEC currency committee began meeting on June 22, offering an opportunity for unofficial discussions with France on shifting to Article VIII status. Here it was confirmed that France had a positive view on a simultaneous shift in status.[61] Emminger and Banque de France Vice-President Pierre Calvet both served as deputy chairs of this committee, and through discussions between these

[56] Vertrauliche Ausarbeitung für Mr. Rooth über "Deutschland und Art. VIII", 23. August 1955. B330/1058. HADBB.

[57] See James (1996), p. 108, concerning the "gentlemen's agreement" with Britain.

[58] Otmar Emminger, Vermerk: Betr. Übergang von Art. XIV zu Art. VIII im Internationalen Währungsfonds, 12. Juni 1959. B330/1058. HADBB.

[59] W. Hanemann an Bundesminister für Wirtschaft, Betr.: Übergang zu. Art. VIII des IWF-Abkommens, 27. März 1959. B330/1058. HADBB.

[60] Otmar Emminger, Vermerk: Betr. Übergang von Art. XIV zu Art. VIII im Internationalen Währungsfonds, 12. Juni 1959. B330/1058. HADBB.

[61] Entwurf einer Weisung an Herrn Dr. Guth, Betr. Übergang von Art. XIV zu Art. VIII, 10. Juli 1959. B330/1058. HADBB.

two it was reported that Germany was asking Britain for its views on a simultaneous shift to Article VIII status. France, which was in the middle of a currency crisis, suggested that a simultaneous shift to Article VIII status would be difficult before 1960.[62]

Germany determined that the response of Western European states depended decisively on Britain's course of action, and that it would not be realistic for it to shift to Article VIII status without Britain.[63] For this reason, it took into account Managing Director Jacobsson's support of a simultaneous shift of Western European states, centered on Britain, to Article VIII status. In October 1960, Irving S. Friedman, Director of the IMF's Exchange Restrictions Department, proposed to Germany the timing for a simultaneous shift in status, with Germany expected to take the initiative.[64] In this way, Germany became responsible for coordinating the shift with Britain and France.

5 Conclusion

How are we to understand Germany's interactions with the IMF from the 1950s through the start of the 1960s? When Germany revalued the mark by 5 % in March 1961, Jacobsson was furious but the IMF Executive Board approved it without objection (Emminger 1986, S. 126–127; James 1996, p. 115; Holtfrerich 1998, S. 413). Emminger assumed heavy responsibilities in the EEC currency committee, and in 1959 he was replaced as Germany's representative director to the IMF by Bundesbank statistics bureau chief Wilfried Guth. In a way that expresses clearly the view in Germany at the time, Guth regarded Managing Director Jacobsson as follows: While he attempted to enhance the existing international currency system, to those who considered it antiquated and those seeking to create a new order he was no more than a conservative Managing Director. From the start, Jacobsson acted based on the assumption of how to put the existence of the IMF to use within the existing framework (Guth 1964, S. 11). Furthermore, Guth understood Jacobsson's convictions to be as follows (in summary): Global economic growth is possible only under a system of stable, fixed exchange rates. A system of floating exchange rates is dangerous. This conviction is reflected strongly in the policies of the IMF Managing Director, and the role of the IMF as an organization is limited to responding to a currency crisis (Guth 1964, S. 11). As is clear from these statements from Guth, as early as the mid-1950s a new movement had begun in Germany arguing for utilizing flexible foreign exchange market policies to avoid inflationary effects on the domestic economy, as seen in Emminger's proposal. However, in fact Jacobsson had tremendous influence as IMF Managing Director. This choice also was influenced by the fact that the first President of the Bundesbank Karl Blessing shared

[62] Germany's Relation to International Monetary Fund, April 28, 1959. RG56. Box 49. NARA.

[63] Wilfried Guth, Betr.: Übergang zu Artikel VIII und damit zusammenhängende Fragen, 17. Juli 1959. B330/1058. HADBB.

[64] Wilfried Guth, Übergang zu Art. VIII, 14. Oktober 1960. B330/1059. HADBB.

Jacobsson's convictions. From the mid-1950s through the start of the 1960s, Germany's views were not united, and the country continued to act through trial and error (James 1996, p. 110–115; Holtfrerich 1998, S. 400–413).

At the end of the 1950s, in a complex situation that involved signs of the weakening of the dollar and the rise of the mark, Germany prioritized political considerations first, implementing capital exports and accepting the postponement of its shift to Article VIII status. After that, through the 1960s the Bundesbank acted as an important international credit institution both inside and outside the IMF. The Bundesbank provided this international credit because it saw itself as having a special responsibility for the survival of the Bretton Woods system (Emminger 1976, S. 550). While international credit from the Bundesbank was able to postpone the end of the Bretton Woods system, it was no more than temporary financial support and was unable to create a new international currency order (Lindenlaub 2008, S. 13–34).

As we have seen in this chapter, Germany's capital exports implemented beginning in the latter half of the 1950s emerged out of consideration for OEEC member states faced with current account deficits. To Germany, which considered its ties to Britain and France to be very important, demands from the OEEC were more influential than the IMF, even as it continued working together with the IMF. On the other hand, discussions on adjusting exchange rates did not advance within the OEEC. As a result, the revaluation of the mark was a decision made by Germany itself. However, this revaluation should be recognized as more than just an example of the currency sovereignty of a single country. It proved an important opportunity for powerfully advancing currency cooperation among EEC Common Market member states beginning in the 1960s, by harmonizing the interests of those member states.[65] Topics for future discussion include the rise of the mark as a central currency and Germany's contributions in currency cooperation.

Primary Sources

International Monetary Fund Archives (IMFA), USA
National Archives and Records Administration (NARA), USA
  RG56, The Department of Treasury
Bundesarchiv (BArch), Koblenz/Germany
  B102, Bundesministerium für Wirtschaft
  B136, Bundeskanzleramt
Historisches Archiv der Deutschen Bundesbank (HADBB), Frankfurt am Main/Germany
  B330, Dienststelle des Direktoriums der Bank deutscher Länder und der Deutschen Bundesbank

[65] See Emminger (1986), S. 129–131; Tietmeyer (2005), S. 23–24; Zimmermann (2008), p. 160, in particular note no. 16. Emminger lists as one of the international impacts of the revaluation of the mark the promotion of currency cooperation among Western European states, and former Bundesbank President Hans Tietmeyer makes the same point in his memoirs.

References

Asai, Yoshio. 2005. IMF8 jōkoku Ikō to Bōeki Kawase Jiyūka: IMF to Nippon 1952–1964 nen (Japan's Participation in the IMF Article VIII Countries: Japan & IMF 1952–1964, Part I). In *The Institute for Economic Studies Seijo University*, No. 42.

Buchheim, Christoph. 1990. *Die Wiedereingliederung Westdeutschlands in die Weltwirtschaft 1945–1958*. München: R. Oldenbourg Verlag.

Bührer, Werner. 1997. *Westdeutschland in der OEEC, Eingliederung, Krise, Bewährung 1947–1961*. München: R. Oldenbourg Verlag.

Dickhaus, Monika. 1996. *Die Bundesbank im westeuropäischen Wiederaufbau: Die internationale Währungspolitik der Bundesrepublik Deutschland 1948 bis 1958*. München: R. Oldenbourg Verlag.

Emminger, Otmar. 1957. Internationaler Währungsfonds und Wechselkurspolitik. In *Zeitschrift für das gesamte Kreditwesen*, 18. Heft, 732–736. Frankfurt am Main: Fritz Knapp Verlag.

Emminger, Otmar. 1976. Deutsche Geld- und Währungspolitik im Spannungsfeld zwischen innerem und äußerem Gleichgewicht: 1948–1975. In *Währung und Wirtschaft in Deutschland 1876–1975*, ed. Deutsche Bundesbank, 485–554. Frankfurt am Main: Fritz Knapp Verlag.

Emminger, Otmar. 1986. *D-Mark, Dollar, Währungskrisen: Erinnerungen eines ehemaligen Bundesbankpräsidenten*. Stuttgart: Deutsche Verlags-Anstalt.

Furuuchi, Hiroyuki. 2007. *Gendai Doitsu keizai no Rekishi (A history of the modern German economy)*. Tokyo: University of Tokyo Press.

Guth, Wilfried. 1964. Per Jacobsson in memoriam (1894–1963). In *Zeitschrift für die gesamte Staatswissenschaft*, Bd. 119, Heft 4, 1–12. Tübingen: J. C. B. Mohr.

Harries, Heinrich. 1998. *Wiederaufbau, Welt und Wende, Die KfW-eine Bank mit öffentlichem Auftrag*. Frankfurt am Main: Fritz Knapp Verlag.

Holtfrerich, Carl-Ludwig. 1998. Geldpolitik bei festen Wechselkursen (1948–1970). In *Fünfzig Jahre Deutsche Mark: Notenbank und Währung in Deutschland seit 1948*, ed. Deutsche Bundesbank, 347–438. München: Verlag C. H. Beck.

Ishizaka, Ayako. 2006. 1950 nendai Nishidoitsu ni okeru Naigaikeizaifukinkō: Shakaitekishijyōkeizai no Kiki (Disequilibrium between National and International Economic Accounts in the 1950s West Germany: Dilemma of the 'Social Market Economy'). In *Shinjiyūshugi to Sengoshihonshugi: Ōbei ni okeru Rekishitekikeiken* (Neo-Liberalism and the Post-War Capitalism: The European and American experiences from historical perspectives), ed. Gonjo Yasuo, 255–299. Tokyo: Nihon Keizai Hyōronsha.

Ishizaka, Ayako. 2012. IMF 14jyōkoku jidai no doitsu: Yōroppa no kurojikoku kara Shihon yushutsu koku he (From regional surplus nation to global capital exporter: German as an Article XIV Member of the IMF (1952–1961)). In *REKISHI TO KEIZAI (The Journal of Political Economy and Economic History)* 217: 16–27.

Jacobsson, Erin E. 1979. *A life for sound money: Per Jacobsson, His biography*. New York: Oxford University Press.

James, Harold. 1996. *International monetary cooperation since Bretton Woods*. New York: Oxford University Press.

Kaplan, Jacob J., and Günther Schleiminger. 1989. *The European payments union: Financial diplomacy in the 1950s*. Oxford: Clarendon.

Lindenlaub, Dieter. 2008, Karl Blessing [1900–1971]. In *Deutsche Bankiers des 20. Jahrhunderts*, ed. Pohl, Hans, 13–34. Stuttgart: Franz Steiner Verlag.

Lindenlaub, Dieter. 2013. Die Errichtung der Bank deutscher Länder und die Währungsreform von 1948: Die Begründung einer stabilitätsorientieren Geldpolitik. In *Schlüsselereignisse der deutschen Bankengeschichte*, ed. Lindenlaub, Dieter, Carsten Burhop, Scholtyseck, Joachim, 297–319. Stuttgart: Franz Steiner Verlag.

Neebe, Reinhard. 2004. *Weichenstellung für die Globalisierung: Deutsche Weltmarktpolitik, Europa und Amerika in der Ära Ludwig Erhard*. Köln: Böhlau Verlag.

Nishimuta Yuuji. 2007. 1953nen London Saimu Kyōtei ni kansuru Saikin no Kenkyū Doukō (Recent studies on the London Debt-settlement Agreement of 1953). In *SHAKAI-KEIZAISHIGAKU (Socio-Economic History)* 73(1): 85–93.

Schlesinger, Helmut. 1976. Geldpolitik in der Phase des Wiederaufbaus: 1950-1958. In *Währung und Wirtschaft in Deutschland 1876–1975*. ed. Deutsche Bundesbank, 555–607. Frankfurt am Main: Fritz Knapp Verlag.

Schmidt, Heide-Irene. 2003. "The Embarassment of Strength": Die deutsche Position im International Monetary System 1958–1968. In *Deutschland, Großbritannien, Amerika: Politik, Gesellschaft und Internationale Geschichte im 20. Jahrhundert*, ed. Lehmkuhl, Ursula/Clemens A. Wurm/Hubert Zimmermann, 155–195. Stuttgart: Franz Steiner Verlag.

Scholtyseck, Joachim. 2013. Das Londoner Schuldenabkommen 1953: Das Tor zur Welt öffnet sich wieder. In *Schlüsselereignisse der deutschen Bankengeschichte*, ed. Lindenlaub, Dieter, Burhop, Carsten, Scholtyseck, Joachim, 334–348. Stuttgart: Franz Steiner Verlag.

Tanaka, Ryoichi. 2000. Seiō Tūka no Kōkansei Kaifuku: Doitsu no Keizai seicyō to EPU mekanizumu no 'genkai' no Kanten kara (Convertibility of European currencies in the 1950s). Ritsumeikan kokusai kenkyu (*The Ritsumeikan journal of international studies*) 13(2): 133–150.

Tietmeyer, Hans. 2005. *Herausforderung EURO: Wie es zum Euro kam und was er für Deutschlands zukunft bedeutet*. München: Carl Hanser Verlag.

Tüngeler, Johannes. 1982. *Die D-Mark im internationalen Währungsgefüge, Rückschau auf Leben und Arbeit*. Teil II, Frankfurt am Main.

Yago, Kazuhiko. 2007. Kokusai Kinyū Kikanshi (History of International Financial Institutions) In Kokusai Kinyū Shi (*History of international financial system)*, ed. Kamikawa, Takao, Yago, Kazuhiko, 321–345. Tokyo: Yuhikaku.

Zimmermann, Hubert. 2002. *Money and security: Troops, monetary policy and West Germany's relations with the United States and Britain, 1950–1971*. Cambridge: Cambridge University Press.

Zimmermann, Hubert. 2008. West German Monetary Policy and the transition to flexible exchange rates, 1969–1973. In *Orderly change: International monetary relations since Bretton Woods*, ed. D. M. Andrews, 155–176. Ithaca, New York: Cornell University Press.

Chapter 9
The IMF and Italy: Trade Liberalization and Return to Convertibility

Kanna Ito

From the beginning of the 1950s to 1963, Italy experienced rapid economic development and eventually declared the external convertibility of its currency with the major European nations in 1958. In this period, Italy participated in the Bretton Woods system and the European integration process. In this chapter, we will review how the Bretton Woods system infected and restricted the economic policy management of the member countries by examining the Italian experience.

1 Italy's Accession to the IMF

In 1943, when the Allies started to talk about constructing a new international monetary regime, this news also reached Italy. After the liberation of Rome on April 25, 1944, the Italian government was eager to participate in the International Monetary and Financial Conference of the United Nations and its allies at Bretton Woods in July, but they were not allowed to participate, even as observers. The Italian government set up a committee of experts that reached a final consensus in September, after several months of discussion, that Italy should be incorporated into the international economy without delay because of its large dependence on the import of raw materials and the export of handicraft products and for the purpose of its political revesting after the long international isolation forced by the fascist regime. In addition, they expected that admission to the Bretton Woods organizations would promote stabilization of the domestic economy.[1] Italy submitted its application for

[1] Regarding the Italian accession to the Bretton Woods Agreement, refer to Cotula (2001), pp. 75–109; Di Taranto (2007).

K. Ito (✉)
Faculty of Economics, St. Andrew's University,
1-1 Manabino, Izumi, Osaka 594-1198, Japan
e-mail: kaito3@andrew.ac.jp

K. Yago et al. (eds.), *History of the IMF*, Studies in Economic History,
DOI 10.1007/978-4-431-55351-9_9

the IMF and the IBRD on February 14, 1946; however, it encountered immediate protests from the representatives of Greece and Yugoslavia. They insisted that since Italy was the former enemy, its application should not be accepted before having signed the peace treaty. Then, the Executive Board of the IMF set up a special committee to discuss this subject, where the American representative took the stance that there were no obstacles for Italy's participation in the IMF because Italy had been admitted as a cobelligerent country in 1943 and had made an important contribution in the fight against Germany. In addition, Italy had reinstituted diplomatic relations with almost all of the Allies that did not intend to obligate Italy to accept every condition of the armistice agreement. The United Kingdom also affirmed this stance. Then, the Executive Board of the IMF admitted Italy to membership on October 2, 1946; Italy joined the IMF and the IBRD on March 27, 1947.

The amount to be paid by Italy as the IMF quota was 180 million U.S. dollars. This was far less than the 300 million dollar cost that was anticipated by the Italian government. Italy's reserve, however, was nearly exhausted; it came up short by approximately 30 million dollars in gold in its payment to the IMF. Therefore, when Donato Menichella[2] visited the USA while attending Prime Minister De Gasperi in January of 1947, his highest priority objective was to negotiate a loan and raise the funds necessary for membership in the IMF. The loan of 100 million dollars, obtained at that time from the Export–import Bank, provided the first pathway to knowing the latest American mechanical products for Italy and the first stimulus toward modernizing the industrial facilities in Italy (see Cotula 2001, pp. 50–51; Segreto 2000).

2 The 1947 Monetary Stabilization

Partnership with the IMF and the assistance of the U.S. government helped Italy to reconstruct its monetary stability. The war had reduced the value of the lira, since wholesale prices were 25 times higher at the end of the war than they had been before it. Then, after a year of monetary calm, another serious bout of inflation began in the second half of 1946. According to Menichella, this new inflation was preceded by a boom in equity prices and foreign exchange quotes. The banks withdrew large deposits from their accounts with the Bank of Italy and expanded their loans for the industrial recovery and speculative dealings of securities and commodities. The government's bread price control policy placed a financial burden on the budget, and the deficit was financed by the monetary base creation through

[2] Donato Menichella assumed the position as the general director of the Bank of Italy on April 19, 1946, by recommendation of Luigi Einaudi, governor of the Bank at that time. He engaged in a bailout and liquidation of the big bank groups in the 1920s, then executed a series of public interventions in the banks and the industrial companies after 1933 as the general director of the Institute for Industrial Reconstruction (Istituto per la ricostruzione industriale, IRI). Carli outlined how the recruitment of Menichella disappointed the industrialists of northern Italy and made them hostile to Einaudi's initiatives. Carli (1993), p. 84.

rediscounts at the Bank of Italy (Fratianni and Spinelli 1997, p. 170; Cotula et al. 2003, p. 464). Although supported by United Nations Relief and Rehabilitation Administration (UNRRA) aid, the shortage of coal, iron, and food was critical. Furthermore, the forecast that the aid would soon end fueled people's fears. Since the rations that could be obtained with coupons were so small, people turned to the free market and the black market, where the biggest rises in food prices occurred. The upswing was strengthened by keen foreign demand for Italian products, especially textiles; at the end of the year, it led to such an appreciable rise in wage rates that the resultant increase in domestic demand for consumer goods far exceeded their supply. Thus, during the 15 months covered by the new inflation process, the wholesale price average climbed from 25 times the prewar level to 60 times and beyond. The expectation of further rises led to large-scale hoarding and stock building on the part of producers, and companies and individuals obtained bank loans and rushed to invest in real estate, gold, and jewelry. The flight of capital gained impetus, and the official reserve declined sharply.[3]

Per Jacobsson, economic advisor and head of the Monetary and Economic Department of the Bank for International Settlements (BIS) at the time, stayed for several months in Rome starting in January of 1947 at the height of inflation in order to study the Italian economic situation.[4] He kept in close contact with the Bank of Italy's research department. Jacobsson observed closely and concluded that the basic cause of the rapid rise in Italian prices was the excessive liquidity remaining after the war. This conclusion coincided with the opinion of the Bank of Italy. That same January, right after returning from his mission in the USA, Menichella spoke at a general meeting of the Italian Banking Association. He reported his conversations in the USA and urged Italy to cope with the problem of paying their balance; to this end, stabilization of the currency would be essential. On that basis, he requested that bankers not accommodate credit for excessive stock accumulation and warned that failure to comply would result in the introduction of the reserve requirement system.[5]

At the end of May of 1947, Luigi Einaudi joined the government as deputy prime minister and minister of the budget, while his friend, Gustavo Del Vecchio, was appointed minister of the treasury, and Menichella replaced Einaudi as governor of the Bank of Italy. The legislature approved the bill that allowed the new monetary instrument; therefore, continuance of the stabilization program was guaranteed. Einaudi, a liberal economist with an academic career as a professor of public finance at Turin University, had commented on the government's economic conduct as a columnist in a widely read Italian newspaper for more than 30 years. Additionally, he wrote articles, showed how fast credit had expanded, and justified the policy of

---

[3] Regarding Einaudi's fight for stabilization, see Archivio Storico Banca d'Italia (ABI), Direttorio Menichella (DM), cart. 98, fasc. 1, pp. 78–88, "Introductory Remarks: Per Jacobsson and Monetary Development in Italy, 1946–1947," 1966; Fratianni and Spinelli (1997), pp. 168–171.

[4] Regarding Jacobsson's study on the Italian problem, see Jacobsson (1979); BIS (1949).

[5] Cotula et al. (1997), doc. 12 "Discorso all'assemblea dell'Associazione Bancaria Italiana," 18 gennaio, 1947.

checking excessive credit expansion by means of the reserve requirements. In this way, Einaudi turned public opinion to his side, as Menichella described.

The new system of compulsory reserves was introduced in August, and the official discount rate was raised from 4 to 5.5 % in September.[6] In the midst of the polemics unleashed by the new provisions, Einaudi resolutely declared that he would not hesitate to raise the reserve ratio even more sharply if the new demand for credit was intended for hoarding. He explained that it included the hoarding of land, houses, jewelry, gold, foreign currency, and stocks and shares, which many firms had been buying as a hedge against further price rises, utilizing bank credits that they had requested ostensibly for production and trade. Thus, Einaudi demonstrated a rigorous and inviolable stance of credit restriction. Banks no longer readily complied with demands for increased credit. The credit restrictions were soon reflected in a large-scale liquidation of stocks held in anticipation of higher prices. Once several key prices fell, consumers expected further price decreases and bought only to meet their immediate needs, and the hoarding stopped. Wholesale prices, which had risen by 70 % in the first 9 months of 1947, showed continuous reduction from the peak in September of 1947 until February 1948. Within 5 months, wholesale prices declined by 14 %, retail prices by 12 %, and the cost of living by 10 %, remaining unchanged since.[7] Inflation was halted. Jacobsson wrote later that it was a violent shock; however, a shock is generally necessary when things have gone so far—as they had done in Italy—that confidence in the currency has been shaken.[8]

The second point of the government's anti-inflationary policy was reduction of the deficit. In October of 1947, Einaudi stated in the Constituent Assembly (functioning at the time as Parliament) that the budget deficit introduced harm, such as the growth of public loans, that amounted to more than 2,000 billion lire at the end of June of 1947. As a result, the value of the currency was declining, and savings and securities holders would suffer losses and be impoverished; therefore, stabilization should be done for them. Then, he declared that the essential condition for stabilization was budget equalization. He cited the statement of Camille Gutt, governor of the IMF, the high authority for international currencies, that in several countries, the large budget debt was the root of inflation. Thus, the start point of monetary and economic reforms should be equalization of revenue and budget expenditures. This must be the real balance, that the real revenue derived from the current national revenue should cover expenditures on the public's behalf. Neither banks of issue nor commercial banks should provide funds for the public expenditure. Einaudi stated that, in Italy, such perfection was too much to ask; however, it would

[6] Regarding the deposit requirement, see Fratianni and Spinelli (1997), p. 174: "Credit institutions had to deposit with BI or purchase government securities for an amount equal to 20 % of the difference between their deposit base and ten times their net worth, and 40 % of any subsequent increase in deposits. Amounts deposited with BI yielded the interest applied on short-term Treasury bills less 25 basis points." Cfr. BIS (1949), p. A3.

[7] IMF SM/248, "The Financial Situation in Italy," June 21, 1948.

[8] ABI, DM, cart. 98, fasc. 1, pp. 78–88; Cotula (2001), pp. 51–53.

suffice if the national budget would equalize not only by tax revenue but also by issuing treasury bonds and government bonds.[9]

Throughout the period from 1945 to 1960, when Einaudi and Menichella governed the Bank of Italy, maintaining the currency's stability was considered to be the top priority; therefore, the authority aspired to constrain the creation of excessive liquidity by banks and to stimulate investment by mobilizing the savings to the public bond market. Actually, introduction of the compulsory reserve made banks invest a part of their liquidity in treasury bonds. Therefore, the compulsory reserve supported the public bond market.[10] The Bank of Italy, the custodian of the compulsory reserve, became a real central bank, and its authority over credit control was consolidated. Furthermore, soon after stabilization of the currency, regulations that restricted financing the budget deficit by monetary base creation were established, giving sufficient autonomy of currency flow control to the central bank.[11]

3 Dispute with the IMF About the Italian Floating-Rate System

Article XIV of the Articles of Agreement of the IMF also applied to the Italian accession to the IMF. As Section 2 of the same article stipulated, Italy, which was admitted "in the postwar transitional period may, notwithstanding the provisions of any other articles of this Agreement, maintain and adapt to changing circumstances (and, in the case of members whose territories have been occupied by the enemy, introduce where necessary) restrictions on payments and transfers for current international transactions." Italy aspired to the application of this article because it adopted the exchange control and floating exchange rate system.

In the middle of March of 1947, on the eve of signing the Agreement, however, an issue was raised in the IMF Executive Board meeting.[12] Ernest de Selliers, the Belgian executive director, raised the question of the introduction by Italy, as lately as 1946, of a legal free market for foreign currencies, which he considered to be contrary to the principles of the Fund's Agreement. He suggested that Italy should not be allowed to become an active member of the Fund until such a time as the free market had been abolished. The consensus was opposed because so long as Italy

[9] Einaudi, "Intervento all'Assemblea Costituente," 4 Ottobre, 1947, in Barucci (2008). For the fiscal year of 1946–47, only 50 % of the expenditure was covered by real revenue. See BIS (1949), pp. A2–A3.

[10] For example, in 1956, approximately 330 billion lire of the reserve deposit with the Bank of Italy was invested in tresuary bonds. IMF SM/57/23, "1956 Consultation—Italy," p. 5.

[11] Regarding the legal reforms of the Bank of Italy, see Fratianni and Spinelli (1997), pp. 174–189; Cotula (2001), pp. 12–18. In the middle of 1945, 97 % of the Bank of Italy's assets was treasury credit. Einaudi, assuming the post of governor in January, criticized the situation at that time, saying that rather limited room was left for the bank of issue's autonomous action.

[12] IMF EBM/Meeting 147—March 18, 1947.

was not a member of the Fund, it was under no obligation with regard to the Fund Agreement and had the full right to adopt any monetary policy it wished. Additionally, since the board of governors determined the terms and conditions upon which Italy would be admitted to membership, the executive board could not presume to modify those terms and conditions. Furthermore, even after Italy became a member, she would be covered by the transitional provision of Article XIV, Section 2. Therefore, the discussion should take place after Italy's joining of the Fund.[13]

The currency reforms from 1926 to 1928 charged the Bank of Italy with managing currency policy and reserves in Italy. Then INCE (Istituto nazionale per i cambi con l'estero, or the National Institute for Foreign Exchange), established by the organizational changes in the 1930s, monopolized all exchange operations and, with ICE (Istituto per il commercio estero or Institute for Foreign Trade), was entrusted with the tasks of regulating the distribution of exchange, coordinating import and export services, and regulating purchases abroad for the accounts of all State departments and agencies. Since 1934, it was prescribed that all foreign currency and foreign assets must be ceded to the government. The licensing systems for all imports and exports were introduced in 1939 and 1940, respectively; every import or export had to be authorized. From that time until the beginning of 1946, the foreign exchange operation was totally monopolized by the government. After the war, the role of the INCE was taken over by its successor, the UIC (Ufficio Italiano dei Cambi, or the Italian Foreign Exchange Office),[14] and the governor of the Bank of Italy doubled as the chief of the UIC. Thus, the Bank of Italy assumed authority for managing the foreign exchange and reserves.

Immediately after landing, the Allies established the official rate of 100 lire to the dollar and 400 lire to the pound sterling. Since the official rates were overestimated, they were raised, so far as merchandise trade was concerned, by 125 % in January of 1946. Then, forced cession of all export proceeds at the official rate was relaxed by legislative decree on March 26, 1946, which installed a free market for the U.S. dollar, the pound sterling and the Swiss franc, and the "50 percent system." Since then, exporters have been required to sell one half of their foreign exchange proceeds earned on exports to countries without a trade agreement to the UIC at the official fixed rate (225 lire to the dollar); the other half might be used for the specified import within the given period or sold for the importers through authorized banks in the legal free market. This was the first step toward liberalizing the foreign exchange in postwar Italy. Since the exchange rate fluctuates in response to the

[13] Regarding Italian exchange control, see IMF, Research Department (RD)—234, "Foreign Exchange Practice in Italy," April 10, 1947; EBM, Meeting 182—July 1, 1947; Meeting 223—November 12, 1947; Cotula (2001), pp. 16, 46–48; Fratianni and Spinelli (1997), p. 170.

[14] The UIC mediated foreign exchange trade directly and indirectly from a period of the absolute monopoly of the foreign exchange until April of 1990, when the restriction regarding foreign exchange was totally abolished. See the UIC (1995), p. 171.

demand and supply of the foreign exchange in the free market, the free rate[15] declined continuously from the first rate of 364 lire to the dollar, reflecting the large Italian demand for imports. In 1947, when the government deficit problem became more acute, the free rate dropped to 690 lire to the dollar in March; the difference from the official rate was widening. An IMF study stated that the legal existence of a "free" foreign exchange market in Italy created, in fact, a multiple-currency system that involved some elements of discrimination between trade-agreement and non-trade-agreement countries and was incompatible with the objectives of the Fund. The IMF showed, however, some understanding that its existence might be a policy of transition toward a new readjustment of the exchange value of the lira, and its elimination must depend on the normalization not only of Italy's position but also of the European exchange market in general.[16]

After Italy's accession to the IMF, Guido Carli[17] became executive director for Italy in May of 1947. On July 1, at the executive board meeting, he reported on recent monetary developments in Italy and pointed out that the existing multiple exchange rate system had been initiated after the War to meet the dual need for a fixed official rate in connection with financial charges imposed by the Armistice and for a fluctuating rate that would facilitate equilibrium between external prices and changing internal prices. To eliminate discrimination, Italy took steps to use the rate average of the official rate and the free rate for all exports and imports in near future (at the time, 100 % of export and all but 15 % of import transactions were settled at or near the average rate). He also said that Italy wanted to establish a single, stable exchange rate as soon as possible; however, because of the continuing upward trend in internal prices, a fixed rate was not desirable at that time. He further pointed out that the balance of payment equilibrium would depend on the possibility of restoring normal intra-European trade, the backbone of Italian trade before the War. Without remedying the dislocations in her foreign trade, there would be few prospects for price stability, and the exchange rate would hardly be stabilized before the economy would be balanced.

Carli's explanations showed that Italy placed greater importance on intra-European trade than on trade with the USA and intended to postpone declaring the par value until the monetary, economic, and balance of payment's stability could be obtained. These policy lines would be points of arguments with the IMF in the 1950s.

Two weeks after Carli's explanation at the executive board meeting, Menichella, governor of the Bank of Italy and chief of the UIC, wrote to Giorgio Cigliana, the

---

[15] The exchange rate in the free market was called the "free rate" (IMF, Bank of Italy), the "export rate" (Bank of Italy), and the "free market rate" (BIS) at the time. In this chapter, we use the term "free rate."

[16] IMF SM/79, "Foreign Exchange Practice in Italy," April 11, 1947.

[17] Guido Carli was an official of the IRI from 1938 and dealt with war planning. He was chosen by Einaudi for the UIC in 1945, served as the executive director for the IMF (from 1947), as chairman of the EPU (1950–1952; as a member until 1958), as Minister for Foreign Trade (1957–1958), as governor of the Bank of Italy (August 1960–July 1965), as President of Confindustria (1976–1980), as a senator (1983–1992), and as Minister of the Treasury (1989–1992). Cfr. Asso (2011).

representative of the New York office of the UIC, and asked him to explain his vision to Edward Bernstein, the chief of the research department of the IMF and other members of the IMF and the IBRD during casual conversation. His vision was to see that the Italian multiple exchange rate regime could fully defend its legitimacy in the sense of Agreement article XIV, Section 2 against criticism from other IMF members and for the evolution of the existing Italian regime toward unified exchange rates and the multilateralization of international trade. If Italy were to fix a single rate for the lira on the basis of a middle rate between the export rate and the official rate, it would be more economical than those of other European countries' rates that were overestimated against the dollar. Taking into account the trend toward unification of the foreign exchange market that was inherent in the evolution coupled with the Italian authorities' discipline on the subject at that time, it might be pointed out that the foreign critics were irrational and intended to impede the Italians' progress. Furthermore, Menichella commented that Bernstein's proposal (refer to Carli 1993, pp. 67–68) for reorganizing the Italian regime was intended to establish a monopoly on the sale of foreign exchanges that would pull Italy backward and inevitably lead to the establishment of monopoly prices. This would probably result in the subsequent distancing of the official exchange rate from the economic rate, which was in opposition to the spirit of the Bretton Woods Agreements.[18]

On the other hand, there seemed to be an attitude at the IMF that, taking into consideration the severe economic conditions in Italy at that time (1947), no other choice could be made to allow for the existing exchange practice. When the IMF's managing director, Gutt, reported on his trip to Italy at the executive board meeting in November, he reviewed the Italian economic situation and credit restraint measures and commented that, as Carli had emphasized, the main need of the existing floating exchange system was to ensure a flow of imports to keep the economy working. For Gutt, the system also appeared to be a necessary balancing mechanism as long as stability was lacking.[19]

At the start of the stabilization program in August of 1947, the official rate of the lira rose from 225 lire to 350 lire to the dollar. At the time, the monthly average of the free market rate was approximately 700 lire.[20] Through reform introduced by the Decree of November 28, 1947, with a view toward unifying the rate structure, the fixed official rates were practically abolished; one half of all foreign exchange receipts ceded to the monetary authorities would be sold at a rate established every

---

[18] Cotula et al. (1997), doc. 16 "Lettera di rappresentante dell'Ufficio Italiano dei Cambi a New York Giorgio Cigliana," Roma 14 luglio, 1947.

[19] IMF EBM 223, November 12, 1947.

[20] The quotes for Italian bank-notes on the free market in Switzerland, corresponding to the quotes for foreign currencies on the black market in Italy, reached their maximum in May of 1947 when, at times, nearly ITL 950 was paid for a dollar, while the official rate was only ITL 225. BIS (1949), p. A3.

month at the average of the free market rates during the previous month, with upper and lower limits of 650 and 350 lire to the dollar, respectively. This brought the end of the multiple exchange rate system, and the current rates were based on the quotes in the free exchange market, subject to official intervention, when necessary. The quotes had been kept extraordinarily stable without any great difficulty, being maintained almost unchanged at approximately 575 lire to the dollar (BIS 1949, p. A6; Cf. Cotula 2001, pp. 53–54).

The IMF executive board discussed these changes in Italian foreign exchange practice several times starting on December 2.[21] Carli pointed out that the primary aim of the changes had been to facilitate finding an exchange level at which the value of the lira could be stabilized. When that took place, Italy hoped to agree with the Fund on a par value and assume the full rights and obligations of Fund membership. Andrew Overby, the IMF's executive director for the USA, considered the new system to be a desirable step toward a greater reality. Various questions were raised as to the workings of the system. Then, the managing director asked the directors what position the IMF should publicly take on the new Italian measures. George Bolton, The IMF's executive director for the United Kingdom, insisted that since he believed such systems were opposed to the basic principle of the Fund Agreement for the stability of rates and to members' obligations to promote exchange stability and maintain orderly exchange arrangements among members, the IMF could not make any statement implying approval or even a lack of objection. A number of related questions were raised, such as whether the changes Italy had made came under Article XX, Section 4(d)(iii); if not, agreement with the IMF was necessary, and in the absence of an agreement, any action would be ultra vires. As to these points, Carli replied that he did not believe that Italy was subject to the obligations of Article XX, Section 4(d)(iii), since it had not communicated a par value. He said that the objective of the Italian government had been to permit the market to establish a realistic exchange rate in the hope that a stable par value could be achieved shortly thereafter and to encourage exports, both of which were in accord with the purposes of the IMF.

In the press release, emended several times based on these discussions, the IMF reported that the Italian modification brought the actual rate of exchange of the lira nearer to the equilibrium of the internal and external price levels, thus encouraging Italy's ability to export. In fact, the arrangements resulted in fluctuating exchange rates that were not in accord with the principles of the IMF. The IMF recognized, however, that members might be required, for temporary periods, to institute extraordinary measures in an attempt to overcome particular difficulties. The IMF felt sure that the Italian government was in full agreement with the long-range purposes of the IMF and would move toward the establishment of fixed and stable exchange rates as quickly as possible.

---

[21] IMF EBM228, December 2, 1947; EBM229, December 2, 1947; EBM230, December 4, 1947; EBD243 "Exchange Actions in Italy," December 3, 1947.

4 Reconstruction of the Foreign Reserve and Trade Liberalization

From the postwar period until the end of the 1940s, the top priority of the Italian currency policy was monetary stabilization and reconstruction of the reserves. Through the stabilization program initiated in September of 1947, confidence in the lira was regained, and exports increased with the devaluation. Therefore, in 1948, the balance of payment improved, and the official reserve became reconstructed. Four years of aid from the USA gave a foothold to the policy of reserve accumulation through the European Recovery Program (ERP). The Italian Government didn't use the counterpart fund, the so-called "fondo lire," the special account belonging to the government opened at the Bank of Italy and fed by the revenue from the sellout of American goods ceded gratuitously under the ERP for the 2 years from 1948 to 1949 to build up the reserves.[22] The Italian reserve accumulation policy generated a long dispute with the USA that strongly requested to use the fund for large-scale investment. The Italian authority insisted, however, that Italy needed to reconstruct abundant reserves so as to face the possible balance of payment difficulties upon termination of the ERP and to promote trade liberalization. Therefore, Italy gave higher priority to inflation control and reserve accumulation than to public investment. The prudent monetary policy of 1948–1949 had proved successful in increasing the volume of the gold and dollar reserves to approximately 600 million dollars, enough to cover 7 months of imports (cf. Cotula 2001, p. 20; Cotula et al. 2003, pp. 461–463). In 1949, industrial production recuperated to the level of 1938, the target of postwar reconstruction; the real national income and savings also increased. The Italian economy got on a definite path of growth.

Since 1949, Italy has proceeded rapidly with trade liberalization. With the maintenance of price stability, the economic growth of major western European countries in the 1950s, and the function of the European Payments Union (EPU),[23] Italian exports increased remarkably. Italy had nearly reached the limit of its EPU creditor quota by the end of October, 1951. To improve this situation, the export restriction was conceived; however, Ugo La Malfa, the Minister of Foreign Trade, decided to eliminate the quantitative restrictions on all of Italy's imports with few exceptions, such as cars, and successfully reduced the average import duties by 10 %. According to La Malfa, liberalization of imports from the OEEC area would alleviate demand pressure, curb price rises, improve living standards, make the Italian industry face competition, and ease the workload at the ministerial officials by handling the applications from importers every day (Martinez Oliva 2003, p. 20). By 1953,

[22] Cotula et al. (2003), p. 462. Einaudi explained the rationale behind the policy of not using the counterpart funds for public investment: As they did not come from loans or taxes, they were equivalent to a net creation of money, having dangerous implications in terms of inflation. See Martinez Oliva (2003), pp. 15–16.

[23] At the EPU, the multiple settlement system created at the end of 1950, each country's foreign position with other countries was to be reported monthly to the BIS and the offsetting claims cleared. Martinez Oliva (2003), p. 19. Carli chaired the managing board of the EPU for its first 2 years.

99.7 % of Italian imports from the EPU area have been freed, and Italy became the standard bearer of import liberalization among OEEC countries.

5 IMF Consultations and Italian Policy Management

Since 1952, the Italian government has consulted with the IMF regarding their continuing retention of the transition measures.[24] In this section, we will examine this consultation and shed some light on how the IMF has influenced Italian policy management.

5.1 Balance of Payments Deficit and Trade Restrictions in the Dollar Area[25] (1952)

The equilibrium of the balance of payments has been the important subject of consultations between Italy and the IMF. From the end of the World War to 1952, Italy had always operated with an overall deficit of goods and services. Until 1947, this deficit existed with both dollar and non-dollar countries. Since then, the general pattern has become one of a deficit vis-a-vis the United States and Canada, partially offset by an overall surplus with other areas. Dollar exports rose by 50 % over the 1950 average due to lower prices in Italy relative to other countries, the existence of some unused capacity, and improved marketing. On the other hand, due to the coal crisis in Europe and poor wheat harvests in Italy, the imports of bread grains and coal from the dollar area expanded significantly, and Italy's dollar deficit increased to some 328 million dollars in 1951, as compared to 209 million dollars in 1950. The Italian representatives stressed that Italy had attempted to achieve balance of payments equilibrium since 1947 through inflation control, reduction of the budget deficit, maintaining a stable dollar-exchange rate, and the accumulation of gold and dollar reserves. Deficit of balance of payments, however, increased to 125.7 million dollars in 1951; Italy's attempts to achieve equilibrium faced many difficulties.

When the IMF queried the comprehensive plan for coping with the overall deficit, the Italian representatives indicated that the policy pursued to that point had been to relax restrictions on imports from different areas in accordance with the availability of various types of exchange. The high degree of liberalization of imports from EPU countries had been made possible by the development of substantial surpluses with

---

[24] Article XIV, Sec. 4 stipulated that "Five years after the Fund begins operations, and in each year thereafter, any member still retaining any restrictions inconsistent with Article VIII, Section 2, 3 or 4, shall consult the Fund as to their further retention." On the consultation methods the Executive Meeting discussed and resolved in January 1952. IMF EBM/52/6, January 24, 1952.

[25] IMF ERD52/53 "Italy – Restrictive System 1952 Consultation," August 4, 1952; European and North American Department (ENA) 52/53 "Italy – Recent Economic Development (Consultation Memorandom)," August 5, 1952; SM52/53, "Italy – Staff Discussions 1952 Consultations," August 5, 1952.

those countries, whereas the limited availability of dollars had dictated the retention of more restrictions from the dollar area. The Italians emphasized that only if the commercial policy of the U.S. were changed markedly would Italy be able to improve its dollar position and substantially reduce the existing restrictions.

Another important subject was the Italian exchange practice. Italy had introduced the 50 % system and the floating-rate system that used the average of the previous day's closing rates of the foreign exchange markets in Rome and Milan as official rate. This rate had been maintained steadily at a level between 624 and 625 lire to the dollar since 1950, after some fluctuation following the devaluations of September–October 1949.[26] The IMF asked the methods by which the dollar rate kept stable at the desired level. The Italian representatives explained that all transactions were to be made through authorized banks; hence, the exchange authorities knew at each moment the availability of exchange retained by the exporters that represented the supply of exchange on the exchange market. By keeping the amount of licensed imports within the limits of such availability, the authorities could avoid excess demand in the exchange market and, thus, an upward trend in the exchange rate.

As illustrated above, the connection was clear between the licensing policy for dollar imports, the exchange rate policy, and the import policy for other areas in the Italian exchange and restrictive system. Hence, with regard to the question of the possible relaxation of dollar restrictions and reduction of discrimination, the Italian representatives maintained their stance that lessening the dollar import restriction would be difficult under existing conditions. The IMF staff concluded that because of the present magnitude of the Italian dollar deficit as well as the overall deficit and its continued dependence on foreign aid, the Fund could not urge Italy to substantially relax its present level of dollar restrictions.

5.2 *Trade Deficit Problems with the EPU Area (Since 1953)*

In 1953, the main subject of discussion was the underlying causes and remedies for the balance of payments deficit.[27] Italy shifted its import from the dollar area to the EPU area in order to solve the serious balance of payments deficit of the previous 2

[26] When Gutt visited Italy in August 1951, he asked the authorities whether, in view of the remarkable stability of the lira for more than two years, they had considered discussing the establishment of an initial par value with the Fund. They replied that the matter had been actively considered but there were a number of difficulties. Italy was concerned about the possible effects of rearmament, trade liberalization measures in connection with the OEEC, and any decline in aid from the ECA (Economic Cooperation Agency). However, the main uncertainty was that a new tariff system was being introduced, and the authorities could not know in advance the impact of the new measures on the cost of living. This topic was discussed again in the executive board meeting; however, Italian Executive Director, Cigliana repeated the same explanations. IMF, EBM/636, January 31, 1951.

[27] A series of meetings were held between delegates of Italy and the IMF staff team in Rome between September 21 and October 9, 1953. The principal delegate of the Italian government was Guido Carli, director of the UIC. Other officials authorized by their governments discussed specific issues with the IMF staff.

years. In the first half of 1953, such a shift occurred in the import of raw materials, equipment, and crude oil; hence, imports from the EPU area increased, and substantial improvements were made on the current dollar accounts.[28] However, the worldwide textiles slump after the post-Korean boom period and increasing competition, the restrictions on intra-European imports imposed by the United Kingdom (November 1951) and France (February 1952), and other factors severely hit important Italian exports such as textiles, fruits, and vegetables. Therefore, the trade surplus with the EPU area ($34 million) changed into a sizable deficit in 1952 ($397 million) and the first half of 1953 ($363 million), due to both a fall in exports and an increase in imports. The deterioration of the balance of payments with EPU countries became a very serious problem. *The Financial Times* reported on August 11, 1953, that the payment position of Italy had been steady deteriorating, changing from a persistent creditor nation to a debtor. Italy's EPU quota might have been exhausted by the following spring if no remedial action had been taken. The authorities in Rome had been considering partly abandoning trade liberalization, which at the time comprised almost 100 % of Italy's imports.[29]

The Italian government, however, decided to leave liberalization of European imports intact as far as possible, intending to deal with the balance of payments problem by attempting to shift imports from the OEEC countries and the dollar area to third countries (countries with bilateral trade agreements, e.g., Argentina, Brazil, and Egypt) from which essential raw materials could be obtained and paid for with increased exports. The IMF stressed that the proposed Italian policy would be moving in a direction away from the objectives of the Fund, that is, to promote multilateral trading arrangements. The Italian representatives emphasized that such measures were to be regarded as a temporary expedient, and possible alternatives would include deliberalization of imports from European countries, a reduction in investment, or a reduction in domestic consumption; however the government didn't hope to take these actions. The IMF concluded that if Italian exports could be expanded and overall restrictions on imports were not increased (in particular, if the present high degree of liberalization vis-a-vis the EPU area was to be maintained), the demand for imports would have to be reduced by a slowing up of the investment program or a reduction of Italian consumption of imported commodities by taxation or other means. The internal policy was always constrained by the objective of the balance of payments equilibrium.

---

[28] Wool had been imported from Argentina before trade liberalization with the EPU, but it no longer was available in sufficient quantities or at competitive prices. Therefore, there was a shift in purchases in the sterling area. There were also shifts regarding certain commodities such as wheat and copper from the dollar area to the EPU supply sources (e.g., Turkey and the Belgian Congo). IMF SM/53/89, p. 3. Exempted items for EPU import liberalization were automobiles (industrial protection), antibiotics (infant industry), and grains. IMF C/Italy/420.1 Box 4, File 1, December 22, 1953.

[29] "More Talks on Convertibility. Coming World Bank and OEEC Meeting," in *The Financial Times*, August 11, 1953. In September, 1952, the Italian minister, "La Malfa's announcement that Italy would retract its trade liberalization in case of need, and in the absence of concrete American support, prompted only generic expressions of appreciation. Further complaints on Italy's precarious situation following the French and British retreat and the threat of reactivating import controls also failed to produce tangible results." Martinez Oliva (2003), p. 21.

The IMF also considered that, to the extent that Italy could not attract foreign investment capital and as direct American economic aid diminished, the balance of payments would have to be improved by increasing exports, and Italy should make every effort to expand exports on a competitive basis. Menichella, governor of the Bank of Italy, shared this policy line and promoted awareness about improving productivity and competitiveness.

5.3 Disputes About Dollar Liberalization and the Re-establishment of Convertibility (1954)

In 1953,[30] the Italian balance of payments had shown a deficit of 460 million dollars on the areas of goods and services. Taking into account the private donations and net inward capital movements (320 million) and the official contractual repayments (some 50 million), the total deficit was 185 million and had been financed mainly through U.S. aid and EPU credit. Given the direct U.S. economic aid of 124 million dollars, Italy's official holdings of gold and convertible currency had shown a net increase of 115 million dollars in 1953.

Italy's trade position with the dollar area was a surplus of 39 million dollars due to a shift in imports from the dollar area to EPU countries and substantially increased dollar earnings from military government service and tourism.[31] On the other hand, Italy ran a deficit of 239 million dollars with the EPU area because of import restrictions and agricultural protection by partner countries, whereas Italian imports originating in EPU countries rose from 53 % in 1952 to 64 % in 1953—nearly 300 million dollars greater than in 1952. Italy had recently carried out measures to stimulate the export of capital goods to underdeveloped countries by way of export credits and credit guarantees. Latin American countries with which Italy had no compensation agreements and could pay in convertible currency were the destination for exports. Latin America welcomed the measures.

Since the year before, pressure by the U.S. government on Italy to eliminate the dollar import discrimination had increased.[32] On August 7, 1954, Italy expanded import liberalization from 10 % to approximately 25 % with the USA and 37 % with Canada. The IMF staffs appreciated this approach; however, at the executive board

---

[30] The IMF staff group visited Rome between July 14 and July 27,1954. The Italian government was represented by Carli, and the IMF staff group had technical discussions with officials of the Bank of Italy and the Ministry of Foreign Trade. IMF SM/54/113 "Italy—1954 Consultations," October 26, 1954; EBM/54/58, November 22, 1954.

[31] Net tourist receipts increased from 75 million dollars in 1952 to 131 million dollars in 1953. The IMF concluded that it was due to the fact that foreigners made increasing use of official channels for exchange conversion that showed the adequacy of the official rate; additionally, Italy had proven to be an attractive destination with relatively cheap prices. IMF C/Italy/1760 Box 18 File 2 "Adequacy of the Present Exchange Rate of the Italian Lire," August 9, 1954.

[32] "Guido Carli had earlier advocated a further tightening of controls on imports from the United States, provoking strong reactions by the American authorities." Martinez Oliva (2003), p. 23.

meeting in November, the directors for the dollar area commented that Italy had been able to accumulate gold and dollar resources and further reduction in discrimination might be in order and advantageous to the Italian economy.[33] The director for Italy, Gragnani, remarked that the Italian government firmly intended to decrease discrimination against dollar imports, but it believed caution had to be exercised in implementing the policy.

In 1954, the European countries disputed over a move to convertibility. In June, as a result of the debate, they decided to prolong the EPU system. On July 15–17, the OEEC ministerial meeting was held in London for a first review of convertibility. The backlash of Italian public opinion about convertibility was limited; however, La Malfa, who had promoted EPU trade liberalization with great enthusiasm for European integration, refuted the remark of Ludwig Erhard, West Germany's Minister of Trade, that the pound sterling and the mark would re-establish convertibility by the summer of that year. La Malfa warned that the French franc and the lira could not stand against such a venture, and the unilateral decision by the countries that could make the move to convertibility would demolish the European integration that had proceeded successfully until that time.[34] This shows that Italian authorities believed that an early move to convertibility and the consequent liberalization vis-à-vis the dollar area would be a major risk. They hoped that elimination of discrimination would be undertaken in the framework of common dollar liberalization measures in collaboration with other European countries. Therefore, the Italian government had submitted a memorandum on this question to the Ministerial Examination Group on Convertibility at its London meeting and proposed the adoption by European countries of a "common list" for the purpose of liberalizing the dollar restrictions and instituting a European Stabilization Fund. The latter idea had been accepted for further study by the Ministerial Group. At an IMF consultation, Italy explained that their proposal aimed, after the disappearance of the EPU, by furnishing adequate credits to the weaker European countries, to make it possible for them to apply the common list of dollar liberalization to the widest extent practicable. The IMF objected that adoption of the common list procedure for dollar liberalization might, at least initially, imply some dollar deliberalization on the part of those European countries that had gone the farthest in relaxing their dollar restrictions. That was not in accordance with the philosophy of the Fund Agreement,

[33] At the previous year's consultation, the IMF staffs noted that under the Italian dollar import restriction, raw materials, machinery, and food were given priority whereas consumption goods were strictly set aside. They considered that there was, no doubt, a great demand in Italy for American consumer products (such as refrigerators) with better quality for the same price and asked Italy to give an estimate of the demand for consumption goods that would be released if dollar imports of such goods would be freed. The Italian representatives, however, declined this request. IMF C/Italy/420.1, Box 4 File 1, September 22, 1953. Regarding liberalization in August of 1954, almost all of the additional goods were raw materials.

[34] La Malfa, Ugo, "La convertibilità della moneta," La Stampa, 25 giugno 1954. Cf. IMF SM/53/28 "Report on Discussions at the OEEC on the Future of EPU, April 9, 1953; SM/54/53 "Discussion on Convertibility in the OEEC Countries, May 12, 1954.

which required that each member country go as far in the direction of abolishing its exchange restrictions as its balance of payments position would allow.

5.4 Monetary Reform and the Liberalization for the Dollar Area (Since 1955)

In 1954, Italy achieved substantial further increases in production.[35] Wages rose while prices remained stable. The balance of payments deficit on goods and services showed considerable improvement. Notwithstanding deterioration of the dollar trade balance due to higher dollar imports, Italy had continued to run a small surplus on goods and services with the dollar area, taking into account the dollar receipts from military expenditures. However, a substantial deficit persisted with EPU countries in goods and services. At the executive director's meeting, the U.S. Director expressed his satisfaction over Italy's maintenance of internal stability. He thought, however, that the Italian authorities had been too cautious in liberalization and non-discrimination, more so than in other European countries. Despite Italy's large payments to the EPU, its gold and dollar reserves had increased by approximately 190 million dollars in the first three quarters of 1955, and the U.S. Director believed the Fund should urge Italy to take more action toward dollar liberalization. The other directors in the dollar area shared this opinion. The directors discussed the pros and cons of Italian policy considerations. Carlo Gragnani, the director for Italy, noted that Italy's total imports had increased 8 % in the first part of 1955, while imports from the dollar area rose to 40 % above those for the corresponding period the previous year. The increase in gold and dollar holdings was offset by a reduction in inconvertible currency holdings and an increase in the EPU indebtedness. He noted that the total amount of reserves had shown very little variation since 1951.

As we shall see below, the impact of the government's investment program on the balance of payments was always a matter of concern that caught the attention of the IMF. Reducing unemployment was an important objective of Italian economic policy. This objective was pursued by actively stimulating mass emigration and by promoting economic expansion through investment. Emigration increased remittances that contributed to solving the balance of payments problem. In 1952, however, because of great difficulties encountered abroad, Italy's efforts in this direction had been successful only to a limited extent (SM/52/53). Therefore, the government launched a long-term investment program. In the 2 years prior, the investment policy had been increasingly geared toward direct job creation for unskilled workers (in home construction and public works) and the development of Southern Italy. A large-scale investment caused the budget deficit to increase, involved a substantial and almost immediate increase in imports of raw materials and equipment, and

[35] 1955 consultation was held in September and discussed at the Executive Board Meeting in December. IMF C/Italy/420.1 Box 4 File 4 "Exchange Restrictions Consultations in 1955 Minutes of Meeting"; SM/55/77 "1955 Consultations – Italy"; EBM/55/62, December 27, 1955.

eventually caused the trade balance to deteriorate. Therefore, the IMF proposed to reduce public investment in 1953. The Italian government responded that they recognized that the investment program being carried out at the time put a serious strain on the balance of payments. It was difficult, however, to restrict the volume of investment because of the urgent social necessity of increasing employment and raising the very low standard of living in the south. The political pressure to maintain the present volume of investment was strong and could not be neglected by the government. Thus, Italy adopted mobilization by the Treasury of an increasing part of the available domestic savings to avoid a budget deficit and to maintain monetary stability (SM/53/89). In 1954, with the prospect that the 10-year-old development program (the Vanoni Plan, from 1953 to 1963) designed to reduce unemployment would cause the balance of payments to deteriorate for the next several years, the IMF staff and the directors questioned what resources Italy would use to finance the deficit. The Italian government pointed out that the main sources were U.S. economic aid, EPU credit facilities, sterling balances, and new additional resources. They emphasized that eventual implementation of the program was conditional on the availability of additional resources to absorb the effects of its balance of payments.[36] The IMF welcomed the Italian stance of maintaining internal stability and gearing any substantial increase in its present investment levels to the availability of additional resources (SM/54/113; EBM/54/58).

Since January of 1955, the government inaugurated the easing of regulations on foreign exchange so as to facilitate the investment of foreign private capital in Italy. First, in January, the tax on foreign exchange transactions was reduced. Exporters were allowed to use as they wished 50 % of their proceeds in Swiss francs. That spring, Guido Carli, president of Mediocredito Centrale (Central Institute for Medium-Term Credit) and EPU director, and Rinaldo Ossola, manager of the Paris branch of the Bank of Italy, made a direct plea to the cabinet to quickly improve the currency legislation. This was caused by the realization and impatience of the fact that a move toward convertibility by European countries had been accelerated unexpectedly, whereas the Italian currency system had not yet reached a level to move toward convertibility; they did not have a foreign exchange market, there was a monopoly on foreign exchange, and the 50 % mechanism for export currency was still valid. At that time, the guideline given by Menichella was to adhere strictly to the Bretton Woods Agreement and not depart from it. Thus, between 1955 and the summer of 1956, currency laws were legislated. In February of 1956, nonresidents who invested in Italy were allowed to repatriate their initial capital and accrued interests at the official exchange rate. In March, the Italian authorities settled the fixed rate between the lira and the currencies of the EPU countries. In June, a free

[36] "It begins to be clear…that the real limiting factor of an expansion of the investment policy in Italy is given by the balance of payments…: no one can misapprehend that we have the chance to borrow abroad…that would be necessary to cover the deficit of the balance of payments…determined and enhanced by the large investment policy." [translated by the author] D. Menichella, Dichiarazioni alla Commissione d'inchiesta sulla disoccupazione, Camera dei Deputari, Roma 1953, pp. 130–132, cited in Cotula (2001), p. 20, n. 58.

market for foreign banknotes was established. In July, credit institutions were authorized to carry out foreign exchange transactions with exporters and importers based on market conditions. Hence, foreign exchange transactions were liberalized, and the monopoly by the Exchange Office was attenuated. Furthermore, exporters were given the option of selling their entire foreign currency proceeds on the free market. This series of reforms created the foreign exchange market and decentralized most of the trade of currencies from a state monopoly to the banks. Therefore, the reforms met with virulent opposition and requests for postponement in the foreign trade bureaucracy, which feared losing exchange control of the currency.[37] These reforms sent out signals that the Italian government had given way to a return to convertibility; furthermore, thanks to the relatively high Italian interest rate, the influx of foreign capital into Italy was stimulated. The huge volume of foreign capital required to continuously implement the long-term investment program had been financed by the government, credit provided by the World Bank, the U.S. government, the EPU and the Swiss market, relatively low-interest bonds issued by private companies abroad (mainly in Switzerland), and banks' short-term borrowings and foreign direct investments.[38] After the currency reforms of 1955–56, the lira's credibility increased, and foreign banks and private institutions showed their confidence in Italy by granting credit and holding deposits with Italian banks in increasing amounts. Also, taking into account the receipt of a large amount of U.S. aid, Italy's official reserve increased continuously, until it amounted to more than 1,100 million dollars in September of 1956. The increase in exports in 1955 and 1956 was most marked for engineering products, iron, steel, metallurgical products, motor cars, office equipment, chemicals, and canned foods, in addition to its traditional exports of foods and vegetables, textiles, and other products. The sharp increase in exports reflected a very high rate of expansion of industrial production (by 9 % in 1955, 8 % in 1956). The economy had been growing steadily (the growth rate was 5 % in 1954, 7 % in 1955, and, due to poor crops, 4–5 % in 1956).

The expansion of the Italian economy continued in 1957. Industrial production had shown a steady and remarkable rise from the beginning of 1956.[39] The increase in employment, together with net emigration, exceeded the natural increase in the labor force, and registered unemployment fell by approximately 10 % from 1956 to

---

[37] Regarding the currency reforms of 1955 – 1956, see Fratianni and Spinelli (1997), p. 198; Carli (1993), pp. 120–123; Cotula (2001), p. 62; IMF C/Italy/420.1 Box 4 File 4, "1955 Consultation with Italy Summary Record of Meeting held on September 21, 1955". With the free market of foreign banknotes established in 1956, the emigrant remittance and foreign currency of tuorists were traded.

[38] IMF SM/57/23 "1956 Consultations—Italy," March 20, 1957; C/Italy/420.1, Box 4 File 5, "Exchange Restrictions Consultations in 1956. Minutes of Meetings"; EBM/57/18, April 24, 1957. 1956 consultations were held from December 3–10, 1956, in Rome. The Italian representative was Guidotti of the Bank of Italy, and the IMF staff also had meetings with Carli and Menichella.

[39] The 1957 consultation meetings were held in Rome from January 27–February 4. IMF SM/58/38 "1957 Consultations–Italy," May 9, 1958; EBM/58/25, June 11, 1958.

1957. Prices showed little change, and wages rose moderately. The Italian government preferred increases in productivity to lead to lower prices of industrial goods rather than to higher wages. Restrictions and discrimination against the dollar area were further reduced, and the percentage of dollar import liberalization was raised from 39 to 71. Both imports and exports expanded substantially. The trade deficit remained in the neighborhood of 700 million dollars, but net income from services, particularly tourism, and private donations rose sharply. The balance of payments on goods, services, and emigrant remittances shifted from a deficit in 1956 to a surplus in 1957. Official reserves of gold and foreign exchange increased by nearly 300 million dollars in 1957 and stood at 1372 million dollars (net) at the end of the year. In accordance with the provisions of the new decree, all restrictions on the repatriation of capital invested in the establishment or expansion of productive enterprises and on the transfer of income from that were abolished; hence, the capital transfer was deregulated. At the executive board meeting in June, the IMF directors expressed appreciation for the Italian successes—steady growth and reduction in unemployment within the context of internal stability—and emphasized that in view of the reserve position Italy had achieved, further trade liberalization should be possible. They requested extension at the same level of import liberalization to the dollar and non-dollar areas, to non-OEEC countries as well as the OEEC area, to reduce agricultural protections as well.

In January of 1958, the European Economic Community (EEC) was inaugurated, and the custom was reduced by 10 % as stipulated by Treaty of Rome. Intra-EEC trades were stimulated and expanded. The most remarkable progress for the Italian economy was the favorable development of the balance of payments. The net inflow of capital (by tourism, emigrant remittances, and private foreign investments) remained substantial, and the official reserves of gold and foreign exchange (net) rose by an additional 850 million dollars to approximately 2,200 million dollars at the end of the year. At the end of 1958, the Italian lira was declared externally convertible.

Additionally, the balance of payments remained strong in 1959, and reserves continued to expand to approximately 2,700 million dollars. With the new decree of June 9, 1959, liberalization of the dollar was raised from 71 to 85 %. Only three bilateral payment agreements remained, and measures to eliminate these were under active consideration. The IMF staff and directors welcomed and praised these developments; however, they noted that discrimination against dollar imports was still substantial and, in view of the improved Italian reserve position, balance of payments reasons no longer justified restrictions on dollar imports. Italy should make rapid progress in eliminating restrictions and discriminations.[40] In November, the Italian authorities put forward liberalization of the dollar to 97 % for the USA

[40] IMF EBM/59/40, October 7,1959; SM/59/55, "1959 Consultations–Italy."

and 99 % for Canada, raising it to approximately the same percentage as for OEEC countries.[41] Italy also paid its quota to the IMF.[42]

The IMF repeatedly asked Italy to declare the establishment of an initial par value leading up to the 1959 consultations. On March 15, 1960, the Italian government eventually communicated to the IMF a proposed par value for the lira of 625 lire to the dollar. The IMF acknowledged that since September of 1949, Italy had maintained this proposed rate as a unitary exchange rate between 624.60 lire and 625.10 lire for the dollar, and since then, Italy had continuously and rapidly developed. The Fund agreed to the communicated par value.[43] In February of 1961, Italy accepted the obligations of Article VIII, Sections 2, 3, and 4.

6 Conclusion

In this chapter, we have examined the impact of the IMF on Italy's economic policy management. The IMF members urged Italy to fulfill its obligations, such as rapid abolishment of the multiple exchange rate system and establishment of a fixed exchange rate, equilibrium of the balance of payments, and elimination of restrictions on foreign exchange and trades. Thus, the IMF kept checking on Italian economic policy management so as to nudge Italy to establish external balance with internal stability. After the war through 1960, when Einaudi and Menichella governed the Bank of Italy, the monetary authority promoted maintaining monetary stability and the foreign exchange rate, inflation control, and reducing the budget deficit as top priorities. Therefore, the IMF and Italy shared the same policy objectives. Actually, as we have seen above, in executing the stabilization program and financial reforms of 1947, Einaudi and Menichella used the IMF name as the international high authority and external pressure to validate their policies and more persuasively push through the necessary reforms with political fermentation.

In discussions with the IMF, the balance of payment equilibrium was the most important objective and restriction; dollar import liberalization was also requested repeatedly. Regarding the latter, Italy maintained a cautious approach. Behind the discrimination for the dollar area, not only was it necessary to save dollars but policies intended to give more weight to the promotion of exports to OEEC countries were also necessary, along with European economic integration. Italy had committed to the creation of the EPU and, through this, tried to expand their intra-European

[41] IMF EBS/61/17 "Italy—Acceptance of Obligation of Article VIII, Sections 2, 3, and 4," February 13, 1961.

[42] Italy paid 1/100th of 1 % of its quota in U.S. dollars on March 27, 1947, and made a gold subscription payment equivalent to 25 % of its quota in April of 1958. Then, in October of 1959, it paid the remaining 75 % and additional currency subscription by lire. IMF EBD/58/63, "Italy–Gold subscription payments," April 15, 1958; EBD/59/125, "1959 Italy–Payment of Original Quota Subscription and Currency Portion of Quota Increase," October 15, 1959.

[43] IMF EBS/60/28 "Italy—Initial Par Value," March 23, 1960.

trade. In 1953, Italy eventually liberalized almost all imports from the EPU area. Even though Italy's trade deficit with this area increased remarkably, it maintained a high percentage of its import liberalization. In the middle of 1950s, when the OEEC discussed whether the EPU would be abolished or extended, Italy insisted on its continuation. There was careful reflection on the move toward convertibility and elimination of dollar discrimination, judging these would obstruct rather than further European economic integration. However, Italy imported goods from the dollar area through OEEC countries; for this reason, the Italian authorities recognized that dollar import liberalization had been realized de facto early on.

The difference between the de facto and de jure conditions was also shown in the foreign exchange system. Italy maintained the floating exchange rate regime and did not establish a par value in the face of repeated calls for improvement by the IMF. The authorities, however, considered that Italy followed the IMF's recommendations and established a unitary exchange rate (cambio unico) in 1949, maintaining it stably during the 1950s; therefore a de facto fixed exchange rate system and external convertibility for EPU had been realized at an early stage.[44] In discussions between Italy and the IMF, we can see that the Italian government had not communicated a par value because they preferred not to be subject to the obligations of IMF full membership so as to ensure the autonomy and flexibility of their domestic monetary policy management. The reason Italy did not shift the de facto fixed rate system to a de jure rate system was that the authorities feared possible future adverse developments in the market. They considered that when a change occurred in the market, they would need to revise the system; however, if it were legislated, it would take time to go through procedures to modify the system, thus, delaying action and jeopardizing political stability. With repeated requests by the IMF and its executive board to take appropriate legal steps, Italy eventually made a legislative confirmation in the late 1950s.

Governor Menichella and the Italian authorities were cautious and hesitant about moving toward convertibility and successive liberalization of short-term capital movements. In the early 1950s, however, the OEEC countries began to review convertibility; at home, demand for public investment increased in response to complaints of people who were excluded from the benefits of trade liberalization; furthermore, with the prospect of the termination of American aid, Italy pushed through the currency reforms and eventually imported a large amount of capital.

Due to space constraints, we could not examine in this chapter the huge influx of foreign capital realized by the move to convertibility that was expected to reduce the relatively high capital costs in Italy and, therefore, contribute to Italian industry. Around the same time, the interest rate was decreased, and public investment and capital investment accelerated. Production was on a growth path in 1959; since then, the authorities have taken precautions against possible inflation and have again switched the expansive monetary policy to a prudent one (Cotula, a cura di 1998, p. 349). External convertibility, however, made it impossible to raise the interest rate

[44] Cotula et al. (1997), doc. 28 "Verbale di riunione presso il ministero degli Affari Esteri," 27/8/1949.

as an austerity measure, as raising the interest rate might promote additional influx of foreign capital and create an adverse effect of increasing internal liquidity. Thus, the Bank of Italy decided to make available to agent banks a part of the official reserves to enable them to reduce their short-term debt to foreign countries, already considerable, so as not to excessively increase the reserve and to restrict bank liquidity (Cotula 2001, p. 62). At the end of 1960, Carli replaced Menichella as governor of the Bank of Italy. In 1962, he reconverted Italy to an expansive monetary policy, and the balance of payments was reversed into the large deficit. After the balance of payments crisis in 1963, the Italian "economic miracle" was slowing down.

References

Asso, Pier Francesco. 2011. Guido Carli Economista internazionale 1945–60. Working Paper Res 01/2011, Fondazione Res.

Bank for International Settlements (BIS). 1949. *Economic and financial problems of Italy in the summer of 1949*. Monetary and Economic Department, C.B.213., Bank for International Settlements.

Barucci, Piero, a cura di. 2008. Luigi Einaudi *Considerazioni finali della Banca d'Italia*. Milano: Treves Editore.

Carli, Guido. 1993. *Cinquant'anni di vita italiana*. Rome: Laterza.

Cotula, Franco, Cosma O. Gelsomino, and Alfredo Gigliobianco 1997. *Donato Menichella: Stabilita' e sviluppo dell'economia italiana, 1946–60 I. Documenti e discorsi*. Rome: Laterza.

Cotula, Franco, a cura di. 1998. *Stabilita' e sviluppo negli anni cinquanta – 2. Problemi strutturali e politiche economiche*. Rome: Laterza.

Cotula, Franco, a cura di. 2001. *Stabilita' e sviluppo negli anni cinquanta – 1. L'Italian nel contesto internazionale*. Rome: Laterza.

Cotula, Franco, Marcello De Cecco, and Gianni Toniolo, a cura di. 2003. *La Banca d'Italia: Sintesi della ricerca storica 1893–1960*. Rome: Laterza.

Di Taranto, Giuseppe. 2007. Italy and the international monetary fund. from multiple exchange rate system to convertibility. *Journal of European Economic History* 35(2): 263–312.

Fratianni, Michele, and Franco Spinelli. 1997. *A monetary history of Italy*. Cambridge: Cambridge University Press.

Jacobsson, Erin E. 1979. A life for sound money: Per Jacobsson – his biography. Oxford: Oxford University Press. Japanese edition: Jacobsson, Erin E. 2010. Sound money (trans: Shinichi Yoshikuni, and Kazuhiko Yago). Hiratsuka: Sōtensha.

Martinez Oliva, Juan Carlos. 2003. Italy and the political economy of cooperation: The Marshall Plan and the European Payments Union. Banca d'Italia, *Quaderni dell'Ufficio Ricerche Storiche*, no. 6.

Segreto, Luciano. 2000. Finanza, industria e relazioni internazionali nella ricostruzione. Il prestito dell'Eximbank all'Italia (1947–1955). *Passato e Presente* 51: 67–94.

Ufficio Italiano dei Cambi. 1995. *Cinquant'anni di storia*. Rome: Laterza.

Chapter 10
The IMF and Canada: From Floating to Fixed Exchange Rates

Ayumu Sugawara

1 Introduction

A key element in the 1944 Articles of Agreement of the International Monetary Fund (IMF) was fixed exchange rates.[1] However, while most IMF member countries sought to establish or maintain fixed exchange rates in the 1950s, the Canadian government placed the Canadian dollar under a flexible exchange rate regime. Canada began using a flexible rate in September 1950 and returned to a fixed rate in May 1962.

According to Canadian Nobel Laureate Economist Robert Mundell, Canada's choice of flexible rates in 1950 was one of four blows to the prestige of the embryonic IMF. The other three were the Marshall Plan by the United States in 1947 and the devaluation of the French Franc and the British Pound Sterling in 1948 and 1949, respectively.[2] All of these four countries had presented their own original plans for the IMF before the Bretton Woods Conference, and their actions, as four important founding members, harmed the prestige of the early IMF (Horsefield 1969c, pp. 3–118). This book considers the relationship between the IMF and the current G7 countries (Canada, France, Germany, Italy, Japan, the United Kingdom, and the United States). In 1976, the G5 countries at the time added Canada and Italy and became the G7. Compared with other G7 members, Canada is far smaller in both population and GDP. In 1950, when Canada introduced a floating exchange rate system, its population (13.7 million) and real GDP comprised only 0.5 and 1.8 % of the world totals, respectively (Maddison 1995, Appendixes A and B).

[1] The Articles of Agreement of the IMF, Article VI, Par Value Currencies, Horsefield (1969c), p. 189.

[2] Mundell (1969), pp. 476–479. Bordo follows the argument. Bordo (1993), p. 46.

A. Sugawara (✉)
Department of Economics, Tohoku University, 27-1 Kawauchi, Aoba-ku,
Sendai 980-0011, Japan
e-mail: sugawara@econ.tohoku.ac.jp

K. Yago et al. (eds.), *History of the IMF*, Studies in Economic History,
DOI 10.1007/978-4-431-55351-9_10

In contrast to these small amounts, however, Canada was responsible for 5.1 % of the world's total exports in 1950; this ranked it fourth in the world, following the United States (18.0 %), Britain (10.7 %), and France (5.4 %) (United Nations 1953). The Second World War brought Canada a chance to become a major trading power, although, from the current viewpoint, it is clear that this was only temporary. As a world trade power, Canada could present its own original IMF plan. Since Canada was a major player in the international economy just after the WWII, its departure from the Bretton Woods fixed rate system was seen as a prominent affront to the 1944–1971 IMF system, representing a major country with a floating rate.[3]

The purpose of this chapter is to address several questions related to Canada's floating rates. Firstly, we consider why they were adopted. Secondly, we examine why this was done even under the IMF agreement. Thirdly, we investigate the impact of the floating system on the Canadian economy. We then examine why Canada returned to the IMF's fixed rate system in 1962 and the implications of the Canadian experience with floating rates for interpreting the old IMF system.

The rest of the chapter proceeds as follows. Section II surveys Canada's exchange rate regime from the nineteenth century to 1962. Section III then explains the reasons for Canada's introduction of floating rates in 1950. Section IV examines the reaction of the IMF to Canada's action, while Section V focuses on Canada's post-1957 economic challenges. Section VI considers Canada's return to fixed exchange rates in 1962, and Section VII concludes.

2 Canadian Exchange Rates, 1854 to 1962

When discussing Canada's floating rates between 1950 and 1962, it is often argued that the 'par value' (i.e. 1 Canadian dollar equal to 1 US dollar) had long been maintained.[4] In order to ground this opinion historically, we will briefly review Canadian exchange rates from a long-term perspective.

Under the Currency Act of 1854, Canada adopted the gold standard. The Canadian dollar exchange rate was set at that time to 4.866 Canadian dollars per British pound sterling; 1 Canadian dollar thus equalled 1 US dollar. From that time until 1948, Canadian dollar exchange rates were kept on par with the US dollar except during four periods (1862 to 1879, 1918 to 1921, 1931 to 1933, and 1939 to 1943) (Fig. 10.1). Between 1854 and 1948, Canada used a gold standard during two periods: 1854 to 1914 and 1926 to 1929. Floating rates were used from 1914 to 1926 and from 1929 to 1939.[5]

[3] de Vries (1969), p. 159. In June 1970, Canada adopted floating rates again within the Bretton Woods fixed exchange rate system. Powell (2005), pp. 71–73; Helleiner (2006), pp. 118–126. The event shows constancy of the Canada's economic structure.

[4] An example is the remark of the Minister for Reconstruction Clarence Howe in June 1950. Plumpre (1977), p. 143.

[5] During 1862 to 1879 the United States suspended its currency's convertibility due to the Civil War and its consequence and the Canadian dollar kept its value more than 1 US dollar. On the other

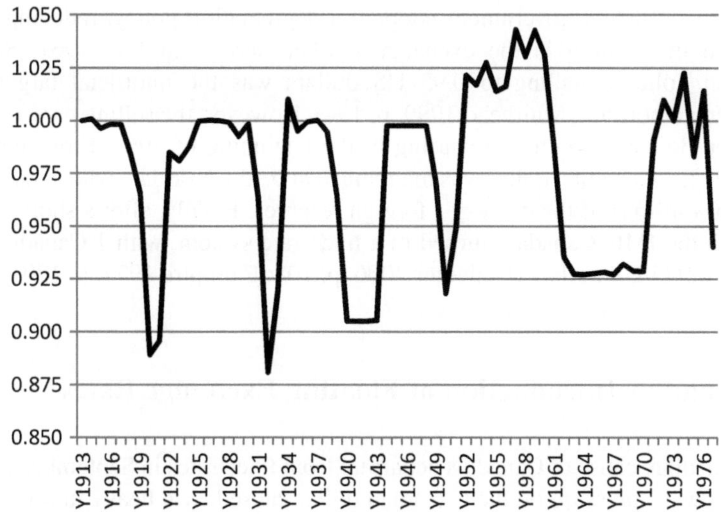

Fig. 10.1 Canadian dollar exchange rates: 1913–1977 (Unit: US Dollars) (*Source*: Leacy 1983)

With the outbreak of the Second World War in September 1939, Canada declared war on Germany at the same time as Britain and simultaneously adopted a fixed rate, 1 Canadian dollar per 0.9 US dollars, with exchange controls. During the war, Canada increased its foreign reserves due to growing exports to the United Kingdom and larger capital imports from the United States.[6] After the end of the war, in July 1946, Canada revalued its currency, increasing its value by 10 % to again be on par with the US dollar. This exchange rate was communicated to the IMF as the 'initial par value' in the Articles of Agreement (Horsefield 1969a, p. 153). The immediate motivation for the revaluation was to prevent inflation in the United States from spreading into Canada (Plumptre 1977, p. 95). In September 1949, following the devaluation of the British pound by 30 %, the Canadian dollar was again devalued by 10 % to 1 Canadian dollar equalling 0.9 US dollars (Plumptre 1977, p. 109).

It was September 1950 when Canada departed from the IMF's fixed exchange rate system in favour of floating rates (Powell 2005, p. 61). After the transition, the Canadian dollar gradually rose to 1 Canadian dollar equalling approximately 0.95 US dollars in 1951 (Powell 2005, p. 97). In March 1952, the Canadian dollar reached 1.003 US dollars and, from 1952 to 1960, continued to float slightly above par with the US dollar.

Both in 1957 and 1960, the Canadian dollar reached a value of more than 1.05 US dollars; simultaneously, unemployment rates in Canada exceeded 7 %. As a

hand, in the other three periods, Canadian dollar's value fluctuated around 0.9 US dollars. Powell (2005), p. 97.

[6] Canada's foreign reserves surged from US$ 188 million in 1941 to US$1,508 million. Powell (2005), p. 56.

result, the Canadian government adopted a depreciation policy, reducing interest rates and intervening in the exchange market starting in July 1961. Setting 1 Canadian dollar equalling to 0.95 US dollars was the unofficial target of the Canadian authorities (Muirhead 1999, p. 194). However, the selling pressure on the Canadian dollar strengthened starting in the beginning of 1962. From January to April 1962, 1 Canadian dollar was maintained at 0.95 US dollars with a loss of 22 % (US$460 million) of the country's foreign reserves. Finally, after a short consultation with the IMF, Canada returned to a fixed rate system, with 1 Canadian dollar equal to 0.925 US dollars (Helleiner 2006, p. 108; Plumptre 1977, p. 170).

3 Canada's Introduction of Floating Exchange Rates

The immediate cause of Canada's departure from fixed rates in September 1950 was strong upward pressure on the Canadian dollar caused by a heavy inflow of short-term capital (Fig. 10.2) (Plumptre 1977, p. 142). This capital flood transpired for two main reasons: the Canadian dollar was regarded as an undervalued currency following the 1949 devaluation, and the outbreak of the Korean War in June 1950 created expectations of increasing natural resource prices. Canada, a traditional natural resource exporter, thus attracted considerable foreign investment.

Amid this heavy capital inflow, Canadian monetary authorities hoping to maintain the fixed rate bought US$534 million between July and September (Plumptre 1977, p. 143). However, in order to intervene in the foreign exchange market the government's Foreign Exchange Control Board raised funds by selling treasury bills to both the central and private banks; Canadian authorities feared this increase

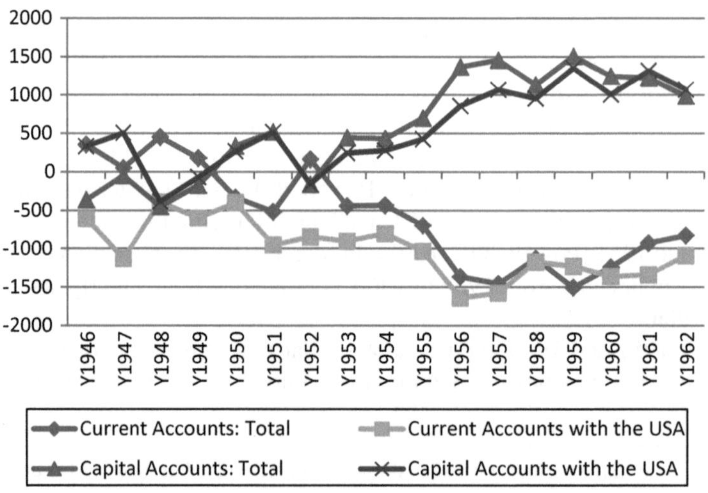

Fig. 10.2 Canada's current and capital accounts: 1946–1962 (Unit: Can$ million) (*Source*: Leacy 1983)

in funds in the banking sector would drive inflation. In order to avoid inflation, the Canadian government was finally compelled to seriously consider altering the fixed exchange rate (Plumptre 1977, p. 144).

The Canadian government chose floating rates as a means of securing currency appreciation rather than changing the par value under the IMF agreement. Helleiner (2006) divided the reasons for this into four groups: the de-politicisation of exchange rate decisions, the decline in regulations on capital movements, the Canadian experience in the 1930s, and the support of the United States.

De-politicising exchange rate decisions was one key aim of the policy. The choice of a fixed exchange rate could be subject to fierce criticism in national politics. In Canada during the balance of payments crisis of 1947, the government's 10 % appreciation of the Canadian dollar was criticised harshly. In 1950, Minister of Finance Douglas Abbott did not want a repeat of this situation (Helleiner 2006, p. 84). Additionally, the Canadian government was concerned that the upward pressure on its currency might be just a temporary effect of the Korean War. They were afraid that if the end of the war coincided with the end of the Marshall Plan's aid, Canadian exports would fall sharply. If this happened when the Canadian dollar was fixed at an appreciated level, it would exacerbate the harm to Canadian exports and the Canadian government (Helleiner 2006, pp. 86–87; Plumptre 1977, p. 145). In addition, another important branch of the Canadian monetary authorities, the Bank of Canada, also voiced in 1949 that it was suboptimal for the government to decide the exchange rate; they regarded floating rates with a lifting of exchange controls as preferable.[7]

The second factor motivating the choice was a decline in regulations on capital movements. As discussed later, when Canadian authorities communicated the decision to adopt floating exchange rates, IMF staff recommended the imposition of capital controls. However, a Canadian IMF director, Louis Rasminsky, refused to do so mainly out of fear that capital controls would hinder the inflow of capital from the United States (Helleiner 2006, pp. 87–88). Historically, Canada tended to fall into current account deficits and needed capital imports to finance these (Fig. 10.2) (Suda 1992).

Third, unlike other Bretton Woods Conference participants, Canadian policymakers thought the 1930s experience of floating rates was a positive one. In this decade of international turmoil, Canada did not resort to manipulating exchange rates to gain export price competitiveness; the currency's exchange rate remained stable after a sharp depreciation from 1931 to 1933 (Fig. 10.1). Contrary to conventional wisdom, Canadian monetary policymakers recognised the floating rate system as compatible with currency speculation to maintain an economic equilibrium. The first Governor of the Bank of Canada, Graham Towers, explained that the deprecation of the Canadian dollar in the 1930s was followed by a cessation of both capital outflows and panicked selling in securities markets.[8]

[7] Bank of Canada Archives, Louis Rasminsky fonds, LR76–115, Vol. 2, A Method of Combining a Free Exchange Rate with the Present System of Exchange Control in Canada, January 31, 1949.

[8] Helleiner (2006), p. 93. The Bank of Canada was established in 1935. Powell (2005), pp. 47–49.

The support of the United States also influenced the decision to adopt a floating rate. For a member country to introduce floating exchange rates in 1950 broke the IMF agreement; in order to achieve both goals, floating exchange rates and IMF membership, Canada had to gain the support of other IMF member countries. Hence, Canada appealed to the United States, which was a prominent IMF sponsor, Canada's main economic partner, and the hegemon of the post-war capitalist world. Rasminsky met US Treasury Secretary John Snyder and US IMF Director Frank Southard, Jnr and secured American recognition for the Canadian floating policy under the condition that the Canadian dollar's exchange rate would continue to rise for the next 3 years. Behind the American support also lay a goal of keeping free capital flows between the United States and Canada. At the IMF Board of Directors meeting in September 1950, Southard insisted that floating rates for Canada were preferable to the capital controls suggested by IMF staff. This is evidence of a divide in exchange rate policy between the American political core and American IMF staff. American multinational business and financial interests also supported the Canadian policy of maintaining capital flows across its southern border (Helleiner 2006, p. 98).

4 The Reaction of the IMF

4.1 Staff Opposition and Directors' Support

Canada was not the only IMF member departing from the par value system. Before Canada, Mexico in 1948 and Belgium in 1949 also adopted floating rates despite being IMF members (de Vries 1969, pp. 153–156). However, Canada was the sole country with floating rates among the contemporary trading powers. As a consequence, Canada's policy upset IMF staff. The head of the Research Department, Edward Bernstein (an American) argued that the IMF agreement did not permit even temporarily floating rates. He feared a potential negative impact of Canada's decision on other countries because of the country's strong position in world trade and moral leadership. Bernstein and other IMF staff were embarrassed: if Canada, as the second-strongest economy in the world, adopted floating rates, they had no idea what to say to weaker, less responsible countries who sought to follow Canada's lead.[9] The IMF staff recommended two alternatives to floating rates: the Bank of Canada should undertake buying operations to absorb excess liquidity and introduce capital controls to check the heavy inflow of capital (de Vries 1969, p. 159). Contrary to the 1990s 'Washington Consensus', support for capital controls was the orthodox view in the 1950s IMF, which was influenced by John Maynard Keynes' legacy.[10]

[9] Bank of Canada Archives, International Department fonds, 4B-220, Vol. 1, Wallace Goforth, Reaction to the New Canadian "Floating" Rate, October 18, 1950.

[10] Helleiner (1994), Chap. 2; Chwieroth (2010), Chaps. 3 and 4. In the Articles of Agreement of the IMF, the Section 3 of the Article VI describes controls on capital movements. Horsefield (1969c), pp. 193–194.

In a discussion with Rasminsky, Bernstein, and others in September 1950, IMF staff argued aggressively that the Canadian action was an infringement on IMF rules, harming trust in the fledgling organisation as well as its larger purpose (Helleiner 2006, pp. 83–84). Furthermore, they criticised the action as an unwarranted destruction of IMF principles that would make the world extremely unstable and the IMF unworkable while also harming Canada. Finally, they insisted that only direct capital controls could solve Canada's problem.[11]

Rasminsky later described the senior IMF staff as being hostile towards him during this discussion.[12] He refuted all their proposed alternatives. Regarding buying operations, he insisted that the Canadian government could not bear additional debts of unknown size (de Vries 1969, p. 160). He asserted that capital controls were unacceptable due to technical difficulties such as identifying investments to be checked by the control as well as the likelihood of offending both American investors and Canadian public opinion, which preferred liberalism (Helleiner 2006, pp. 87–89). At a later IMF board meeting, Rasminsky insisted that Canada was unique in that American investors did not regard it as a completely foreign country; this underlined the importance of capital movements between the two countries (Helleiner 2006, p. 84).

At the September 1950 board meeting, the United States, based on the arguments of Rasminsky and Southard, was the first to voice support for Canada's floating rate policy. They were followed by the United Kingdom, the Netherlands, and France (Helleiner 2006, p. 98). Many directors recognised Canada as being in a special situation and hence approved the floating rates as a temporary solution; they expected Canada to return to fixed rates immediately after this brief exceptional period ended (de Vries 1969, p. 160). Within the IMF there was an enormous contrast between the expert staff and the member country directors. The former were opposed to floating rates while the latter were sympathetic to the Canadian situation.[13] The IMF annual report, written by the staff, voiced no judgment on Canada's switch to floating rates and merely described the decision (Helleiner 2006, p. 98).

4.2 *The IMF and Floating Rates from a Canadian Viewpoint*

In the end, the IMF as a whole thus acquiesced to Canada's floating exchange rates. Canadian authorities had their own views and expectations regarding the introduction of floating rates under the IMF Articles of Agreement, which excluded the float. Interesting documents from the Bank of Canada archives shed light on these

[11] Bank of Canada Archives, LR76-522, Vol.1, Louis Rasminsky, Report on Washington Discussions, Re Floating the Canadian Dollar, October. 21, 1950.

[12] Bank of Canada Archives, LR76-522, Vol.1, Louis Rasminsky, Report on Washington Discussions, Re Floating the Canadian Dollar, October. 21, 1950.

[13] Bank of Canada Archives, International Department fonds, 4B-220, Vol.1, Wallace Goforth, Reaction to the New Canadian "Floating" Rate, October 18, 1950.

opinions. In September 1950, Bank of Canada Governor Towers and Rasminsky met IMF Managing Director Camille Gutt (a Belgium) in Paris to give advance notice of the introduction of floating rates. At that time, Gutt mentioned that Canada had opposed Belgium's adoption of floating rates in 1949. To this, Rasminsky replied that Canada had merely opposed to providing official IMF permission, as this would constitute a violation of the Articles of Agreement. Rasminsky added that, for the same reason, Canada did not want to seek official IMF permission for its own floating rates.[14]

Other records support Rasminsky's argument. In October 1949, regarding Belgium's floating rates, Rasminsky told National Bank of Belgium Governor Hubert Ansiaux that what he wanted to say on the subject at the IMF board meeting was that the IMF should not punish Belgium for adopting floating rates but merely avoid official recognition of the choice, which would be a violation of the IMF agreement.[15] Further, in October 1950, Rasminsky told Gutt that the Canadians did not need the IMF to officially permit Canada's shift toward floating rates during the IMF board meeting.[16] Rasminsky argued that the IMF both could and should acquiesce to the floating rate introduction.

Canada's floating rates proved to be far from a temporary measure, as discussed at the September 1950 IMF board meeting. A year and a half later at the February 1952 board meeting, British director Arthur Maxwell Stamp expressed concern that Canada's floating rates might continue beyond the short term. In response, Rasminsky again emphasised the uniqueness of the Canadian situation. He admitted that Canada's action was against the core IMF goal of maintaining fixed exchange rates for member countries. However, he also insisted that Canada was different from other member countries in that it had achieved the other two IMF goals: removing exchange controls and restoring convertibility (de Vries 1969, p. 161; Plumptre 1977, p. 149). Again, as in September 1950, Rasminsky was able to persuade the directors. They expressed an official opinion that, given the current situation, floating exchange rates were useful for many countries seeking to remove various currency restrictions (de Vries 1969, p. 161). Even the IMF expert staff representative, Bernstein, who had been the leading Canadian opponent in September 1950, recognised Canada's argument in 1952 (Helleiner 2006, p. 101).

Under higher but stable exchange rates from 1952 to 1956, Canada achieved economic growth driven by large-scale capital imports (Figs. 10.2 and 10.3). Until 1956, the Canadian dollar exchange rate remained stable, within a band between US$1.00 and US$1.05, despite departing from fixed rates in 1950. Therefore, the Canadian situation was regarded not as a clean float but as a managed one.[17] In fact, the Bank of Canada had aimed for a floating but managed system even before 1950.

[14] Bank of Canada Archives, LR76-522, Vol.1, Louis Rasminsky, Report on Washington Discussions, Re Floating the Canadian Dollar, October 21, 1950.

[15] Bank of Canada Archives, LR76-269, Rasminsky to Ansiaux, October 17, 1949.

[16] Bank of Canada Archives, LR76-269, Rasminsky to Gutt, October 18, 1950.

[17] Siklos (2009) empirically clarifies that in the Canadian float from 1951 to 1957 the foreign exchange interventions well contributed to stabilize the Canadian dollar's volatilities.

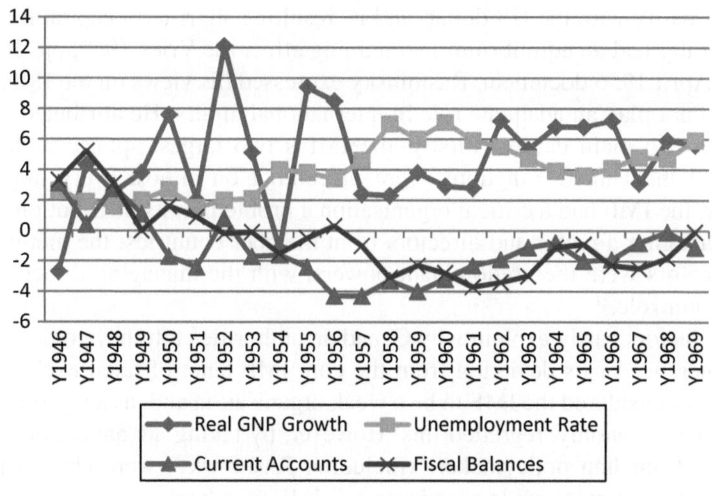

Fig. 10.3 Main economic indicators of Canada: 1946–1969 (Unit: %) (*Source*: Leacy 1983). Notes: Real GNP growth means annual growth rates. Current accounts and fiscal balances are shown in the ratio to GNP

As early as 1949, authorities considered introducing floating rates and concluded that, in the early stages of a float, the Bank of Canada should prepare to smooth daily exchange markets in order to avoid large fluctuations.[18] Here, too, Rasminsky was involved. As a deputy governor of the Bank, he argued to the Minister of Finance and other Bank staff in March 1951 that the Bank should counter large fluctuations in exchange markets (i.e. a more than one quarter of a per cent movement within a single day).[19] In March 1953, Rasminsky precisely identified the bounds for Canadian dollar fluctuations, insisting that the Exchange Funds Account should be used to minimise fluctuations around a centre point of US$1.02 (Fig. 10.1).[20] This is consistent with actual data: the Canadian dollar fluctuated between US$1.00 and US$1.05. As a consequence, Canadian floating rates did not disturb either the international or Canadian economies until 1956, in contrast to the Bretton Woods architects' negative expectations for floating rates.

Finally, even the IMF staff officially admitted the economic success of Canada's floating rates, given the country's unique circumstances. The IMF staff saw Canada as unique due to its credibility in both fiscal and monetary policies, even though the Canadian economy was characterised by trade deficits and capital imports. Furthermore, the Canadian dollar had convertibility, no restrictions on its trade, and

[18] Bank of Canada Archives, LR76-115, Vol. 2, A Method of Combining a Free Exchange Rate with the Present System of Exchange Control in Canada, January 31, 1949.

[19] Bank of Canada Archives, LR76-522, Vol.1, J.E.C., Exchange Policy, March 5, 1951.

[20] Bank of Canada Archives, LR76-522, Vol.1, Note on discussion with Coyne, Rasminsky and Turk, March 24, 1953. On the Exchange Fund Account, see Neufeld (1955), pp. 29, 140.

historical parity with the US dollar, and its resulting short-term capital movements had generally had an equilibrium-maintaining effect (de Vries 1969, pp. 161–162).

In an April 1956 document, Rasminsky expressed his views on the IMF, arguing that it did not play an adequate role in international affairs. He attributed this inadequacy to two main causes. Firstly, the IMF's two largest sponsors, the United States and the United Kingdom, were in conflict on almost every major issue. Secondly, the IMF had a critical organisational problem in its distribution of power to the managing director and directors from member countries: the member countries' directors were the predominant powers, with the managing director playing only a minor role.[21]

These factors partly explain why Canadian authorities felt they could expect the IMF's tolerance of its deviation from the core IMF tenet of fixed exchange rates. Rasminsky considered the IMF to be a weak organisation and, as a representative of a small open economy, regretted this. However, by taking advantage of the IMF's weakness, Canadian policymakers (including Rasminsky) were able to maintain floating exchange rates while remaining full IMF members.

5 Deteriorating Economic Growth and Employment, 1957 to 1960

Canada returned to a fixed exchange rate in 1962, driven by lowered economic growth and a rise in unemployment after 1957(Fig. 10.3). In order to understand Canada's return to fixed rates, it is essential to probe the reasons for the deterioration of the Canadian economy after 1957.

In 1957, not only the Canadian economy but also Canadian politics reversed course. The general election for the Canadian House of Commons took place in June 1957, with the Progressive Conservative Party, led by John Diefenbaker, defeating the Liberal Party to regain power for the first time since 1935 (Ohara 1981, pp. 188–190, and Appendix p. 43). The new Progressive Conservative government carried out expansionary fiscal policies, such as providing financial support to the low-income Atlantic and western provinces, increasing pensions, and reducing taxes (Smith 1995, pp. 218, 224–225, 230). The Conservatives' fiscal expansionism became one of two critical issues in the Canadian economy after 1957 (Figs. 10.3 and 10.4).

The high interest rates set by the Bank of Canada proved to be another critical issue (Fig. 10.5). These, combined with the eccentricity of the second governor of the Bank of Canada, James Coyne, caused serious antagonism between the Conservative government, which demanded an interest rate reduction in order to improve employment, and the governor of the central bank, who raised the rates. The government envisioned a relationship wherein high interest rates led to increased capital imports, followed by (in causal order) appreciation of the exchange

[21] Bank of Canada Archives, LR76-284, Louis Rasminsky, Functioning of IMF, April 20, 1956.

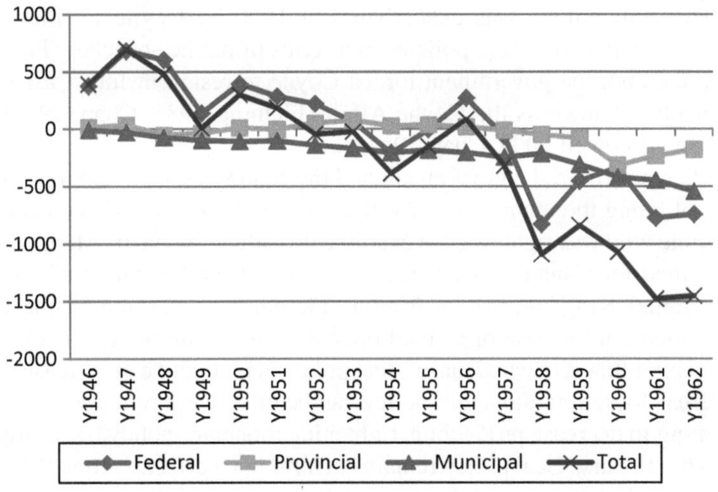

Fig. 10.4 Canada's fiscal balances: 1946–1962 (Unit: Can$ million) (*Source*: Leacy 1983)

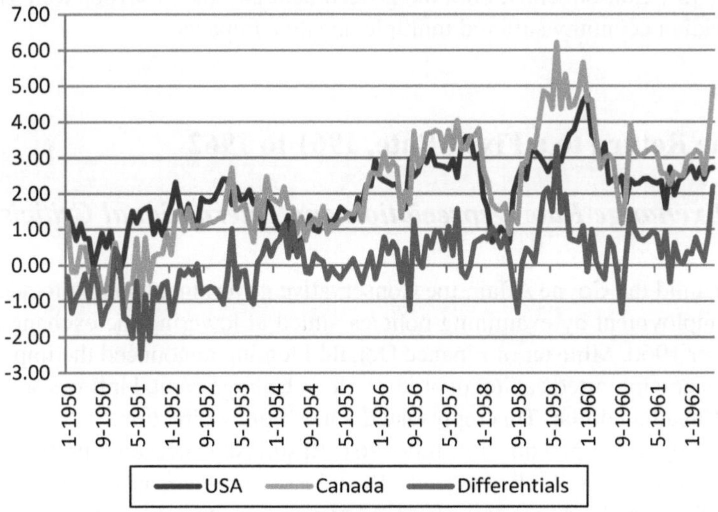

Fig. 10.5 Real 3 months interest rates in Canada and the USA (Unit: %) (*Sources*: For Canada's 3 months interest rates and consumer prices in Canada and the United States, Statistical Canada Website. For America's 3 months rates, Federal Reserve System Website). Note: Real interest rates are calculated by deducing consumer price growth rates from nominal 3 months interest rates. Interest rate differentials are calculated by deducting American rates from Canadian

rate, growth of the current account deficit, shrinking production, and increased unemployment. On the other hand, Coyne argued that, in order to offset the inflationary pressure brought by the government's budget deficits, interest rates must be raised. This antagonism was exacerbated in 1960 by Coyne's criticism of the government's expansive fiscal policies in a series of public speeches (Powell 2009, p. 95). In the end, the government forced Coyne to resign in July 1961 in a well-known incident known as the Coyne Affair (Fleming 1985, Chap. 29; Grantstein 1986, Chap. 4; Powell 2009, Chaps. 9–13).

In the Coyne Affair, the government and the central bank governor each accused the other of being the main culprit for the deterioration of the Canadian economy. To determine who was right, we can examine this situation via the Mundell-Fleming model (named for Canada's Mundell, mentioned at the beginning of this chapter, and the United Kingdom's John Marcus Fleming). According to the Mundell-Fleming model, in the case of a small open economy with floating exchange rates and free capital flows, expansionary fiscal policy is ineffective at increasing production, whereas loosening monetary policy can be effective. From the opposite view-point, aiming to decrease production, tightening monetary policy has a large impact while contractionary fiscal policy remains neutral in its effect.[22] After 1957, Canada adopted a policy mix of expansionary fiscal and contractionary monetary policies. The former had no impact on production but brought on inflationary pressure. The latter succeeded at reducing production (Bordo et al. 2009, pp. 13–14; Rhomberg 1964, p. 15). Consequently, both the government and the governor were right, and the Canadian economy suffered multiple negative impacts.

6 The Return to a Fixed Rate, 1961 to 1962

6.1 Exchange Rate Depreciation and International Criticism

In 1960 amid the Coyne Affair, the Conservative government sought to address rising unemployment by examining policies aimed at lowering the exchange rate. In December 1960, Minister of Finance Donald Fleming announced the imposition of a 15 % tax on imported capital in order to slow the large capital inflows and appreciate the Canadian dollar. This represented a new policy direction.

After Coyne stepped down in July 1961, Rasminsky succeed him, becoming the third Governor of the Bank of Canada. Rasminsky simultaneously remained an IMF director for Canada. At the same time, Minister of Finance Fleming stated publicly that an exchange rate depreciation was necessary and directed the Exchange Funds Account to intervene in the exchange markets. In contrast to earlier events, the Bank of Canada under the new governor cooperated closely with the government, reducing interest rates. Given the new political circumstances, the Ministry of Finance aimed at setting a depreciated exchange rate centred on US$0.95 (Muirhead 1999, p. 194).

[22] Bordo et al. (2010) and Siklos (2010) respectively prove by simulations that financial policies after 1957 was too tight.

In 1950, support from the directors of the member countries enabled Canada to smoothly transition from a fixed rate to a float within the framework of the IMF agreement, even though IMF staff fiercely attacked Canada's policy. Regarding the new Canadian policy of lower exchange rates in 1961, however, the reactions within the IMF were vastly different. Canada was now subject to a barrage of criticism from all quarters: not just the IMF staff but also the member countries' directors, the powerful managing director Per Jacobsson of Sweden (who took the post in 1956), and the US Treasury. At a special directors' meeting in July 1961, the member countries' directors expressed concern and recommended Canada return to a fixed rate. Jacobsson then criticised Canada as potentially gaining unfair benefits from the change. Finally, US Under Secretary of the Treasury Robert Rosa, an American IMF director, insisted that manipulating exchange rates was tantamount to a beggar-my-neighbour policy and it should not be allowed to take place, though he did not refer to Canada by name (Muirhead 1999, pp. 194–195). Two months later, at the IMF's annual directors' meeting in September 1961, Canadian Minister of Finance Fleming defended the country's position by saying that Canada was not aiming for a competing devaluation (Fleming 1985, pp. 376, 490). However, his words had no effect: Canada's 1961 exchange rate policy was regarded as being against the IMF's founding doctrine of 'to avoid competitive exchange depreciation'.[23]

6.2 The 1961 IMF Consultation

In January 1962, IMF staff interviewed Canadian monetary authorities as part of a routine IMF consultation of the Article VIII countries; due to the IMF fiscal year, this is known as 'the 1961 consultation'. In the ensuing report to Canada, IMF staff officially criticised Canada's floating rates. The report firstly described Canada's 1961 depreciation policy as 'individualistic' and against the rules codified in the IMF Articles of Agreement. The report then said that, although the Canadian Minister of Finance had defended Canada to the managing director by explaining that the policy was not intended to harm other countries, such a statement offered no final solution to the issue.[24]

Next, the report summarised the total experience of Canadian floating rates: such a disappointing performance of the Canadian economy 'may be viewed against the background of the earlier period from 1948 to 1956. It is instructive to view this period as one of the abnormally high growth and expansion because of the exceptional circumstances which prevailed'. This was followed by the words: 'taking a backward look at Canada's experience under a freely fluctuating rate from October 1950 to June 1961, the staff has concluded that it is not at all apparent that this system served Canada well and was of ultimate benefit to her'.[25]

---

[23] The Articles of Agreement of the IMF, Article I, Purposes (iii). Horsefield (1969c), p. 188.

[24] IMF Archives, Canada-1961 Article VIII Consultation, January 30, 1962, p. 20.

[25] IMF Archives, Canada-1961 Article VIII Consultation, January 30, 1962, p. 22, 24.

Finally, the report concluded by clearly counselling Canada to return to a fixed rate, insisting 'the re-established of an effective par value within a reasonable period should be made a priority objective by the Canadian government'.[26] In 1950 IMF staff reluctantly accepted Canada's float; in 1956, they then had no choice but to admit the float was working well. In the end, however, they were able to return to their strong criticism of Canada's floating rates, now identifying the period between 1950 and 1956 as also a part of their target.

Based on the 1961 consultation report, the IMF directors discussed Canada's exchange rate policy during their meeting in February 1962. Again, the directors of member countries criticised Canada, arguing that depreciation could not be done without damaging other countries. Some directors further criticised Canada's policy as too expansive. Consequently, the directors supported the 1961 consultation report although they avoided officially counselling Canada to return to a fixed rate.[27]

There was thus a key difference between the first and second halves of the 1950s. The work of a Canadian official of the time sheds some light onto why. In August 1961, under severe criticism of the depreciation policy, Canadian Under Secretary of Finance Arthur Plumptre examined whether Canada should maintain the float or return to a fixed rate. In his report, Plumptre wrote, 'in the immediate post war world, when Canada was in a uniquely favoured economic position and when we were distributing military and economic aid in very large amounts, other countries were quite willing to put up with abnormal action on our part; but it is clear that irregularities on our part are not readily accepted today'.[28] In 1957, Canada's position in the world economy started to decline while that of the IMF began to strengthen (Horsefield 1969a, p. 426).

6.3 *Canada's Foreign Reserve Crisis and the Return to a Fixed Rate*

Starting in January 1962, there was considerable selling pressure on the Canadian dollar. The Canadian government lost US$460 million of their foreign reserves between January and April 1962, or 22 % of the total. Furthermore, after the end of April, when the dissolution of the House of Commons was decided, the size of the foreign reserve outflows grew due to expectations that the Conservative Party would continue its expansionary fiscal policy. Canada's foreign reserves fell by US$35 million on 27 April, US$20 million on 28 April, and US$36 million on 1 May, at which point New York newspapers reported the weakness of the Canadian dollar (Fleming 1985, p. 493).

---

[26] IMF Archives, Canada-1961 Article VIII Consultation, January 30, 1962, p. 25.

[27] de Vries (1969), pp. 163–164.

[28] Bank of Canada Archives, LR76-522, Vol.2, A.F.W. Plumptre, Exchange Rate Policy, August 23, 1961. On the strengthening of the IMF after 1956, see the Chapter 3.

In order to address the foreign reserve crisis, emergency meetings were organised by Minister Fleming, Under Secretary Kenneth Taylor, and Governor Rasminsky (also an IMF director) from 28 April to 1 May. Fleming thus decided to return to a rate fixed at US$0.925. The policymakers also considered US$0.90, but Fleming was afraid of resistance by the United States to such a low rate. On 2 May, Rasminsky attended an emergency board meeting of the IMF and enacted the new fixed rate of US$0.925. This was immediately approved by the directors (Fleming 1985, pp. 494–495). Nevertheless, the return to a fixed rate could not stop speculative attacks against the Canadian dollar because the rate still seemed too high. Therefore, in June 1962, Canada withdrew US$300 million from the IMF. In addition, the country was able to obtain a US$400 million credit line from the Export-import Bank of Washington and make swap agreements for US$250 million with the Federal Reserve Bank of New York and US$150 million with the Bank of England. After concluding these international arrangements, Canadian authorities were able to restore confidence in the currency (Fleming 1985, pp. 517–519).

Recollecting the events of 1962, Fleming said 'we were able to act with the full support of the IMF, which we would have lacked had we not pegged the dollar on May 2. Such a plan of massive external borrowing would have taken time to arrange… It could not possibly have been done on May 1 or 2, and any delay might have precipitated a crisis'. Fleming placed a high value on the IMF (Fleming 1985, p. 497). In 1961 and 1962, as shown by the international critiques of Canada's depreciation policy and support for Canada's return to fixed rates, the IMF was able to play the important role envisioned by the Bretton Woods architects.

7 Conclusion

The conflict between Canadian officials and IMF staff when Canada moved to a floating exchange rate in 1950 clarified the roles of the IMF and Canada in international finance. The goal of the IMF was to maintain the fixed rate system, and IMF officials regarded capital controls as orthodox methods for achieving this. On the other hand, Canada set free capital movements as its goal and adopted a float as a solution for a specific situation. In different situations from Canada and of similar mind-sets to the IMF staff, policymakers in the major Western European countries in the 1950s pursued a policy combination of fixed exchange rates and capital controls. In this sense, Canada had a unique experience.

In the relevant literature, Canada's float between 1950 and 1962 is valued highly as a forerunner that shows the effectiveness of floating exchange rates.[29] However, emphasising only the successful side of Canada's float ignores the other side–the meaning of Canada's return to a fixed rate in 1962.

[29] Friedman (1953) is a classic case for the Canadian float. A new case is Helleiner (2008). On the other hand, Mundell regarded the Canadian experience as a failure of experiment. Mundell (1961), p. 664. When he wrote the paper, Mundell was an economist at the IMF Special Research Section.

Canada was a forerunner of not only floating rates but also free capital movements. In the current sense, the latter is more important, as free capital flows relax limitations on foreign borrowing and enable a country to widen its current account deficit via capital imports. Still, Canada's current account deficits of over four per cent of its GNP were unsustainable, as shown in 1962 (Fig. 10.3). That experience can be seen as a forerunner to the US dollar depreciation via the Plaza Accord in 1985 and to the US dollar just before the sub-prime crisis in 2007.[30] In addition, Canada's slower economic growth after 1957 can be interpreted as a savings-short country going through an investment boom entailing capital imports, then facing decreased investment profitability until the increasing exchange rates became too much for the country to withstand. In that sense, the Canadian case foreshadows the 1997 Asian currency crises.[31]

However, Canada in 1962 was different from the cases from the 1990s in that it was able to relatively smoothly return to a fixed rate via a devaluation (Figs. 10.1 and 10.3). This was facilitated by the different international financial situation in 1962 as compared to the 1990s, particularly in terms of the size and speed of international capital flows. Within the historical context, the IMF in 1962 was able to fulfil its mandate when Canada returned to the fixed rate system.

Acknowledgments The author thanks the Bank of Canada for permission to access the Archives. I am also grateful to Mariko Hatase, Masato Masuda, Tomonori Naito, Masanori Sato, Masato Shizume, and Yasuo Takatsuki for their helpful comments to the earlier drafts.

References

Bordo, Michael, Tamara Games, and Lawrence Schembri. 2009. Canada and the IMF: Trailblazer or Prodigal Son? *Bank of Canada Discussion Paper*, 2009–1

Bordo, Michael, Ali Dib, and Lawrence Schembri. 2010. Canada's pioneering experience with a flexible exchange rate in the 1950s: [Hard] lessons learned for monetary policy in a small open economy. *International Journal of Central Banking* 6(3): 51–99.

Chwieroth, Jefferey. 2010. *Capital ideas: The IMF and the rise of financial liberalization*. Princeton: Princeton University Press.

de Vries, Margaret G. 1969. Fluctuating exchange rates. In *The international monetary fund 1946–1965: Twenty years of international monetary cooperation, volume II analysis*, ed. Horsefield, John Keith. Washington DC: International Monetary Fund.

Fleming, Donald. 1985. *So very near; the political memoirs of the honourable Donald M. Fleming, volume two, the summit years*. Toronto: McClelland and Stewart.

Friedman, Milton. 1953. The case for flexible exchange rates. In *Essays in positive economics*, ed. Milton Friedman. Chicago: University of Chicago Press.

---

[30] On American cases, see Sugawara (2007), p. 158. In 2006, the United States swelled its current account deficits to 6.8 % of its GDP. The United States in the 2000s could run larger deficits compared to its GDP than Canada could run in the 1950s because the former have issued the key currency.

[31] The idea of economic growth depending on capital imports and its collapse comes from Takemori (2008), pp. 135–137.

Grantstein, J.L. 1986. *Canada 1957–1967: The years of uncertainty and innovation*. Toronto: McClelland and Stewart.
Helleiner, Eric. 1994. *State and the reemergence of global finance: From Bretton Woods to the 1990s*. Ithaca: Cornell University Press.
Helleiner, Eric. 2006. *Towards North American monetary union?: The politics and history of Canada's exchange rate regime*. Montreal: McGill-Queen's University Press.
Helleiner, Eric. 2008. Ambiguous aspects of Bretton Woods: Canadian exchange-rate policy in the Marshall system, 1950–1962. In *Orderly change: International monetary relations since Bretton Woods*, ed. M. Andrews David. Ithaca: Cornell University Press.
Horsefield, John Keith ed. 1969a. *The international monetary fund 1956–1965: Twenty years of international monetary cooperation, Volume I: Chronicle*. Washington D.C.: International Monetary Fund.
Horsefield, John Keith ed. 1969b. *The international monetary fund 1956–1965: Twenty years of international monetary cooperation, Volume II: Analysis*. Washington D.C.: International Monetary Fund.
Horsefield, John Keith ed. 1969c. *The international monetary fund 1956–1965: Twenty years of international monetary cooperation, Volume III: Documents*. Washington D.C.: International Monetary Fund.
Leacy, F.H. (ed.). 1983. *The historical statistics of Canada*, 2nd ed. Ottawa: Statistics Canada.
Maddison, Angus. 1995. *Monitoring the world economy 1820-1992*. Paris: The OECD Development Centre.
Muirhead, Bruce. 1999. *Against the odds: The public life and times of Louis Rasminsky*. Toronto: University of Toronto Press.
Mundell, Robert A. 1961. A theory of optimal currency areas. *American Economic Review* 51(4): 657–665.
Mundell, Robert A. 1969. The international monetary fund. *Journal of World Trade Law* 3: 455–497.
Neufeld, E.P. 1955. *Bank of Canada operations 1935–54*. Toronto: University of Toronto Press.
Ohara, Yuko. 1981. *Kanada Gendai Shi [A history of the modern Canada]*. Tokyo: Yamakawa Syupan Sha.
Plumptre, Arthur F. W. 1977. *Three decades of decision: Canada and the world monetary system 1944–75*. Toronto: McClelland and Stewart.
Powell, James. 2005. *A history of the Canadian dollar*. Ottawa: Bank of Canada.
Powell, James. 2009. *The Bank of Canada of James Coyne: Challenges, confrontation, and change*. Montreal: McGill-Queen's University Press.
Rhomberg, Rudolf R. 1964. A model of the Canadian economy under the fixed and fluctuating exchange rates. *Journal of Political Economy* 72(1): 1–14.
Siklos, Pierre .L. 2009. Not quite as advertised: Canada's managed float in the 1950s and Bank of Canada intervention. *European Review of Economic History* 3(3): 413–435.
Siklos, Pierre. L. 2010. Rivisiting the Coyne Affairs: A singular event that challenged the course of Canadian monetary history. *Canadian Journal of Economics* 43(3): 994–1015.
Smith, Denis. 1995. *Rogue Tory: The life and legend of John G. Diefenbaker*. Toronto: MacFarlane, Walker and Ross.
Suda, Miyako. 1992. Kanada No Keizokuteki Keijyousyushiakaji: Kako To Genzai [Canada's persistent current account deficits: Past and present]. In *Taigai Fukinkou No Keizaigaku* [*An economic analysis on external imbalance*], ed. Miyako Suda. Nihon Keizai Shinbun Sya. 127–168.
Sugawara, Ayumu. 2007. Taigai Kinyu Seisaku: Shihon Ryunyu No Jizoku Kanousei [External economic policy of the United States: An analysis on the sustainability of capital imports]. In *G W Bush Seiken No Keizai Seisaku* [*The economic policy of G.W. Bush: Ideas and realities of an American conservative*], ed. Kawane Takuro. Kyoto: Mineruva Shobo. 157–195.
Takemori, Shunpei. 2008. *Shihonsyugi Wa Kirai Desuka: Soredemo Manei Wa Sekai O Ugokasu [Don't you like capitalism?: But money drives the world]*. Tokyo: Nihon Keizai Shinbun Sya.
United Nations. 1953. *Yearbook of international trade statistics 1952*. New York: The Statistical Office of the United Nations

Chapter 11
Japan's Participation in the IMF and Settlement of Its Prewar Foreign Debt

Makoto Kishida

1 Introduction

During the time of the prewar international gold standard, Japan had issued large amounts of external bonds, mainly in London and New York financial markets, as the balance of Japanese external bonds issued peaked in 1930 at JPY2,268 million, accounting for about 15 % of Japan's estimated GNP. But Japan's access to raising such bonds was closed off by the Great Depression and the collapse of the international gold standard. After the end of World War II and 6 years of occupation led by the General Headquarters, Supreme Commander for the Allied Powers (GHQ/SCAP), Japan regained independence in April 1952 and joined the IMF and the World Bank in August of that year. Japan's participation in the Bretton Woods system had been realized with the strong support of the U.S. government, which had desired an independent Japanese economy after a turnabout in its postwar policies toward Japan. At that time, expectations had risen in Japan that this would open a path toward access to foreign capital for purposes of economic restoration and development in place of American aid. While its participation in the Bretton Woods system enabled Japan to raise long-term funds from the World Bank, to do so it needed to resolve the issue of repayment of outstanding prewar external debts on which it effectively had defaulted during World War II. In July 1952, a conference on resolution of these debts was held in New York between the Japanese government and representatives of British, French, and the United States' bondholders under the terms of the San Francisco Peace Treaty, and an agreement was reached in September of that year, under which Japan resumed payment on nearly all government bonds, not including those issued in France. The success of negotiations on resolution of external debts was important in that it meant Japan had regained the

M. Kishida (✉)
College of Economics, Nihon University, Tokyo, Japan
e-mail: kishida.makoto@nihon-u.ac.jp

K. Yago et al. (eds.), *History of the IMF*, Studies in Economic History,
DOI 10.1007/978-4-431-55351-9_11

trust of international society and served as the starting point for Japan's postwar access to foreign capital.

This chapter will describe the process of Japan's entry to the Bretton Woods system and its return to international financial markets, by looking at the course by which Japan joined the IMF and analyzing the process of the New York Debt Conference based on primary sources from the participating countries.[1] Previous studies on the issue of resolution of Japan's prewar external debts have referred to the memoirs of Juichi Tsushima, who served as the representative of the Japanese government in the conference, which describe the facts of the meetings in detail (Tsushima 1966). The official history of the Japanese Treasury also relies on his memoirs (Ministry of Finance, Financial History office 1997, pp. 57–75). However, these are written only from Japan's point of view, and until now there has been no empirical study of the negotiations and of the attitudes of the other countries party to the meetings, the U.S. and Britain, toward the issue of resolution of external debts. This chapter will consider political and economic interests in the countries party to the negotiations in light of the international economic situation in the formative period of the Bretton Woods system, using materials from sources including Japan's Ministry of Foreign Affairs, the British Foreign Office, and the U.S. Department of State to examine the process of negotiations.

2 Japan's Participation in the IMF and the Plan for the Introduction of Foreign Capital

2.1 The Debate on Japan's Entry to the IMF

Information on the Bretton Woods Conference and its proposed agreement began to make its way to Japan via the overseas institutions of the government, the Bank of Japan, and others during World War II. After the end of the war the Ministry of Finance and the Bank of Japan studied this information internally. Initially Japan was interested in whether entering the Bretton Woods system would restrict its existing policies of managed currency and foreign-exchange controls. This also was connected to the issue of whether to see the Bretton Woods system as a revival of the gold standard or to interpret it as involving a Keynesian aspect of tolerating discretionary action to achieve domestic equilibrium (Asai 1998, pp. 93–97). A Bank of Japan document written in January 1946 describes the Bretton Woods system as "a plan to realize a gold standard without the freedom to change par value," commenting, "there is little hope for demanding a new international equilibrium point for purposes of domestic economic growth."[2] At the same time, the document

[1]Asai (2005, 2007) examines in detail the process of the consultations on Japan after it joined the IMF, while Itoh (2009) discusses comprehensively Japan's external financial policies from its joining the Bretton Woods system through the shift to floating exchange rates.

[2]Bank of Japan Research Bureau, *Bureton Uzzu Tsūka Kyōtei to Nihon Sanka no Hōto* [The Bretton Woods agreement and means of participation for Japan], January 1946, Bank of Japan

supported Japan's entry to the Bretton Woods system, arguing, "In exchange for contributing a certain amount of gold participating countries would gain several times that amount in capacity to settle their international balances of payments, and they would be able to access long-term foreign capital from the World Bank without regard to the amount of their contribution." It pointed out the need for the preparatory measures of improving the international balance of payments and accumulating gold reserves, thorough fiscal austerity, and reorganizing the Bank of Japan.

As the activities of the IMF and the World Bank took on concrete form, both the Japanese government and the Bank of Japan came to see the Bretton Woods system as something that would not restrict domestic policy. An internal document prepared by the Bank of Japan in April 1948 stated that the Bretton Woods system "is applied in a flexible and realistic manner through implementation of the text of the agreement, and it can be expected that measures such as foreign-exchange controls would be permitted relatively easily in the future as well when unavoidable such as in the case of an imbalance in the international balance of payments", and concluded that there were no barriers to Japan's entry to the Bretton Woods system and that Japan should join it as quickly as possible.[3] Behind this change of view in the debate were the "Intermediate Stabilization Plan" being promoted by the Economic Stabilization Agency and SCAP, and the plan for attracting foreign capital by the Ashida Cabinet, established in March of that year (Itoh 2009, pp. 54–57). They saw that the Bretton Woods system did not conflict with the intermediate stabilization plan, which prioritized maintenance of domestic equilibrium for the time being over international equilibrium, and restoration of international credit through joining the IMF and the World Bank was expected to provide support for access to foreign capital.

However, the U.S. National Advisory Council (NAC), in particular the Department of the Treasury and the Federal Reserve Board (FRB), strongly opposed SCAP's plan of Intermediate Stabilization (Itoh 2009, pp. 58–59; Miwa 2002, pp. 59–61). The Young Mission, headed by Ralph A. Young of the FRB, visited Japan in May 1948 and recommended the prompt setting of a single exchange rate and strengthening of financial stabilization measures, describing the multiple exchange rate system and effective trade subsidies as themselves impeding currency stability. In October 1948, the U.S. National Security Council (NSC) approved "Recommendations with Respect to U.S. Policy toward Japan" (NSC-13/2), and U.S. policy toward Japan shifted from a focus on demilitarization and economic democratization to a policy of helping Japan's economic recovery and reentry into the international economy as a member of the Western bloc. Based on this shift, the Nine-Point Program for Japan's Economic Recovery and Stabilization was transmitted from Washington to SCAP and Prime Minister Shigeru Yoshida, calling for enactment of an economic stabilization plan including balancing the budget,

---

Institute for Monetary and Economic Studies (1983), pp. 1–16.

[3] Bank of Japan Foreign Affairs Department, *Bureton Uzzu Kikō Sanka ni Kansuru Jakkan no Mondai* [Minor problems concerning participation in the Bretton Woods system], April 1948, Bank of Japan Institute for Monetary and Economic Studies (1983), pp. 34–38.

enhancing tax collection, and restricting lending as well as the goal of setting a single exchange rate within 3 months. In February 1949, Joseph M. Dodge, President of the Detroit Bank, was sent to Japan as a financial adviser in charge of the nine-point plan. He directed the deployment of the austerity policies known as the "Dodge Line" and a single exchange rate of 360 yen to the dollar was established in April of that year.

In response to this shift in U.S. policy toward Japan, the debate on joining the IMF was rekindled within the Japanese government and the Bank of Japan. In October 1949, a Bank of Japan document reached the conclusion that the burdens on Japan of joining the IMF (e.g., the requirement of foreign-exchange stability, the elimination of foreign-exchange controls, and the required financial contributions to the IMF) would be tolerable and that Japan should ask to join the IMF for the four reasons that the country would be able to borrow foreign currency from the Fund, it would have access to loans from the World Bank, entry would make it possible to encourage private-sector foreign investment, and it would serve as a confirmation of Japan's status as a member of the international economic community.[4] The visit to the U.S. of Minister of Finance Hayato Ikeda from April through May 1950 had the missions of negotiating on the peace treaty, promoting economic reconstruction, and making a tentative overture concerning Japan's entry to the IMF and the World Bank. These were intended to help resolve some of the key policy issues faced by the Yoshida Cabinet. When visiting the IMF and the World Bank Ikeda demonstrated Japan's proactive attitude toward joining both.[5]

2.2 *Japan's Entry to the IMF*[6]

The visit of U.S. Secretary of State John Foster Dulles to Japan in January 1951 spurred the progress in peace negotiations with Japan and a plan for U.S.–Japan economic cooperation involving the use of Japan's industrial might to supply the U.S. military was discussed.[7] With that background, the movement toward Japan's entry to the IMF would come into full swing in the spring of 1951. In May

[4] Bank of Japan Research Bureau, *Sengo ni Okeru Kokusaitsūkaseido no Hatten – Kokusai Tsūka Kikin Kanyū Mondai ni Kanren shite* [Development of the postwar international currency system: In connection with issues related to joining the International Monetary Fund], October 1949, Bank of Japan Institute for Monetary and Economic Studies (1983), pp. 40–61.

[5] In March 1950, prior to Ikeda's visit to the U.S., Finance Commissioner Takeshi Watanabe of the Ministry of Finance visited the IMF, where the process of entry to the IMF and the World Bank was explained to him. This was Japan's first point of contact toward entry. (Asai 1998, p. 97)

[6] Except as noted otherwise, the descriptions in this paragraph are from Asai (1998).

[7] While the plan for U.S.–Japan economic cooperation got its start in talks with Prime Minister Yoshida during Dulles' visit to Japan in January 1951 as a means by which Japan would contribute to the Western bloc, in Japan it came to be discussed in connection with the nation's postwar recovery plans. Regarding U.S.–Japan economic cooperation, see Ministry of Finance, Financial History Office (1976) and Nakamura (1982), and regarding plans to attract foreign capital see Asai (2001a, b).

W.W. Diehl of the SCAP diplomatic bureau met with Ikeda to encourage Japan to prepare for entry, and in early July the Department of State approved Japan's quick entry for reasons including the political influence it would give Japan and to implement economic development policies after the peace. The Japanese government asked to send observers to the general meetings of the IMF and the World Bank held in September 1951, and on August 9 it formally applied to join the IMF and the World Bank.

On September 18 the IMF set up a membership screening committee to discuss conditions for Japan's entry. While none in the committee opposed Japan's entry, there was a conflict of opinion on the size of Japan's quota, with the U.S. arguing for a quota in the range of USD265–270 million while Britain and Australia, which did not favor expanding Japan's voice in the IMF, argued for one no higher than 200 million. In January 1952, the decision calling for a quota of USD250 million and payment of 62.5 million in gold was sent to Japan. While the Japanese government argued for a reduction in the amount of gold it needed to pay in, in the end it accepted the IMF proposal. On April 18 the Japanese cabinet decided to join the IMF and the World Bank. Following an entry process that included a report from the screening committee and procedures with the Executive Board and others, on May 28, 1952 all IMF member states voted on Japan's entry, which was approved with the support of 94 % of all ballots. On August 13, Japan formally joined the IMF and the World Bank. In March of the following year Japan notified the IMF of a par value of 360 yen to the dollar, and in May the IMF Executive Board approved this value. Thus Japan, guided by the U.S., entered the Bretton Woods system soon after regaining its independence and the pathway opened toward economic cooperation with the U.S., particularly access to foreign capital, that Japan had hoped for. But in order to realize these aims the issue of Japan's prewar external debts needed to be addressed.

3 The Issue of Defaulted Prewar External Debts and Responses After Conclusion of the Peace Treaty

3.1 The Default of Japanese External Debts and Wartime Measures Taken by the Japanese Government[8]

With the outbreak of the war in the Pacific in December 1941, Japan suspended payment of both interest and principal on its debts to belligerent nations, effectively defaulting on these external debts. As shown in Table 11.1, Japan's balances of foreign-currency debts at the start of the war were GBP88.52 million of sterling debt, USD283.49 million of debt denominated in dollars, and FRF663.79 million of debt in French francs. Of these, Japanese individuals and corporations held foreign

[8] Regarding measures for Japanese foreign-currency bonds during the war, see Takaishi (1974) and Ministry of Finance, Financial History Office (1983).

Table 11.1 Unredeemed amounts and accumulated unpaid interest on prewar external debts (in thousands of currency units)

		Unredeemed amount at start of war [A]	Amount disposed of under Act on Treatment of Foreign Currency-Denominated Bonds (1943) [B]	Unredeemed amount at end of April 1952 [C]	Unredeemed amount at end of June 1952 (under agreement on resolution of external debts) [D]	Accumulated unpaid interest at end of June 1952 (under agreement on resolution of external debts) [E]
GBP bonds	Government bonds	77,225	25,586	51,500	64,500	36,157
	Municipal bonds	8,094	1,508	6,596	6,599	4,173
	Corporate bonds	3,208	200	3,007	5,175	3,432
	Total	88,528	27,296	61,103	76,275	43,764
USD bonds	Government bonds	152,808	131,300	25,797	28,376	18,829
	Municipal bonds	24,993	18,591	6,430	6,505	3,992
	Corporate bonds	105,751	65,855	39,924	41,479	27,217
	Total	283,492	215,746	72,151	76,361	50,039
FRF bonds	Government bonds	415,980	–	(383,266)	383,221	54,178
	Municipal bonds	(247,819)	–	(195,169)	n/a	n/a
	Total	663,799	–	(578,435)	n/a	n/a

Sources:
[A] [B] Ministry of Finance, Financial History Office (1983), Table 1–17. Figures in parentheses from Takaishi (1974), pp. 466–468
[C] Ministry of Finance, Financial History Office (1983), Table 9-9. Figures in parentheses from Ministry of Finance, Financial Bureau, "Foreign-denominated bonds in Japan (estimated as of March 31, 1952)"
[D] [E] Ministry of Finance, Financial Bureau, "Principal and unpaid interest on Japan's foreign-currency debt (as of June 30, 1952)"; Tsushima (1966), Appendix 1
Notes:
Since amounts are rounded down to the nearest 1,000 currency units, totals may not always match
South Manchuria Railway Sterling bonds paying 5 % interest are included under government bonds
[B] Represents the total of amounts of external bonds held by issuers subject to forced extinguishment and amounts converted to yen bonds
[C] Represents the amount including validated foreign-currency bonds owned by nationals of the U.S. and its allies that had been converted to yen-denominated bonds without permission under the Law relating to the Treatment of Foreign Currency Bonds
[D] [E] The amounts of Sterling bonds represent the equivalent values in pounds after application of optional currency clauses under the agreements on resolution of external bonds

debts of GBP26.79 million and USD211.68 million. On December 29 the Japanese government decided on emergency measures for payment of interest and principal on Japanese external debts, under which payment of interest on debts would continue formally, with payment of interest and principal on external debts held by Japanese and nationals of non-belligerent countries being made in yen and payment of interest on bonds held by nationals of belligerent countries being remitted in yen to the Special Property Administration Account opened in the Yokohama Specie Bank under the provisions of the Enemy Property Administration Law.

In March 1943, the government passed the Law relating to the Treatment of Foreign Currency Bonds (Law No. 60, 1943) to resolve thoroughly the issue of foreign-currency bonds. The law called for conversion of all foreign-currency bonds held by Japanese and nationals of non-belligerent countries to yen-denominated bonds (Article 2), extinguishment of foreign-currency bonds held by issuers themselves, under government order (Article 8), and succession by the government of obligations to pay interest and principal on municipal and corporate bonds, by which the original contracts would cease to have any effect on matters other than the obligations to pay interest and principal, such as mortgages (Article 9). As a result, debts of GBP27.08 million and USD191.42 million were converted to yen bonds and GBP190,000 and USD23.75 million were extinguished. The unpaid balances of external debts succeeded by the government in April 1952 stood at GBP61.10 million, USD72.15 million, and FRF578.43 million, as shown in Table 11.1[C].

3.2 The San Francisco Peace Treaty and the Responses of Creditor Countries

In Article 18 of the San Francisco Peace Treaty, signed in September 1951, Japan acknowledged that prewar external debts remained in effect (Paragraph a) and the government pledged promptly to begin negotiations on resumption of payments on those debts (Paragraph b). The U.S. government's consideration of the issue of resolution of prewar debts took place as part of the process of preparation of a recommendation to the Interdepartmental Ad Hoc Committee on Japan Property and Claims Questions (JAPQ), which took place as a preparation to draft the peace treaty beginning in 1951. The State Department's draft recommendations for JAPQ prepared in December 1951 identified the following as basic policies that the U.S. government should take: (i) While it would be desirable to conduct negotiations after reaching agreement in the negotiations on U.S claim for postwar economic assistance and the financial arrangements for the support of U.S. troops in Japan, this should not hinder an early resolution; (ii) The debt settlement arrangements should not unduly drain Japan's foreign exchange resources or add considerably to the financial burden of any Allied Power; (iii) Bonds of former dependent territories issued with guarantees from the Japanese government also would be included; (iv) Extinguishment of mortgages under the Law relating to the Treatment of Foreign

Currency Bonds would be accepted; (v) The claims of nationals of the U.S. and its allies that had been converted to yen-denominated bonds without permission would be restored; and, (vi) The U.S. should oppose application of the gold clauses in bond contracts.[9] The State Department adopted a cautious attitude to the issue of resolution of external debts, one premised on avoiding an impact on Japan's dollar balances while also linking it to the issue of repayment of postwar U.S. aid.

After the treaty was signed the U.S. government showed no intention to begin discussion of the issue of resolution of external debts immediately.[10] But the British government, in particular HM Treasury, took proactive action for the prompt settlement of the resumption of payment on Japan's external debts. On January 18, 1952, D.W. Serpell of HM Treasury telephoned C.P. Scott of the Foreign Office's Far East Department, telling that HM Treasury and the Bank of England were highly interested in the worsening of the sterling balance of payments with Japan and that the government should approach the Japanese government directly to resolve the issue of Japan's external debts.[11] In response, the Foreign Office issued instructions on an official approach. On February 6, the United Kingdom Liaison Mission in Japan submitted a written proposal concerning resumption of payment on Japan's prewar debts.[12] HM Treasury and the Bank of England were most interested in guarantees of optional currency clauses (payable in U.S. dollars).[13] Since Britain was in the midst of a severe shortage of dollars, HM Treasury strongly insisted on performance of optional currency clauses as stipulated in the original contracts.

In response to the British approach, Prime Minister (and Minister of Foreign Affairs) Yoshida issued instructions to propose a plan to deposit with the Bank of England GBP10–20 million of the sterling funds held by the Japanese government.[14]

---

[9] NARA, RG59, Subject Files Relating to International Economic Development, Revised Recommendations for JAPQ D-3/7, December 3, 1951 (abbreviated NARA hereinafter).

[10] Letter from Director of the Japanese Overseas Agency in Washington (Ryuji Takeuchi) to Minister of Foreign Affairs (Shigeru Yoshida), No. 155, November 19, 1951; No. 161, November 22, 1951, in the Ministry of Foreign Affairs document *Honpō no Senjichū Mibarai Gaisai Shori Kaigi Kankei* [Japanese wartime unpaid external debt resolution conference-related materials] (abbreviated "Conference-Related Materials" hereinafter).

[11] TNA, FO371/99421, Minute by C. P. Scott "Japanese Bonds", 18 January 1952 (abbreviated TNA hereinafter).

[12] Ministry of Foreign Affairs, Economic Affairs Bureau, *Senzen Gaisai no Shori ni Kansuru Igirisu Misshon no Mōshiire ni Kansuru Ken* [On the proposal by the British mission concerning resolution of prewar external debt], February 6, 1952, Conference-Related Materials.

[13] Optional currency clauses in a bond contract permit the recipient to choose the currency in which interest and principal will be paid. Specifically, those in which conversion to foreign currency is pledged at a fixed exchange rate (such as GBP1 = USD4.86) are referred to as "fixed rate clauses" and those pledging payment converted at the prevailing exchange rate on the date of payment are referred to as "current rate clauses". Since Britain had devalued the pound against the dollar since 1931, it could demand to receive dollars at a more advantageous rate than the current market exchange rate by applying these optional currency clauses. This is why the British government strongly demanded performance of optional currency clauses.

[14] Telegram from Minister of Foreign Affairs (Yoshida) to Director of the Overseas Agency in Geneva (Keiichi Tazuke), No. 10 (addressed to Director Koichiro Asakai of the London office), January 27, 1952, Conference-Related Materials.

Yoshida described the purpose of this overture as follows: "Aside from the political point of view, recently not a few bondholders have indicated concern about Japan's intentions regarding payment of its external debts. We consider it important to give the holders of government bonds some peace of mind through central-bank deposits."[15] Following negotiations between Japanese and British authorities, a 2-year deposit of GBP20 million with the Bank of England was announced on March 29.[16] Later, the U.S. too requested similar measures,[17] and a deposit of USD20 million with the New York Fed was announced on April 16. As these deposits with the British and American central banks were an attempt to regain the trust of the markets, the movement toward resolution of the issue accelerated in Britain and the United States.

3.3 The Japanese Government's Approach Toward Negotiation on Resolution of External Debts

Thus proposed by the British government, the Japanese government began considering practical resolution of resumption of payment on its external debts. A document prepared by the Ministry of Foreign Affairs' Economic Affairs Bureau on March 4, 1952, insisted on the need for a prompt decision on a policy in light of the importance to perform the terms of the peace treaty, to maintain the trust of holders of external debts, and to attract private-sector foreign investment in the future, and it called for beginning advance discussions with creditor countries once the peace treaty took effect.[18] That document indicated the following as policies for resolution of external debts: (i) While Japan would not ask for reductions in principal or accumulated unpaid interest, it would request exemption from interest on accumulated unpaid interest; (ii) Payments methods to be considered would be those of (a) bulk conversion to new bonds the principal and accumulated unpaid interest on both debts that had matured already and those that had not matured already, and (b) converting accumulated unpaid interest to new bonds or paying it in future installments, and extending the maturity date of principal into the future by the same period of time for which payment of interest was suspended; (iii) Mortgages on bonds would be extinguished and the government would guarantee payment; (iv) Gold clauses would not be in effect; and, (v) The applicable exchange rate would be the going rate as of the time of payment in the future.

[15] Telegram from Minister of Foreign Affairs to Director of the Overseas Agency in Geneva, No. 14 (addressed to Director of the London office), February 8, 1952, ibid.

[16] Press Release Document, *Pondo Shikin no Azukeire ni Tsuite* [On deposit of sterling funds], announced by the Ministry of Foreign Affairs Information Bureau, March 29, 1952, ibid.

[17] Telegram from Minister of Foreign Affairs to Director of the Overseas Agency in Washington, April 1, 1952, ibid.

[18] Ministry of Foreign Affairs Economic Affairs Bureau, *Gaisai Shori ni Kansuru Ken* [On resolution of external debts], March 4, 1952, Conference-Related Materials.

This proposal by the Ministry of Foreign Affairs can be considered to have reflected Yoshida's strong desire to attract foreign investment for reconstruction of the Japanese industry. But the Ministry of Finance adopted a more cautious point of view. A written reply prepared by Director-General Ishida of the Ministry of Finance's Financial Bureau in response to an inquiry from the Overseas Agency in Washington, while agreeing with the above Ministry of Foreign Affairs proposal in calling for bulk resolution of debts without reducing their amount, noted, "We believe at present that it might be more realistic to address the issue of repayment of U.S economic assistance to Japan first, then to resolve external debts, and then to decide on and move forward with reparations."[19] On payment methods Ishida's reply took into consideration the method of separating the debts and unpaid interest [as under (b) above], but it noted that at present the Ministry of Finance was inclined toward the method of bulk conversation of debts [as under (a) above], noting, "At this time we have not yet reached the point of deciding on the timing and declaring an intention to resume negotiations."

In response to the Ministry of Finance's reply, Yoshida instructed that the issue of external debts be resolved quickly, writing in the margins of the Ishida's letter, "I would like us to begin solving the issue of external debts as soon as possible. The only way for early resolution is through conversion of debts. Whatever the case we need to give the impression to creditor countries that we are beginning preparations for resolving external debts by appointing (Juichi) Tsushima or other specialists on external debt as advisory council members in preparation for enactment of the treaty." On March 25 the cabinet decided to establish a temporary advisory council to the Minister of Finance on resolution of prewar foreign bonds, appointing as members Juichi Tsushima (advisor to the Ministry of Foreign Affairs), Hisato Ichimada (Governor of the Bank of Japan), Takeo Kato (former President of Mitsubishi Bank), Jiro Shirasu (President of Tohoku Electric Power Co.), and Nobutane Kiuchi (chairman of the Foreign Exchange Control Commission), and as expert advisers Jiro Oka (from the Tokyo Electric Power Co.), and Jiro Honda (from Ibigawa Electric Industry Co.).[20] The council met five times over the period April 1–30, with the Minister of Finance in attendance. As a result, the members were of the view that a final draft should not be prepared in the council. They agreed to consider multiple proposals and reached the following tentative conclusions[21]:

(i) The amount that could be paid in 1 year would be roughly USD30 million, and it would be kept to no more than USD50 million at the highest.

(ii) Regarding the contracts of old bonds, (a) security clauses and gold clauses would be canceled, and (b) although clauses on payment currency would be a

[19] Letter from Director of Ministry of Finance Bureau (Tadashi Ishida) to the Director of the Ministry of Foreign Affairs Economic Affairs Bureau, March 11, 1952, ibid.

[20] *Rinji Gaikasai Shori Taisaku Kyōgikai Secchi Yōryō* [Outline of establishment of emergency council on resolution of external debt], ibid.

[21] Letter from the Director of the Ministry of Finance Bureau to the Director of the Ministry of Foreign Affairs Economic Affairs Bureau, May 21, 1952, ibid.

subject for future consideration, the conversion loan for sterling bonds all would be paid in pounds.

(iii) After consideration of the following proposed resolution methods, plan (a) below would be desirable under current conditions:

(a) Double conversion (issue of new conversion bonds individually for principal and accumulated unpaid interest; this method would require USD30 million in the first fiscal year)

(b) Conversion of principal for bonds that have matured already or will mature soon (issue of new conversion loans for principal and all accumulated unpaid interest on bonds that had already matured or would mature soon, while payments of bonds that would mature in the distant future would be resumed in accordance with the terms of their original contracts; this method would require USD43 million in the first fiscal year)

(c) Adjustment of principal for bonds that have matured already or will mature soon (adjustment of principal only on the bonds covered by proposal (b), to defer payment by 10 years on average; this method would require USD62.5 million per year)

(iv) Proposal for single conversion (conversion of interest and unpaid interest in bulk) or bulk deferment (resumption of payment in accordance with the old contracts, deeming the wartime period as a blank period) would be abandoned as impractical.

Through the course of discussions in the council, on May 17 the government gave instructions to consult with creditor countries that preparations had been made for meeting with creditor representatives on the settlement of Japanese prewar foreign debts,[22] and a proposal was approved to meet jointly in New York with representatives of British, American, and French bondholders in the latter half of July.[23] The government announced officially that Juichi Tsushima would be dispatched to the meeting with full authority. On June 10 Tsushima and high officials of the Ministry of Finance and Ministry of Foreign Affairs held a meeting at the official residence of the Minister of Finance. In discussion it was agreed that "it was necessary to explain fully to creditor representatives the fact that the outlook for the Japanese economy is uncertain, and strive to gain their understanding on matters such as the fact that the amount paid per year must not be too high, the need for conversion to new long-term bonds, and the fact that the interest rates on new bonds must be low."[24] The participants also agreed to explain that the tax-bearing capacity of the Japanese public was reaching its limit due to burdens such as the costs of repayment of Government and Relief in Occupied Areas (GARIOA) funds, repara-

[22] Telegram from Minister of Foreign Affairs (Katsuo Okazaki) to Chargés d'affaires to the U.S. (Ryuji Takeuchi) and Chargés d'affaires to Britain (Koichiro Asakai), No. 91, May 17, 1952, ibid.

[23] Telegram from Chargés d'affaires to Britain to Minister of Foreign Affairs, No. 271, June 7, 1952, ibid.

[24] Ministry of Foreign Affairs Economic Affairs Bureau, *Gaisai Kaigi Taisaku Uchiawasekai ni Kansuru Hōkoku* [Report on meeting on external bonds talks], June 10, 1952, ibid.

tions, and development of self-defense forces. It is clear that at that time the government was considering the proposal of conversion to new bonds as a method of resolution of external debts—the method that would be least costly to Japan.

However, in a meeting right before Tsushima was dispatched to New York, the final proposal chosen for resolution of the debts was not conversion to new bonds but bulk deferment, a proposal that had been rejected by the council described above. Tsushima later describes in his memoirs the reason for this choice that while issue of new conversion bonds would involve complex procedures such as organizing an underwriting syndicate as well as new costs such as issuing fees and stamp tax, it would be easier to reach agreement on the method of bulk conversion in light of its clear and simple procedures and the way it did not discriminate among bondholders, and thus it would make possible a quick resolution of the debts (Tsushima 1966, pp. 50–60). Minister of Finance Ikeda entrusted Tsushima with development of practical methods of resolution as long as the amount needed per year for payment of interest on external debts was in the range of USD40–50 million.

4 Discussions in the New York Debt Conference

The Debt conference was held at the Association of the Bar of the City of New York beginning July 21, 1952. Discussions continued for more than 2 months through the signing of an agreement on September 26. Representatives taking part in the Conference were Juichi Tsushima of the Japanese government, Sir Thomas Frazer of the Council of Foreign Bondholders from Britain, James Grafton Rogers of the Foreign Bondholders Protective Council from the U.S., and Andre de Chalender of the Association Nationale des Porteurs Français de Valeurs Mobililiers from France. Below we will examine the negotiations between Japan, Britain, and the U.S., focusing chiefly on the matter of optional currency clauses on bonds denominated in sterling, the greatest point at issue in the negotiations.[25]

4.1 Conflict Between Britain and the U.S. on Optional Currency Clauses

The conflict of opinion on optional currency clauses (permitting payment of sterling debts in dollars) surfaced early, in the second general meeting held on July 22 when substantial discussions began. Frazer strongly urged performance of optional currency clauses in accordance with the original contracts, describing this as a strong

[25] While the dispute between Japan and France concerning resolution of bonds denominated in francs was another point of contention in these negotiations, this chapter looks only at negotiations between Japan, Britain, and the U.S. because talks between Japan and France broke down at the start of the meeting and negotiations carried over until after the meeting.

demand from HM Treasury. Rogers declared his opposition to this proposal, arguing that performance of optional currency clauses would be unfair to American creditors, and said that he had received from the U.S. government a notice instructing him to oppose payment of sterling bonds in dollars.[26] Following the meeting, Rogers reported on the course of the discussions to Hamlin Robinson of the State Department by telephone, saying that the American Council intended to oppose payment in dollars. In response, the State Department provided indirect support for Rogers' policy by repeatedly expressing concerns about the outlook for Japan's dollar balances, although it did not express its views on the surface.[27]

Rogers' declaration that the U.S. government supported his opposition on optional currency clauses was a major shock to the British government, and the Foreign Office checked the veracity of this statement with the State Department through the British embassy in Washington. The State Department avoided making a formal declaration of its attitude, replying, "The U.S. Government had not formulated a position on this subject, although there is considerable concern within the Government at the prospect of Japan making dollar payments on sterling obligations – for reasons which have been elaborated elsewhere. In any case, Mr. Rogers had not been authorized to express a Government opinion on this point".[28]

Unofficial talks took place between Japan and the U.S. on both July 25 and July 26, in which Tsushima unofficially presented Japan's proposal on resolution of external debts, which Rogers welcomed.[29] The content of the proposal was communicated to the State Department right away, and Robinson suggested resolving the matter of optional currency clauses through payment in pounds at a premium.[30] This referred to payment of the face value in dollars converted at the prevailing exchange rate between the dollar and the pound on the payment date of the original contract, converted to pounds at the current prevailing exchange rate. This meant that the amount of payment would increase by a premium that would compensate for the loss of gains due to the fall in the pound exchange rate. Even before the conference this solution had already been discussed in the State Department, which had

[26] Telegram from Consul General in New York (Hisahiro Shimazu) to Minister of Foreign Affairs, No. 150 (*Gaisai* no. 4 from Ambassador Tsushima), July 23, 1952, Conference-Related Materials.

[27] RG59, Central Files, 894.10/7-2352, Memorandum of Telephone Conversation between James Rogers and Hamlin Robinson, July 23, 1952.

[28] RG59, Central Files, 894.10/7-3052, Memorandum of Conversation between Rogers and Robinson, July 30, 1952.

[29] Tsushima (1966), pp. 133–136. While Tsushima's memoire states that the meetings took place on the 24th and the 25th, according to an official Ministry of Foreign Affairs telegram (telegram from Consul General in New York to the Minister of Foreign Affairs, No. 153 [*Gaisai* no. 6 from Tsushima], July 28, 1952) they took place on the 25th and the 26th. Hereinafter we will use the dates of the official telegram.

[30] RG59, Central Files, 894.10/2552, Memorandum of Telephone Communication between Rogers and Robinson, July 25, 1952.

anticipated the British government's strong demand for payment in dollars through optional currency clauses and Japan's rejection of this demand.[31]

In unofficial tripartite talks between Japan, Britain, and the U.S. on July 29, Japan presented its proposal for resolution of the debts, based on bulk deferment. According to Tsushima, while "there did not appear to be any particularly strong opposition to the plan itself on the whole",[32] the arguments of Japan and Britain on the matter of optional currency clauses remained just as far apart. In this meeting Tsushima also proposed cancellation of the security clauses on government-assumed bonds, adjustment of sinking funds, and naming the Bank of Tokyo as a fiscal agent to replace the Yokohama Specie Bank but was unable to get the creditors to agree to these proposals at that time (Tsushima 1966, p. 154). On July 30, Official four-party talks were held between Japan, Britain, the U.S., and France, in which Tsushima submitted Japan's tentative proposal in writing. Its main points were: (i) repaying the principal of the external debts without reducing it, paying interest in accordance with the interest rates of the original contracts, and not discriminating between holders of external debts in the way they would be treated; (ii) deferring the deadlines for repayment of principal in the original contracts by 10 years; (iii) paying interest coupons with payment deadlines arising after conclusion of the agreement on those payment dates; (iv) paying interest coupons whose deadlines already have passed on, in principle, payment dates deferred by 10 years from the specified payment deadlines; (v) cancelling the security clauses specified for government assumed bonds; and, (vi) not citing optional currency clauses.[33] Noting that this proposal likely would satisfy American creditors, Rogers supported Japan's position on the matter of optional currency clauses as well. Frazer strongly refuted Rogers, rejected Japan's claim that application of the clauses would lead to a severe outflow of dollars, and repeated the argument that Britain could accept no proposal that did not permit optional currency clauses.[34]

After the four-party talks, Britain–U.S. talks were held and Frazer requested Rogers to ask what Japan thought about resolution through payment in pounds at a premium instead of in dollars, seeking out the possibility of compromise. When Rogers informed him of this, Tsushima said that Japan was ready to pay in pounds at a premium for sterling bonds with clauses specifying fixed conversion rates (Tsushima 1966, pp. 162–163). When Rogers reported this to the State Department by telephone, Robinson pointed out that Britain was insisting stubbornly on payment in dollars and was unlikely to accept the above proposed compromise, instead demanding payment in pounds at the prevailing exchange rate on the payment date

[31] RG59, Subject Files Relating to International Economic Development, Memorandum, April 17, 1952.

[32] Telegram from Consul General in New York to the Minister of Foreign Affairs, No. 154 (*Gaisai* No. 7 from Tsushima), Conference-Related Materials.

[33] Telegram from Consul General in New York to the Minister of Foreign Affairs, No. 156 (*Gaisai* No. 8 from Tsushima), Conference-Related Materials.

[34] FO371/99423, Telegram: Consul General in New York to FO, No. 21, 31 July 1952.

in the original contract of bonds with current rate options.[35] While Tsushima presented the above proposed compromise in talks between Japan and Britain held on August 6, Britain held fast to its demand for payment in dollars, arguing that even if optional currency clauses were fully applied the amount of dollars Japan needed per year would not become too high.[36]

4.2 *Diplomatic Negotiations Between Britain and the U.S. on Optional Currency Clauses*

As seen above, a conflict of opinions continued between Japan and Britain on the matter of optional currency clauses, or payment of sterling bonds in dollars, in the negotiations on resolution of Japan's external debts. While both Tsushima and Frazer were seeking a path to compromise through payment in pounds at a premium instead of payment in dollars, HM Treasury remained unyielding in its demands for full performance of the original contracts and payment in dollars. Since to Britain the matter of optional currency clauses was related not just to negotiations on resolution of Japan's external debts but also to the simultaneous negotiations under way on resolution of Germany's external debts, HM Treasury steadfastly maintained a policy of accepting no compromise. At the same time, Britain's Foreign Office attempted to find out the State Department's official view by pressing to reply to an aide-mémoire of June 27, in which the British Government had requested to announce U.S views on the optional currency problem in the case of Peruvian bonds.[37] However, the State Department put off a reply for reasons of coordination of opinions within the U.S. government.[38] HM Treasury expressed its strong displeasure, stating, "We fear that by procrastination they are avoiding causing themselves embarrassment while at the same time serving the interests of the United States Bondholders Protection Council. Until the State Department comes into the open the United States Bondholders Protective Council can continue to justify opposition to dollar options by reference to the State Department's alleged views and the Japanese derive great bargaining strength from this. Moreover the Peruvian and German dollar option bonds will also be affected by the reply."[39]

In the fifth session of formal talks, held on August 20, Frazer expressed the unyielding policy of refusing to consider various proposals unless a full proposal

[35] RG59, Subject Files Relating to International Economic Development, Memorandum of telephone communications between Rogers, J. C. Jones and Robinson, August 4, 1952.

[36] Telegram from Consul General in New York to the Minister of Foreign Affairs, No. 164 (*Gaisai* No. 14 from Tsushima), August 6, 1952, Conference-Related Materials: FO371/99423, Telegram: Consul General in New York to FO, No. 24, 6 August 1952.

[37] FO371/99423, Telegram: FO to Washington, No. 3131, 1 August, 1952.

[38] FO371/99423, Telegram: Sir O. Franks (Washington) to FO, No. 1514, 12 August 1952.

[39] FO371/99423, Telegram: FO to Washington, No. 3337, 15 August 1952.

was indicated for optional currency clauses.[40] Tsushima countered that it would be pointless to propose a compromise if Britain did not express its views concerning points other than optional currency clauses.[41] After the end of the formal talks, on August 22 Rogers visited the State Department to meet with Hamlin Robinson. In the conversation, Rogers said that the negotiations had reached a complete deadlock, as the British representatives, whom he had thought were ready to withdraw their demand for payment in dollars, repeated their original argument at the last moment. He also suggested the possibility of concluding a bilateral agreement between Japan and the United States. Robinson mentioned the British aide-mémoire on Peruvian bonds and stated, "we were about to deliver a reply to the British in which we would say that we 'do not favor' dollar payments on sterling obligations in a way which would make it clear that we had the Japanese negotiations in mind", and Rogers agreed to this proposal.[42]

On the afternoon of August 22, Corbett of the State Department visited the British embassy to deliver the reply to the June 27 aide-mémoire. In this reply, after a preliminary note that the federal government was not a party to the debt negotiations, the State Department stated, "This Government is, of course interested in avoiding any impression that it is not concerned with the fulfillment of contractual obligations. However, it cannot ignore the fact that circumstances may have changed very materially since the time when the obligations were entered into. ... In the opinion of this government, the optional currency provisions referred in the Ambassador's aide-mémoire are not immune from re-examination in the light of existing circumstances. In this connection, the government feels obliged to state that it does not favor the implementation of such provisions as to require substantial dollar payments on sterling obligations contracted during a period when the world's major currencies were freely convertible, where such payment would be detrimental to the interest of the United States."[43] Corbett pointed out that this reply was intended to pertain not just to Peruvian government bonds but to negotiations on Japan's external debts as well, identifying as the reason the government could not support payment in dollars the fact that if Congress were to notice that Japanese dollar holdings had been reduced by payments to British bondholders at a time when Japan held a high level of Sterling it would be difficult to secure passage of the generous resolution to the GARIOA obligations that the State Department desired.[44] Christelow of the British embassy replied that the embassy here had opposed London's position of steadfastly insisting on payment in dollars and would recom-

[40] FO371/99423, Telegram: Consul General in New York to FO, No. 24, 6 August 1952.

[41] Telegram from Consul General in New York to the Minister of Foreign Affairs, No. 174 (*Gaisai* No. 21 from Tsushima), August 20, 1952, Conference-Related Materials.

[42] RG59, Central Files, 894.10/8-2252, Memorandum of Conversation between Rogers and Robinson, August 22, 1952.

[43] FO371/99423, Telegram: Franks to FO, No. 1559, 22 August, 1952.

[44] FO371/99423, Telegram: Franks to FO, No. 1600, 22 August, 1952.

mend to withdraw the demand for dollar payment.[45] British Ambassador to the U.S. Sir Oliver Franks asked the Foreign Office and Treasury to change its policy on payment in dollars, saying, "Unless Frazer's instructions on this head [payment in dollars] can be substantially modified we fear that we may have to withdraw from the negotiations. If he is permitted to press for payment in sterling written up to $4.86 we may be able to enlist support."[46]

However, HM Treasury strongly rebuffed the reply from the State Department and the recommendations of Britain's Ambassador in support of the U.S. In a reply telegram to Washington it drafted itself, HM Treasury strongly criticized the State Department's reply that it prioritized expediency over the spirit of the law and fairness and claimed that there were no realistic problems that would hinder performance of the dollar clauses. Treasury asked the Embassy to seek out the possibility of direct negotiations between the governments by contacting the State Department and Tsushima on that issue.[47] In response, Franks made tentative overtures to the U.S. Departments of State and the Treasury, describing the results in a reply telegram as follows:

> ... Our conclusion on the basis of such soundings is that we are most unlikely to obtain any support for our demand for settlement of sterling indebtedness in terms of dollars. ... The American position is (i) that the present level of Japanese dollar holdings is due to the Korean war and to American assistance; (ii) that it is therefore fortuitous and the Japanese have a reasonable claim to reserve to support them during less favourable terms; (iii) they ought to maximize that part of their reserves which is in convertible currencies, i.e. dollars; ... The situation is, moreover, further complicated by the fear of provoking difficulties with Congress in a campaign period. This may seem like the old Congressional bogey. But the fact is that the departments concerned, even if we can convince them of the justice of our case, are not going to risk any Congressional complications for the remainder of this year. Given the wider issues involved this expedient course is in our own best interest.[48]

British Ambassador to Japan Sir E. Dening agreed with Franks, noting that Japan's present dollar position depended on expenditure on the Korean War and no guarantee could be given that this state would continue.[49] T. Peters of the Far Eastern Department noted, "The Treasury are considering what further action should be taken. When they make their proposals we should back up the views expressed by Tokyo and Washington."[50]

On September 6, HM Treasury decided on a new policy regarding the handling of optional currency clauses. This policy consisted of the following elements: (i) Britain's position that it could not accept the U.S. State Department's argument would be sent in writing in response to the August 22 reply, and (ii) Britain was prepared to agree to a compromise in the conference on government bonds subject

[45] RG59, Central Files, 894.10/8-2252, Memorandum of Conversation between Rogers and Robinson.

[46] FO371/99423, Franks to FO, No. 1600.

[47] FO371/99423, Telegram: FO to Washington, No. 3545, 26 August 1952.

[48] FO371/99423, Telegram: Franks to FO, No. 1642, 28 August, 1952.

[49] FO371/99423, Telegram: Sir E. Dening (Tokyo) to FO, No. 1519, 30 August, 1952.

[50] FO371/99423, Minutes by T. Peters, 2 September, 1952.

to the following conditions: (a) British bondholders' claim to the full sterling value of all foreign exchange options would be accepted, and (b) the United States, French, and Japanese governments would agree to set four-party talks concerning optional currency clauses in the future. This can be described as Britain's acceptance of payment in pounds at a premium on a temporary basis, on the condition of guaranteeing the possibility of payment in dollars in the future, without backing down from its previous argument on the legal binding force of optional currency clauses in government bond agreements. While the Foreign Office was not enthusiastic about arguing for the first part of this proposal, it instructed Frazer to submit the content of the second part to Japan in the sixth general meeting to be held on September 8.[51] J. A. Pilcher of the Far Eastern Department noted, "I should have thought, therefore, that, if we obtain an admission of the sanctity of the contract and then demand payment in sterling, honour would be satisfied and no-one's nose put out of joint."[52] Frazer introduced this counterproposal in the September 8 meeting, describing details including the fact that this proposal applied not just to fixed rate clauses but also those on current rate clauses and would remain in effect even of the pound exchange rate were to fall in the future. Tsushima asked Britain to make clear its attitude toward Japan's proposal on matters other than optional currency clauses, and Frazer replied that Britain had no objections other than those concerning the issue of the fiscal agent.

The negotiations on external debts made considerable progress toward a compromise with the British government's agreement to the basic points of Japan's proposal on resolution of external debts and conditional approval of payment of optional currency issues in pounds at a premium. As the U.S. State Department, which despised political intervention in external debt negotiations, opposed Britain's proposal for intergovernmental talks between the four countries,[53] HM Treasury withdrew the proposal for four-party talks and instead submitted a new proposal: (i) Sterling bonds with optional currency clauses would be paid in sterling so long as payment relation accruing from payment agreements were on sterling basis. However, in the event of a future change in the payment relation the Japanese government must authorize the right of holders of government bonds to receive payment in other currencies. (ii) The British government would recognize the agreement of the Japanese government to pay the equivalent value in pounds as an essential requirement for all government bonds with optional currency clauses.[54] While the Japanese government opposed Britain's proposal to link the issue of external debts with the payment agreement between Japan and Britain, in the end agreement was reached to hold future bilateral talks on the subject between Japan and Britain.[55]

---

[51] F371/99423, Telegram: FO to Consul General in New York, No. 662, 8 September, 1952.

[52] FO371/99423, Minute by J. A. Pilcher, 8 September, 1952.

[53] F371/99424, Telegram, Franks to FO, No. 1751, 15 September, 1952.

[54] Telegram from Consul General in New York to the Minister of Foreign Affairs, No. 196 (*Gaisai* No. 25 from Tsushima), September 8, 1952, Conference-Related Materials.

[55] RG59, Central Files, 894.10/9-1952, Memorandum of Conversation between Mr. Macay (British Embassy) and Robinson, September 17, 1952.

4.3 *Compromise on an Agreement on Resolution of External Debts*

Now that Britain had agreed, albeit conditionally, to payment of dollar bonds in pounds, only two issues remained to be resolved in the negotiations on resolution of Japan's external debts: the successor fiscal agent to the former Yokohama Specie Bank and the exchange rate used when paying bonds with current rate clauses. On the subject of the former issue, since the start of negotiations Japan had called for naming the Bank of Tokyo as the fiscal agent, but the creditors wanted to name banks in their own countries as the agents. As a result, discussion of this matter had been put off until later. While Tsushima discussed the issue of the fiscal agent in a meeting with Rogers on September 15, he could not obtain the agreement of the American Council.[56] Tsushima continued efforts to persuade Rogers, and in the September 19 Japan–U.S. talks Rogers announced that the Council had decided to accept Japan's request.[57] As a result, agreement had been reached on the main points of Japan–U.S. negotiations on resolution of external debts, and preparations toward signing an agreement began.

On the issue of government bonds with current rate clauses, Britain demanded payment in the equivalent amount in pounds at the current prevailing exchange rate of the dollar amount converted at the prevailing exchange rate of dollars to pounds as of the payment date in the original contract, rather than conversion at the current market exchange rate as of the new payment date after conclusion of an agreement on resolution of external debts. In response, in talks between Japan and Britain on September 17 Tsushima submitted a proposal for compromise on the applicable rate for government bonds with clauses calling for conversion at market rates and asked for Britain to negotiate on the proposal.[58] However, in a telegram to the Minister of Foreign Affairs Tsushima noted, "I suspect that they will not give up their argument through now." In fact, the reply from the British government submitted on September 22 steadfastly stuck to its previous view of demanding full performance of optional currency clauses, proposing that (i) payment in sterling would be authorized under the best possible conditions for all agreements on sterling bonds with optional currency clauses, with the deadline for such payment deferred by 15 years, and (ii) Japan and Britain would meet to discuss optional currency clauses at a later date.[59] Frazer declared that if Japan accepted Britain's demands on optional currency

---

[56] Telegram from Consul General in New York to the Minister of Foreign Affairs, No. 210 (*Gaisai* No. 32 from Tsushima), September 15, 1952, Meeting-Related Materials.

[57] Telegram from Consul General in New York to the Minister of Foreign Affairs, No. 219 (*Gaisai* No. 36 from Tsushima), September 19, 1952, ibid.

[58] Telegram from Consul General in New York to the Minister of Foreign Affairs, No. 214 (*Gaisai* No. 33 from Tsushima), September 17, 1952, ibid. The compromise proposal was for an intermediate value between the exchange rate on the payment date in the contract and the current exchange rate.

[59] Telegram from Consul General in New York to the Minister of Foreign Affairs, No. 228 (*Gaisai* No. 44 from Tsushima), No. 229 (*Gaisai* No. 45), September 23, 1952, ibid.

clauses then he was prepared to accept all of Japan's proposals, including those on the issue of the fiscal agent, seeking to advance to the final stage of negotiations with Japan. In the final negotiations between Japan and Britain on September 23, Tsushima replied that Japan would accept Britain's demands concerning optional currency clauses, subject to conditions including the following: (i) deferral for 15 years of sterling government bonds with optional currency clauses, (ii) acceptance of Japan's proposal concerning bilateral talks between Japan and Britain, (iii) close examination of the draft of the agreement on optional currency clauses, (iv) acceptance of Japan's proposal for resolution submitted on July 30 regarding matters other than the above, and (v) simultaneous signing of the agreements between Japan and the U.S. and between Japan and Britain. When Frazer agreed to these terms, the negotiations on resolution of external debts between Japan and Britain had ended in compromise.[60]

The resulting agreements between Japan and the U.S. and between Japan and Britain on the resolution of Japan's external debts, signed on September 26, consisted mainly of the following points[61]:

- Finalization of the bonds covered by the agreement (Article 1)
- Approval of assumption of liabilities for corporate bonds by the government and elimination of security and other clauses of these bonds (Article 2)
- Extension of the maturity dates by 15 years for government bonds with optional currency clauses and 10 years for others (Article 3)
- Resumption of use of sinking funds and adjustment of amounts, dates, and periods of them (Article 4)
- Payment of interest at the same rates specified in the original contracts during the extended period after the original maturity dates (Article 5)
- Extension of payment dates of interest and its payment method: interest coupons during the period of no payment (1942–1952) in principle would be paid on the new payment dates extended by 10 years, while interest coupons after conclusion of the agreement would be paid on the payment dates shown on the coupons (Article 6)
- Succession by the Bank of Tokyo of the status of fiscal agent for those government bonds for which the Yokohama Specie Bank was designated (Article 7)

[60] Telegram from Consul General in New York to the Minister of Foreign Affairs, No. 233 (*Gaisai* No. 48 from Tsushima), September 23, 1952, ibid.

[61] Negotiations between Japan and France did not reach a compromise in New York due to conflicts on the gold clause for 4 % government bonds denominated in francs (issued in 1910) and on the handling of franc-denominated municipal bonds from the City of Tokyo (issued in 1912) that the Japanese government excluded from resolution. Later both governments asked IMF Managing Director Rooth to mediate, and a mediation proposal by Stein of the Stockholm Enskilda Bank, recommended by Rooth, served as the basis of an agreement on resolution of external debt signed in Paris in July 1956 (Ministry of Finance, Financial History Office 1997, pp. 75–81). Compromise on the City of Tokyo bonds was reached with the conclusion of a payment agreement in October 1961 based on a mediation proposal from World Bank President Black, who was asked to mediate in 1958 (Tsushima 1966, p. 213).

- Maintenance of the terms of the original contracts for matters not changed through this agreement (Article 8)
- Respecting the optional currency clauses of sterling bonds. Although whether or not to permit payment in foreign currency would be determined in later talks between Japan and Britain, until then the dollar payment amounts in the contracts would be paid in the equivalent value in pounds. (Article 9 in Anglo-Japanese agreement)

This agreement finalized Japan's unredeemed balance of currency-currency bonds and its accumulated unpaid interest, as shown in Table 11.1[D] [E]. Payment of interest resumed in London and New York on December 22, 1952.

5 Conclusion

In this chapter, we have looked at the process of Japan's entry to the Bretton Woods system and the resolution of its prewar external debts in the New York Debt Conference. A major issue involved in recovering Japan's economy in the postwar period was how to balance the supply of money needed to resume production, price stability, and the international balance of payments. In considering Japan's entry to the IMF and the World Bank, Japanese authorities expected the nation's entry to the Bretton Woods system to enable it to access foreign capital, to fund the capital investment needed to restore production as well as to obtain the foreign currency needed to pay for imports. At the same time, they were concerned about the possibility of balancing the maintenance of par value against the dollar and the obligation of liberalizing foreign exchange advocated by the IMF with domestic inflationary economic policies. Ultimately the barriers to IMF entry disappeared when Japan curbed inflation and realized a single exchange rate through implementation of the Dodge Line, and it joined the Bretton Woods system at the same time it regained independence. These developments also followed the course of a 1948 shift in U.S. policy toward Japan.

Prime Minister Yoshida was highly aware of the need to attract foreign capital needed to fund the growth that was essential to an economic recovery. He attempted to join the IMF and the World Bank and resolve the issue of resolution of prewar external debts as steps toward this goal. In the process of the domestic debate in Japan, in contrast to the Ministry of Finance, which wanted to keep the burden of payments as low as possible out of foreign currency reserve and fiscal concerns, Yoshida considered the prompt resolution of the issue to be important. The fact that even though a proposal to resolve the issue through conversion, which would not have been very costly, was considered in preliminary discussions, the government shifted to a bulk deferment proposal immediately prior to the start of the talks can be said to indicate that Yoshida's plan to aim for prompt resolution of the issue had borne fruit.

The biggest concern in the negotiation of the Debt Conference was the matter of optional currency clauses for sterling bonds, or in other words whether to permit payment in dollars. With Britain's severe dollar shortage and the sterling crisis in the background, the British government, particularly HM Treasury, issued a strong demand for payment in dollars through performance of optional currency clauses. However, the U.S. State Department did not want the issue of resolution of external debts to increase the fiscal and funding burden on Japan, out of concern for matters such as Japan's burden of external payments after the peace, including those related to GARIOA repayment and rearmament issues. While through the mediation of the U.S. State Department the conflict of opinion between Japan and Britain on optional currency clauses ended in a compromise that successfully contained Britain's demands for payment in dollars, this was not merely a case of the U.S. supporting Japan's economic recovery. Rather, it reflected American domestic interests (particularly demands from Congress) that desired to lessen Japan's burden on the United States. In addition, although the British government's demand for payment in dollars was not accepted, it continued its strong insistence on performance of its contractual rights, ultimately succeeding in getting Japan to agree to pay in pound values equivalent to the amount that it would have received in dollars under the original contracts (in other words, payment at a premium equal to the amount lost due to exchange-rate fluctuations).

In this way, the issue of resolution of Japan's prewar external debts symbolizes the economic interests of each country in the period the Bretton Woods system was established, and the results of the process of related talks showed the predominance of the U.S. in the international economic order. Under these conditions, Japan was able to regain international credit by resuming payment of foreign-currency bonds and entered a period of access to foreign capital, chiefly in the form of World Bank loans that came into full swing beginning in the 1950s. In its relationship with the IMF, Japan was able to achieve liberalization of foreign exchange in stages, while using IMF standby lines of credit in the 1953 and 1957 foreign currency crises, and to shift to Article VIII status in 1964. Japan during the 1950s moved from an economic recovery to rapid economic growth by putting to maximum use the framework of the Bretton Woods system in coordinating domestic and international equilibrium.

References

Asai, Yoshio. 1998. *Nihon no IMF, Sekaiginkō eno Kamei ni Tsuite* (Japan's membership in the IMF and the World Bank). *Soka Keiei Ronshu* (Soka University The Review of Business Administration), 23–2. Tokyo.

Asai, Yoshio. 2001a. *1950-nendai Zenhan ni Okeru Gaishi Donyu Mondai (Jō)* (Issues in attracting foreign capital during the first half of the 1950s (I)). *Seijo Daigaku Keizai Kenkyu* (Seijo University Economic Papers), 153. Tokyo.

Asai, Yoshio. 2001b. *1950-nendai Zenhan ni Okeru Gaishi Donyu Mondai (Chū)* (Issues in attracting foreign capital during the first half of the 1950s (II)). *Seijo Daigaku Keizai Kenkyu* (Seijo University Economic Papers), 154. Tokyo.

Asai, Yoshio. 2005. *IMF 8-jōkoku Ikō to Boeki/kawase Jiyūka (Jō): IMF to Nihon: 1952-64-nen* (Japan's participation in the IMF Article VIII countries: The IMF and Japan: 1952–64 (I)). Research reports of the Seijo University Institute for Economic Studies, No. 42. Tokyo.

Asai, Yoshio. 2007. *IMF 8-jōkoku Ikō to Boeki/kawase Jiyūka (Ge): IMF to Nihon: 1952-64-nen* (Japan's participation in the IMF Article VIII countries: The IMF and Japan: 1952–64 (II)). Research reports of the Seijo University Institute for Economic Studies, No. 46. Tokyo.

Bank of Japan Institute for Monetary and Economic Studies. 1983. *Nihon Kinyushi Shiryo Showa Zokuhen* (Materials on Japanese monetary history-Showa Era, 2nd series), vol. 14. Tokyo: Ministry of Finance Printing Bureau.

Itoh, Masanao. 2009. *Sengo Nihon no Taigai Kinyu: 360-en reto no seiritsu to hokai* (External finance in postwar Japan: The rise and fall of the 360-yen exchange rate). Nagoya: University of Nagoya Press.

Ministry of Finance, Financial History Office. 1976. *Showa Zaiseishi: Shusen Kara Kowa Made* (The financial history of Showa Era: The allied occupation period, 1945–1952), vol. 3, *Amerika No Tainichi Senryo Seisaku* (The U.S. occupation policy toward Japan) (Written by Ikuhiko Hata). Tokyo: Toyo Keizai Shinposha.

Ministry of Finance, Financial History Office. 1983. *Showa Zaiseishi: Shusen Kara Kowa Made* (The financial history of Showa Era: The allied occupation period, 1945–1952), vol. 11, *Seihu Saimu* (Governmental Debts) (Written by Saburo Kato). Tokyo: Toyo Keizai Shinposha.

Ministry of Finance, Financial History Office. 1997. *Shōwa Zaiseishi: Showa 27-48 Nendo* (The financial history of showa era: From FY1952 to 1973), vol. 7, *Kokusai* (Government Bonds) (Written by Yuji Yui and Hiromitsu Ishi). Tokyo: Toyo Keizai Shinposha.

Miwa, Ryoichi. 2002. *Nihon Senryo no Keizai Seisakushi Teki Kenkyu* (A study of the history of economic policies in occupied Japan). Tokyo: Nihon Keizai Hyoronsha.

Nakamura, Takafusa. 1982. Nichibei "Keizai Kyoryoku" Kankei no Keisei (Formation of Japan-- U.S. "Economic Cooperation"). In Kindai Nihon Kenkyu (Modern Japanese studies), *The Pacific War: From the start of war to the peace*, vol. 4, ed. Kindai Nihon Kenkyukai, 279–302. Tokyo: Yamakawa Press.

Takaishi, Sueyoshi. 1974. *Tekisan Gaisai Shimatu* (Resolution of enemy property and external bonds), vol. 1. Tokyo: Zaimu Shuppan.

Tsushima, Juichi. 1966. *Gaisai Shori No Tabi* (The road to resolution of external debts), Hōtō Zuisō, vol. 16. Tokyo: Hōtō Kankōkai.

Chapter 12
The IMF and Japan: Liberalization of Foreign Exchange and Pursuit of High Growth

Yoshio Asai

1 Introduction

Japan joined the IMF in August 1952, 8 years after the Bretton Woods Conference. Germany joined the IMF in that same month. About 12 years later, in April 1964, Japan's status shifted to that of an IMF Article VIII nation. The leading Western European member states already had acceded to Article VIII status 3 years earlier. While under Article XIV status, Japan had borrowed funds from the IMF in 1953 and 1957 and concluded standby line of credit agreements in 1962 and 1964, but since acceding to Article VIII status it has not borrowed from the IMF once. Japan's shift to Article VIII status was carried out when the time was fully ripe.

Assessment of Japan during its time as an Article XIV member state will vary depending on the time of assessment. When it first joined the IMF, Japan was isolated within international settlement as a whole and within the Asian economy in particular. Japan faced some very large difficulties, and everybody agreed that it would be impossible for the nation to liberalize foreign exchange and realize multilateral trade over a short period of time. Stressing this point, we can describe Japan's time as an Article XIV member as a painful process of achieving trade and foreign-exchange liberalization while repeatedly facing international balance of payments crises. However, looking back from the period after Japan's postwar rapid economic growth, Japan appears to have strived devotedly for economic growth under protectionist policies while gaining time through securing concessions from the IMF by intentionally overstating its difficulties, even though the obstacles it faced actually were not that large. While when considering history we must not be so arrogant as to judge the past from the point of view of the present, at the same time we need to

Y. Asai (✉)
Faculty of Economics, Seijo University, Setagaya-ku, Tokyo, Japan
e-mail: asai@seijo.ac.jp

K. Yago et al. (eds.), *History of the IMF*, Studies in Economic History,
DOI 10.1007/978-4-431-55351-9_12

remember that the assessments of people at the time were not necessarily accurate descriptions of the actual realities that they faced.

Below, in Sect. 2 we will describe the international conditions in which Japan found itself in the 1950s, within the context of its relationship with the IMF. Section 3 will analyze the process by which Japan, forced to liberalize as liberalization advanced in trade and foreign exchange with the restoration of convertibility of the leading Western European currencies at the end of 1958, reached the stage of full-fledged trade and foreign-exchange liberalization efforts. In Sect. 4 we will examine the impact on Japan of changes in international conditions, such as the development of international financial markets and the worsening of the U.S. international balance of payments, and describe the process by which it secured the status of a developed country as it acceded to IMF Article VIII status in 1964 and joined the OECD at roughly the same time.

2 Division of Japan's Settlement Area and Issues of Economic Independence

2.1 A Divided Settlement Area

2.1.1 International Isolation

In 1951, although Japan's industrial production already had recovered to its prewar (1934–1936 average) level, its exports stood at only about one-third their prewar level and its imports at about one-half the prewar level. The causes of this delay in recovering trade levels are discussed below.

First, Japan's international relations had undergone a dramatic change after its loss in the war. The "yen bloc" that Japan had built up on the Korean Peninsula and in China during the 1930s had collapsed. The Cold War that began in 1947 and the Korean War that broke out in 1950 made trade with Mainland China, Japan's greatest source of raw materials, difficult. In particular, the U.S. embargo on trade with China implemented after the latter entered the Korean War effectively severed trade between Japan and China. While the Korean War caused Japan's economy to flourish through special procurement by the U.S. military, diplomatic relations between Japan and South Korea were not restored until 1965, and trade between the two countries remained largely nonexistent. It also took time to restore relations with Southeast Asian countries that had been subjected to Japanese military occupation during W W II.

The second cause was a transformation in the system of international division of labor due to the changing industrial structure. While Japan's chief exports prior to World War II had been textile goods, centered on cotton fabrics, in the postwar period the rise of the textile industry in other Asian countries led to advancing import substitution. For this reason, Japan needed to transition its exports to products of the heavy and chemical industries. However, even though they had progressed considerably during the war Japan's heavy and chemical industries still had not reached an internationally competitive level, and they had been late to start modernizing their machinery and equipment.

Third, the division of foreign-exchange areas into the dollar and sterling areas hindered expansion of trade. In the postwar years Japan was forced to import from the dollar area the raw materials it previously had imported from colonies and occupied territories. This resulted in a massive trade deficit. However, it was unable to cover its trade deficit with the dollar area with British pounds earned through exporting to the sterling area, because currency convertibility had not been restored. What's more, exports to the sterling area were unstable due to import restriction measures and advancement of import substitution in that area. Bilateral open account trade was used as a means of avoiding these difficulties.

2.1.2 Trade with the Sterling Area

The inability to restore convertibility of the pound over a lengthy time after World War II was a major impediment to growing trade with Southeast Asia, which was important to recovering Japan's economy. After the failed attempt to restore convertibility of the pound in 1947 Britain shifted to a policy of gradual liberalization of foreign exchange, gradually expanding the regions with which transfer of pounds was permitted, and after about 10 years it realized convertibility of the pound at the end of 1958.

Japan, under Allied occupation, resumed full-fledged international trade in 1950. Japan had great expectations for trade with Southeast Asia. As used at the time, the term Southeast Asia referred to the region from Taiwan to Pakistan, and most of those countries and territories were part of the pound area. However, Japan's diplomatic relations with the sterling area were not favorable. In Britain, the scars suffered by the Lancashire cotton industry as a result of an inundation of cotton products exported from Japan in the 1930s were still fresh. Also, in Australia, which had been threatened by a military invasion by Japan during World War II, feelings toward Japan were tense. Even after the signing of the Peace Treaty of San Francisco in September 1951, negotiations with sterling area countries on conclusion of trade agreements failed to advance, so that trade continued only under agreements on payment and trade subject to annual renewal.

In addition to these factors, sterling areas had implemented foreign-exchange controls in response to Britain's foreign-exchange crisis and to maintain the value of the pound. The barrier of preferential tariffs for Commonwealth nations, erected at the 1932 Ottawa Conference, actually was strengthened by the barrier of sterling area foreign-exchange controls formed in response to the devaluation of the pound in 1949. In particular, the strict import controls adopted by sterling area countries in cooperation in the spring of 1952 in response to the worsening of the sterling area's balance of trade in the second half of 1951 impeded expansion of Japan's exports to the sterling area (Schenk 1994, pp. 62–78).

In May 1948, while Japan was still under occupation, the General Headquarters, Supreme Commander for the Allied Powers (GHQ/SCAP) concluded an Overall

Payment Agreement (OPA) with the sterling area. While this agreement called for trade between Japan and the sterling area to be settled in British pounds, it also stipulated that Japan's sterling balances could be converted to dollars at any time (the "dollar clause"). Since the dollar clause could have led to an outflow of dollars from Britain, the sterling area restrained trade with Japan, and as a result trade with the sterling area failed to grow.

Seeking the abolition of the dollar clause with the end of the occupation, in September 1951 Britain concluded the new Anglo-Japanese Payments Agreement with Japan. Although Japan hoped that the new agreement would expand trade with the sterling area, it also was concerned that Japan could end up burdened by its holdings of pounds at risk of a drop in exchange rates. As expected, exports to the sterling area jumped after conclusion of the new agreement. At the same time, imports from those regions failed to grow as a result of a drop in the market exchange rate of the pound, so that Japan's pound balances swelled, more than tripling from GBP38 million (USD106 million) in August 1951 to GBP127 million (USD355 million) in June 1952 (this was referred to as the issue of accumulated sterling balances).

However, beginning in March 1952 Japan's balance of trade with the sterling area fell into a massive deficit in an instant as that area implemented uniform strong restrictive measures against imports from non-sterling regions. By the end of March 1953, Japan's balance of pounds had decreased to below the level needed for settlement of trade with the sterling area. Japan asked Britain to relax import restrictions through negotiations on revisions to the Anglo-Japanese Payments Agreement, and it also asked for assistance with the shortage of funds for settlement purposes. Britain, which already had escaped its foreign-currency crisis, promised to relax import restrictions and authorized capital support (of up to GBP35 million over the period May 1953 through April 1954) through swaps guaranteed by the Bank of England.[1] As a result, exports to the sterling area began to recover in 1954 and Japan's pound balance also recovered to GBP100 million in March 1955.

The repeated severe fluctuations in Japan's balance of pounds held illustrate vividly the instability in trade relations between Japan and the sterling area (See Fig. 12.1a, b). However, from an overall perspective trade with the sterling area improved over the 1950s. We can identify the following three reasons for this improvement. First, Britain was interested most in restoring the pound's status as a currency of international settlement, and forces seeking to restrict trade with Japan were not dominant within the British government (Yokoi 2003). Second, through the mid-1950s an effective restoration of convertibility of the pound had advanced through the expansion of regions with accounts having Administrative Transferability. Third, as nations in the sterling area grew more independent the area's cohesion weakened. The conclusion in 1957 of a trade agreement between Australia and

[1] "Anglo-Japanese Payments Agreement: December 27, 1953 payment agreement", "Anglo-Japanese Trade and Payments Agreement: January 29, 1954 payment agreement," Diplomatic Archives of the Ministry of Foreign Affairs of Japan, B'5.2.0.J/B2-4 (hereafter Diplomatic Archives).

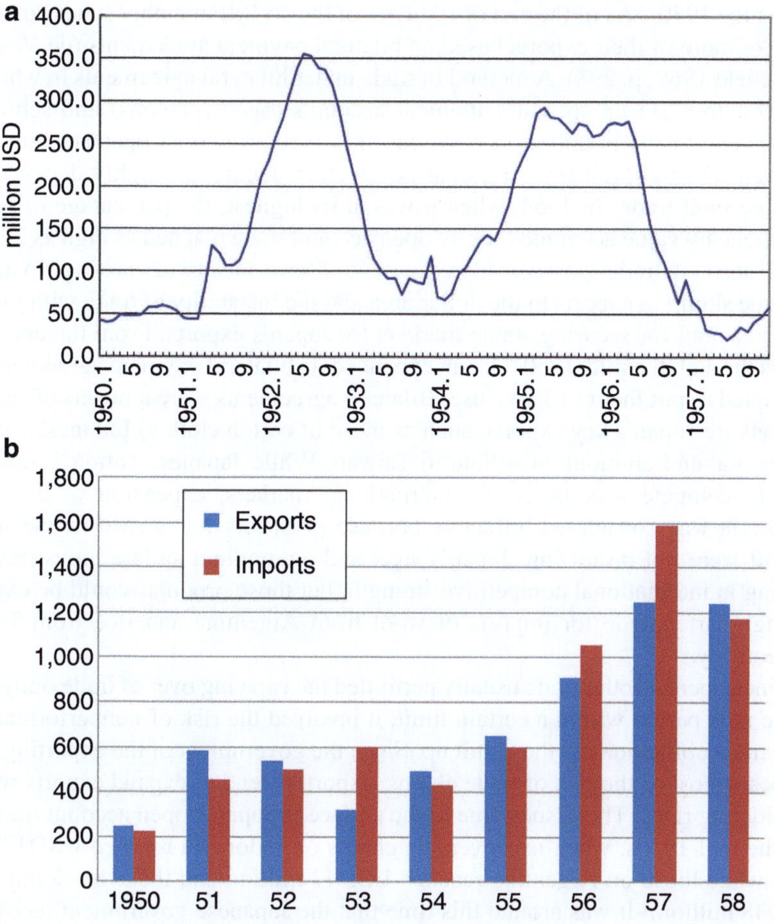

Fig. 12.1 (**a**) Trends in pound balances. Note: 1 USD=0.3571 GBP (Source: Ministry of Finance, *Showa zaisei-shi, 1952–73* (*History of fiscal and monetary policies in Japan, 1952–1973*), Vol. 19, p. 525, Economic Planning Agency, *Sengo keizaishi, boueki kokusaishushi-hen* (*Postwar economic history, foreign trade and balance of payments*), pp. 475–476) (**b**) Japan's trades with the sterling area. Note: million USD (Source: Ministry of Finance, *Gaikoku boueki gaikyou* (*Survey of the foreign trade*), various issues)

Japan based on most-favored-nation treatment proved an epochal event in the normalization of relations between Japan and the sterling area (Rix 1986; Mori 2011).

2.1.3 Open Account Trade

Trade through bilateral agreements conflicts with the IMF's ideal of multilateral settlement. However, in response to pronounced shortages of dollars in the immediate postwar period even more countries traded through bilateral agreements than did during the 1930s. As of the end of 1954, 41 of the 56 IMF member states conducted 10 % or more of their exports based on bilateral payment agreements (de Vries and Horsefield 1969, p. 298). A method of trade under bilateral agreements in which the two countries set up special settlement accounts (open accounts) and settle payments periodically in dollars or other currency is referred to as open account trade.

Even when viewed from a global perspective, Japan was highly dependent on open account trade. In 1954, when it was at its highest, the percentage of Japan's total trade by value accounted for by open account trade reached as high as 29.2 %.[2] Open account trade was considered essential as a means of making up for the extreme slump in exports to the dollar area and the instability of trade with the sterling area, and for securing stable markets for Japan's exports. From the end of the 1940s through the mid-1950s, Japan expanded its bilateral payment agreements and attempted to put them to active use. Bilateral agreements were a means of securing markets for Japan's key exports, such as those of cotton cloth to Indonesia, steel to Argentina, and ammonium sulfate to Taiwan. While Japanese cotton goods were able to compete adequately on international markets, expansion of exports to Indonesia was considered attractive because prospects for growth of the market overall were not promising. Japan's steel and ammonium sulfate industries were lacking in international competitive strength, but those products could be exported through barter trade for imports of wool from Argentina and rice from Taiwan, respectively.

Since open account trade usually permitted the carrying over of trade obligations to the next period within a certain limit, it involved the risk of nonperformance of such trade obligations as they built up. Since the government of the exporting country bears most of the risk of trade claims, exporters tend to expand exports without considering risks. This issue came to the surface in Japan's open account trade during the mid-1950s, when irrecoverable claims on Indonesia reached USD177 million, while those on Argentina reached USD47 million and those on South Korea USD48 million.[3] It was around this time that the Japanese government recognized that it should discontinue use of open accounts because their disadvantages outweighed their advantages.

Beginning in the mid-1950s the IMF shifted to a policy of actively promoting the discontinuation of bilateral payment agreements. Until then the IMF had demonstrated an attitude that saw a degree of dependence on bilateral agreement as unavoidable in light of the worldwide dollar shortage. However, with the expansion of the pound transfer system and the advancement of the European Payments Union (EPU), the IMF determined that the time was approaching for a shift to a multilateral payment system. In June 1955 the IMF Executive Board passed a resolution calling for the IMF to discuss with member states the discontinuation of bilateral agreements to enable the members to break free from dependence on bilateral

[2] While open accounts were not used for trade with the sterling area, they were a type of trade under bilateral agreements. However, since this agreement covered the entire sterling area it differed completely in nature from open-account trade.

[3] "Japan-Argentina Trade Agreement", "Japan-Indonesia Trade Agreement", "Japan-China Trade and Payments Agreement," Diplomatic Archives, microfilm B'0092-0093.

agreements quickly.[4] While Japan had concluded 16 bilateral agreements by that time, these were cut massively in 1956–1957, and by the end of 1958 the number had fallen to 4.

2.1.4 The Possibility of an Asian Payments Union

Around the time exports to the sterling area became difficult in 1952 some in Japan proposed the idea of attempting to break free from international isolation in foreign-exchange settlement by creating a regional foreign-exchange settlement system like the European Payments Union (EPU). Referred to as the Asian Payments Union (APU), this idea was proposed in 1953–1954 at the Economic Commission for Asia and the Far East (ECAFE), a regional commission of the Executive Board of the United Nations' Economic and Social Council (ECOSOC).[5] While the creation of a payments union was proposed at the Simla Conference held in 1955 at India's initiative to discuss use of the U.S. President's Fund for Asian Economic Development, the majority of participating countries showed no interest.[6]

While the IMF avoided expressing a point of view publicly,[7] the IMF Secretariat viewed the APU idea favorably if it would serve as a first step toward multilateral settlement.[8] However, the APU idea can be described as having been considerably wanting in practicality from the start. This is because the majority of Asian nations belonged to Western settlement areas such as the sterling area, trade within the region accounted for only a small share of Asia's trade, and furthermore there was little hope for aid from the US comparable to the aid it provided to the EPU (USD300 million). Even Japan, which had first proposed the APU, no longer felt a need for a regional payment union once convertibility of Western European currencies was restored in the latter half of the 1950s. Japan would not propose this idea again.

2.2 *The Foreign-Currency Crisis of 1953–1954 and Dependence on the US*

The severe dollar shortage expected to occur after the end of economic assistance during the occupation was patched up temporarily by a sudden burst of special procurement by the U.S. military caused by the outbreak of the Korean War in 1950. However, it was inevitable that special procurement would drop sharply once the war ended. It would be the 1953–1954 foreign-currency crisis that exposed the two

[4] "Bilateralism and Convertibility, IMF Board Decision No. 433," June 22,1955.

[5] "Report on attendance at the ECAFE regional payments union specialists committee," Bank of Japan Counselor Ko Yoshizawa, August 19, 1954, Bank of Japan Archives A4866.

[6] "Simla Conference," Diplomatic Archives of the Ministry of Foreign Affairs of Japan, B'6.3.0.16.

[7] IMF EBM54/34, July 7, 1954.

[8] "Payments Problems of Japan," IMF Asian Department [IMF SM/54/74], "Report on attendance at the ECAFE regional payments union specialists committee," Bank of Japan Counselor Ko Yoshizawa, August 19, 1954.

weaknesses in the Japanese economy of instability of trade with the sterling area, as discussed above, and the fragility of an international balance of payments that depended on special procurement.

The foreign-currency crisis first appeared in the form of a shortage of pounds. Since the sterling area enacted powerful restrictions on imports from Japan for purposes of the international balance of payments at the same time Japan was advancing policies of encouraging imports from sterling areas to decrease its accumulated pound balances, a massive trade deficit arose, causing a sudden drop in pound reserves.

At the start of April 1953, pound balances fell to below the level of working capital needed for trade settlement, and the Japanese government responded to the shortage for the time being by procuring sterling funds urgently through swaps guaranteed by the Bank of England. However, since the British government appeared reluctant to expand these swaps, Japan decided at the end of August to borrow pounds from the IMF, and in its September 4 meeting the IMF Executive Board approved the drawdown of GBP22.3 million (USD62.5 million), an amount equivalent to the gold tranche.[9] Since at this time Japan held USD870 million in U.S. dollars, allowing it some leeway in foreign reserves, it also could have sold dollars and purchased pounds. However, the government decided to borrow from the IMF because it preferred not to decrease Japan's dollar reserves.

The Japanese government prized the nation's dollar reserves due to uncertainty about the future prospects for dollar revenues from special procurement. Special procurement refers to procurement in Japan by U.S. military stationed in the country as well as consumption in Japan by civilian military employees and their families. This special procurement began with the outbreak of the Korean War and reached a level of USD800 million/year in 1952 and 1953. Since Japan's exports in those 2 years totaled about USD1.2 billion/year, in scale special procurement was equivalent to about two-thirds of exports. The massive inflow of dollars due to special procurement led Japan's balance of dollars held, which had been no more than USD156 million at the end of 1949, to rise to USD883 million by September 1953. However, negotiations on a ceasefire to the Korean War had begun in June 1951, and the government was concerned that an end to the war would mean the loss of special procurement. (A ceasefire agreement was concluded in July 1953.)

The U.S. government too had strong concerns about a Japanese economy dependent on special procurement. It feared that a Japanese economic crisis could lead to political disorder and that Japan could join the Communist bloc as a result. Making Japan's economy self-sufficient was important from the point of view of U.S. national security policy as well. In June 1953 the U.S. government pressured the Japanese government to implement policies to restrain inflation. It decided on a policy of reducing the trade deficit by decreasing domestic demand as well as expanding trade by supporting Japan's accession to the General Agreement on Tariffs and Trade (GATT) and promoting industrial development by supporting Japan's securing of loans from the World Bank and the Export-import Bank of

---

[9] IMF EBM53/66, September 4, 1953, EBM53/69, September 23, 1953.

Washington (EXIM).[10] U.S. ambassador to Japan John M. Allison believed that in order to restrain inflation in Japan it would be necessary to prescribe "another dose of Dodge's medicine".[11] The Japanese government accepted the U.S. demands, and beginning in September 1953 it shifted to tightening policies, implemented monetary policy based on discontinuation of measures such as preferential measures for import finance, and fiscal policy in the form of an austerity budget of JPY1 trillion, lower than the budget of the preceding fiscal year.

Despite Japan's shift to tightening policies, it recorded a deficit of USD151.5 million in its dollar balance of payments from January through March 1954. The main reason for this was the sudden drop in income from special procurement. Income from special procurement was projected to fall rapidly from USD800 million in the previous year to USD500–600 million in 1954, and there were concerns that this could hinder imports of raw materials and food. Japan's balance of dollars held began to decrease at the end of 1953, falling to USD530 million by June 1954, leading to rumors of a devaluation of the yen. In fact, in September 1954 the IMF and the U.S. government seriously discussed the pros and cons of devaluation of the yen. While the majority opinion in the U.S. State Department supported devaluation of the yen, the IMF was opposed, arguing that the effects of a devaluation would be only temporary.[12] The Japanese government consistently advocated a policy of maintaining the value of the yen, and it rejected the proposal for devaluation.

The Japanese government strived to put a stop to the decrease in special procurement by negotiating with the U.S. on the matter, while also planning to procure an exchange stabilization fund in preparation for a rapid drop in foreign reserves. It had no plans for further borrowing from the IMF, from which it already had borrowed up to the level of its gold tranche, and instead considered means such as EXIM loans, agricultural product loans under the Public Law 480 (Agricultural Trade Development and Assistance Act), and setting up lines of credit with U.S. commercial banks.[13] However, since the cash flow of foreign currency improved beginning around August 1954 no emergency fund-raising measures actually were implemented.

Since as seen above the largest problem related to Japan's international balance of payments during the 1953–1954 foreign-currency crisis was the continuation of special procurement, negotiations were held with the U.S. on improving the international balance of payments. The IMF played only a secondary role.

---

[10] "Note by the Acting Executive Secretary (Gleason) to the National Security Council," June 29, 1953, *Foreign Relations of the United States,1952–54,Vol. XIV*, pp. 1448–1452 (hereafter FRUS).

[11] "The Ambassador in Japan (Allison) to the Department of State," September 7, 1953, FRUS 1952–54, Vol. XIV, pp. 1497–1502.

[12] "Meeting Held at the State Department on Tuesday, September 7, 1954," IMF C/Japan/820, "Japanese Economic Situation," September 7, 1954, NARA RG59 894.00.

[13] "Prime Minister's visit to the U.S." June 4, 1954, Diplomatic Archives of the Ministry of Foreign Affairs of Japan, E'4.1.0.2.1, "The Ambassador in Japan (Allison) to the Department of State," May 18, 1954, FRUS 1952–54, Vol. XIV, pp. 1040–1042, "Economic Consultation with Japan," June 28, 1954, NARA RG59 894.00.

3 Progress on Liberalization of Foreign Exchange and the International Balance of Payments Ceiling

3.1 *The 1957 Foreign-Currency Crisis*

Following the quantitative boom of 1955 through the first half of 1956, the Japanese economy entered a period of unprecedented boom from the second half of 1956 through 1957 (the "Jimmu boom"), accompanied by a large-scale boom in capital investment. The Jimmu boom spurred a massive modernization of machinery and equipment, and Japan would proceed along the path of rapid economic growth until the 1973 oil shock. However, economic growth did not proceed along a completely straight course. Accelerated economic growth led to growth in imports and worsening of the international balance of payments. An economic cycle of 3–4 years appeared in which each time the international balance of payments got worse the Japanese government and the Bank of Japan would implement tightening policies, and the economic boom would hit the ceiling of the international balance of payments. (See Table 12.1)

The foreign-currency crisis of 1957, spurred by the overheating of investment as a result of the Jimmu boom, differed in its nature from the 1953–1954 foreign-currency crisis. The cause of the 1953–1954 foreign-currency crisis had been the long-term, structural issue of the decrease in special procurement, rather than a

Table 12.1 Balance of international payments and foreign reserves (1950–1965) (million USD)

Year	Trade balance	Exports	Imports	Current balance	Overall balance	Gold and foreign exchange reserves
1950	38	924	886	476	434	516
1951	Δ 287	1,358	1,645	329	370	795
1952	Δ 407	1,294	1,701	225	186	979
1953	Δ 790	1,260	2,050	Δ 205	Δ 379	823
1954	Δ 427	1,614	2,041	Δ 51	2	738
1955	Δ 53	2,008	2,061	227	285	768
1956	Δ 131	2,482	2,613	Δ 34	1	941
1957	Δ 401	2,855	3,256	Δ 620	Δ 503	524
1958	368	2,871	2,501	264	393	861
1959	362	3,414	3,052	361	143	1,322
1960	268	3,979	3,711	143	105	1,824
1961	Δ 558	4,149	4,707	Δ 982	Δ 952	1,486
1962	402	4,861	4,459	Δ 49	236	1,841
1963	Δ 165	5,391	5,556	Δ 779	Δ 161	1,878
1964	375	6,703	6,328	Δ 480	Δ 130	1,999
1965	1,901	8,332	6,413	932	405	2,107

Source: Ministry of Finance, *Showa zaisei-shi, 1952–73* (*History of fiscal and monetary policies in Japan, 1952–1973*), Vol. 11, p. 491, Vol. 12, p. 3, Vol. 19, p. 523

temporary worsening of the international balance of payments. For this reason, the government had focused more on negotiations with the U.S. than the IMF. Also, it had been pressure from the U.S. government that forced Japan to implement tightening policies. In contrast, measures in response to the 1957 foreign-currency crisis were centered on loans from the IMF, with EXIM loans playing a complementary role.

As a result of the rapid increase in imports of raw materials and other items spurred by the Jimmu boom, Japan's balance of trade fell into a surplus of payments beginning in the summer of 1956, and its foreign reserves decreased to approximately USD600 million by the end of May 1957. The government, which had given top priority to growth, was hesitant to shift to tightening policies even as the current account balance worsened. Finally in May 1957 the Bank of Japan raised the official discount rate to 8.40 %, and in June the government announced emergency measures to improve the international balance of payments, including budget cuts. In July, Prime Minister Kishi replaced the expansionist Ikeda, and appointed Finance Minister Ichimada, an advocate of stability.

In June 1957, the Japanese government requested from the IMF a loan of USD125 million, up to the limit of the first credit tranche. In response to feelers from Japan's IMF Executive Director Takeshi Watanabe about the possibility of borrowing up to the second and third credit tranches, Managing Director Jacobsson replied that loans in excess of the first credit tranche would be difficult in consideration of balance with other countries. Also, U.S. Executive Director Southard expressed the opinion that if Japan used short-term loans from the EXIM then lending up to the first credit tranche should be enough.[14] At the end of June the U.S. approved an EXIM short-term loan of USD175 million (including refinancing of USD60 million in raw-cotton loans), so that combined with the IMF loan Japan was able to secure USD300 million in short-term funds.

The IMF did not consider the 1957 foreign-currency crisis to be a structural economic crisis. It judged the Japanese economy to be sound, since the cause of the worsening of the international balance of payments had been a rapid rise in imports and exports remained at a high level. It also regarded highly the fact that Japan had implemented measures to address the international balance of payments centered on fiscal and monetary policy and had not relied on trade or foreign-exchange restrictions.[15] However, some doubt remains concerning this assessment. While it is a fact that Japan did not implement in 1957 the discriminatory foreign-exchange restrictions it had implemented in 1953–1954, such as strengthening of the retention quota system, expansion of the system of linking exports with imports, and expansion of barter trade, the measure that proved most effective in improving the international balance of payments during the 1957 foreign-currency crisis was the direct trade restriction of limiting issuance of import letters of credit.

---

[14] "Japanese Interest in IMF Assistance," June 18, 1957, NARA RG59, 894.

[15] Bank of Japan, eds., *Nihonginko enkakushi* ("Chronological History of the Bank of Japan"), Vol. 5, No. 16, pp. 585–587.

3.2 *Liberalization of Foreign Exchange and Trade*

3.2.1 Foreign-Exchange Regulations

Japan's foreign-exchange controls during its period of Article XIV status were based on the Foreign Exchange and Foreign Trade Control Act enacted in December 1949. The IMF had taken part behind the scenes in the passage of this act, through IMF staff member Jan Mladek providing guidance to SCAP and the Japanese government.[16] Mladek submitted a report to the GHQ/SCAP arguing that since for the time being Japan could not secure through exports the foreign currency needed for imports of food and raw materials, it should implement foreign-exchange controls together with import controls. The reason for this was because it would not be possible to correct Japan's surplus of imports using inflation controls (i.e., total demand controls) based on fiscal and monetary policy since the surplus resulted from insufficient supply due to decreased production levels in postwar Japan.[17]

The system of foreign-exchange controls established based on Mladek's proposal was one of foreign-exchange controls combined with trade controls under an exchange budget system, and as such it differed from prewar foreign-exchange controls intended mainly to prevent capital flight. The exchange budget system was a system under which the government estimated foreign-currency income for each individual period (quarterly from January 1950 through March 1952 and semiannually from April 1952 through March 1964) and distributed foreign currency to each imported good and the invisible balance depending on its priority. It was intended to conserve foreign currency by prioritizing its allocation to necessary imports.

In addition to quotas by which foreign currency was allocated to individual products and accounts (Fund Allocation [FA] System budget), the exchange budget also established quotas under which importers could choose imports freely (Automatic Approval [AA] System budget). The AA budget would expand automatically when an abundance of foreign currency was expected and shrink when the international balance of payments worsened. Growth in the percentage of the exchange budget made up of the AA budget was an indicator of progress in liberalization of trade and foreign exchange. Increasing this percentage became a focal point in negotiations on foreign-exchange liberalization in IMF consultations.

Let's take a look at trends in the percentage of the exchange budget accounted for by the AA budget. (See Fig. 12.2) Spurred by the outbreak of the Korean War, in the second half of 1950 the AA budget leaped to a share of more than 50 %. This was due to an ample supply of foreign currency as a result of special procurement and to promotion of imports in anticipation of expected difficulties in obtaining raw materials during the Korean War. However, proactive measures to promote imports led to speculative imports, leading to foreign-currency funds bottoming out in February 1951 and forcing a temporary full suspension of the AA System in March. As a result,

[16] "Mr. Mladek's assignment with SCAP," June 15, 1955 [IMF Archives, C/Japan/830].

[17] "Report on Exchange and Trade Controls in Japan," November 18, 1949, NARA, SCAP Papers.

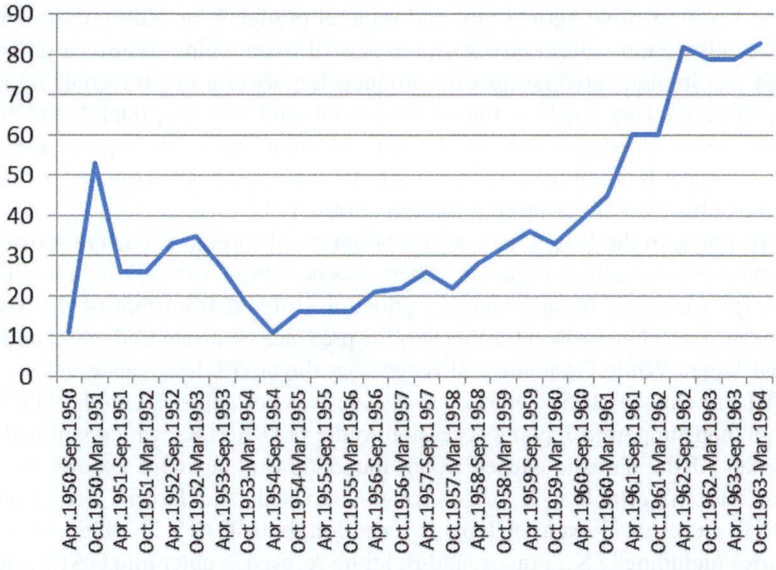

Fig. 12.2 AA budget as a percentage of the exchange budget [Confirmed amounts] (Source: Bank of Japan (1979), Vol. 17, pp. 733–734)

the AA budget's share of the FY1951 budget contracted to 26 %. Later, in 1952, in an effort to resolve the issue of accumulated pound balances the portion of imports corresponding to imports from the sterling area was shifted to the automatic approval system, so that the AA percentage recovered to 35 % in the second half of 1952. However, the 1953–1954 foreign-currency crisis led to a massive decrease in the AA budget, and in the first half of 1954 its percentage returned to its level from prior to the Korean War. The expansion of the AA budget during the Korean War had been only temporary and did not constitute liberalization of foreign exchange. Strong foreign-exchange controls were in place until 1955, and it was only beginning in that year that the Japanese government recognized the necessity of foreign-exchange liberalization.

The liberalization of trade and foreign exchange from 1955 through 1964 can be divided at the year 1959 into two phases. The pace of liberalization through 1959 was very slow, and the AA budget's percentage of the total budget was only 33 % in the second half of that year. Liberalization had failed to advance not solely because of restrictions on foreign currency usable for imports but also because allocation of foreign currency had been employed as a means of domestic industrial policy. Allocation of foreign currency was used as a means of quantitative allocation to protect domestic industry, to protect products of industries having future potential such as motor vehicles[18] and products of industries unable to compete with imports,

[18] The import quota on passenger vehicles was 898 vehicles in 1959 (Iwakoshi 1963, pp. 178–179).

such as uncompetitive agricultural and mineral products. In addition, the foreign-currency allocation system also was a means of maintaining industrial order. The system was implemented not just for products but also for raw materials important to Japanese industry, such as raw cotton, wool, and iron ore, intended to restrict competition in industries and avoid overproduction and overcompetition through the government holding the power to allocate raw materials to companies, in addition to its objective of conserving foreign currency.[19]

In response to the IMF's demand for abolition of foreign-exchange restrictions, the Japanese government argued that there was no reason for hurrying liberalization of foreign exchange because Japan's situation differed from that of the Western European states. One reason for this was the presence of strong trade discrimination against Japan. While Germany had acceded to the GATT in advance of its joining the IMF (in October 1951), Japan's accession was not approved until 1955. While the U.S. had supported Japan's accession to the GATT, U.K., which still had vivid memories of the damage caused by an inundation of Japanese exports of cotton goods before World War II, was strongly opposed, and Japan's accession was delayed as a result. Even after Japan's accession to the GATT in 1955 a total of 14 countries including U.K., France, and Belgium refused to enter into GATT relations with Japan, citing GATT Article XXXV (Akaneya 1992). The Japanese government argued that Japan could not be asked to liberalize foreign exchange as long as it was unable to receive most-favored-nation treatment under Article 1 of the GATT from powerful GATT member states.[20]

In this way, Japan can be seen as having mildly resisted IMF pressure toward liberalization of foreign exchange until 1958.

3.2.2 Liberalization of Trade and Foreign Exchange

The restoration of convertibility of the leading Western European currencies in December 1958 and the U.S. falling into an international balance of payments deficit beginning in 1958 greatly changed the international environment in relation to liberalization of trade and foreign exchange. In 1959 Japan too shifted course in the direction of advancing trade and foreign-exchange liberalization in response to calls for liberalization from the IMF and GATT as well as pressure from the United States.

In the June 1959 consultation, the IMF strongly encouraged Japan to move forward with liberalization, without falling behind the foreign-exchange liberalization of the Western European states.[21] In October of that same year, the IMF Executive

---

[19] However, it also has been pointed out that the system of allocation of foreign currency did not function effectively to regulate capital investment (Korenaga 2000).

[20] By the end of the 1950s Japan's major trading partners such as Australia and India had granted the nation most-favored-nation treatment and claims under Article XXXV impeded trade only with Western European countries.

[21] "IMF Minutes of the 1959 Consultations with Japan, June 1–10, 1959," IMF C/Japan/810.

Board passed a resolution calling for abolition of discriminatory restrictions imposed for balance of payments reasons, demonstrating its posture of fully addressing the abolition of dollar discrimination (de Vries and Horsefield 1969, pp. 281–283). In the GATT consultation on Japan in October the GATT criticized Japan's liberalization policies as overly cautious, arguing that Japan's liberalization rate was too low and that discriminatory measures against the U.S. continued.[22]

Pressure from the U.S. government toward liberalization also increased in 1959. Since a surplus of imports to Japan had continued in Japan-U.S. trade, the U.S. until then had not made strong demands on Japan for liberalization. However, beginning around 1955 Japan's exports of products such as textile goods and sundry goods to the U.S. increased rapidly, leading to frequent trade frictions. Also, in the first half of 1959 Japan's balance of trade with the U.S. showed a surplus, albeit a temporary one, for the first time in the postwar period. Under such conditions, in July and August 1959 U.S. ambassador to Japan Douglas MacArthur II asked the Japanese government to abolish discriminatory practices against U.S. products and to make progress on trade liberalization.[23]

In light of the sudden intensification in 1959 of external pressure demanding liberalization of trade and foreign exchange, the Japan Business Federation (Keidanren) came out clearly in support of liberalization. In February 1960 the Keidanren submitted to the government and the Diet a written opinion stating that the progress of liberalization would serve to propel rationalization and structural improvements in businesses.[24] The business world had determined that if liberalization was inevitable then it would be prudent to ask the government to implement measures to strengthen businesses so that they could deal with liberalization. This judgment also reflected the fact that in addition to Japan's shipbuilding industry, which had achieved an internationally competitive level in the mid-1950s, by around 1960 the nation's steel industry also had secured a sufficient degree of international competitive strength, and aside from the machine and chemical industries Japan's leading industries had reached the same levels of productivity as those in the leading industrialized countries, so that the conditions were falling into place for acceptance of liberalization.

In January 1960 the Japanese government set up a ministerial conference to promote liberalization of trade and foreign exchange, and in June it announced a program of exchange and trade liberalization describing a rough schedule that called for increasing the current liberalization rate from 40 to 80 % (or 90 % if petroleum and coal were liberalized) in 3 years (through April 1963). However, these goals were expressed in vague terms, and adjustments between industries remained as an

[22] "*GATT ni okeru wagakuni no yunyuseigen ni kansuru kyogi ni tsuite*" ("Consultation on Japan's import restrictions in the GATT"), *Gaikoku kawase* (Foreign exchange), no. 223, December 1959.

[23] "Telegram from the Embassy in Japan to the Department of State," August 27, 1959, FRUS, 1958–60, Vol. XVIII, pp. 214–218, "Representatives to Japanese Cabinet Ministers on Japanese Trade Restrictions," September 8, 1959, NARA RG59 494.

[24] *Jiyuka ni taisuru shiken* ("Personal views on liberalization") (April 19, 1960, Nippon Keidanren), *Keidanren geppo*, Vol. 8, no. 5, May 1960.

issue to be addressed later. The liberalization of imports of raw cotton and raw wool in April 1961 increased the percentage of liberalized goods (AA goods) in the exchange budget from 45 to 60 % in a single leap. The April 1961 liberalization was meaningful in that the government had accepted the fact that it no longer was possible to use foreign-exchange allocation as a means of industrial policy. At this stage, the government was not yet able to address the issue of liberalization of imports of final products, or of the protection and nurturing of domestic industry.

4 Accession to Article VIII Status

4.1 Inflow of Short-Term Funds from Overseas and the 1961–1962 Foreign-Currency Crisis

4.1.1 Inflow of Short-Term Funds from Overseas

The inflow of short-term funds from overseas that became more active at the end of the 1950s eased restrictions on foreign currency and raised the ceiling of the international balance of payments. This inflow of short-term funds brought about favorable conditions for Japan, which considered the realization of a high rate of economic growth a top priority.

While Japan's restrictions on movement of short-term funds were strict even by international standards and nearly all such movement was constrained through 1959,[25] from 1959 through 1960 measures that made movement of short-term funds possible were implemented gradually, resulting in more active inflows of short-term funds (See Table 12.2).

Usance borrowing from U.S. banks accounted for the largest share of short-term funds from overseas. From the immediate postwar years through the first half of the 1950s, the main means of settlement used internationally was a bill at sight, and Japan too restricted use of usance notes.[26] As part of foreign-exchange liberalization measures in April 1959 use of import usance was permitted for items covering 60 % of the total value of imports, and in August 1960 the restriction on applicable products was abolished as well, so that the usance system underwent rapid liberalization in the years 1959 and 1960. Usance funds were raised primarily from the American banker's acceptance markets, mainly by U.S. banks.

[25] Until 1959, almost the only means of raising short-term foreign funds in the private sector was borrowing by Japanese foreign-exchange banks of usance funds from foreign banks. Year-end balances of usance loans from foreign banks were only roughly USD100-200 million from 1955 through 1958. ("*Wagakuni no taigai tanki saimu ni tsuite*" ["Japan's short-term foreign debt"], June 27 1964, International Department, Bank of Japan).

[26] While usance settlement in pounds was authorized in 1953 and usance settlement in dollars in 1954, applicable products and periods were restricted, so that usance was not put to full use.

Table 12.2 Trends in short-term funds from overseas [1960–1969] (million USD)

	Short-term funds from overseas							
	Euromoney							
End of year	Eurodollar	Other foreign currency deposit	Loans without collateral	Free Yen	Total	Import usance	Short term impact loan	Total
1960	192	31	18	86	327	692	15	1,034
1961	199	53	68	174	494	1,222	15	1,731
1962	392	108	99	245	844	1,227	63	2,134
1963	357	158	77	352	944	1,698	96	2,738
1964	474	131	89	515	1,209	1,904	143	3,256
1965	543	130	82	403	1,158	2,035	59	3,252
1966	821	81	52	259	1,213	1,806	11	3,030
1967	998	98	46	259	1,401	2,211	15	3,627
1968	1,121	58	69	284	1,533	2,302	47	3,882
1969	804	17	44	283	1,147	2,280	0	3,427

Source: "Kaigai tanshi zandaka no suii (Trends in short-term funds of overseas)," January 19, 1967 & August 1970 (Ministry of Finance)

The balance of usance acceptance by foreign banks grew rapidly from USD129 million at the end of 1958 to USD692 million at the end of 1960 and USD1.222 billion at the end of 1961. Lending of trade funds to Japan came to account for a large share of the U.S. financial markets. Japan's share of the balance of banker's acceptance credit provided by American financial institutions to overseas borrowers reached 46.5 % in 1960.[27]

Another route taken by this inflow of short-term funds from overseas was the Euromoney market. The route toward adoption of Euromoney was opened with the July 1960 adoption of yen foreign exchange and establishment of free yen accounts for nonresidents. These measures restored yen convertibility for nonresidents only. They were similar to the measures taken at the end of 1958 by Western European states to restore convertibility of their currencies. However, since unlike the British pound the yen was almost never used in trade settlement, the adoption of yen foreign exchange did not have much practical significance. The establishment of free yen accounts, however, made possible the inflow of Euro funds. Japanese foreign-exchange banks used these accounts to obtain Euromoney through their branches overseas (mainly their London branches). The balance of Euromoney reached USD328 million at the end of 1960, USD494 million at the end of 1961, and USD944 million at the end of 1963.

At the end of 1961, the balance of foreign short-term funds reached USD1.731 billion, vs. foreign reserves of USD1.486 billion. The Japanese government welcomed the short-term capital from overseas for the way it raised the ceiling of the international balance of payments and facilitated the implementation of long-term

[27] United States Treasury Department, *Treasury Bulletin, 1962*.

growth policies. In the early 1960s there was little wariness about the instability of short-term capital from overseas, and usance funds in particular were considered highly stable funds since they were backed by actual trade transactions.

4.1.2 The FY1961 Consultation and the 1961–1962 Foreign-Currency Crisis

In December 1960 the Japanese government made a cabinet decision on a plan to double the national income. Setting the goal of doubling real GNP over the 10-year period beginning FY1961, this was a bold policy that sought to draw out potential productivity to the maximum extent. While the goal of a 7.2 % growth rate when converted to an annual rate was a lofty one, Prime Minister Ikeda planned to accelerate growth further, setting a target growth rate of 9 % over the first 3 years. While during the 1950s advocates of growth had clashed with advocates of stability within the government, when growth advocate Hayato Ikeda took office as Prime Minister in July 1960 the advocates of growth had taken control decisively.

The Income-Doubling Plan was positioned at the highest level of policy, and other policies were expected to contribute to its realization. Prime Minister Ikeda's cherished opinion was that Japan needed to lower its interest rates, which were higher than international levels, and the government's intentions can be considered to have affected the cuts in the official discount rate in August 1960 and January 1961 (Bank of Japan 1986, pp. 20–27). While the current account balance had fallen to a massive deficit beginning in January 1960, right after the announcement of the Income-Doubling Plan, the government expressed the optimistic view that there was no concern about prospects for the international balance of payments. Both the government and the business world wanted to avoid putting the brakes on economic growth through restraint in capital investment. This optimistic view found support in the steady increase in foreign reserves, which surpassed USD2 billion in April 1961. This temporary increase resulted because the worsening of the current account balance was not reflected directly in foreign reserves due to the inflow of short-term capital. However, the inflow of short-term funds from overseas also reached its limit, and then foreign reserves decreased rapidly after peaking in April 1961.

In June-July 1961, when concern about the international balance of payments began to surface, the FY1961 consultation was held. This consultation would be the climax of negotiations on accession to IMF Article VIII status. The IMF had recommended Germany's accession to Article VIII status in June 1957 and then recommended accession for a succession of Western European states, and in February 1961 nine Western European states acceded to Article VIII status at once. It was thought widely that in the 1961 consultation Japan, the last remaining leading nation that had not yet acceded to Article VIII status, was certain to be judged by the IMF not to have any BP reasons (reasons for restricting foreign exchange for purposes of the balance of payments).

The Japanese government asked the IMF not to recommend accession to Article VIII status, arguing that it would prefer not to receive such a recommendation while its international balance of payments was worsening and that increasing the speed of liberalization would hinder its efforts to advance the industrial structure. In response, the IMF argued that the worsening of Japan's international balance of payments was a temporary phenomenon and that it should balance growth and equilibrium in its international balance of payments through reducing total demand. Since Japan was behind the Western European states in liberalization as well, it asked Japan to increase the liberalization rate to 95 % within 1 year.

The Japanese government approached the U.S. government in an attempt to prevent the IMF Executive Board from recommending accession to Article VIII status. The U.S. opposed Japan's request, arguing that in light of the true power of Japan's economy it could not agree to a failure of the IMF Executive Board to reach the conclusion that there were no BP reasons involved in Japan's case. However, ultimately the Japanese government succeeded in persuading the U.S., and the recommendation of accession to IMF Article VIII status was postponed for 1 year, in exchange for moving forward by half a year the goal established in 1960 of 90 % liberalization after 3 years, pledging to achieve this goal by October 1962.[28]

4.1.3 IMF Standby Line of Credit

In July 1961 the Bank of Japan raised the official discount rate as it began a shift to tightening policies. This shift had been encouraged by the IMF's demands in the consultation for an increase in the official discount rate and fiscal measures to reduce total demand, in addition to the continued worsening of the international balance of payments.

Anticipating that if foreign reserves continued their decrease they would reach the critical level of USD1.3 billion around March 1962, the Japanese government requested in the September 1961 IMF annual meeting the cooperation of the IMF, EXIM, and U.S. private banks in its international balance of payments policies. Since conclusion of a standby line of credit with the IMF would reveal the fact that Japan was in a foreign-currency crisis, the government planned first to borrow USD300 million from three U.S. private banks (Chase Manhattan Bank, First National City Bank, and Bank of America) and then to use USD300 million in IMF funds and a USD100 million EXIM short-term loan to cover its international balance of payments deficit through FY1962. On November 24 the Bank of Japan concluded an agreement with the three banks on a USD200 million loan (with a term of up to 1 year).[29] Then, on January 9, 1962, the government applied to the IMF for a standby line of credit, and on January 19 it concluded an agreement on a standby line of credit of USD305 million, equivalent to the first credit tranche. In addition, due to a shortage of funds at EXIM the EXIM loan was replaced by a loan

[28]"*1961-nendo IMF tainichi consaruteshon kanrenshiryo*" ("Materials related to the FY1961 IMF consultation on Japan"), (Ministry of Finance 1998, pp. 41–42).

[29]The terms of these loans were disadvantageous to Japan for reasons including strict collateral conditions and high real interest rates.

of USD125 million from seven U.S. private banks (with a term of 1 year), backed by an EXIM guarantee. In the end, the IMF standby line of credit was never exercised, and Japan was able to overcome this foreign-currency crisis through borrowing USD325 million from U.S. private banks.[30] Japan did not draw on the IMF funds so it could avoid restrictions on its economic policies.

However, in the process of concluding the standby line of credit agreement Japan did modify its growth policies. When it asked for the IMF's cooperation in September 1961 the Japanese government decided on comprehensive measures to improve its international balance of payments, announcing a strengthening of tight monetary policy (increasing the official discount rate, strengthening the higher interest rate application system, and increasing the deposit reserve rate) and partial deferment of some government loans and investment programs as well as public-works projects. Furthermore, when concluding the IMF standby line of credit in January 1962 the government pledged to lower the rate of growth in the economy to 5.4 % in FY1962. In response, the IMF acknowledged that the policies of the Japanese government were adequate and did not demand any specific additional policies. After peaking at the end of 1961 the economy entered a slowing phase, with real GNP growth slowing in 1962 to 6.4 % and per-capita GNP growth to 5.4 %, so that Japan fulfilled this pledge. If Japan had drawn funds under the standby line of credit the IMF likely would have made additional policy demands.

4.2 Accession to Article VIII Status and to the OECD

4.2.1 Recommendation of Accession to Article VIII Status

In the November 1962 IMF consultation, Director of the Exchange Restrictions Department Irving S. Friedman encouraged the Japanese government to make preparations for accession to Article VIII status, and in its meeting on February 6, 1963 the IMF Executive Board passed a resolution to the effect that no BP reasons remained in existence in Japan's case (i.e., recommended accession to Article VIII status).[31] In response to this resolution, the Japanese government immediately began preparations for accession to Article VIII status.

Japan needed to increase its liberalization rate and achieve something close to full liberalization by the time of accession to Article VIII status. In October 1962 the liberalization rate was only 88 %, lower than the rate of 90 % after 1 year promised in the previous year, and this did not include machinery such as passenger vehicles, computers, large machine tools, heavy electrical machinery, and color

[30] "*Gaika shikinkuri no kanwa no tame no tanki shakkan ni tsuite*" ("Short-term loans to ease foreign-currency cash flow conditions") (Foreign-currency funds, September 4, 1961), "*Gaika shikinkuri taisaku*" ("Foreign-currency cash flow measures") (Foreign-currency planning, January 8, 1964), "*Zainichi beikei sanko yori no shakkan ni tsuite*" ("Loans from three U.S. banks with locations in Japan") (December 25, 1961) (Ministry of Finance 1998, pp. 160–161).

[31] IMF EBM63/4, February 6, 1963.

televisions, in which the U.S. was strongly interested. In the FY1962 consultation the IMF demanded that Japan achieve the target liberalization rate of 90 % within a few months.[32] This rate of 90 % was reached at the end of August 1963. The Ministry of International Trade and Industry (MITI) felt the need to create a new industrial order to replace allocation of foreign exchange in energy industries and to take measures to protect and nurture machinery industries with future potential prior to acceding to Article VIII status. However, although the Petroleum Industry Act promulgated in 1962 introduced regulations to replace foreign-exchange allocation, these regulations proved ineffective and a bill on special temporary measures to stimulate specific industries, aimed at strengthening the international competitive abilities of the machinery and petrochemical industries, suffered a setback. Ultimately, at the time of Japan's accession to Article VIII status the liberalization rate was only 93 % and 178 product categories, including machine tools, passenger vehicles, and light oil, remained exempt from liberalization. After accession to Article VIII status the venue for discussion of these products would shift to the GATT consultation process.[33]

Initially, the Japanese government had planned on accession to Article VIII status in the summer or autumn of 1964. However, it moved up the timing of accession in order to better move forward negotiations on OECD accession. In its last Article XIV consultation in November 1963 Japan pledged to abolish the exchange budget system by the time of its accession to Article VIII status, and that system was abolished in April 1964 at the same time Japan acceded to Article VIII status.[34]

4.2.2 The 1964 IMF Standby Line of Credit

Japan's international balance of payments began to recover rapidly in mid-1962, and the tightening measures introduced during the 1961–1962 foreign-currency crisis were released beginning in September 1962.[35] While the economic recovery in 1963 was supported by strong exports, the growth in exports led to a rapid increase in imports, centered on raw materials, so that the current account balance quickly fell into deficit. In 1963, Japan recorded a current account deficit of USD779 million due to a trade deficit of USD165 million plus a substantial deficit in the balance of maritime transport. In December 1963, the Bank of Japan returned to tightening of monetary policy just a little more than 1 year after it had ended the previous tightening policies.

---

[32] "Meeting Wednesday November 14, 1962", "Procedural questions (excluded how to proceed)," IMF C/Japan/420.1.

[33] At the same time the Article XIV countries acceded to Article VIII status in the IMF, they shifted from GATT Article XII countries (those able to restrict imports for balance of payments reasons) to Article XI countries (those unable to restrict imports for balance of payments reasons).

[34] "Minutes of Meeting," November 1963, IMF C/Japan/420.

[35] The official discount rate was lowered three times, in October 1962, March 1963, and April 1963.

Wanting to do whatever it could to avoid falling into a foreign-currency crisis immediately after accession to Article VIII status, the Japanese government aimed to keep foreign reserves to no less than USD1.8 billion at the time of accession. A system was formed for close cooperation between the government and the Bank of Japan, and three methods were considered for reinforcing foreign reserves: borrowing from U.S. private banks, an IMF standby line of credit, and swaps with the Federal Reserve Bank of New York. The resulting decision was on a policy of concluding a standby line of credit with the IMF but giving preference to swaps with the New York Fed to replenish foreign reserves for the time being, with loans from U.S. private banks as the second preferred option.[36]

First, the Japanese government concluded a standby line of credit in the amount of USD305 million with the IMF on March 11, 1964. In accordance with the chosen policy, before drawing on the IMF funds it reinforced foreign reserves through swaps between the Bank of Japan and the New York Fed (implementing swaps for USD50 million in April and an additional USD30 million in July). Since March 1962 the New York Fed had concluded swap agreements with Western European countries in order to stabilize the dollar. In October 1963 a standby arrangement was concluded for yen-dollar swaps with a limit of USD150 million (and a term of 3 months, renewable). When the swap agreement was concluded between the Bank of Japan and the New York Fed, the Bank of Japan had not expected to use it to address the international balance of payments, but in 1964 it noticed that this agreement could be used to reinforce foreign reserves.

In the 1959 IMF capital increase, Japan's contribution increased from USD250 million to USD500 million, and in 1963 a swap agreement was concluded between the New York Fed and the Bank of Japan. This greatly increased Japan's ability to raise funds in the event of a worsening of the international balance of payments. However, at the same time the rapid inflow of short-term funds from overseas beginning in 1960 led the balance to reach as high as approximately USD3.2 billion as of March 1964. It was thought that IMF funds and swaps would not be enough in the event of an outflow of short-term funds.

4.2.3 Accession to the OECD and Joining the Group of Leading Industrialized Countries

Japan's external relations underwent some massive changes beginning in 1961.

First, the claim against Japan under Article XXXV of the GATT was withdrawn. The GATT responded to Japan's repeated calls for withdrawal of Article XXXV with the decision by the GATT general assembly in May 1961 to establish a working committee to examine the Article XXXV claims against Japan. Starting around the same time, Western European countries began to look more positively on withdrawal of the Article XXXV claims. With the conclusion of the Anglo-Japanese

[36] "*Gaika junbi hokyo no tame no shokento*" ("Considerations on reinforcement of foreign reserves"), 1964, Bank of Japan, Bank of Japan Archives, 13579.

Treaty of Commerce and Navigation in November 1962 commercial relations between Britain and Japan finally were normalized after a period of roughly 20 years starting with the beginning of World War II, and Britain too withdrew its Article XXXV claim. The three Benelux countries and France did the same in 1964.

The second major change was Japan's accession to the OECD in April 1964. Since around 1960 the U.S. had considered Japan a member of the group of leading industrialized countries together with the U.S., Western Europe, and others, and as it strived to work out policies for strengthening the ties among the leading industrialized countries it actively worked toward Japan's accession to the OECD (Winand 1993, p. 129; Griffiths 1997, Chapter 18). Japan too considered accession to the OECD to be essential to the nation's upgrading from middle-tier status to the ranks of the leading industrialized countries. In 1962 Prime Minister Ikeda visited Western Europe, where he asked for cooperation in Japan's accession bid. As a result, in March 1963 the OECD ministerial council declared its support in principle for Japan's accession, and in April 1964 Japan officially became an OECD member.

5 Conclusion

During Japan's 12 years of IMF Article XIV status, the slow liberalization of foreign exchange through 1958 contrasts sharply with the rapid progress of 1959 and later.

At the start of the 1950s Japan was isolated within the Asian economic sphere and was unable to receive most-favored-nation treatment from most countries in the world. The external conditions that made it possible for Japan to achieve rapid economic growth under such disadvantageous circumstances were direct and indirect support from the U.S. together with conservation of foreign currency and protectionist trade based on strict foreign-exchange controls. The fact that the IMF prioritized foreign-exchange liberalization in Western Europe and did not actively demand liberalization from Japan enabled Japan to maintain its foreign-exchange controls over a longer period of time than did the countries of Western Europe.

While the Bretton Woods system had been intended to enable member countries to pursue autonomous economic policies, after the creation of the IMF its quality changed to something closer to an international gold exchange standard. But did the restrictions on international balances of payments under the Bretton Woods system, similar to those of a gold-exchange system, hinder Japan's pursuit of economic growth? The fact that in Japan during the 1950s there was a rivalry between those who advocated stability, focusing on equilibrium in the international balance of payments, and growth advocates who gave priority to economic growth would suggest that there was a strong element involved of restriction of growth for purposes of stability. Through its consultations, the IMF supported the advocates of stability in Japan. The reason Japan was able to start a period of rapid economic growth smoothly even though its macroeconomic policies focused on stability was because the nation put the transitional provisions of the IMF Articles of Agreement to effective use, encouraging investment through allocation of foreign currency and capital controls, supplementing macroeconomic policy with microeconomic industrial policy.

At the start of the 1960s, the path opened toward introduction of short-term funds from overseas, easing restrictions on the international balance of payments. As a result, the growth advocates secured the advantage over the stability advocates. The appearance of the Income-Doubling Plan at the end of 1960 showed that the growth advocates had captured the initiative. However, within the framework of the Bretton Woods system Japan could not simply implement economic policies without any regard for international balance of payments restrictions.

It should be noted that throughout the period of the fixed exchange-rate system the Japanese government consciously sought to maintain the yen exchange rate. It would appear that the rate was comparatively high at JPY360 to the dollar from the outbreak of the Korean War through the 1950s, while it was comparatively low at any point in time during the 1960s (Eichengreen 2007, Chapter 3). For this reason, the option of devaluing the yen should have been available during the 1950s. One reason Japan did not devalue the yen was because it preferred to be able to procure imported raw materials at relatively low prices since it depended on overseas supplies for nearly all its industrial raw materials. Another reason was the fact that with the exception of the first half of the 1950s there were no structural imbalances in the international balance of payments, so that a worsening of the international balance of payments could be overcome simply by slowing the pace of economic growth.

Under the Bretton Woods system, IMF funds were expected to play a buffering role by alleviating temporary imbalances in the international balance of payments. But did IMF funds serve as such a buffer in Japan's case? Due to the small scale of the IMF's funds it proved unable to supply ample quality of funds that Japan needed, and Japan needed to supplement these with U.S. government funds such as EXIM loans and with funds from swaps with the New York Fed. However, since EXIM and the New York Fed did not have the authority to supervise the borrowers of the Japanese government and the Bank of Japan, the IMF did have an effect, to some degree, on macroeconomic policy through its lending policies.

References

Akaneya, Tatsuo. 1992. *Nihon no GATT kanyu mondai (The problem of Japanese accession to the GATT)*. Tokyo: University of Tokyo Press.

Bank of Japan. 1979. *Nihonginko Enkakushi* (Chronological history of the bank of Japan), Part 5, vol. 16, Tokyo: Bank of Japan.

Bank of Japan. 1986. *Nihon Ginko Hyakunenshi (One hundred-year history of the Bank of Japan)*, vol. 6. Tokyo: Bank of Japan.

de Vries, Margaret G., and J. Keith Horsefield. 1969. *The International Monetary Fund, 1945–1965*, vol. 2. IMF, Washington.

Economic Planning Agency. 1962. *Sengo keizaishi, boueki kokusaishuushi-hen* (Postwar economic history, foreign trade and balance of payments). Tokyo: Ministry of Finance Printing Office.

Eichengreen, Barry. 2007. *Global imbalance and the lessons of Bretton Woods*. Cambridge: MIT Press.
Griffiths, Richard T. (ed.). 1997. *Explorations in OEEC history*. Paris: OECD.
Iwakoshi, Tadamichi. 1963. *Jidosha kogyoron (A study of the auto industry)*. Tokyo: University of Tokyo Press.
Korenaga, Takafumi. 2000. Sengo nihon no gaika yosan seido to menbosekigyo (The exchange budget system and the cotton-spinning industry in postwar Japan). *Toyo Daigaku Keizaigaku Ronshu* (University of Tokyo Journal of Economics) 66(1).
Ministry of Finance. 1992. *Showa Zaiseishi 1952–1973* (History of fiscal and monetary policies in Japan, 1951–1971), vol. 12. Toyo: Tokyo Keizai Inc.
Ministry of Finance. 1998. *Showa Zaiseishi 1952–1973* (History of fiscal and monetary policies in Japan, 1952–1973), vol. 18. Tokyo: Toyo Keizai Inc.
Ministry of Finance. 1999a. *Showa Zaiseishi 1952–1973* (History of fiscal and monetary policies in Japan, 1951–1971), vol. 11. Toyo: Toyo Keizai Inc.
Ministry of Finance. 1999b. *Showa Zaiseishi 1952–1973* (History of fiscal and monetary policies in Japan, 1951–1971), vol. 19. Toyo: Toyo Keizai Inc.
Mori, Tateshi. 2011.1950-nendai no nichigo tsusho kankei (Japanese-Australian commercial relations in the 1950s). *Toyo Daigaku Keizaigaku Ronshu* (University of Tokyo Journal of Economics) 76(4),77(1),77(2).
Rix, Alan. 1986. *Coming to terms: The politics of Austria's trade with Japan, 1945–57*. Sydney: Allen & Unwin.
Schenk, Catherine R. 1994. *Britain and sterling area, from devaluation to convertibility in the 1950s*. London: Routledge.
Winand, Pascaline. 1993. *Eisenhower, Kennedy and the United States of Europe*. London: Macmillan.
Yokoi, Noriko. 2003. *Japan's postwar economic recovery and Anglo-Japanese relations, 1948–1962*. London: Routledge.

Chapter 13
China and the International Monetary Fund 1945–1985

Catherine R. Schenk

1 Introduction

The history of China's engagement with the IMF was complicated by China's broader political and economic relations with the capitalist world during the first three decades of the IMF's operations. At the time of the Bretton Woods negotiations in July 1944, Chiang Kai-shek's Guomintang (KMT) ruled China, but the onset of the civil war in 1947 and the subsequent victory of Mao Tse-Tung's Chinese Communist Party in 1949 led to the interruption of international economic relations between the mainland of China and most 'western' states during the Cold War era. Chinese officials, government ministers and bankers were prominent at the Bretton Woods conference in 1944, enjoying the support of the Allied powers while the Japanese war still raged. During the early years of the Fund's operations, the civil war in China preoccupied the KMT regime. But China's territorial boundaries were not resolved with both the KMT and the PRC claiming to be the legitimate government of 'China'. In the early 1970s, Mao reached out to the US President Nixon to begin to re-engage with the global system, a process that culminated in Deng Xiao-ping's Open Door Policy in December 1978. After 30 years of gradual opening to international trade and investment, China joined the IMF in April 1980, unseating the Republic of China (ROC). Although Chinese experts influenced the design of the Bretton Woods institutions, the PRC was thus a late-comer to the IMF, joining when many key structures were already in place and left with the legacy of China (Taiwan)'s policy choices over 25 years.

Despite Lardy's assertion that 'the story of China's entry into and initial involvement with the key international financial organizations is well known' (Lardy 1999. p. 208), there is a surprisingly limited range of accounts of China's historical

C.R. Schenk (✉)
School of Social and Political Sciences, University of Glasgow, Lilybank House,
Bute Gardens, Glasgow G12 9RT, UK
e-mail: catherine.schenk@gla.ac.uk

K. Yago et al. (eds.), *History of the IMF*, Studies in Economic History,
DOI 10.1007/978-4-431-55351-9_13

engagement specifically with the IMF (Ferdinand and Wang 2013, p. 895). China's position at the Bretton Woods meeting forms a peripheral part of wider descriptions of this formative congress by Van Dormael (1978) and Steil (2013). Some greater detail is revealed by Helleiner as part of his exploration of the role of developing and peripheral states at the meeting (Helleiner 2014). The most authoritative and exhaustive account of the subsequent replacement of the KMT by the PRC is now somewhat dated (Jacobson and Oksenberg 1990). Their work was based on interviews with a range of Chinese and IMF officials and completed just when the Tiananmen incident appeared to mark a turning point in China's policy reform. They conclude that there was a convergence of policy approaches between the IMF and the PRC during the 1970s that supported the strong political leadership on both sides to manage the transition from ROC to PRC successfully. The international political economy literature, focussed more broadly on China's engagement with international organisations, has drawn on this account (e.g. Kent 2009, Pearson 1999). Boughton's (2001) official IMF history supplements this with evidence from the IMF archives to provide an introduction to the relevant issues in the negotiations with the PRC and a brief overview of China's role in the Fund in the 1980s. Nevertheless, the role of ROC, the reasons why the accession of the PRC was so prolonged and the detail of the early confrontations between the PRC and the IMF and has not been fully explored and this has led to some confusion. For example both Ferdinand and Wang, and Bottelier underestimate China's use of the Fund's resources in the 1980s (Ferdinand and Wang 2013, p. 900; Bottelier 2007, p. 241). Monami (2013, p. 126) used archive evidence to argue that China 'attempted to reinstate itself at the IMF throughout most of the Cold War period'. In contrast, this chapter demonstrates the hesitancy of the PRC to claim its seat on the IMF and the complications that this generated for the IMF management. This chapter also examines in greater detail the era when the Republic of China (ROC) represented China and the ways that this affected the PRC's later position. Understanding these early years are important because of the controversial and complex relationships that China has developed in the IMF since the late 1990s when the Chinese economy began accelerate its international engagement. This chapter demonstrates the extent to which these patterns of relations were evident much earlier, before China had resumed great economic power status. Indeed, continuities are detectable from the time when the ROC represented China in the Fund.

The first section examines China's role in the origins of the IMF by focussing especially on the Bretton Woods meeting. The second section addresses the decisions of the KMT in the IMF during the 35 years when it represented China. The third section introduces new evidence to explain the prolonged transition in China's representation in the IMF, which accelerated as the Open Door Policy gained traction in the PRC. This is followed by a survey of the main challenges faced by the PRC in the 1980s, particularly over conditionality, exchange rate policy and quota size. A final section concludes.[1]

[1] This chapter does not deal with China's role in the IBRD, which occurred in parallel, but which involved distinct challenges.

2 China at Bretton Woods

Already in 1944, at the time of the Bretton Woods meeting, the KMT regime was under threat externally from Japanese invasion and internally from Mao's Chinese Communist Party, so the Bretton Woods meetings came at a time when the Chinese state was especially eager to garner support from the international community and prove its legitimacy in the global political system. The country's struggles through the 1930s and 1940s against a common external enemy had prompted considerable financial support from the West (particularly from the USA), although relations between the KMT regime on the one hand and Washington and London on the other were beginning to cool as Chiang Kai-shek's economic and military management unravelled. Indeed, a special meeting was convened in the middle of the Bretton Woods conference on 7 July to commemorate the beginning of the eighth year of the Sino-Japanese war. In his speech at this event H.H. Kung (China's Finance Minister and lead delegate) linked Japanese aggression against China directly to Japan's global threat after 1940 and stressed the future strategic importance of China in East Asia. He then called for more supplies for China to defeat Japan and for capital and technical assistance in the postwar effort 'to carry out a vast program of industrialization'.[2]

Helleiner observed that 'China's role in the creation of the Bretton Woods system has received little attention in existing academic literature' and has sought to fill this gap (Helleiner 2014, p. 185). It can certainly be considered a neglected story since China sent a very large delegation to the Bretton Woods meeting (second only to the USA), drafted an alternative vision for the Fund in advance of the meeting and was allocated the fourth largest quota (after the USA, UK and USSR). From Helleiner's perspective, the Chinese approach clearly sought to redress imbalances in economic development after the war through international institutions inspired by Sun Yat-sen's International Development Organisation and the anticipated need for long term foreign capital for development (Helleiner 2014, pp. 187–90).[3] The Chinese response to the Keynes and White Plans in 1943 leaned closest to the Keynes Plan in its ambitious scale but also emphasized the need for the international community to support monetary stabilisation; a looming challenge for China as inflationary pressure increased in the 1940s (Helleiner and Momani 2014). The need to address unequal development was an important theme of the Bretton Woods meetings, although the records of the meeting suggest that this campaign was mainly led by India's delegation.

Some indication of the specific role of Chinese officials is possible through the recent release of secret transcripts of the meeting (Schuler and Rosenberg 2013). Tsiang Tingfu chaired the Committee 1 (Purposes, Policies and Quotas of the Fund)

[2] Address by Dr. H.H. Kung, Chairman of Chinese Delegation, 7 July 1944. *United Nations Monetary and Financial Conference, Bretton Woods, Proceedings and Documents*, Vol. 2, p. 1165.

[3] Helleiner and Momani (2014) cite correspondence between H.H. Kung (and other Chinese officials) and US authorities in advance of the Bretton Woods meeting.

of Commission 1, which would seem a prominent and prestigious task. Tsiang was Chief Political Secretary of the Executive Yuan in the KMT Government and was later the ROC representative to the UN and Ambassador to the USA (Schuler and Bernkopf 2014, p. 5). Committee 1 considered the text for the first two sections of the Joint Statement that would form the basis for the Articles of Agreement including a section on quotas, so it seemed to have a prominent place. But the proceedings of this committee exemplify the way that the negotiations were constrained in practice. Tsiang began with consideration of Article I, but the meeting quickly descended into disagreement over the wording of 'institution' vs 'machinery'. When he proposed a vote, the US and UK supported his motion but it was not carried by the majority of members. At this point, Lionel Robbins of the UK objected that discussion of each proposed amendment would take too long and moved to establish a permanent subcommittee to deal with drafting changes where there was likely to be a 'substantial change'.[4] This had already been proposed at the start of the meeting by Ecuador, but rejected because there was no seconder to the motion. Despite some disquiet about accountability the motion was carried this time with US support. Fred Vinson of the USA then remarked 'his understanding that differences of opinion in the Committee would be reported fully to the Commission' rather than resolved in Committee. Tsiang 'replied that the Committee was not under obligation to report on all purposes of differences since in that case it would not fulfil its purpose of saving time for the Commission'. Tsiang then turned to the next alternative texts but at this point Vinson asked that Harry White, Chairman of the Commission, be given the floor. White made clear 'his feeling that a vote on each question would be undesirable and would slow down the Committee's progress and asked whether in cases where the Chair recognized the differences of opinion, the Chair would not refer the matter to the Commission' rather than take a vote. Tsiang responded that 'on matters of importance it was his intention that the Committee should have free expression of its views and that all shades of opinion should be reported fully'. But he agreed 'it would probably be satisfactory if the Chair would consult the Committee on whether or not there should be a vote'. In practice many issues were referred either to a Drafting Sub- Committee for reconsideration or to the Commission for decision and the power of the Committee was thus minimised. Likewise, the designation of quotas was quickly deferred and ended up controlled by the USA and UK (Van Dormael 1978, p. 180; Steil 2013, p. 231). This example shows the limits on the influence that delegations such as China could have at Bretton Woods despite having prominent positions in the conference apparatus and confirms Steil's characterisation of the Bretton Woods congress as essentially designed to protect the integrity of the draft articles devised by the Americans (Steil 2013).

Although this episode demonstrates that there were limits to China's influence over the Articles of Agreement, they were clearly favoured in the allocation of quotas. Steil argued that the quotas were essentially determined by the US authorities

[4]Minutes of Meeting of Commission I – Committee 1, 10 am 4 July 1944. The Bretton Woods Transcripts, Chapter 11.

on the basis of political and strategic considerations and that the Russian quota was the most controversial, although noting that 'China demanded to be number four, ahead of France' (Steil 2013, p. 230; Helleiner 2014, p. 199). Quotas were based on estimates of pre-war national income, foreign trade, gold and dollar holdings, but in the maelstrom of wartime, the data required to be precise were often missing and this was certainly the case for China, which had been involved in formal warfare since 1937. The estimates for China's national income using current prices and merely converting through to US$ for 1936 varied from $ 8 billion to 9 billion, including Manchuria but not Taiwan.[5] Estimates of gold and dollar assets as of July 1943 were agreed to be $624.4 million based on an agreed figure by the US Treasury and the Chinese government. But this total included $260 million in credit extended to China from the USA in March 1942 that was 'considered at the time [1944] both by the Chinese Government and the US Treasury as the equivalent of dollar deposits'.[6] Trade figures for 1934–1938 were distorted because of the Sino-Japanese War, but with Manchuria and Formosa included as part of China, accounted for 2.2 % of world imports and 1.6 % of world exports. The ratio of exports to national income was only 3.4 %. Despite these modest measures, China was allocated the largest quota outside the great powers of the USA, UK and USSR, more than France, India or Canada. This maximised China's voting, representation and borrowing rights.

The allocation of quotas (then as now) was particularly controversial because of the link between the governance of the IMF and the size of quota, so the algorithm for determining each member's contribution was somewhat opaque to allow for some manipulation to meet political or economic questions. The formula was devised by Raymond Miksell of the US Treasury with the express aim of ensuring c.$2.5 billion for the USA, c.$1.25 billion for the UK and a third and fourth place respectively for USSR and China (Horsefield 1969, p. 95). Table 13.1 shows that during the course of drafting the terms of the IMF, China's proposed share grew from an initial $350 million in June 1943 to $550 million agreed at Bretton Woods. Both the USSR and China negotiated quotas 157 % larger than the US delegation had planned on the eve of the conference, at the expense of the occupied states of France and Netherlands. Table 13.1 shows the distribution of quotas for the top ten members in 1944 and their quotas in 2013.

China's role in the Bretton Woods meeting might be considered highly successful. The delegation succeeded in demonstrating their importance in the future peace among nations and leveraging their relations with both the UK and USA to achieve a relatively large quota and, thereby, were assured an appointed Executive Director on the IMF Board. In the end, however, the large quota allocated to China at Bretton Woods became an albatross around the neck of the successor ROC China until the 1970s, when China became eligible to draw on Fund resources. But by this time the first steps toward the transition from the KMT government to the new People's Republic of China (PRC) in the Fund had already begun.

---

[5] Committee on Quota for China, Document No. 1, 23 September 1946. RD/46/39. IMF Archives [hereafter IMFA].

[6] Ibid.

Table 13.1 Suggested and actual quota distribution

	US June 1943	US Jan. 1944	UK March 1944	Brought to Bretton Woods by USA	Final	%	2013 %	Difference from 1944
USA	2,929	2,900	2,900	2,929	2,750	31.25	17.69	−13.56
UK	1,275	1,300	1,300	1,275	1,300	14.77	4.51	−10.26
USSR	763	900	900	763	1,200	13.64	2.5a	−11.14
China	350	600	500	350	550	6.25	4	−2.25
France	–	500	500	620	450	5.11	4.51	−0.60
India	367	300	400	367	400	4.55	2.44	−2.11
Canada	278	300	300	278	300	3.41	2.67	−0.74
Netherlands	–	250	300	325	275	3.13	2.17	−0.96
Belgium	–	235	300	250	225	2.56	1.93	−0.63
Australia	149	150	300	149	200	2.27	1.36	−0.91
TOTAL	10,064	8,490	9,800	8,490	8,800			

Source of proposed quotas: Horsefield (1969), Vol I, p. 96
[a]Russian Federation only

3 China and the IMF 1945–1980

China was an original member of the IMF and committed to take up its quota of US$550m in December 1945, although it took 15 years to complete its payment. Almost immediately after the end of the Second World War, the monetary and economic situation in China deteriorated sharply as the civil war between the KMT and the CCP intensified. When devaluations of the Taiwan dollar became more frequent and urgent, in June 1948 YC Koo of the KMT government requested special procedures to overcome the requirement of members to consult with the IMF prior to changing exchange arrangements. Thus Koo argued that 'China's exchange situation is in an extremely fluid state, requiring the closest watch and often necessitating prompt action on the spot when violent waves of speculation set in as a result of military and economic difficulties' and asked for a special procedure that would allow faster prior consultation than going through the Executive Board.[7] Shortly afterward, in August 1948 the government introduced the Gold Yuan in an effort to stem inflation (issued at an exchange rate of 3 million: 1 against the old fapi). From this time, the Executive Board agreed a 'special procedure' for consultation with China about changes in the exchange system whereby 'the Chinese authorities are to notify the Managing Director in advance of contemplated changes in China's exchange rates and exchange structure; the Managing Director may reply at once on behalf of the Fund, unless he prefers to raise the matter with the Executive Board'.[8] This allowed China to avoid formal discussion and approval of changes in the

[7]Memo from YC Koo to Camille Gutt, Chairman of Executive Board IMF, 3 June 1948. EBD/48/278. IMFA.

[8]August 1948.

Executive Board. The procedure followed the evacuation of the KMT to the island of Taiwan and was only ended at the end of 1960 at the request of the ROC authorities.[9]

Despite the transition of government of Mainland China in 1949, the KMT regime kept its seat in the Executive Board to represent China. Several countries, including the UK, recognised the legitimacy of the PRC in 1949 but the PRC was increasingly ostracised with the outbreak of the Korean War in mid-1950 and the deepening of the Cold War in Asia. The US government continued tosupport the KMT regime, supplying sustained economic and military aid to support its claims to re-take control of the mainland from Mao's Communist Party. The UN embargo on strategic trade with the PRC from May 1951 and the continuation of the KMT government's representation of China in the UN formalised the exclusion of the PRC from post-war international institutions.

In this political context, the transitional arrangements for the representation of China in the IMF were uneventful. In February 1950 the Czech representative, Bhumil Sucharda protested on behalf of Czechoslovakia and Poland that he 'could not recognize any action undertaken by the people of the Kuomintang group concerning the activities of the Fund'.[10] In August 1950, Zhou En-Lai, Minister of Foreign Affairs of the Central Peoples Government of the PRC protested that 'the so-called "delegates" of the Chinese Kuomintang Reactionary Remnat [sic] Clique have no longer any qualification for participating in the International Monetary Fund and must therefore be driven out from its various organs and meetings'.[11] But when the Czechs finally managed to bring a resolution to replace the KMT representation in September 1951, it was roundly rejected.[12] The Czechs protested again in August 1952 'proposing exclusion of the Kuomintang group from all organs of the Fund and of the Bank' but they gained no traction in the context of the Cold War.[13] Even the Eastern Bloc's support ended after the withdrawal of Czechoslovakia in December 1954 and the PRC's political break with the USSR in 1960 (Luthi 2008). During the 1960s the intensification of Mao's radical economic and social policies intensified the PRC's isolation.

In early 1951, the IMF staff continued to consider both PRC and ROC together in their standard annual economic reviews, although in separate sections.[14] In September 1951, the KMT government requested a visit from IMF staff, who reported in December on a 'Survey of Economy of Taiwan'[15] and when the Executive Board discussed the paper in early January 1952 there was no mention of the

[9] Memo, 20 December 1960. EBD/60/154. IMFA.

[10] Letter from B. Sucharda to Camille Gutt (IMF), 3 February 1950. EBS/50/135. IMFA. See also, (Boughton 2001, p. 970).

[11] Cable from Chou En-Lai, Beijing, 26 August 1950. EBD/50/733. IMFA.

[12] Press Report, New York Times, 11 September 1951. PREP/51/291. IMFA.

[13] Memo to Executive Board, EGD/452/167. IMFA

[14] Review of Economic Developments in China, 1949–50, by Ching Gwan Chang, 14 February 1951. SM/51/563 IMFA. Data on mainland China were collected from Hong Kong.

[15] Survey of Economy of Taiwan, 11 December 1951, SM/51/639. IMFA.

Mainland economy.[16] Although the Staff Report on China's 1952 Article XIV consultation referred to 'China (Taiwan)', the minute of the discussion of this consultation does not mention the word 'Taiwan', but refers only to 'China' and the 'Government of China'.[17] Mainland China had gradually disappeared from the view of the IMF.

This lacuna eventually drew the attention of the IMF staff. At the beginning of 1966, DS Savkar, Director of the Asian Department (from India) approached the Acting Managing Director to ask 'whether so long as Nationalist China is recognized as the rightful representative of China we should not collect information about developments in Red China'.[18] While 'we cannot establish official relations with Red China for collecting data,' other organisations such as the UN and ECAFE included 'Red China' in their analyses and there were published sources available, particularly 'a good deal of information is seeping through Hong Kong'. One IMF staffer was 'unofficially collecting some information but because of lack of status to such work, she is very hesitant'. There is no reply to this memo in the file and economic reports on Mainland China to do not appear in the Asian Department's Non-Members files until February 1974.[19]

Taiwan's relations with the IMF were uncontroversial through the 1950s and 1960s as the mainland PRC economy lurched from the Great Leap Forward to the Cultural Revolution. Boughton describes the ROC as 'sensitive to the need to maintain a low profile and to recognize the limits of its economic power' during this period (Boughton 2001, p. 971). The ROC did not declare a par value for the New Taiwan currency as it was obliged to under the Articles of Agreement, and also operated a range of restrictive exchange practices including multiple exchange rates that the IMF was willing to tolerate in the short term while the economy was rebalanced and inflation contained.[20] They continued in a 'transitional' stage without a par value and subject to 'consultations' on the progress towards the principles of the Articles of Agreement under Article IV. By May 1954 they had eliminated the multiple exchange rates that had been in place to channel resources into particular sectors, but a year later an 'emergency situation in balance of payments' prompted a new system that introduced exchange certificates for private trade at rates set by a central committee.[21] In subsequent consultations the multiple currency system continued to be scrutinised; by August 1959 there were only two rates and the exchange rate gap was reducing.[22] At the end of July 1960 the ROC Finance Minister notified

[16] Executive Board Meeting 52/2, 9 January 1952. EBM/52/2. IMFA.

[17] Executive Board Meeting 52/44, 30 July 1952. EBM/52/44. IMFA.

[18] DS Savkar to Acting Managing Director, 25 January 1966. ADIO, Country Files, Box 19, Non-Member Countries, China, 1971–1977. IMFA.

[19] The Economic System of the PRC, February 1974, ADIO), Country Files, Box 19, Non-Member Countries, China, 1971–1977. IMFA.

[20] 1952 Consultations China (Taiwan), 22 July 1952. SM/52/41. IMFA. The multiple exchange rates were eliminated by May 1954.

[21] Memo from Beue Tann, Executive Director for China, 3 March 1955. EBD/55/33. IMFA.

[22] Minutes of Executive Board Meeting 18 September 1959, EBM/59/35. IMFA.

Table 13.2 China's quota calculation

Indicator	Value/estimate	Contribution to quota calculation
National income	$13 billion	2 % = $260 m
Gold and dollar assets	$624.4 million	5 % = $31.2 m
Ratio of average exports to national income	3.4 %	
Imports	$581 ($673.4 including smuggling)	10 % = $58.1
Exports	$441.6 ($473 including smuggling)	10 % of variation = $13.3b
Total		$362.6

Source: Committee on Quota for China, Document No. 1, 23 September 1946. RD/46/39. Sum not shown in document

the IMF that new reforms would push almost all private and official foreign exchange trading to exchange certificates, which would trade in a free market, thus creating a single floating rate alongside the official parity with the latter creating a ceiling for appreciation.[23] A similar strategy for moving gradually from a pegged, overvalued exchange rate to a fluctuating, market determined rate using exchange certificates was used 20 years later by the PRC.

Some of Taiwan's interactions with the Fund had longer term consequences for the PRC's position. This is especially true for the size of the quota, and China's consequential role in the governance of the Fund. In September 1946 the Chinese government sought to increase in their quota by 30 %.[24] The matter was referred to a Committee chaired by Saad of Egypt and including Bolton (UK), Gomez (Mexico), White (USA) and Koo (China).[25] Table 13.2 shows the calculations that the IMF used setting out the basis of the quota computations for China in 1944, which did not provide any support for an increase, although the calculations included all of mainland China.

Conversely, in September 1959 when the Executive Board passed a resolution to increase members' quotas by 50 % to increase the resources of the Fund, the KMT Minister of Finance informed the IMF that 'due to present special circumstances, my Government is not in a position to increase its quota'.[26] China's quota was left at SDR550m despite an increase in others' quotas so that China's share fell steadily to 3.4 % in 1965 and 1.9 % by 1971. China's profile in the Fund receded as a result, as is shown in Table 13.3. Since Russia did not in the end join the IMF, Table 13.3 shows that China had the third largest individual share of voting rights until the enlargement of quotas in 1959, although this was only 5.52 %. From 1960, West Germany replaced China as a member entitled to appoint an Executive Director and from this date Beue

[23] Memo from Beue Tann, 6 July 1960. EBD/60/97. IMFA.

[24] YC Koo to Gutt, 18 September 1946. EBD/46/65. IMFA.

[25] Minutes of Executive Board Meeting, 19 September 1946. EBM/46/61.IMFA.

[26] Letter Chia Kan Yen to Roman Horne, Secretary IMF, 27 April 1960. EBD/60/57. IMFA.

Table 13.3 Voting power as percentage of total votes (%)

Executive directors	1946	1950	1956	1960	1964
USA	33.52	30.46	26.62	25.63	22.63
UK	16.0	14.54	12.71	12.18	10.77
China	6.95	6.31	5.52	3.55	3.14
France	5.73	6.04	5.28	5.02	4.43
India	5.13	4.66	4.08	3.86	3.41
West Germany	–	–	–	5.02	4.43
Others	32.67	37.99	45.79	44.74	51.19
Total	100	100	100	100	100

Source: Horsefield (1969), Vol II, p. 353

Tann was an elected member of the Board rather than an automatic appointment. China never regained the status of an appointed executive director; when the reforms of 2010 are implemented all Executive Directors will be elected.

The ROC did not deposit its full quota in gold and Taiwan dollars until September 1970, which finally allowed it to meet the conditions for drawing on the Fund's resources. Although China's continued low quota levels restricted representation on the Executive Board and voting rights, from 1966 the ROC did manage to represent an East Asian group of members including South Korea and Vietnam (Philippines joined in 1970) but even this position was snatched away in 1972 when Indonesia took leadership of a range of developing economies. From this point, China had no direct representation on the Executive Board and could only vote as one of a group of countries. In 1978 the ROC did not take part in the election of Executive Directors and itself was no longer represented even indirectly on the Board. As its presence became increasingly vulnerable, ROC made a final drawing from the reserve tranche in June 1978 of SDR29.9 million and subsequently received two allocations of SDRs in January 1979 and January 1980 amounting to SDR114.4 million.

In October 1971 the UN voted to expel ROC and to bring the PRC in to represent China, but it took a further 9 years for the PRC to take over the representation of China in the IMF and the IBRD. The IMF was a Specialised Agency of the UN but legally functioned as a separate and independent organization. The IMF Articles of Agreement did not allow a member to be expelled unless they had violated the rules, which ROC had not done. Membership of the IBRD and IMF also brought significant financial obligations and rights associated with that made it challenging technically to change representation, although this was achieved much faster for the unified state of Vietnam in 1976. Beneath this apparent blindness to the changing direction of Chinese politics, the Fund staff and management were keenly aware of the implications for the Fund.

A few days after the UN resolution, the IMF Managing Director met with senior staff members and concluded that the IMF Management should not be pro-active about China's representation, but would instead 'engage in informal discussions with individual directors in order to attempt to ascertain the attitude of members on the question'.[27] If there was a majority in favour of keeping the ROC, this was preferred. The PRC was unlikely to be able to meet the obligations of membership 'and it would be embarrassing to have to begin registering violations almost from the outset' so if a majority was against ROC's continued membership then 'China' should withdraw rather than be replaced by the PRC.[28] The IBRD wanted to publish a 'statement of facts' to 'avoid the appearance of procrastination' but the Fund staff encouraged them to make an even simpler statement to avoid controversy.[29]

Southard and Gold (Chief Counsel) met individually with the 20 executive directors or alternates over the next 10 days.[30] It was explained that if the Fund followed the UN in recognising the PRC as representing 'China', the PRC would have to be able to meet the membership obligations. These included repurchase of the gold tranche, a contingent obligation to repurchase down to 75 % of quota, to provide economic data, to seek approval for exchange practices inconsistent with the Articles. If the PRC accepted these obligations and joined but was 'a wholly passive member, taking no part in the activities of the fund', this would complicate voting and the achievement of special majorities (required e.g. for SDR issue). This was a rather weak obstacle since China had just under 2 % of the Fund's voting power. If the membership merely transferred to the PRC but they refused the obligations, China might need to be expelled, causing fresh political difficulties. A better option, therefore, was that the PRC should apply for membership – this would allow discussion of how to meet the obligations over time (as was the case for ROC) and would signify that the PRC would not be a passive member. This might be achieved by 'a finding that in the course of time the membership of "China" in the Fund had become the membership of the R[epublic] of C[hina], or more properly the international entity governed by the R.C.'. Thus the PRC and ROC would both sit independently as members. This seems a remarkably naïve solution given the political animosity and territorial dispute between the two governments. But Southard and Gold dismissed concerns about the territorial claims of the government of Taiwan as 'a political question that was not within the Fund's purview, and that the RC might be induced quite readily to forebear from making any such claim in the Fund.'

The Directors expressed 'a virtually unanimous reaction that there should be no haste in raising the matter in the Fund… This was the attitude even of directors who were appointed or elected by members that had been in the vanguard in promoting the cause of the PR in the UN'.[31] The political as well as financial problems were

---

[27] Memorandum for Files, 2 November 1971, Asian Department Immediate Office (ADIO), Country Files, Box 19, Non-Member Countries, China, 1971–1977. IMFA.

[28] Ibid.

[29] Memorandum for Files by Joseph Gold General Counsel IMF, 9 November 1971. ADIO, Country Files, Box 19, Non-Member Countries, China, 1971–1977. IMFA.

[30] Memorandum for Files by J. Gold, 10 November 1971. ADIO, Country Files, Box 19, Non-Member Countries, China, 1971–1977. IMFA.

[31] Ibid.

clear to all, but 'there was nevertheless a feeling that the situation was by no means under control' since governments might instruct their delegates to raise the matter at any time, or the PRC might request to be accepted as a member and this would have to be discussed at the Board. The last meeting was with P.Y. Hsu, China's Executive Director, who was briefed on the discussions with other directors. He offered no comment on the political or territorial issues or the quota but stated that his government wished to remain in the Fund. The directors and the management of the Fund were therefore unanimous in procrastination over the status of the PRC. When Hsu and ROC Ambassador Wong met with Managing Director Pierre-Paul Schweitzer and Southard a month later, Schweitzer expected the issue to come up at the next Annual Meeting of Governors in 1971 and he warned that 'almost certainly if there was a vote on a motion to recognise a governor designated by the PRC, it would win'.[32] Wong suggested that ROC could retain their seat as a representative of the territorial area covered by the New Taiwan Dollar, although he was disappointed to be told that this would likely mean a quota of less than $100 m. In the event, there was no such vote. The PRC was not in a rush to join the IMF, contacting the Managing Director only once in 1973 calling for the 'Chiang Kai-Shek clique' to be expelled.[33] As we shall see below, there was no further correspondence from the PRC until September 1976.

An important issue affecting the PRC's position in the Fund was the decision taken in May 1976 to sell a proportion of the Fund's gold back to members at the original parity of SDR35/oz as part of the demonetization of gold. Since the market price of gold was significantly higher, this so-called 'restitution' offered members an important windfall. To restrict this benefit to those members that had originally contributed gold to the IMF, the scheme included only those members as of end August 1975, which included China represented by the ROC, which had deposited SDR60 millions of (borrowed) gold in August 1970.[34] China's share of the gold to be sold based on their quota was 470,708 oz, equivalent to SDR16.5 million at the official rate of SDR35/oz. Since the market price was about $125 per ounce, this scheme would net about $90 per ounce and be very profitable to the original members of the Fund.[35] Suddenly the stakes for claiming the Chinese 'seat' in the IMF had increased.

[32] Memo for File by Frank Southard, Chinese Membership, 9 December 1971. ADIO, Country Files, Box 19, Non-Member Countries, China, 1971–1977. IMFA.

[33] Letter from Chi Peng-Fei, Minister of Foreign Affairs of the PRC, to H.J. Witteveen, Managing Director IMF, 24 September, 1973. ADIO, Country Files, Box 19, Non-Member Countries, China, 1971–1977. IMFA.

[34] Summary of Discussion at Executive Board Meeting 5 January 1977. China – Sale of Gold for Distribution, IMF Staff Paper, 24 March 1980. EBS/80/65.IMFA.

[35] China – Sale of Gold for Distribution, IMF Staff Paper, 24 March 1980. EBS/80/65. IMFA.

4 Battle over Representation of China

The process of PRC representation of China in the IMF was extraordinarily long drawn out in comparison with participation in other agencies such as the UN. But were the delays mainly on the Chinese or the Fund's instigation? Jacobson and Oksenberg note that there was internal disagreement within the PRC over membership of the IMF and IBRD. Mao appeared to countenance PRC participation in 1973, but in 1974 the Ministry of Finance and Ministry of Foreign Affairs rejected pursuing membership on the basis that the Chinese quota (and voting power) would be very small and that the rules of the IMF would require interference on exchange rate policy (Jacobson and Oksenberg 1990, pp. 63–64). The two key areas of controversy for China from the 1980s to the 2010s were already clearly identified. Subsequently, the internal contests over the leadership succession after Mao's death in 1976 and the ascendancy of Deng Xiaoping, with his outward looking vision for China's future, no doubt preoccupied policy-makers and made IMF representation rather peripheral to the existential struggles taking place at home. The launch of the Open Door Policy in December 1978 marked the commitment to modernisation of the Chinese economy through greater reliance on international capital and technology. This new direction reinvigorated China's external engagement and the attractions of the resources (both technical and financial) from the IMF (Jacobson and Oksenberg 1990, pp. 66–72).

Within a month of Mao's death in early September 1976 the issue of representation was renewed when the President of the People's Bank of China Chen Hsi-Yu wrote to the Witteveen, IMF Managing Director, claiming the rights to China's assets and quota in the IMF, at the same time signalling a return to Zhou En-Lai's modernisation programme.[36] This took the PRC's claims beyond the previous call to expel the ROC, although the staff believed that the PRC leadership was not yet ready to join the IMF because of the financial obligations.[37] Membership of the UN had delivered important political benefits, but the IMF and the IBRD were believed to be a lower priority for the PRC leadership. The first stage of the distribution of the IMF's gold was set to begin in January 1977, but the Managing Director Witteveen preferred that the arrangements for China should be postponed while the appropriate representative of China was determined.

After several discussions (including an offer by Martin Wong, ROC Ambassador in Washington, to donate the profit on gold sales to the IMF Trust Fund for developing countries) Witteveen proposed in January 1977 to delay decision on restitution to China on the basis that 'if by April 1 1977 a response has been received from the Government of the People's Republic of China expressing its wish to be represented in the Fund, the gold could be retained until the question of representa-

[36] Memo, PRC: Issues and Outlook, 3 November 1976. ADIO, Country Files, Box 19, Non-Member Countries, China, 1971–1977. IMFA.

[37] Ibid.

tion had been resolved'.[38] Boughton records that there was 'a sizable number of Directors favouring an even more positive response: expulsion of the ROC prior to any further talks' but a majority voted to support Witteveen's more cautious position (Boughton 2001, p. 975, fn 25). The ROC members obviously complained, particularly after the deadline had passed for the PRC to take up the offer, but they were no longer directly represented on the Executive Board. At this point the IMF Management and Executive Board were waiting for the PRC to declare its intention to represent China at the IMF, but this declaration was not forthcoming.

The prospect of a considerable gold profit should have been an extra incentive for the PRC to take over representation in the IMF, but the PRC was not quick to respond to the timetable set at the Executive Board. On 5 March 1977, the President of the PRC wrote to Witteveen suggesting that he arrange discussions with the PRC's mission to the UN in New York. This meeting only took place on 31 March, one day before the deadline. The IMF staff asked Nan Chou, Counsellor to the PRC's UN delegation, bluntly whether the PRC wished to represent China in the Fund.[39] Chou responded that he had two points to make; that the Fund should first expel the ROC in accordance with UN Resolution of October 1971, and secondly that the assets and rights of China in the IMF belonged to the PRC. Chou insisted that 'the Fund should implement the UN Resolution, and only then would the People's Republic decide on what course of action the Peoples' Republic would adopt with respect to membership in the Fund'. The IMF staff explained that if the PRC was not ready to commit to take over representation, expelling China as a member from the Fund would require a new application for membership from the PRC if they subsequently wanted to join. As regards China's 'assets' in the Fund, these amounted to an amount of Taiwan dollars held with the Central Bank in Taipei equal to China's quota [the gold and dollars had been drawn]. The withdrawing member could only claim this amount in national currency.[40] The staff also explained the gold restitution scheme making clear that the gold did not comprise an 'asset' of China; it was being sold to replenish the Fund's holdings of national currencies. Chou seemed surprised and responded that 'he was not familiar with the technical aspects of these transactions' and that he would need to consult with his government. Since these initial discussions were inconclusive, the Managing Director was forced to recommend yet a further delay 'as it appears that the question of the effect of a change in the representation of China in the Fund may need to be considered

[38] China – Sale of Gold for Distribution, IMF Staff Paper, 24 March 1980. EBS/80/65. IMFA.

[39] Memo by David Williams for Files, Discussion with Representatives of the Permanent Mission of the PRC, 1 April 1977. ADIO, Country Files, Box 19, Non-Member Countries, China, 1971–1977. IMFA. A shorter version of this minute is included as appendix of China – Sale of Gold for Distribution, IMF Staff Paper, 24 March 1980. EBS/80/65. IMFA IMF Staff included Tun Thin (Director of Asian Dept), James G Evans, David Williams.

[40] Statement by Staff on Discussions with the Representatives of the PRC on 31 March 1977. EBS/80/65. IMFA. ROC had made 2 gold tranche purchases in January and June 1975 (SDR59.84 million) that were due to be repurchased in 1978 but which could be scheduled for repurchase through 1980. The memo noted that 'circumstances did not permit these technical aspects of the financial obligations of China to be discussed'.

further by the authorities in Peking'.[41] The PRC did not in the end respond and the situation remained in limbo until the acceleration of Deng's policy reforms in 1978. Boughton has concluded that there was no further significant progress until 1980, but the archives reveal ongoing expectations that PRC representation at the IMF was imminent from early 1979 (Boughton 2001, pp. 976–977).

On the eve of the resumption of formal diplomatic relations between the PRC and USA at the start of January 1979, there was an indirect contact with the IMF office in Geneva from Wu, a PRC member of the UNCTAD secretariat.[42] At this point the PBC, Ministry of Finance and Ministry of Foreign Affairs had prepared a report on joining the IMF and IBRD that recommended seeking information from other Eastern Bloc members, Yugoslavia and Romania (Jacobson and Oksenberg 1990, p. 70). On 12 January 1979, Managing Director Jacques De Larosiere held a secret meeting with staff and the US Executive Director to prepare 'for an approach at any time' since 'matters concerning mainland China (PRC) were progressing fast'.[43] For Joseph Gold as IMF legal counsel, 'the underlying concern was to ensure that the fundamental principle that new governments are responsible for the obligations of their predecessors should not be undermined'. At this time, the obligations included two repurchase obligations; SDR30 million to be repurchased in 3–5 years and SDR77 million to reduce the Fund's holdings of Taiwan dollars to 75 % of the quota by 1 April 1982.[44] There was a suggestion of encouraging ROC to repurchase its obligations to meet the 75 % threshold and then an immediate purchase to bring the Fund's holdings of Taiwan's currency to 100 % (Boughton 2001, p. 977). This would mean that there was no financial obligation to pass on to the PRC, but De Larosiere noted that 'desirable though it might be, it required a degree of friendliness and cooperation on the side of the ROC which might not be forthcoming'. On the gold restitution, Gold stated 'the legal position on restitution was clear – the gold should have been restituted to the RoC' since the PRC had not stepped up to claim its place in the Fund within a 'reasonable time', but he was aware that the Board would probably reject this outcome. If ROC withdrew unilaterally from the Fund it would claim the gold and this could open a difficult legal situation for the Fund. There was also a danger that the ROC could use its SDRs at any time and then these could not be transferred to the PRC. William Dale (Deputy Managing Director) then 'wondered whether restituting the gold to the ROC could perhaps be the price of its cooperation in other matters, though he realized that this would imply – perhaps unrealistically – cooperation from the PRC'. Cross, the Executive

[41] China – Sale of Gold for Distribution, IMF Staff Paper, 24 March 1980. Quoting Managing Directors' statement to Executive Board 11 April 1977. EBS/80/65. IMFA.

[42] Letter from Fernando Vera (IMF Geneva) to William Dale (IMF Washington), 14 December 1978. Memo by E Maciejewski for Tun Thin, 27 December 1978. ADIO, Country Files, Box 20, PRC, Correspondence 1978–80. IMFA.

[43] Memo for Files, R.G. Ware, 12 January 1979. ADIO, Country Files, Box 20, PRC, Correspondence 1978–80. IMFA.

[44] ROC had made a purchase of SDR29.9 in the reserve tranche in June 1978 that did not need to be repurchased.

Director for the USA, commented that the US administration 'had not yet come to grips with the problem properly and [he] was sure that his authorities would be responsive to any ideas we could give them'. The meeting concluded that a repurchase-purchase scheme followed by unfettered succession to the PRC was the favoured outcome.[45] The second best option would be for the ROC to withdraw and settle its obligations and then for the Executive Board to make a resolution in the Board of Governors to re-establish membership for China represented by the PRC. This discussion laid the seeds for the eventual settlement with ROC a year later. Although the expected approach from the PRC was not forthcoming over the next few months while the missions to Romania and Yugoslavia took place and a further report was prepared for the party leadership in August 1979, newly hired specialist staff of the Asian Department undertook an extensive and detailed study of the economic system of the PRC in preparation.[46]

In September 1979, Gu Mu, the Vice Premier of the PRC (and supporter of reform) signalled during a press conference that his government would request representation in the IMF, although the timing was left open. In the end, it was informal contact between relatively junior IMF staff from the Asian Department and the Chinese Embassy that accelerated the negotiations. In early December 1979 at a seminar on the Chinese economy held at the Smithsonian Institution, the specialist China staff Francoise Le Gall and Luc de Wulf met Cao Guisheng, Political Counsellor of the Embassy of the PRC in Washington, who 'indicated a personal interest in discussing Fund related matters'.[47] De Wulf followed up with an 'informal dinner' at his house where they suggested that Cao should contact the IMF Secretary Van Houtven. A week later, on 21 February 1980 Cao visited Leo Van Houtven and finally expressed his government's desire to take up China's membership in the Fund by the Fund's Annual Meeting in September/October of 1980. Cao recognised 'that membership entailed both rights and obligations' and while the PRC was not willing to take on liabilities incurred by ROC, 'his government would take a "reasonable" stance toward such questions'.[48] To prepare for the transition, Cao agreed to prepare a mission from Beijing to visit Washington and he concluded by remarking that 'his visit could be expected to be the start of a long and fruitful relationship between the PRC and the Fund'. On 11 March, Cao returned to van

[45] These preferences were then discussed with the General Counsel of the IBRD (Brochas) to ensure that either of these routes would not 'embarrass' the IBRD and were consistent with the PRC joining the IBRD on their terms. Unlike the IMF, the IBRD had an informal agreement that the ROC would honour the guarantees it had given for IBRD lending of US$275 million to companies in Taiwan 'whatever the circumstances might be', so these obligations would not pass to the PRC if representation changed. Memo for Managing Director by Joseph Gold, 12 January 1979. ADIO, Country Files, Box 20, PRC, Correspondence 1978–80. IMFA.

[46] Background Paper on the PRC, by Luc de Wulf and Francoise Le Gall, 15 February 1980. ADIO, Country Files, Box 20, PRC, Correspondence 1978–80. IMFA.

[47] Memo from F. Le Gall to Narvekar, 20 April 1981. ADIO, Country Files, Box 20, PRC, Correspondence 1980–81. IMFA.

[48] Memo for Files by van Houtven, 21 February 1980. ADIO, Country Files, Box 20, PRC, Correspondence 1978–80. IMFA.

Houtven (this time with Tun Thin also present) and formally requested an IMF mission to visit Beijing and made formal his government's wish to discuss the full range of rights and obligations of Fund membership.

In the morning before Cao's formal visit, De Larosiere met with the Executive Directors of the five largest quota holders (US, UK, West Germany, France and Japan) to warn them of the meeting and the impending IMF mission and to gather their views about increasing the Chinese quota.[49] De Larosiere expected that the PRC would accept the terms of representing China in April and negotiations to increase their quota would follow over the following 3 months, ending in July of 1980. But there was a general convention that quotas were frozen for a year from the beginning of July in years when there was election of Executive Directors (to avoid complicating voting rights with new quotas). De Larosiere was seeking support to expedite the quota negotiations for China to meet this deadline. Sam Cross, the US Director, responded first that he 'thought it would be wrong to proceed precipitately with the quota review with a view to achieving approval before July 1 1980' and the others agreed. Hirao of Japan noted 'his authorities adopted a favourable attitude to membership of the PRC' but 'it should be borne in mind that membership of the PRC would naturally affect the present balance in the Board; once a member the PRC might emerge as a leader of the LDCs within the Board.' His own experience was that PRC officials 'were shrewd and tough negotiators' so 'it would be desirable to adopt a cautious attitude in carrying forward discussions with the PRC'. The IMF staff sent to Beijing the following week were carefully briefed to engage in technical questions and fact-finding only and were forbidden to discuss any increase in quota, representation on the Executive Board or restitution of gold. With respect to the quota, they were told to explain that 'an increase is unlikely to be concluded quickly'.[50]

Meanwhile, on 17 March 1980, KH Yu, Governor of the Central Bank of the Republic of China restated his claim to the gold restitution, noting that 'the continued postponement of the restitution of gold to the Republic of China in proportion to what has been delivered to other accredited governments of members contravenes the ...entitlement of the Republic of China and constitutes discriminatory treatment'.[51] The ROC then requested that the Managing Director should put restitution onto the agenda of the Executive Board meeting scheduled for 4 April (the day that the IMF Mission in Beijing was due to conclude).

While the mission was still in Beijing, William Dale (Acting Managing Director) met with all the Executive Directors together confidentially on 31 March 1980 to brief them on the discussions and warn them that the PRC might send their acceptance of obligations to the IMF in advance of the next meeting of the Board (at which

[49] Memo for Files 11 March 1980. ADIO, Country Files, Box 20, PRC, Correspondence 1978–80. IMFA.

[50] Briefing Paper: Staff Mission to the PRC, 13 March 1980. ADIO, Country Files, Box 20, PRC, Correspondence 1978–80. IMFA.

[51] Text of a telex from KH Yu, Governor of Central Bank of Republic of China, 17 March 1980. EBS/80/59.

restitution was to be discussed).[52] Cross of the USA again took the lead and expressed that he 'was anxious to ensure that the process toward the PRC's entry would be orderly and that no hasty action would be taken' while the complexities of financial obligations and capital structure [quota] were resolved. Moreover Cross added that 'it would be desirable not to settle the matter of restitution of gold on April 4'. All other Executive Directors concurred and several questioned whether the PRC was rushing the agenda in order to anticipate the discussion of the gold restitution at the 4 April meeting. If the Board accepted PRC representation in the Fund before taking any decision on restitution, then the gold could only go to the PRC. But if the PRC sent a letter in advance of the 4 April meeting, the Managing Director would have to circulate it to Executive Directors and 'the Fund could not procrastinate'. After further discussion, it was clear that the PRC need not be admitted on 4 April even if a letter were received, although the decision could only be postponed a further 2–3 weeks while a staff paper was prepared. Cross continued to seek further delay and Dale 'then prodded Mr. Cross strongly to be more open with his colleagues regarding the problems which the United States authorities had with an early seating of the PRC'. Cross responded that US Congress needed to pass legislation for a general quota increase and also to increase the US subscription to the IDA (part of IBRD) and 'an early decision on the seating of Peking could have deleterious effects on this legislation'. Nevertheless Cross asserted that his government would support PRC representation of China in the IMF. When Dale asked if all others agreed with Cross, 'no negative replies were given'.

The American position had been set at a meeting of a Presidential Review Committee a few days earlier, on 27 March.[53] The meeting included the Treasury, State Department, Defence, Commerce, Joint Chiefs of Staff and Whitehouse staff among others. They agreed that the US should support PRC claims on the China seat if the PRC raised the issue, and that trying to persuade the Chinese not to go ahead would damage PRC-US relations. But they also agreed that such an initiative should not be encouraged until the FY81 International Financial Institutions legislation had been passed by Congress. The concern was that Congress might not support the $5.5 billion quota increase President Carter was requesting for the IMF and the $3.2 billion he sought as a contribution to the International Development Agency. They were also 'concerned that the Congress might adopt some anti-Chinese amendments barring the IMF or IDA funds for the PRC'.[54] Treasury Secretary Miller agreed to meet with the IBRD president McNamara to try to get him to delay his visit to Beijing scheduled for April, or if this was not likely, to 'convince him that the entry of China into the Bank and Fund this year would not be in the interest

[52] Summary of Confidential Meeting of Executive Directors, 31 March 1980. ADIO, Country Files, Box 20, PRC, Correspondence 1978–80. IMFA.

[53] Foreign Relations of the United States [FRUS], Summary of Conclusions of a Presidential Review Committee Meeting 27 March 1980. FRUS 1977–80 Vol. XIII, China, Doc. 305.

[54] FRUS, memo from President's Deputy Assistant for National Security Affairs (Aaron) to President Carter, 2 April 1980. FRUS 1977–80 Vol. XIII, China, Doc. 306.

of either the institutions or China'.[55] Ambassador Woodcock was instructed to meet with PRC officials to warn them of the drawbacks to taking over the seat while making clear that 'whatever the PRC decision we will support it'.[56] By this time, however, the Chinese had already communicated their intentions to the IMF Managing Director.

On 1 April 1980 Foreign Minister Huang Hua wrote to De Larosiere establishing his government as the 'sole legitimate Government of China' and accepting the responsibility to 'exercise the rights and meet the obligations of China as an original member in the Fund'.[57] The PRC delegation also expressed its desire to request an increase in quota, although the IMF staff warned that the prospects for this were conditional on the extensive economic data required for quota calculations and that quota adjustments tended to take time to determine and agree.[58] The leader of the delegation, Tun Thin, concluded that 'in all its contacts with the Chinese authorities, the mission found them appreciative of the fact that they still had much to learn, not only about the Fund itself, but also about the working of the international monetary system. At the same time, the mission found them determined to work toward active collaboration within the Fund in the context of their goal of modernizing their economy'.[59] But there was still support to protect the interests of the ROC among several Executive Board members and sympathy for their claim of ill treatment.

Wong's request to discuss the restitution of gold to the ROC was fulfilled at the Executive Board meeting of 4 April 1980 where he made the case that the delay was now beyond a 'reasonable time' and that the gold should be restituted to the ROC as a matter of equity, especially since it was the ROC that had met the gold subscription in 1970.[60] Most members sympathised with the ROC's situation but voted to continue to delay restitution while China's representation was clarified. Cross (USA) and Mahsoun Jalal (Saudi Arabia) expressed their country's views that the gold should be restituted to the Republic of China. In contrast, Thierry Aulagnon (Alternate for France) expressed the French government's view that 'any restitution of gold to the representatives of Taiwan would deny the rights of the PRC to the benefits of membership in the Fund'. An important consideration, however, was that the ROC had used its national currency to purchase all the gold from its quota and

[55] FRUS, Summary of Conclusions of a Presidential Review Committee Meeting 27 March 1980. FRUS 1977–80 Vol. XIII, China, Doc. 305. Miller also tried to prolong the IMF mission in Beijing (Jacobson and Oksenberg 1990, p. 74).

[56] FRUS, memo from President's Deputy Assistant for National Security Affairs (Aaron) to President Carter, 2 April 1980. FRUS 1977–80 Vol. XIII, China, Doc. 306.

[57] Quoted in Memo from Secretary to Executive Board, 30 June 1980. ADIO, Country Files, Box 21, PRC, Correspondence 1978–80. IMFA.

[58] Representation in China, 8 April 1980. EBS/80/79. The IMF Mission had taken with them a draft letter for the PRC to agree. Draft letter 13 March 1980. ADIO, Country Files, Box 20, PRC, Correspondence 1978–80. IMFA.

[59] Statement by Tun Thin on notification from the PRC, Executive Board Meeting 7 April 1980. EBM/80/62. IMFA.

[60] Executive Board Minute, 4 April 1980, EBM/80/61. IMFA.

had an obligation to repurchase this currency with gold.[61] Jalal objected most strongly to further delay or the possibility that the gold would go to the PRC, asking 'How can the Board ignore the equity and legal aspects of this case and deny the Republic of China restitution?' He also clarified that if China's membership was terminated, the gold would go to the ROC as the Government representing China; this seemed to open a route for ROC to claim the gold while still allowing the PRC to apply to reinstate China as a member. Whitelaw of Australia questioned whether further delay in transferring the gold would be prejudicial to ROC's interests since the gold would only be released to China as soon as the PRC became the government representing China. In this case, delay would likely mean that the ROC would not get the gold. The Director of the Legal Department confirmed this was the case, causing the Acting Chairman (Dale) to propose a splitting of hairs to meet the legal requirements. He suggested that the Board agree to delay the decision of restitution for the time being, but to commit to take the decision BEFORE the PRC was recognized as the representative of China in the Fund. This would remove the legal prejudice on the delay. Dale also clarified that the profit on the restituted gold at current prices was \$208 million and that the ROC owed \$200 million to the World Bank. Jalal 'pointed out that although there was no legal connection between the Fund and the World Bank on the question of China's liabilities and assets…members could make sure that decisions reached would combine to ensure an equitable solution to the problem'. The mood of the Executive Board seemed ripe for a compromise that would allow the PRC to take over China's membership while still allowing Taiwan an opportunity to exit without substantial losses.

The PRC Minister of Foreign Affairs' letter to De Larosiere dated 1 April was brought to the Executive Board on 7 April and it was agreed that China's representation would be discussed on 16 April and the issue of restitution on the 14 April. This was described as too hasty by some members who questioned the need to have the matter settled before the Interim Committee meeting in Hamburg (they usually had 2 weeks to digest staff papers) and in the end it was agreed to take the matter up on 17 April to give 'at least a little more time to study the staff paper'.[62] Boughton has recorded that in the meantime the USA 'suddenly' proposed an alternative restitution deal (Boughton 2001, p. 978) although we have seen that there were alternatives discussed at the end of March. At the meeting on 14 April, Cross suggested that restitution should go to the ROC on the condition that they used just over 60 % of the value of the gold at market prices to cover their repurchase obligations in the Fund, which would leave just under \$100 m for the ROC.[63] This would leave the PRC with a legacy of about \$136 million that it could draw automatically as its reserve tranche. Wong reported that he was authorized by his government to accept

[61] Statement by Director of Legal Department, EBM/80/61.

[62] Executive Board Minutes, 7 April 1980. EBM/80/62, EBM/80/63. Executive Board Minute 9 April 1980. EBM/80/67. IMFA.

[63] Executive Board Minute, 14 April 1980. EBM/80/72. IMFA. Because the gold transaction could not take place before the PRC took over representation of China, it was agreed that the repurchase could be in US dollars.

the deal but it still only passed by a small margin with seven Directors holding 42.47 % of the voting power supporting Cross and eight directors with 30.63 % of voting power wanting to postpone. S.D. Deshmukh (India) and Price (UK) abstained, which allowed Cross' suggestion to be carried.[64] Thus, on 14 April 1980 the Executive Board agreed to give the 'government on Taiwan' 470,708 oz on condition that it was used to repurchase the currency element in their quota.[65] Li Baohua, President of the People's Bank of China predictably wrote that his government 'deeply deplores this decision'.[66] Three days later, after years of negotiations and delay, as of 17 April 1980 the PRC represented China in the IMF, with only a few cautious comments about the obligation to supply accurate economic information. Boughton suggests that Taiwan's resistance waned as the years passed so that Wong agreed in January 1979 to 'help the Fund staff in reaching an amicable settlement of the dispute over representation' (Boughton 2001, p. 977). But the response from KH Yu of the central bank was robust: 'I am greatly shocked…under the circumstances it is my solemn responsibility to declare that the Government of the Republic of China lodges the strongest protest against this action and will take all necessary measures to protect its legitimate rights'.[67] The new evidence presented here has highlighted the importance of the US position and the sensitivities of Congress as well as the split over the gold restitution, with Saudi Arabia emerging as a strong supporter of the ROC.

5 People's Republic of China and the IMF 1980–85

Immediately after the PRC took up its representation of China in April 1980, the economy began to reap the benefits of the Open Door Policy and accumulated substantial foreign exchange surpluses. Figure 13.1 shows the accumulation of foreign exchange reserves from 1972 until 1989. As the PRC's reserves accumulated, the Executive Board applied greater pressure to crack the air-lock between the domestic and external sectors.

The Fund's first Article IV consultation in early December 1980 was tasked with discussions of the terms for China's first credit tranche drawing as well as a loan from the IMF Trust Fund for poorer countries of SDR300 million. The priority for Fund staff was to ensure that the negotiated program during a 12-month drawing would 'be aimed at sustaining China's domestic and external stability' during the period of restructuring in order to 'support China's increasing integration with the world economy' particularly through expanding exports and restraining fiscal defi-

[64] Ruding, Mentre de Loye, Muns, Al-Eyd, Alfidja, Kiingi, Blondal and de Groote were among those wanting to postpone restitution further.

[65] Communication to PRC from Tun Thin, 16 April 1980. EBS/80/91.IMFA.

[66] Letter Li Baohua to IMF, 28 June 1980. EBS/80/147. IMFA.

[67] Letter from HK Yu to Managing Director, 21 April 1980. EBD/80/111. IMFA.

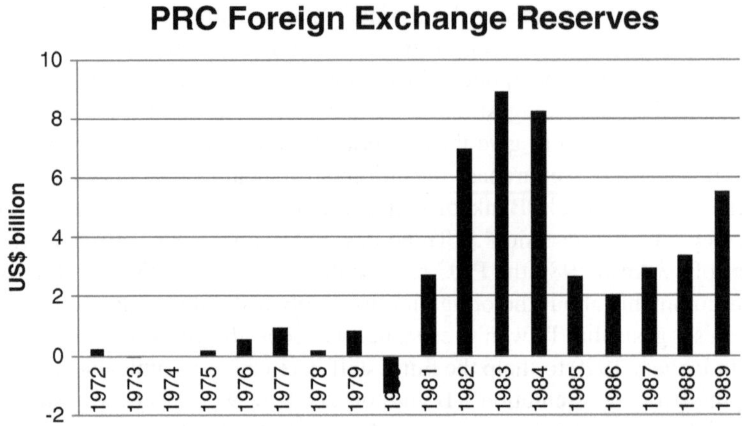

Fig. 13.1 PRC foreign exchange reserves (*Source*: State Administration of Foreign Exchange, People's Republic of China)

cits.[68] Fund staff noted that the government was already in the process of implementing 'a reasonably tight stabilization effort' and so 'should have little difficulty in formulating and agreeing on a policy program with the staff team'. When the mission arrived, however, they found many senior officials preoccupied with a Sino-Japanese ministerial meeting and then with responding to a new more restrictive economic policy announced on 1 December.[69] They also found most agencies reluctant to supply data (other than the PBC) so that 'the consultation was not as thorough as it might otherwise have been'. Mark Allen, of the Exchange and Trade Relations Department and a member of the mission, was not enthusiastic about the reforms announced since 'contrary to what might be expected, the central authorities' control over the economy appears weak' and the new policy appeared mainly focussed on recentralisation and price controls so that 'it is difficult to say whether the new policy is appropriate or whether it will be effective.'[70] The next year, the mission similarly reported that 'the steady stream of regulations issued by the central authorities to influence decisions of lower level authorities are frequently ignored.'[71] The data on balance of payments was very sketchy, but Allen determined that there would be a balance of payments need for resources as required by the Fund to authorise credit. Peter Heller, also part of the mission, similarly complained that 'in many cases, the authorities are simply unaware of many statistical concepts

[68] Brief for IMF Mission, November 1980. ADIO Country Files, China, Box 24, 1982–83. IMFA.

[69] Note by Mark Allen (ETR) for Palmer, 16 December 1980. ADIO Country Files, China, Box 24, 1982–83. IMFA.

[70] Note by Mark Allen (ETR) for Palmer, 16 December 1980. ADIO Country Files, China, Box 24, 1982–83. IMFA.

[71] Hubert Neiss to Acting Managing Director, China 1983 Article IV Consultation, 12 August 1983. ADIO Country Files, China, Box 24, 1982–83. IMFA.

critical to macroeconomic policy formulation'. The relevant data to determine balance of payments need and the program to underpin the proposed drawing on the Fund was only made available the day before the mission left.[72]

Despite these uncertainties, the Chinese authorities accepted the Fund's draft letter of intent with only minor amendment and the PRC made its first request for a 12-month standby arrangement for SDR450 million in January 1981.[73] This opened China to regular consultations with the Fund while the stand-by was outstanding and to a commitment about its economic policy for 12 months. The statement by the Government to support the application for the Stand-by was self critical noting that 'we did not make adequate appraisal of the difficulties and shortcomings caused by 10 years of disruption' and committed the government 'fully and resolutely to implement the policy of readjustment' by dramatic cuts in capital construction (from Y50 billion in 1980 to Y30 billion in 1981) and the government deficit (from Y12 billion in 1980 to Y5 billion in 1981). They also pledged not to introduce new multiple currency practices nor restrict exchange controls any further on current account transactions nor restrict imports for balance of payments purposes. In the end, the cut in construction expenditure was less than planned but the budget deficit fell faster.[74] China's first foray into conditionality seemed unproblematic, but the next in 1986, described below, was more controversial.

In May 1982, Boughton notes that China approached the Fund for a further drawing, but this was rejected on the basis that there was inadequate 'balance of payments need' (Boughton 2001, p. 980, fn 45). Indeed, by October 1982, the Fund was ready to determine that China's reserves position and balance of payments was so healthy that China should be required to make an early repurchase of SDR223 million in its outstanding credits from the Fund during December 1982-February 1983.[75] But this requirement was not in the end implemented. Instead, China repaid early in two stages in May (SDR333.8 m) and August 1983 (SDR116.2 m). At the same time in November 1982, China met the terms of designation for accepting SDR, but this was also postponed.[76] The rapid transformation of China's economy also complicated consideration China's quota position in the Fund.

---

[72] Peter S Heller (FAD) to Goode, Back-to-Office Report, 17 December 1980. ADIO Country Files, China Box 24 1982–3 IMFA.

[73] Letter Li Baohua, President PBC to J. de Larosiere, 26 January 1981. Memo for Executive Board, 17 February 1981. EBS/81/35.

[74] PRC Staff Report for 1982 Article IV Consultation, 6 July 1982, SM/82/129. IMFA.

[75] Memo A.F. Moustapha to Gupta, 29 October 1982. Memo W. O. Habermeier to Neiss, 5 November 1982. ADIO Country Files, China, Box 22 1982–86. IMFA The calculation was made on the basis of 1.5 % of gross reserves plus 5 % of the change in gross reserves over the past 6 months.

[76] Memo by De Wulf to Tun Thin, 1 February 1983. ADIO Country Files, China, Box 22 1982–86. IMFA.

5.1 *Quota*

China's first request to increase its quota came at the end of May 1980, somewhat later than originally expected.[77] An IMF staff mission visited Beijing in the first two weeks of July to gather the information necessary for calculating the quota and an increase to SDR1,200 million (increase of 218 %) was hastily agreed in September 1980, with a recommendation for a further SDR600 million by the end of the year to make up for China falling behind while the ROC was the representative.[78] This allowed the PRC to elect its own Executive Director at the 1980 Annual Meeting. Within a few months the PRC requested a purchase of SDR218,140,081 bringing the Fund's holdings of RMB to 100 % of its new quota.[79] This was followed in January 1981 by a purchase of a further SDR150 million when the quota was increased to SDR1,800 million.[80] The enlarged quota thus cost the PRC little in dollars or gold since the Fund holding of RMB was 100 % and the larger quota increased the reserve tranche available without conditions.

The next general review of quotas began in early 1982 and was not finalised until April 1983. At the Joint Annual Discussion meeting in September 1982, Wang Bingqian, Minister of Finance and Governor of the IBRD for China emphasised the needs of developing countries (such as China) and described an increase in quotas as 'an issue of the utmost importance… which must be undertaken in an appropriate manner as soon as possible' and endorsed a call for total quotas to be doubled and to increase the overall share held by developing countries.[81] But there were obstacles to enlarging China's quota since the calculations were based on data from 1976 to 1980 when China's external sector was relatively small compared to GDP. Thus the calculated quota for Belgium and Luxembourg was more than twice that of China despite the fact that the GDP of these two countries together was less than half of China's GDP.[82] Moreover, the rapid growth in international trade and total reserves from 1980 to 1982 meant that China's calculated quota based on 1980 data depressed the overall calculation.[83]

At this point, China's actual quota in the Fund was only 60 % of what it would be if the mathematical algorithm to determine quotas was applied. However, this was much higher than the ratio for other countries; the average for Fund members was 29 % as is shown in Table 13.4 below. This meant that China's actual share in

---

77 Letter from Li Bao Hua, Governor for China of IMF, to J. De Larosiere Managing Director, 28 May 1980. EBD/80/153. IMFA.

78 China- Report of the Committee on Increase in Quota, 6 August 1980. EBD/80/213. IMFA.

79 Memo from Acting Managing Director, 31 October 1980. EBS/80/237. IMFA.

80 Memo from Managing Director, 9 January 1981. EBS/81/1. IMFA.

81 Press Release, statement by Want Bingqian, 7 September 1982. ADIO Country Files, China, Box 22. IMFA.

82 Memo by K. Al-Eyd for Tun Thin, 2 February 1983. ADIO Country Files, China Box 22. IMFA.

83 The quota calculations were initially based on GDP, total reserves, current receipts and payments from 1976–80 and the variability of current receipts from 1968–80. Eighth General Review of Quota – Quota Calculations with Data ended in 1980, 7 April 1982. EB/CQUOTA/82/4. IMFA.

Table 13.4 Actual and calculated quota as of January 1983

	Actual quota	Calculated quota	Actual as % of calculated
Total	61,034.8	209,133.9	29.2
China	1,800.0	2,998.6	60.0
India	1,717.5	1,975.5	86.9
Saudi Arabia	2,100.0	8,468.8	24.8
USA	12,607.5	35,109.5	35.9
UK	4,387.5	11,716.9	37.4
Germany	3,234.0	18,722.6	17.3
Industrial countries	37,410.0	139,317.0	26.9
Oil exporters	6,662.1	29,665.2	22.5
Non-oil developing countries	16,962.7	40,151.4	42.2

Source: Memo from Secretary to Members of the Committee of the Whole on Review of Quotas, 17 January 1983. EB/CQuota/83/1. IMFA

the Fund's resources was considerably higher than the share of calculated quotas (2.5 % vs 1.4 %).[84] Table 13.4 also shows that greater weight on calculated quota would benefit oil exporters and industrial countries more than most less developed countries (including India and China). The method of allocating quotas was a mixed model; all countries would enjoy an increase in their quota relative to the increase in the overall size of the Fund's resources, but the calculated quotas would be used to identify and calibrate selective increases for particular members where their actual quota was most out of line with the calculated quota.[85] Since China would not benefit as much from the calculated quota, it was apparent already in early 1983 that China's share in total quotas and therefore in voting would likely fall under the Eighth Review.

After much wrangling, the total resources of the Fund were increased from SDR61.03 to SDR90 billion (rather less than China had hoped at the start of negotiations) and allocated based on a 40/60 split of equi-proportional distribution of the quota increase and selective increases. The outcome for the largest quota holders is shown in Table 13.5. China's share of the total fell from 2.948 % of total quotas to 2.656 % with a consequent reduction in voting shares from 2.820 to 2.579 %. But China maintained its ranking as ninth largest quota holder and held the largest quota among non-oil developing countries. The Chinese Executive Director voted in favour of this overall distribution.[86]

This analysis has shown that the late internationalisation of the Chinese economy meant that China lagged behind smaller economies in their participation in the Fund

[84] Memo by L. De Wulf for Tun Thin, Topics for Discussion during visit of Shang Ming, VP of PBC, 1 February 1983. ADIO Country Files, China Box 22. IMFA.

[85] Memo by K. Al-Eyd for Tun Thin, 2 February 1983. ADIO Country Files, China Box 22. IMFA.

[86] Memo from Secretary to Executive Board members, 1 April 1983. EBD/83/51. IMFA. Antigua and Barbuda, Gambia, St. Vincent, Singapore and Vietnam did not respond to the call to vote, but did not formally abstain.

Table 13.5 Quotas and voting share for largest 11 members of IMF

	Quota (SDR millions)		Share of total quotas (%)		Voting share (%)	
	1981	1983	1981	1983	1981	1983
USA	12,607.5	17,918.3	20.648	19.902	19.522	19.153
UK	4,387.5	6,194.0	7.186	6.88	6.819	6.638
Germany	3,234.0	5,403.7	5.296	6.002	5.036	5.795
France	2,878.5	4,482.8	4.714	4.979	4.487	4.812
Japan	2,488.5	4,223.3	4.076	4.691	3.884	4.535
Saudi Arabia	2,100.0	3,202.4	3.439	3.557	3.284	3.445
Canada	2,035.5	2,941.0	3.334	3.267	3.184	3.166
Italy	1,860.0	2,909.1	3.046	3.231	2.913	3.132
China	**1,800.0**	**2,390.9**	**2.948**	**2.656**	**2.82**	**2.579**
India	1,717.5	2,207.7	2.813	2.452	2.693	2.383
Netherlands	1,422.0	2,264.8	2.329	2.515	2.236	2.444

Source: Memo from Secretary to Members of the Committee of the Whole on Review of Quotas, 1 March 1983. EB/CQuota/83.5. IMFA

Fig. 13.2 China's share of total IMF quotas 1948–2013 (*Source*: IMF International Financial Statistics)

and that the method of calculation based on historic measures of openness disadvantaged China in the early 1980s. The potential to increase China's share in the 1990s was then complicated by the collapse of the Soviet Union and the accession of Russia and other east European states, so that after the Ninth General Review in 1994, China ranked eleventh with a quota share of 2.315 %. In 2001 China increased its quota by 36 % as a result of the resumption of sovereignty over Hong Kong, but the major breakthrough was in 2010 with the reapportioning of quota that would result in China regaining its historic position as third largest quota and voting power in the Fund. At the time of writing this reform had yet to be approved by the USA. Figure 13.2 shows that China's share in total IMF quotas fell steadily from 1981 to 2001 before reforms brought the share back to 4 % in 2011, about the same as in 1960.

5.2 RMB Exchange Rate

One of the longest running areas of dispute between China and the IMF was the reluctance to introduce a market exchange rate during the period of transformation of the economy through export-led growth (Heep 2014). IMF surveillance of exchange rates was a persistent challenge to the PRC's gradualist strategy when introducing market prices and stabilising its exchange rate against the US dollar.

The remit for the IMF's surveillance of member countries was expanded while ROC still represented China. In 1978, The Second Amendment to the Articles of Agreement included both multilateral surveillance of the global monetary system and bilateral surveillance of individual members' adherence to IMF approved exchange arrangements (Foot and Walter 2011, pp. 79–80). The renewed emphasis on surveillance arose partly from the increasing global imbalances that followed the OPEC oil price increase of 1973/4 and the realisation that the economic adjustment strategies, particularly of developing economies, threatened systemic stability. In addition, the pegged exchange rate system that had defined the IMF's remit since the 1940s had ended in 1973 and was ratified in the Jamaica Agreement in January 1976. In this new floating exchange rate environment, the IMF was tasked with 'firm surveillance over the exchange rate policies of members, and shall adopt specific principles for the guidance of all members with respect to those policies', although this paragraph ended with the caveat that '[T]hese principles shall respect the domestic social and political policies of members, and in applying these principles the Fund shall pay due regard to the circumstances of members.[87] Particular emphasis was placed on avoiding currency wars, such as had characterised the 1930s floating era, so that 'A member shall avoid manipulating exchange rates of the international monetary system in order to prevent effective balance of payments adjustment or to gain an unfair competitive advantage over other members'.[88]

Relative price stability in China (during the long inflation elsewhere in the 1970s) as well as the depreciation of the US$ after the end of fixed exchange rate system and the desire to keep imports relatively cheap in terms of domestic currency prompted a persistent revaluation of the RMB from RMB2.46 per $ in 1970 to RMB1.50 at the end of 1979. This left the RMB considerably overvalued and so there were losses on exports that were not covered by profits on imports.[89] The accounts of state Foreign Trading Companies (FTCs), through which all trade was channelled, had to be balanced by drawing on the government budget and this introduced a strong fiscal motivation to depreciate the currency closer to its market value. In August 1980 the IMF agreed the 'representative rate' for the RMB as the mid-way point between the buying and selling rates of Y1.4719–1.4793/$ and declared

[87] Articles of Agreement of the IMF, Article IV, Section 3. https://www.imf.org/external/pubs/ft/aa/#art4

[88] Articles of Agreement of the IMF, Article IV, Section 1. https://www.imf.org/external/pubs/ft/aa/#art4

[89] Lardy cites losses in foreign trade of RMB3.18 trillion that had to be covered by the central budget in 1980 (Lardy 1992, p. 67).

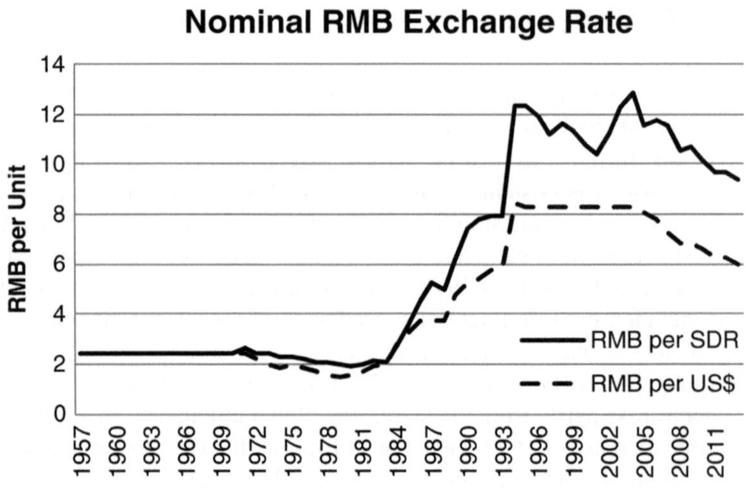

Fig. 13.3 Nominal RMB exchange rate (*Source*: IMF International Financial Statistics)

that the RMB was 'linked to a basket of internationally-traded currencies, weighted with reference to their importance in China's external transactions and their trends in their relative values'.[90] The components and operation of the basket were left opaque, which allowed some flexibility but the fragility of the modernisation process and reliance on central planning meant that the link between domestic and international prices through the exchange rate regime became increasingly complex. Figure 13.3 shows the nominal appreciation of the official exchange rate of the RMB against the dollar and SDR from 1972 to 1981, followed by rapid depreciation from 1985 to 1994 when the exchange rate was unified and pegged to the US dollar. But there were two other versions of the RMB exchange rate.

From 1978, a Foreign-Exchange Retention System allowed the proceeds of some exports to be retained by provincial and local governments, FTCs and producers of exports through an entitlement to buy a proportion of their earnings back from the Bank of China at the official exchange rate (which overvalued the RMB) (Gao and On 1995, pp. 154–155). The amount that could be retained was set in complicated negotiations to try to encourage exports from particular sectors or geographical areas and the amount initially ranged from 5 to 50 % depending on type of activity and location of exporter. There developed a market for these entitlements based on greater demand for foreign exchange from producers who sold mainly to the domestic market but required imported inputs, and extra supply of entitlements from exporters who did not need all of their allocation. In 1980 a foreign exchange trading room opened in the Bank of China's Guangzhou branch to create a central market in entitlements where foreign exchange usually traded at a premium on the

[90] Letter Li Baohua, President of PBC to Managing Director of IMF, 4 August 1980. EBD/80/225. IMFA.

official rate. Similar arrangements began in Shanghai in 1981. The IMF staff, in reviewing China's exchange arrangements and restrictions, took the view that all restrictions in force on the day that the representation of China changed would be considered to be transitional and only new measures introduced after that date required specific approval under Article VIII. The swap market was therefore tolerated by the IMF.

In January 1981, to try to reduce the losses due to an overvalued exchange rate, the government introduced an Internal Settlement Rate (ISR) of 2.8/$ for all international trade transactions (set according to the estimated cost of earning 1 $US) while the official rate for other transactions (mainly with non-residents) stayed at 1.53/$ (Gao and On 1995, p. 158). At the overvalued official rate, Foreign Trading Companies incurred losses on exports that were not balanced by profits on imports and these losses were covered by the government. As foreign trade was decentralised, the Bank of China began to absorb these losses through the ISR in its transactions with FTCs and other regional trade authorities. When the ISR was first introduced, the rate was about 80 % lower than the official rate, although the gap narrowed to 60 % by mid-1982.[91] This dual exchange-rate system made exports more profitable since they generated more Yuan per US$. The rate was only used in transactions between the Bank of China and the FTCs, so it was labelled a 'price' and not an exchange rate, and was only used for visible trade, not tourism, aid or remittances, which continued at overvalued official rate. The IMF estimated in 1982 that only 13–14 % of current account receipts and a very small proportion of payments took place at the official rate.[92] They also determined that 'there is no evidence that the internal settlement rate system gives China an unfair competitive advantage'.[93] Lardy notes that the ISR did not resolve the problems of an overvalued currency because of huge losses on imports so that overall trade losses continued to accumulate during the early 1980s (Lardy 1992, pp. 66–73). Meanwhile, administrative practices for controlling the internal circulation of foreign exchange also generated a separate exchange market.

When the ISR was proposed in December 1980, IMF staff were on a mission to Beijing as part of the Article IV consultations and as part of negotiating China's first credit tranche drawing. Mark Allen noted that on the penultimate day of the mission an article appeared in the Asian Wall Street Journal describing the new scheme but the Bank of China Vice-Chairman only raised it informally after the mission had submitted its final report and 'he characterized it as a purely internal administrative matter'.[94] By the time the mission returned to Washington, the scheme was in place

[91] PRC – Staff Report for 1982 Article IV Consultation, 6 July 1982. SM/82/129. IMFA.

[92] Ibid.

[93] Memo Mark Allen to Tun Thin, 17 November 1983. ADIO Country Files, China Box 22, 1982–86. IMFA.

[94] Mark Allen memo for Palmer, 16 December 1980. ADIO Country Files, China Box 24, 1982–83. IMFA.

and 'this puts us in a most awkward situation. The measure will require Board approval and we have not discussed it at all with the Chinese. Furthermore, the Chinese have, albeit reluctantly, subscribed to the standard paragraph on restrictions in their Statement of Policy, which includes the absence of intent to introduce new multiple currency practices'.

In January 1981, Tun Thin wrote to the People's Bank of China suggesting a draft communication that they could send back to the IMF setting out the details of the ISR reform.[95] The PBC insisted that there was only a single official exchange rate for the RMB and that the experimental internal settlement 'price' was not an exchange rate, but the IMF staff noted that 'one thing is clear – there is certainly at least one new exchange rate for trade.[96] As in the earlier case of the ROC, since there was no 'assurance from the authorities of their ultimate intention to reunify the exchange system, it is not possible to recommend that the Board approve the measure'.[97] As Allen had noted, the issue was further complicated since the new multiple currency practice arose just as the PRC signed a letter of intent related to its tranche drawing that it would not introduce such practices. Mark Allen noted that 'longstanding policy shows that the presence of unapproved exchange practices constitute no bar to a Fund drawing' but advised that the Chinese Executive Director would need to make some form of justification in the Executive Board. [98]

These two forms of multiple exchange rates were strictly against the IMF rules for orderly exchanges and China came under increasing pressure to unify its exchange rate through the mid-1980s. The dual exchange rate contradicted Article VIII Section 3 of the IMF Articles of Association, which forbids members 'to engage in any discriminatory currency arrangements or multiple currency practices'. IMF Staff recommended in July 1982 that China's system should not be approved by the Executive Board because China's external balance was strong enough not to need it and there was no indication of when it would be removed.[99] After some debate, the Executive Board agreed not to approve the multiple exchange practice and noted that it was important to develop 'an effective link between domestic and international prices through the exchange rate. They expressed the hope that the authorities would, in time, be able to establish an exchange rate regime that would correspond to Chinese development needs and be consistent with the principles of the Fund'.[100] The recommendation not to approve China's exchange rate system was repeated in the 1983 Article IV consultations. In discussion, the

95 Telegram from Tun Thin to Shang Ming, PBC, 16 January 1981. ADIO, China Box 21, 1980–81. IMFA.

96 Telegram from Shang Ming to Tun Thin, 23 January 1981. M Allen to Palmer, 23 January 1981. ADIO, China Box 21, 1980–81. IMFA.

97 Mark Allen to Gui Tian, 25 February 1981. ADIO, China Box 21, 1980–81. IMFA.

98 Ibid.

99 PRC – Staff Report for 1982 Article IV Consultation, 6 July 1982. SM/82/129. IMFA.

100 Chairman's summing up at the conclusion of the 1982 Article IV Consultation with the PRC, 11 August 1982. BUFF/82/143. IMFA.

Executive Board members again emphasized the need to reform the price system to link domestic and international prices through the exchange rate and pressed China to increase imports rather than accumulate reserves.[101] Over time the official rate and the ISR converged and from January 1985, the ISR was abolished, but the swap rate market continued, covered by the pre-existing scheme exemption. The PRC then followed a strategy similar to the ROC of gradually depreciating the official rate and then joining it to the free market rate. Lardy argues that 'the IMF was instrumental in convincing China to abandon… the ISR' but this was rather a long campaign (Lardy 1999, p. 210) in an even longer battle.

Criticism of the multiple exchange rate system from IMF Executive Board intensified in the late 1980s as trading volume in the swap centres grew and reserves accumulated, but the Fund had little leverage over China's policy unless China drew on a credit tranche (Ferdinand and Wang 2013, p. 900). The reversal of balance of payments surpluses in 1985 provided an opportunity. In April 1986 the IMF was aware that China would seek another drawing on the credit tranche (expected to be SDR600m) and the Chinese had been seeking indications of the likely conditions that might be attached since earlier in the year.[102] The Managing Director was advised that 'the message that would be useful for you to give to Governor Liu [PBC] at this stage is that in our view the situation in China is rather worrisome' given the growing balance of payments deficit. Tun Thin, head of the Asian Department continued that 'Clearly, we shall have to improve our understanding and be satisfied that a sufficiently firm grip over this situation has been secured… before we could recommend to the Board use of the Fund's resources'. This required a programme including domestic credit restraint, exchange rate depreciation and reducing external borrowing. Tun Thin suggested that a stand-by might need to be delayed past the next IMF mission scheduled for June to agree these terms.

In June 1986, IMF staff advised the Chinese Executive Director Huang Fanzhang that a rate of at least RMB4-5/$ was needed to restore Chinese export competitiveness (rather than the rate of RMB3.2).[103] On 5 July 1986, the RMB was depreciated 15.8 % against the US dollar, but only to RMB3.70/$.[104] Lardy suggests that this decision was supported by IMF advice, but clearly the IMF staff would have preferred a larger devaluation (Lardy 1999, p. 210). China also expressed a need for a credit tranche drawing and this opened an opportunity to

---

[101] Report on the Article IV Consultation by H. Neiss for Acting Managing Director, 12 August 1983. ADIO Country Files, China, Box 24, 1982–83. Executive Board Minute, 21 November 183, EBM/83/157-1 Final. IMFA. The American Association of Textile Manufacturers also objected formally to the ISR in 1983 as a subsidy to Chinese Exports (Lardy 1992, pp. 73–74).

[102] Memo Tun Thin and E Brau to Managing Director, 3 April 1986. ADIO Country Files China Box 22. IMFA.

[103] Kunio Saito to Yang Jiangping (cc to Huang Fanzhang Executive Director), 25 June 1986. ADIO Country Files, China Box 23.. IMFA. This memo also advised that PBC lending rates should be increased so that they were above deposit rates to enhance monetary control. These recommendations were also discussed with Shang Ming of PBC.

[104] Memo to Executive Board, 8 July 1986, EBD/86/191. IMFA.

exert greater pressure. The IMF wanted further depreciation as a condition of a drawing on the first credit tranche in September 1986, but 'the Chinese remained adamant throughout that they could not give a specific assurance as to the timing and extent of the next exchange rate change'.[105] In the end their assurances about future 'flexibility' in exchange rate policies and a cumbersome contingent commitment that

> We will make further exchange rate adjustments as warranted by the implications of price reforms to be introduced in early 1987, as well as export performance, developments in the net foreign assets of the banking system and movements in the exchange rates and prices of our major trading partners and competitors.[106]

was deemed 'satisfactory' and China requested a second 12-month stand-by from November 1986 for SDR598 million. This early skirmish seems to have ended in China's favour since the exchange rate against the dollar was not adjusted until the end of 1989.

During 1989, trading volume in the swap centres reached $8.5 billion, 36 % higher than 1988 and at the end of the year the official rate of the RMB was devalued by a further 21 % in December 1989 and again by a further 10 % in November 1990. In response to the 1989 devaluation, the Chinese Executive Board member Dai remarked that 'this is an important step in pursuing a managed floating exchange rate policy and also a sign of the authorities' determination to consistently carry forward the reform'.[107] By 1991, the exchange rate regime became much more central to the Executive Board's criticism of PRC economic reforms as foreign exchange reserves increased. The Chinese moved to a managed float in April 1991 with an 'ultimate goal' of a unified exchange rate, but were unable to set a 'definite time frame for unification'.[108] Throughout 1993 the RMB depreciated sharply on the swap market due to inflationary pressure and a 60 % increase in the currency in circulation during that year. In response, the Chinese government substantially devalued the official exchange rate in January 1994 and introduced a managed floating system, which essentially unified the exchange rates.

---

[105] Memo Tun Thin to Managing Director for his meeting with Deputy Governor Liu Hongru of PBC also advises that the official rate should be devalued. 3 April 1986. ADIO Country Files, China Box 22. Quote from Memo from PR Narvekar to Managing Director, 29 September 1986. ADIO Country Files China Box 23. IMFA.

[106] Ibid. Attachment with the paragraph on exchange rate policy from the draft Letter of Intent related to the drawing.

[107] Minutes of Executive Board, 28 February 1990. EBM/90/27.

[108] PRC – Staff Report for the 1991 Article IV Consultation, 15 April 1992. SM/92/85.

5.3 *Technical Assistance*

One final aspect of China's relations with the IMF during the first stage of the Open Door policy was the extensive training and technical assistance that it received from IMF staff (Jacobson and Oksenberg 1990, pp. 122–123) although this paled by comparison to development assistance from the IBRD. The transition to PRC representation at the IMF corresponded with an acceleration of economic reform both internally and externally. In the international sector, four Special Economic Zones were identified in 1979 to experiment with more market-oriented models of production based on trade and foreign investment and they proved successful enough during the ensuing 5 years that the exercise was expanded to include 14 cities and Hainan Island in 1984. In 1986 China announced that it would seek to join the GATT, although it took a further 15 years to accomplish this goal. IMF staff supported reforms of the monetary and banking system through training programmes and hosting a China Colloquium in October 1982 to bring expertise to bear on an analysis of the Chinese economy. The Chinese representatives used this opportunity inter alia to question the relatively small role of developing countries in the governance of the Fund given that they comprised 86 % of the members of the Fund but only 40 % of voting power (Hook 1983, p. 53). By mid-1983, seven officials of the Bank of China, eight from the PBC, two from the Ministry of Finance and one each from the State Statistical Bureau and the General Customs Administration had participated in courses organised by the IMF Institute.[109] In order to support the required production of data for the IMF's own publications, advice was given on the development and collection of statistical series to support monitoring of the economy, in particular the balance of payments, by IMF staff sent to Beijing.

6 Conclusions

This chapter has drawn on archival records to demonstrate new complexities in China's role in the IMF. At the Bretton Woods conference China had a large delegation and was keenly interested, as Helleiner has shown (Helleiner 2014, pp. 186–200). But their actual influence at the meeting was stymied by the Anglo-American control of the process described by Steil (Steil 2013, pp. 228–9). The benefits of the relatively large quota allocated on the basis of China's future strategic importance was quickly eroded after 1946 when the Republic of China took 25 years to pay in its obligations and then could not enlarge its quota during the first 34 years of the Fund's existence. In the end, the ROC was unable to fulfil China's role in the IMF as envisaged at Bretton Woods. China's voting power quickly receded, but the ROC was able to draw on the resources of the Fund to support their rapid industrialisation

[109] Briefing Paper for 1983 Article IV Consultation, 5 July 1983. ADIO Country Files, China Box 24. IMFA.

once the quota was fully paid in from 1970. In the meantime, China won special dispensation to alter its exchange rate without prior approval of the Executive Board, and until 1960 operated a multiple exchange rate system that was not condoned by the Fund. This set a precedent for China's later role in the Fund.

The Fund's attitude to the seismic changes happening in East Asia after 1970 was very cautious and heavily influenced in its timing by US policy constraints. Even the United Nations expulsion of ROC did not prompt more affirmative action. This chapter has shown that the management and executive board members of the Fund were initially loathe to open up a highly political and divisive issue in the absence of external pressure for change from the People's Republic of China itself. In turn, the PRC was slow to take the initiative because of the complexity and ambiguity over the rights and obligations of Fund membership. As the question rested in limbo, plans for restitution of the Fund's gold under the second amendment to the Articles of Agreement complicated the representation of China in the Fund even further. But it was clear from the management's insistence that the restitution should not go to the ROC (even though this contravened their own legal opinion) that the Fund leadership favoured PRC representation, if only the PRC would claim it. Meanwhile, the IMF management carefully negotiated among its members to prepare them for PRC membership, facing particular challenges with the US representatives. Torn between long-standing support for the KMT and new opportunities from the rapprochement with the PRC, the US administration walked a middle ground, eventually settling upon a compromise way to transition from the ROC to the PRC that carried a small majority of the Executive Board. Even once majority opinion was ready to consider PRC representation in 1977, there was considerable delay while the Fund waited for the PRC to take the initiative. This chapter has filled in the details of how the PRC was engaged into the Fund's operations through tentative contacts at a humble economics seminar at the Smithsonian Institution.

The initial years of PRC representation coincided with dramatic reforms in China's economic system as the Open Door Policy evolved. The lag in the size of China's quota was quickly redressed so that China's share of fund resources reflected their calculated quota rather better than was the case for other countries. Being a latecomer thus had its advantages. China's balance of payments constraints were eased by accessing Fund resources based on this enlarged quota in 1981 and the first round of conditionality was easily negotiated because the aims of the Fund and the central government were aligned. When the time came for the review of quotas, however, the Chinese position was disadvantaged by the rapid increase in trade and accumulation of reserves since the quota calculations were made on historic data. But the substantial balance of payments surpluses accumulated in these early years decreased the likelihood that China would need to draw on its quota. The main issues in these early years were over the generation and sharing of economic data and over the exchange rate. As China's foreign exchange reserves accumulated, IMF staff became impatient with the pace of market price reform (and therefore the transition to a market exchange rate) and with the rate of imports, but had no discernible influence on economic policy. When China made its second credit tranche drawing in 1986, there was an opportunity to use this leverage, but the IMF was unable to prevail on China to adjust its exchange rate at a pace and to the level that it wanted. Being a late-comer had important implications for the PRC's position in the Fund, but the shift of representation to the PRC finally fulfilled the ambitions for China's place that had been negotiated by the KMT during the Bretton Woods meetings. The early years of PRC membership also presaged the thorny issues that would create difficult relations for China and the IMF 20 years later.

References

Bottelier, P. 2007. China and the World bank: How a partnership was built. *Journal of Contemporary China* 16(51): 239–258.

Boughton, J. 2001. *Silent revolution; the IMF 1979–1989*. Washington: IMF.

Ferdinand, P., and J. Wang. 2013. China and the IMF; from mimicry towards pragmatic international institutional pluralism. *International Affairs* 89(4): 895–910.

Foot, R., and Andrew Walter. 2011. *China, the United States and the global order*. Cambridge: Cambridge University Press.

Gao Xiao, Hang, and Tam On Kit. 1995. China's foreign exchange system. In *Financial reform in China*, ed. Tam On Kit, 143–180. London: Routledge.

Heep, S. 2014. *China in global finance; domestic financial repression and international financial power*. Cham: Springer.

Helleiner, E. 2014. *Forgotten foundations of Bretton Woods; international development and the making of the postwar order*. Ithaca: Cornell University Press.

Helleiner, E., and B. Momani. 2014. The hidden history of China and the IMF. In *The great wall of money; power and politics in China's international monetary relations*, ed. E. Helleiner and J. Kirshner. Ithaca: Cornell University Press.

Hook, A.W. (ed.). 1983. *The fund and China in the International monetary system*. Washington: IMF.

Horsefield, J.K. 1969. *The international monetary fund 1945–65*. Washington: IMF.

Jacobson, H.K., and M. Oksenberg. 1990. *China's participation in the IMF, the World Bank, and GATT*. Ann Arbor: University of Michigan Press.

Kent, A.E. 2009. *Beyond compliance: China, international organizations, and global security*. Singapore: National University of Singapore Press.

Lardy, N. 1992. *Foreign trade and economic reform in China 1978–1990*. Cambridge: Cambridge University Press.

Lardy, N. 1999. China and the International financial system. In *China joins the world: progress and prospects*, ed. E. Economy and M. Oksenberg, 206–230. New York: Council on Foreign Relations Press.

Luthi, L.M. 2008. *The Sino-Soviet split: cold war in the communist world*. Princeton: Princeton University Press.

Momani, B. 2013. China at the IMF: continued engagement in its drive for membership and added voice at the IMF Executive Board. *Journal of Chinese Economics* 1(1): 125–150.

Pearson, M. 1999. The major multilateral economic institutions engage China. In *Engaging China: the management of an emerging power*, ed. A.I. Johnston and R.S. Ross, 212–240. London/New York: Routledge.

Schuler, K., and A. Rosenberg. 2013. *The Bretton Woods transcripts*. New York: Centre for Financial Stability.

Schuler, K., and M. Bernkopf. 2014. *Who was at Bretton Woods*. New York: Center for Financial Stability, papers in Financial History.

Steil, B. 2013. *The battle of Bretton Woods; John Maynard Keynes, Harry Dexter White, and the making of a New World Order*. Princeton: Princeton University Press.

Van Dormael, A. 1978. *Bretton Woods; birth of a monetary system*. London: Macmillan.

Epilogue: How Should We View the Transformation of the IMF? Looking at the Collapse of the Bretton Woods System

Masanao Itoh

1 Findings from This Book

While there is not necessarily a consensus of opinion on what should be considered the classical period of the IMF under the Bretton Woods system, the dominant view holds this to be the period from 1958 to roughly 1968, or from the restoration of convertibility of European currencies to the time of around the adoption of the dual gold-price system. Another view, based on the perspective of the fixed dollar standard and gold dollar standard, sees the classical period as beginning around 1960 and extending until around 1971. Each of these views sees the period of roughly 10 years starting from the founding of the IMF (and the World Bank) as a transitional period. This probably is why the 1950s have been called a period of dormancy for the IMF.

This book has critiqued and reconsidered this view through means including analysis of the IMF's activities and interactions between it and the leading countries. While it mainly covers the 1950s, the content of many of the papers included herein extends to a time around the mid-1960s. This process began in Part I by considering the interconnections between the system, structure, policies and functions of the IMF itself, and the intents and objectives of the leading actors in the creation of the systems and leading players in its management. Then, in Part II we analyzed subjects including the relations between the leading countries' domestic economic policies and responses to the IMF and the connections between the international currency system and each country's financial system. While the results of

M. Itoh (✉)
School of Social Information Studies, Otsuma Women's University,
2-7-1 Karakida, Tama, Tokyo 206-8540, Japan
e-mail: masaitoh@e.u-tokyo.ac.jp

K. Yago et al. (eds.), *History of the IMF*, Studies in Economic History,
DOI 10.1007/978-4-431-55351-9

this analysis have made a number of things clear, here we will identify just one point each from Parts I and II.

The first concerns the governance of the IMF after its establishment and organization. This can be described as the question of whether the IMF was an international public good or a tool of the key countries. While the views of the authors on this point are not necessarily in agreement, most of the chapters in Part I consciously addressed this issue.

Chapter 1 traced the process by which both Keynes and White, who began as universalists and idealists, came to be constrained by the interests of their own countries as the system to be established gradually took on concrete form. Chapter 2 stresses how the USA, which at the time of the IMF's establishment attempted to control the IMF as a whole, including its secretariat, and had felt it had both the responsibility and ability to do so, was unable to dominate the IMF exclusively in the actual process that developed, and was forced to pay close attention to the interests of other leading countries and to tolerate more flexible lines of policy.

Chapter 3 showed how, although the organization of the IMF in the second half of the 1950s had been achieved under the faith and credit of the USA, the IMF framework later turned into shackles on the leading countries of Europe, which had resolved their dollar shortages and achieved foreign-exchange liberalization, and their focus broadened to include the G10 and the WP3 in addition to the IMF. Chapter 4 introduced Per Jacobsson, the third Managing Director of the IMF, focusing on his earlier experiences in the European reconstruction. Chapter 5 stressed that during the formative years of the postwar international currency system, the IMF did not necessarily subordinate itself passively to the mission identified by the leading countries or to rules on the operation of the international currency system.

Furthermore, in Chap. 5 we saw how the IMF and the key currency approach, which had been in conflict at the time of the IMF's establishment, converged on the international financial center approach with the development of international financial markets during the 1950s, and how the restoration of convertibility meant the dollar had an advantage over the pound at the starting line of the race for key currency status. That chapter also emphasized how the resulting free movement of short-term capital would advance even further than the Bretton Woods system, from management of foreign exchange to liberalization of current account balances and, furthermore, to liberalization of capital and financial accounts. Chapter 6 argued that there were limits to the attempt to resolve the actualization of the international liquidity issue known as the Triffin dilemma within the IMF framework through the creation and expansion of special drawing rights (SDRs) even though such a shock to the international financial system could not be addressed without a system to regulate the banks that handle foreign-exchange operations.

Each of the chapters of Part I showed how IMF policy was formed amid tugs of war between the USA and other leading countries and between the USA and specialist bureaucrats within the IMF after its creation; that in this sense the IMF was a tool of its leading member states; and that, however, amid such tugs of war the IMF did achieve policy autonomy, although restricted, and the formative years of that autonomy were the 1950s, said to be a dormant period for the IMF. Thus, these chapters can be described as suggesting the need to break free from the dualistic view of the IMF as either a tool or a public good. The question of whether to see the IMF's history as a process of evolution from a tool to a public good or to consider the IMF to be merely a tool that adopted the outward appearance of a public good or to have had a dual nature of both a tool and a public good probably will have to await future study.

The second issue concerns the framework for coordination between the domestic policies of individual countries and the Bretton Woods system or the international currency system of the time, and how it was reflected in the IMF as a system within such a structure. Put another way, this can be described as the question of how the leading member states adapted to the adjustable peg system that was the essence of the IMF at that time. This point is elucidated through practical analysis of the connections between each government's domestic and external policies and negotiations and consultations with the IMF in each of the chapters of Part II, which looks at the leading IMF member states that later would form the Group of Seven. These papers describe the actual state of IMF operation, looking at the questions of why the postwar transitional phase (i.e., maintenance of foreign-exchange controls on current transactions) ended up lasting longer than initially expected and why a system in opposition to the IMF's principles of floating exchange rates and multiple exchange rates came to be accepted.

Chapter 7 suggests that the relationship between France and the IMF was cooperative, rather than one of fierce antagonism as usually described, and that this cooperative relationship helped to realize the adoption of flexible exchange rates and promotion of expansionary fiscal and monetary policy. Chapter 8 shows how Germany decided to revalue the Deutschemark based on its own judgment, in opposition to the conservative approach of the IMF, which was not in favor of changing exchange rates. Chapter 9 identified Italy's policy of postponing the setting of fixed exchange rates while working aggressively toward the restoration of external equilibrium. Chapter 10 looks at the case of Canada, which employed a floating exchange-rate system for a long period (1950–1962), considering why the IMF tolerated such a floating exchange-rate system, in violation of the IMF Articles of Agreement, in Canada's case in 1950 and had Canada return to a fixed exchange rate in 1962. Chapter 11 described the process by which Japan's entry to the Bretton Woods system and its return to international financial markets were realized amid a conflict between American and British interests. Chapter 12 describes the Japanese case in the 1950s and the 1960s: In a rivalry between the "growth" advocates and the "stability" advocates during the 1950s in the Japanese economic decision-makers, the IMF supported the latter. In the 1960s, however, the "growth" side secured the advantage over the "stability" camp due to the introduction of overseas short-term funds. The role played by the IMF during the period was relatively minor in relation to the EXIM and other fund-suppliers. Chapter 13 explored the long-standing relations between the IMF and China. Although the ROC was an active participant in the Bretton Woods Conference, the position of the Taiwanese Government in the 1950s has been limited: the Taiwanese Government took 25 years to pay in its obligations and then could not enlarge its quota during the first 34 years of the Fund's existence. The PRC joined the IMF in April 1980 unseating the ROC, but the PRC's position in the IMF, including the confrontation between this new-comer nation and the fund, had been affected by the earlier action of the ROC.

For now, we can describe the IMF under the Bretton Woods system as being based essentially on the following three points: (1) use of the US dollar as the international settlement currency, reserve currency, and exchange currency; (2) linkage of each country's own currency to the dollar, in principle, at fixed parity; and (3) exchange of dollars for gold by the USA at the value of USD35 per ounce. When doing so, how we understand the second of these points is critical. Traditionally, the adjustable peg system has been understood to be based on the peg rate system. However, each of the chapters of Part II shows instead that the adjustable system was the basis. In narrow terms this calls for a reconsideration of our understanding of the 1960s as a time when the Jacobsson line of policy of maintaining fixed exchange rates through promotion of liberalization was accomplished. In broader terms, it demands reconsideration of the view that the Bretton Woods system was an extension of the gold exchange standard or a gold dollar standard.

2 What Were the Roles of the IMF?

As Kindleberger said, the postwar IMF was a systemic reform to the exchange-rate system based on reflection on the race to devalue currencies and the blocism of the 1930s. Under this system, the postwar capitalist world achieved macroeconomic stability and high rates of economic growth. This period had higher degrees of both stability and growth than did the period under the classical gold standard or the period that began in the 1970s. This achievement was supported by the adjustable peg rate system. In this sense, the results of the analysis in this book ask anew the question of whether autonomy in each country's own fiscal and monetary policy was increased and price stability, expanded production, and increased productivity achieved by fixed parity and the commitment of each country's government to it or by the commitment of each government in the form of flexible responses, including resistance, to pressure toward such fixed parity.

Viewed from the perspective of the IMF after its creation, this was a mechanism for maintaining the international currency system, cutting the costs of maintaining free trade and multilateral settlement, and preventing the adoption by each country's government of policies of boosting the economy through inflationary policies, adjusting for current account imbalances among member states, supplying the liquidity that each country's economy needed, and maintaining confidence in the dollar as the key currency that enabled these functions to work.

The period from the 1950s through the 1960s was one of advancing liberalization of trade, increasingly active investment, and employment growth. While this book does not consider this topic fully, in fact this system was supported by capital controls. In the process of establishment of the IMF, both Keynes and White believed that capital controls increased the autonomy of individual currencies and stabilized exchange rates, although they differed in that Keynes saw them as a permanent feature of the postwar system while White saw them as a necessary evil and the best out of a range of bad options. In fact, it was not only Britain, which faced numerous international balance of payments crises, that enacted capital controls. So did the key country of the USA (with the 1963 interest equalization tax) and Germany (in 1961), even though it had a surplus. Capital controls can be described as having been used to achieve harmony between exchange-rate stability and the autonomy of each country's economic policies. This too is a major difference from the period beginning in the 1970s.

3 Why Did the Bretton Woods System Collapse?

It is well known that this Bretton Woods system collapsed following the so-called Nixon Shock of August 1971. Originally the Bretton Woods system had been an asymmetrical system premised on the overwhelming economic power and gold holdings of the USA. The USA sought domestic equilibrium while maintaining gold parity, while other countries sought external equilibrium while maintaining parity against the dollar. This led to what came to be known as the "n-1" problem. While frictions already had started to appear within this system at the end of the 1950s, through the first half of the 1960s these were adjusted for temporarily through the Jacobsson line of maintaining the adjustable peg through liberalization and the shift of countries to Article VIII status. However, in the second half of the 1960s it no longer would be possible to adjust for these frictions through sticking to the Jacobsson line alone. Exchange-rate adjustments would begin among the leading states, and at the same time there was no choice but to implement a "Bretton Woods patchwork" through means including conclusion of general agreements to borrow (GAB), the establishment of special drawing rights (SDRs), and the abolition of the gold pooling system and adoption of the dual gold-price system. Concerns came to be pointed out regarding all the elements of harmonization, liquidity, and confidence. The rapid growth of the Eurodollar markets was a direct response of the markets to this crisis.

The suspension of convertibility of dollars to gold due to the August 1971 Nixon Shock brought about the collapse of this Bretton Woods system. But even today no consensus of opinion has yet formed on the real reasons the Bretton Woods system collapsed. At this point in time, we should use Bordo and Eichengreen (1993) as a standard of reference. That work, a collection of papers from a National Bureau of Economic Research conference, answers the question "What brought about the demise of Bretton Woods?" with "Even today there is no consensus answer" and then sums up the matter with the statement, the question of "Why the pegged-rate system collapsed is among the most contentious and confusing debates in the literature on Bretton Woods system."

Eichengreen, one of the editors of the above-mentioned work, describes how there are six views on what led to the collapse of Bretton Woods: (1) differences in currency policy between the USA and other countries, (2) differences in fiscal policy between the US and other countries, (3) the failure of currency devaluation by debtor countries, (4) the failure of currency revaluation by surplus countries, (5) a decline in the international competitiveness of the USA, and (6) structural flaws of the system, as seen in the Triffin dilemma. Noting that "Ultimately, then, the collapse of Bretton Woods was attributable as much to the structure of the system as to the specific policies pursued," he argues, "Structural flaws dictated collapse sooner or later, policies at home and abroad determined only the timing of the event."

Regarding this subject of timing, in the same work monetarists argue, for example, that the collapse of Bretton Woods was due to the lagging effects of expansionary currency policy in the USA, through a process by which (1) the increase in US currency caused inflation in the USA, as a lagging effect, (2) the US currency increase was independent of any change in international reserves, (3) the US currency increase brought about powerful and significant increases in currency in the other seven leading countries, although with a fairly long-term lag, and (4) the currency increases in the seven leading countries led to inflation in those countries, again with a lag. Others argue that the collapse was due to incompatibility between the exchange rates of the USA and other countries and to differences in their rates of growth in productivity, stress the importance of the rapid increases in productivity in Germany and Japan, or emphasize currency and monetary policy, which brought on overvaluation of the US dollar in the second half of the 1960s.

The other editor Bordo argues that the following three factors were the main causes of the collapse of the Bretton Woods system: (1) the two systemic flaws of the gold exchange standard (causing a US convertibility crisis) and the adjustable peg (increasing the cost of individual parity adjustments as a result of intensification of movements of capital), (2) US currency policy not suited to a key currency country, particularly Nixon's inflationary policies after effectively shifting to a dollar standard system in 1968, and (3) resistance to rate adjustments on the part of other leading industrialized states, particularly those with surpluses.

Whatever the case, the Bretton Woods system as an adjustable peg system collapsed at the start of the 1970s. The IMF proved unable to play the leading part in the coordinating role during the chaotic period from Nixon's announcement that the USA would abandon the gold standard on August 15, 1971, through the Smithsonian Agreement at the end of that year to the joint floating of the currencies of the six European Community states in March 1973. At that time it was the Group of 10 and Working Party Three of the Organization for Economic Cooperation and Development that played key roles. However, the USA was dissatisfied with this state of affairs, arguing that Europe had too much influence in international currency matters and that European states were meeting privately with each other in advance of G10 meetings to coordinate their opinions and form a common front. Developing countries too were highly critical, arguing that both in the past, with the creation of special drawing rights, and in these reforms to the international currency system only ten developed countries met and discussed matters in advance and then forced their conclusions on the developing countries. Furthermore, within the developed countries as well strong criticisms were expressed by countries such as Austria and Australia that were not made G10 members. These dissatisfactions on the part of the USA and criticisms from non-G10 member states and developing countries erupted in the May 1972 OECD Ministerial Council Meeting, which saw fierce debate on forum-related issues. Ultimately, agreement was reached to not form new forums on matters related to currency and trade and instead to form an ad hoc committee in the IMF Board of Governors on reforms to the international currency system and discuss those matters there. This was where the establishment of the Committee of 20 (C20) was agreed upon.

However, discussions in the C20 did not go smoothly. It became a three-way battle between the USA, which although a deficit nation was an exporter of capital, other advanced industrialized nations that were surplus nations and restricted capital imports, and developing countries that were deficit nations and hoped to attract inflows of aid more than capital. A continuous tangle was driven by the conflict between France, which argued for the quick restoration of fixed exchange rates, and the USA, which argued for fully floating exchange rates. With this conflict remaining unresolved, the IMF approved the first Outline of Reform at its Annual Meeting in Nairobi in September 1973, and then in June 1974 the Outline of Reform was finalized and the C20 dissolved. The work would be carried on by a provisional committee of the IMF, and after five meetings a basic agreement was reached in January 1976, followed in March by the approval by the IMF Executive Board of the second revisions to the IMF Articles of Agreement. A key point of these revisions was the fact that while each country would be able to choose its exchange-rate system freely, the IMF would establish guidelines for the operation of a floating exchange rate system and consult on and monitor the actions of each country's government. This envisioned a fairly strict managed float system with an obligation of intervention. The turmoil surrounding the international currency system that had continued since the Nixon Shock in 1971 had reached a conclusion, for the time being, in the form of a shift to a managed float regime.

However, this managed float system could not be maintained over even the medium term, let alone the long term. The direct cause of its failure was the fact that the assumption in the IMF guidelines that fluctuations in exchange rates caused by speculative factors could be offset for the most part through intervention by currency authorities was undermined by the actual scale of the turbulence in movements of short-term capital. At a more fundamental level, however, it was due to the facts that the IMF was unable to supply international liquidity in place of the dollar even as it called for shrinking the role of gold and focusing on SDRs and that the short- and medium-term causal relationship between exchange rates and current account balances was weakened by the growth in the size of the domestic economies of the leading countries and their swelling public finances. With the addition of oil money and the issues of aid and loans to developing countries, instability was amplified in the subsequent operation of the international currency system. This was met with a continual patchwork of responses that swayed back and forth like a pendulum between free float and managed float approaches. This is why the period after the suspension of dollar convertibility to gold has been called a period of "non-system" (Williamson 1976).

Financial globalization would advance rapidly beginning in the 1980s, greatly increasing financial instability both within individual countries and internationally. Today one hears renewed calls for reviewing the functions of the Bretton Woods system, which once was sustained as a stable system for a period of time, and for comparative study of international monetary policy in the national economies of the countries that made up that system, as one way of reducing such instability and contributing to the rebuilding of an international financial system grounded in rules and mechanisms. This book is one attempt at such a study.

References

Bordo, M.D., and B. Eichengreen (eds.). 1993. *A retrospective on the Bretton Woods system: Lessons for international reform*. Chicago: The University of Chicago Press.

Williamson, J. 1976. The benefits and costs of an international monetary nonsystem. In *Essays in international finance*, vol. 115, ed. E.M. Bernstein et al. Princeton: Princeton University Press.

Index

K. Yago et al. (eds.), *History of the IMF*, Studies in Economic History,
DOI 10.1007/978-4-431-55351-9

V

W

Y

Z

MIX
Papier aus verantwortungsvollen Quellen
Paper from responsible sources
FSC® C105338

If you have any concerns about our products,
you can contact us on
ProductSafety@springernature.com

In case Publisher is established outside the EU,
the EU authorized representative is:
Springer Nature Customer Service Center GmbH
Europaplatz 3, 69115 Heidelberg, Germany

Printed by Libri Plureos GmbH
in Hamburg, Germany